# Personnel Management
# and Human Resources

# Personnel Management and Human Resources

**C S Venkata Ratnam**

*International Management Institute*
*New Delhi*

**B K Srivastava**

*Behavioural Sciences Consultant*
*New Delhi*

**Tata McGraw Hill Education Private Limited**

NEW DELHI

*McGraw-Hill Offices*

**New Delhi** New York St Louis San Francisco Auckland Bogotá Caracas
Kuala Lumpur Lisbon London Madrid Mexico City Milan Montreal
San Juan Santiago Singapore Sydney Tokyo Toronto

**Tata McGraw-Hill**

This edition can be exported from India only by the publishers,
Tata McGraw Hill Education Private Limited

**ISBN-13: 978-0-07-460460-1**
**ISBN-10: 0-07-460460-0**

Published by Tata McGraw-Hill Publishing Company Limited,
7 West Patel Nagar, New Delhi 110 008, and printed at
Print Shop Pvt. Ltd., Chennai 600 096

*The* **McGraw-Hill** *Companies*

# Preface

This book is intended to be a basic text for all postgraduate courses where "Personnel/Human Resource Management" is offered as a course of study. It could be useful to professional managers in personnel and other staff and line functions as well.

Our objective is to provide a framework of knowledge relating to the concepts and practice of personnel management in the Indian context, which could also be relevant to other developing countries, particularly those in the South Asian region.

Our approach has been to look at personnel in a systemic perspective; to relate the role of personnel to overall business goals; to underline the interlinkages in all subfunctions of personnel as subsystems of an organic whole; to incorporate the essence of the recent contributions of behavioural sciences as is appropriate; and to provide an overview of legal framework at relevant places, while avoiding legalistic approach.

This book differs from other Indian textbooks in giving a decisive behavioural science orientation to the treatment of the subject. For instance, as a prelude to the discussion of human resource planning (Chapter 3), we have examined approaches to analysis and design of jobs (Chapter 2). The discussion on aspects relating to human behaviour and personnel's role (Chapter 10) and employee relations (Chapter 11) will also be found atypical.

We have tried to deal with the subject somewhat comprehensively even as we tried to be concise. Some of the topics discussed in the text are not covered in most Indian textbooks on the subject. Such topics include: MBO and Quality of Work Life (Chapter 10), Stress Management and Counselling (Chapter 11), Industrial Relations: Implications of Personnel Policies (Chapter 12), Alternative Approaches to Participation (Chapter 13), Measurement in Personnel (Chapter 14), and Future Scenario (Chapter 15).

Every chapter has outlined learning objectives, summary, key words, review questions and suggestions for further reading. Each chapter, with the exception of the last one, presents either one or more cases and/or company experiences. The case discussions and review questions are expected to help synthesize and test the knowledge and understanding of the conceptual and practical aspects of the subject.

The use of male gender in this book is neither intended to be discriminatory nor is it to project personnel/human resource management as a male activity.

We hope readers will find the book relevant and useful and we would welcome their comments, criticism and suggestions.

C S Venkata Ratnam<br>
B K Srivastava

# *Acknowledgements*

We wish to express our appreciation to all those with whom we worked/interacted and whose thoughts and insights helped us in furthering our knowledge and understanding of the subject.

We thank the Director, School of Management Studies, Indira Gandhi National Open University; Chairman, Board of Studies, Indian Society for Training and Development; Editors of *Indian Management* and *Personnel Today*, for permission to reproduce part of our contribution to their course materials/publications. We also thank National Institute of Personnel Management and Steel Authority of India Limited for permission to reproduce cases published by them. We also thank numerous other authors/publishers for some quotations which have enriched the quality of this book. Our special thanks to Russi Mody, Chairman, Tata Iron & Steel Company Limited for permission to reproduce excerpts from his speech, 'No Greater Reward'.

A book of this nature is the product of the ideas and experiences of several persons, accumulated over the years, besides the two of us. Though we are unable to mention all of them individually, our debt of gratitude to them is no less. However, we alone take responsibility for any shortcomings.

We deem it our privilege to acknowledge the encouragement and facilities provided to us by the International Management Institute and particularly to Prem Pandhi, Director-Emeritus and Sushil Chandra, Director.

Finally it gives us great satisfaction to record our deep sense of appreciation of the excellent secretarial help provided by Ms Leena Prakasan.

C S Venkata Ratnam
B K Srivastava

# Contents

# Personnel Management in Organizational Context

Organizations exist for people. They are made of people and by the people, and their effectiveness depends on the behaviour and performance of the people constituting them.

There was a time when people were considered a liability. Now they are mostly considered as a resource and an asset. Today reckoned as partners, employees were earlier considered as adversaries by their employers. The transformation in the attitude and outlook towards people in organizations, variously called employees, human resources, etc. has been made possible by the evolution in the field of personnel management, the function with responsibility for managing human resources in any organization.

This chapter, in fact the entire book, is about this function whose preoccupation is with people. Terms such as personnel, human resource management, and employee relations are used to describe the unit, department, group of specialists or the function concerned with people. For our purpose, we shall use them synonymously. Terms and aspects relating to industrial relations and human resource development are integral to the personnel function.

# PERSONNEL ENVIRONMENT

Organizations are becoming large and complex, with progressive industrialization and advent of new technologies. Over the years, government intervention in regulating organizational purpose and performance has increased. Social obligations, legal aspects and trade union pressures are actively shaping the environment. Here we consider some of the environmental trends in terms of five principal environmental aspects:

- Economic
- Demographic
- Socio-cultural
- Politico-legal
- Technological

## Economic

Low growth (3.5% long-term average), high rate of inflation (8.5%), and spreading unemployment have been principal sources of concern in the Indian economic scene. To achieve full employment at 2.4% growth in population, the number of jobs should rise by 3.9%. The International Labour Organization estimated that US $ 6250 is needed to create a new job in developing countries like India. Capital-employment and capital-output ratios have declined progressively during the entire plan period. Inequities in income and wealth distribution have increased over the years, despite government initiatives to combat them. Affirmative actions for the disadvantaged groups brought in their wake new pressures for reservations in education and employment based on heredity, domicile, sex, caste and creed. Employment is sought and created in most of public sector units for its own sake. Together these factors and forces have put the nation on a reverse gear, leading to backwardness.

## Demographic

Over a period of time, the profile of the employees, industrial workers in particular, has been changing. Labour force is now not restricted to certain castes and communities. Social mobility accounts for the emergence of a mixed industrial work force. While in traditional industries this change is slow, it is highly visible in relatively sophisticated industries such as engineering, oil refining and distribution, chemicals and petro-chemicals, machine-tools, etc. The background of the intermediate and lower cadres in the latter industries is overwhelmingly urban; their level of education is higher; they come from middle or lower middle classes. Moreover, the old social barriers are breaking down. The disinterest among certain groups for manual work is gradually wearing off because the groups themselves have not retained their separate identity and also because jobs are now not wholly manual.

Higher skills and educational requirements expected of workers in modern factories and better wage levels have tended to blur further the traditional distinction between manual and non-manual workers. Employees are seeking and demanding parity in employee benefits among different categories and levels. The evolving social and political climate in the country also has its impact on shaping and expediting these changes in the composition of work force and their attitudes at the workplace.

The sex composition of the workers has also been changing. Earlier, women were recruited mainly as labour in agriculture and related traditional industries like plantations, etc. Now they are increasingly occupying white collar and managerial positions. Working women, especially in developing countries like ours, are beginning to resist discrimination against them by employers and sexual harassment at workplace.

## Socio-cultural

Religion and culture do not teach people to be idle. They enjoin that one should do one's duty not in return or in expectation of its fruits but because it is one's *Dharma*. High quality work without supervision over long hours, almost unrelated to its fruits in monetary terms, is done by the self-employed, craftsmen, fishermen, housewives, and employees of small unorganized units in towns and villages. On the other hand, the question of lack of work culture or ethics is discussed largely in the context of large-scale organized industry primarily in urban areas. Some questions arise in this context. Does the joint-family system encourage dependency in work culture? Are people looking for security in modern industry that is comparable to the one found in joint-family system? What are people interested in? In money or what money buys? In being or in having? What importance do people give to the more fulfilling aspects of work like job enrichment? To what extent are our socio-cultural traditions compatible with the modern organizational structures? There is a need to understand these and other related aspects.

## Politico-legal

Political independence and the democratic process have raised the expectations of our people. Compared to most other developing countries in Asia and Africa, the democratic institutions in India are more developed, strong and active. There is an increasing demand from our people for a greater degree of involvement and participation in matters that concern and affect them.

Government intervention in regulating employment relationships and organizational performance have been on the increase, in accordance with the ideals enshrined in our Constitution and the objectives of five-year plans.

We have had much progressive legislation since independence to regulate working conditions and employment relations, abolish bonded labour, check contract labour, ensure equal pay for equal work, guarantee minimum wages, provide social security, etc. We also have some stringent legislations like Essential Services Maintenance Act (ESMA) and the Maintenance of Internal Security Act (MISA), which trade unions and civil liberty organizations abhor.

Employers and unions are critical about much of the legislative framework because it controls and regulates their functions. Non-compliance of legislation is fairly widespread because 'state ways' alone cannot change 'folk ways'; besides, weaknesses in administering the laws and loopholes in the provisions have aggravated the situation. While increased legislation playing a positive role in bringing about desired changes in the direction of social justice, also made employers and employees legalistic.    In the organized manufacturing sector alone, over 3000 man days per every 1000 persons employed are lost every year in industrial disputes where both the parties seek to assert their respective rights.    Litigation has grown due to increase in number of disputes and delays in adjudication.  Over 1.5 lakh labour disputes are pending in courts.

## Technological

Technological imperatives are limiting the options available.  However, modernization and automation lead to fewer job losses than supposed.  Delays in absorption, failure in adaptation, absence of economies of scale, high costs and cost-push tendencies due to the nature of competition have restrained the positive features of technology.

Nevertheless, technological changes have reduced the dependence on muscle power in manual jobs, and manual labour in clerical and other white collar occupations. Modern technology has rendered work on the shop-floor and the office more alike. Job content and methods of production are changing, with modifications in the size and composition of work groups.  The network of social relations among employees is also affected.  Shifts in consumption patterns and technological developments have displaced artisans such as weavers, potters, fishermen, washermen, etc.  Technical training institutions began to impart training in skills such as carpentry and weaving which once used to be the exclusive domain of people belonging to certain castes. In retrospect, these changes had the following effects on the individuals: the link between caste and occupation was broken, the skill of artisans which was more personal and manual was replaced with the skill of technicians which is more impersonal and mechanical; job performance depended more on dexterity in handling machines than exercising one's skill or craft and thus the individual's pride in his contribution to the final output, for which Indian artisans were renowned, had been reduced.

## CHANGING ROLE OF PERSONNEL MANAGEMENT IN INDIA

In India the origins of personnel management could be traced to the concern about labour welfare in factories since 1920s. It resulted in State intervention in the aftermath of the difficult conditions after World War I, and the emergence of trade unions. In 1931 the Royal Commission on Labour recommended the appointment of labour welfare officers to deal with the recruitment of labour and to settle their grievances. The Factories Act (1948), laid down qualifications and duties of welfare officers and made it mandatory for companies employing 500 or more workers to appoint welfare officers with requisite qualifications and training.  Social work education which was started in the country in 1936, soon realized the relevance and significance of social work practice to personnel functions.

Soon two professional bodies emerged:  The Indian Institute of Personnel Management (IIPM) with Calcutta  as the headquarters and the National Institute of Labour Management (NILM) with Bombay as the headquarters.  These two places were the premier centres of traditional industry (jute and cotton respectively) in pre-independent India.  Corporate power was sought as a means of effective performance of the welfare function. In the years immediately after the Second World War and Independence, the welfare needs of the working class grew along with their rising expectations. During the 1960s, the personnel function began to expand beyond the welfare aspect, with the three areas of Labour Welfare (LW), Industrial Relations (IR) and Personnel Administration (PA) developing as the constituent parts of the emerging profession of Personnel Management (PM). Simultaneously, the massive thrust given to heavy industry in the context of planned economic development, particularly since the Second Five Year Plan (1956–61), and the accelerated growth of public sector in the national economy resulted in a shift in focus toward professionalization of management.

By the 1970s a shift in professional values was discernible. It shifted from a concern for welfare to a focus on efficiency. In the 1980s, professionals began to talk about new technologies, Human Resource Management (HRM) Challenges, and Human Resource Development (HRD). The two professional bodies, IIPM and NILM, merged in 1980 to form the National Institute of Personnel Management (NIPM).

Today there is a growing awareness of the importance of the human side of organizations as a vital factor in overall progress. It is clear that even in the sphere of technology, apprehension about treating people as automators within organisations, as extensions of machines, is large. There are no two opinions about the fact that people, not science and technology, will determine the future, both, of organizations and the world. In that sense, as seen in Table 1.1, the personnel function, which had a humble beginning in the 1920s will blossom into a profession, with a philosophical outlook and a focus resting on upholding human values.

**Table 1.1   Evolution of the Personnel Function in India**

| Period | Development Status | Outlook | Emphasis | Status |
|--------|-------------------|---------|----------|--------|
| 1920s – 1930s | Beginning | Pragmatism of capitalists | Statutory, welfare, paternalism | Clerical |
| 1940s – 1960s | Struggling for recognition | Technical, legalistic | Introduction of techniques | Administrative |
| 1970s – 1980s | Impressing with sophistication | Professional, legalistic, impersonal | Regulatory conformance, imposition of standards on other functions | Managerial |
| 1990s | Promising | Philosophical | Human values, productivity through people | Executive |

## IS PERSONNEL A PROFESSION?

What makes a professional? What distinguishes professionals from other occupations? We can on analysis, discern three distinct characteristics of professionals:

- their qualifications, usually of a specific body of knowledge,

- their membership of a professional association to improve professional skills, and
- their code of ethics, which guides them towards the desired goals.

## Academic Qualifications

Occupations pursuing professionalizing strategies have sought the cooperation and legal backing of the State in their attempts to gain a monopoly of control over training. For instance, to qualify in other well-established professions like medicine and law, members must first meet definite academic requirements. In the sphere of management, certain specializations like chartered accountancy and company secretaryship have grown to be professions, in the sense that members must first acquire the formal qualifications specified for entry. The hegemony of professions has been challenged by increased pressures on them and by State intervention. Bare-foot doctors, informally trained nurses and informally trained teachers attempted to break the hegemony of their respective professions. But the trained elites resisted such intrusions through the creation of a hierarchical system of *trained* and *untrained* personnel with better pay and accelerated promotional opportunities for the former. The State, using its regulatory power, has generally endeavoured to keep open a plentiful supply of cheap labour. For instance, though Company Secretaries succeeded in obtaining a charter for their profession through legislation in Parliament in early 1980s, firms with paid up capital of less than Rs 25 lakh are permitted by law to have ordinary commerce graduates as company secretaries.

There are no definite academic requirements for personnel executives in India as also in most other countries. The exception, however, is with regard to the legislation regulating employment of welfare officers under the Factories Act. Formal qualifications and criteria for recognition exist merely for the posts of welfare officers under the Factories' Act, but not for others in the personnel function. Although there are many courses of study available to personnel executives, it is not necessary to complete any one of these in order to hold responsible positions in the personnel function. Preparing for personnel management has been considered more a process of osmosis. Education, training facilities and practices have been highly fragmented.

Personnel specialists expanded their sphere of influence by cashing in on the *inadequacies* and *trained incapacities* of engineers in line management. Most of the functions now performed by personnel were once the forte of line managers. The growth of unionism, State intervention through a spate of legislation and code of practices, the stress on statutory welfare, and need for broader and consistent policies in large and complex organizations made it easy for personnel specialists to expand their role and enhance their status. The increasing incidence of conflict with a better organized work force, and the threat of legal prosecution have enabled the personnel managers to acquire additional clout in the organizational power structure. The knowledge of human relations and social skills which are part of the profession's stock-in-trade are too indeterminate to form a sufficiently exclusive and distinctive basis on which to claim a monopoly. In personnel selection, psychological testing has become a separate specialization. With HRD becoming a fad, training and development is burgeoning into an autonomous discipline, unmindful of the disillusionment and resentment of line management over the stripping of their role in developing people. On the other hand, designing and evaluating jobs which provide incentives to motivate people, and adapt to changes in technology, expert knowledge of industrial and human engineering is required. The wheel of personnel function seems to have taken a full circle since Taylor, and at least part of the work that personnel usurped from engineers in line management is going back to engineers now in staff function.

The maze of labour legislation made legal qualifications imperative to handle the industrial relations function. A critique of personnel education in the country referred to the students of personnel as the children of Industrial Disputes Act and called for de-emphasizing the legal aspects of industrial relations in the function. A similar view was endorsed at the National Workshop on Industrial Relations Teaching and Research conducted by the National Labour Institute at Delhi in February, 1982.

With advances in the information technology, the personnel specialists are now increasingly using computers. Going far beyond traditional pay roll preparation, computers are being used for human resource inventories, for facilitating collective bargaining, thus becoming a vital input for strategic human resource planning and management.

Today, the expanding role of personnel in organizations is accompanied by visible developments in its sub-functions towards the creation of autonomous disciplines. Some of them are now striving to achieve the status of a profession, which for long eluded the personnel function itself.

## Professional Association

Personnel specialists and practitioners formed associations decades ago. In the recent past, two such major professional bodies merged to form a single professional body, National Institute of Personnel Management (NIPM) at the national level. But, the sphere of influence of NIPM is rather limited and unlike other professions, particularly chartered accountancy and company secretaryship, personnel does not possess a charter for its profession.

NIPM conducts pre- and post-training programmes and organizes seminars and conferences to update members on current issues and techniques. But it has virtually no say in the accreditation of academic courses, and the government does not consult NIPM on this. The Indian Medical Association, the Bar Council, the Institute of Chartered Accountants and others have jurisdiction on limiting the entry of people into respective professions, but NIPM or any other personnel professional body does not have similar jurisdiction in personnel education.

NIPM's record of contribution to relevant policy-making, representation in tripartite fora, and authority to morally bind its members to certain basic professional values is extremely limited. Even expulsion from NIPM membership does not disqualify the person from continuing in the profession.

Thus, while it may be unfair to underestimate the positive contributions made by NIPM to the cause of personnel, it is equally hard to concede that it meets the requirements expected of a professional association, as yet.

## Code of Ethics

To be in a profession means to profess, to take a vow of service, to live one's career by a higher standard than is expected of others. The medicos have their Hippocratic oath, but personnel has none except that the National Institute of Personnel Management requires its members to declare allegiance to its code of ethics (Exhibit 1.1). A certificate or a degree can at best serve as a professional identification, but there is a marked difference between professional identification and professional conduct.

The central theme of any profession is unselfish service to mankind, not service to self. Personnel can and should seek to achieve professionalization through performance marked by progressive outlook, attitude and practice. At a recent convention on excellence in personnel, some senior personnel managers admitted the need, in the first instance, for setting out minimum desirable standards of performance and attaining them before one could talk about excellence.

**EXHIBIT 1.1**

---

**National Institute of Personnel Management**
**Code of Ethics**

As a member of the National Institute of Personnel Management, I declare that I shall—

- Subscribe to the aims and objects of the National Institute of Personnel Management and be bound by its Constitution;
- Recognise and accept the dignity of an individual as human being, irrespective of religion, language, caste or creed;
- Maintain high standard of integrity and behaviour demanded by the profession;
- Conduct myself as a responsible member of the management team committed to the achievement of the organizational goals;
- Take keen interest in the establishment of healthy personnel practices and development of the profession;
- Try to win confidence and gain respect of the employers and employees and make myself available to them so as to provide formal and informal intervention to resolve industrial conflicts;
- Endeavour to enhance the good name of my profession in dealing with other professional bodies, government departments, and employers' and employees' organizations;
- Cooperate in maximizing the effectiveness of the profession by exchanging freely information and experience with other members;
- Not allow any interest other than professional to interfere with my official work;
- Not interfere with the right of association of the employees;
- Not disclose any information of a confidential nature that I may acquire in the course of my professional work without obtaining the consent of those concerned and not to use confidential information for personal gains;
- Not accept or offer any improper gratification in any form or manner whatsoever in connection with or in the course of my professional work; and
- Not take or acquiesce in any such action which may bring the Institute and/or the profession into disrepute.

## OBJECTIVES OF PERSONNEL MANAGEMENT

The primary purpose of personnel management is to contribute to the profitability and survival of an organization by effective management of its total human resources. In doing so, however, it seeks to strike a balance, often delicate and complex, of the macro (societal), micro (organizational), functional and personal objectives:

### Societal

Personnel management should recognize the changes in the nature of employment contract, and ideals such as social justice defined in the constitution, objectives set out in the national economic plans and legislation limiting the employer prerogatives and managerial discretion in personnel policies and decisions.

### Organizational

Personnel management contributes to organizational effectiveness by building up employee motivation, commitment and role effectiveness through sharing of information regarding mutual rights, obligations and the philosophy underlying personnel policies, procedures and practices.

### Functional

Personnel management's  functional objective is responsibility for:

(i)  initiating and formulating personnel policies, preferably on the basis of consensus and with the approval of the chief executives;

(ii) advising line managers and operating through, not around them;

(iii) providing support services such as recruitment, selection, training, development, reward systems, etc;

(iv) developing collaborative and problem-solving approaches in union-management relations; and

(v) monitoring, controlling and providing feedback relating to personnel policies and activities and implementing organization development and human resource development programmes.

### Personal

To assist employees in developing congruence between individual goals and organizational objectives and in striving for realizing higher standards of performance, satisfaction and quality of working life.

## THE ROLE OF PERSONNEL FUNCTIONS

All managers have direct responsibility for the human assets (people) in an organization and are responsible for activities and decisions concerning personnel.  In this sense all managers are personnel managers. Still most organizations have a separate personnel department whose main job is to coordinate all personnel activities. There is need for a close interaction between the personnel department which has the responsibility for the administration of personnel and line managers who have responsibility for optimizing the use of their resources, viz., physical, financial and human. The Personnel department is then required to maintain personnel information systems and comply with government's legal regulatory framework and union-management agreements.

While the environmental factors and historical developments discussed earlier influenced and expanded the role of personnel function, it would be useful to conceive the role of personnel in a client-centred perspective. It is possible to identify some major client groups within the organisation and which are not necessarily mutually exclusive. They are top management, line managers, employees and other clients and customers. Personnel activities also involve interface with unions and the government. Ideally the role of personnel should evolve from the expectations of these interacting groups.

Top management expects personnel specialists to devise ways and means for better utilization of human resources, in collaboration with line managers. It expects them to develop cost-effective means to help maintain highly motivated, satisfied and productive human resources. Other expectations include ensuring harmony in its relations with individual employees and unions, anticipating the future areas of concern in managing human assets and preparing itself to meet challenges productively. Personnel specialists should, however, be prepared to face situations where top managements expect them to deliver goods without letting them know what is actually expected of them. There would often be occasions when professional ethics may come into conflict with the business goals of the employer. This problem is common to organizations where the culture and climate are not supportive of professional conduct and where the sole preoccupation is to increase the profits or expand the wealth-base.

The line managers expect personnel staff to advise and assist them in personnel matters, but leave decisions on promotions, job assignments and other people-related matters to themselves. The personnel staff's authority is to advise, not direct, other managers. When line managers choose to reject personnel staff's advice, they must agree to bear full responsibility for the outcome. It is not healthy for any organization if personnel specialists expand their area of power and authority because of the trained incapacities or weaknesses of line managers. Such a trend, if not arrested, will lead to line-staff conflict. It is possible to delineate the line-staff role in different aspects of personnel as shown in Table 1.2. In the personnel department itself, personnel specialists will have line authority to direct operations. And in situations which are technically complex requiring specialist knowledge of personnel staff it will have functional authority to decide for example, while negotiating a pay revision at the instance of top management. Like all organizational decisions, here too such functional authority of personnel is subject to review by the top management.

Employees may have their own expectations from and perceptions about the role of personnel department. For instance, they may want to be heard, involved and are made to feel important; their grievances need to be redressed and their jobs made interesting and purposeful. They expect the personnel to initiate and implement reward and recognition systems. Personnel executives should express concern and take up activities that integrate rather than alienate employees into organizational purposes. Employees feel the need for a trade union to protect their interests because personnel policies and practices in organizations are usually not adequately geared to make employees feel that the management genuinely cares for them. The role of the personnel then is to develop employees as partners in the firm's cause, not as adversaries.

**Table 1.2   Personnel Functions and Responsibilities of Line and Personnel Managers**

| Function | Line Management Responsibility | Personnel Department Responsibility |
|---|---|---|
| Recruitment and selection | Provide data for job analysis and descriptions and specify desired qualifications and skills<br><br>Interview candidates and decide about suitability of candidates | Job/role analysis, HRP, administering recruitment and selection process, compliance with legal and organizational rules/regulations |
| Retention | Fair treatment of employees, open communication and recognition for good work | Equitable, fair and consistent policies and practices; competitive pay and benefit programmes |
| Training and development | On-the-job training, coaching, feedback and motivation | Career planning, Management and Organisation Development |
| Performance appraisal | Performance and potential appraisal, feedback and counselling | Development of performance appraisal system, maintenance of personal records and feedback to line managers |
| Grievance handling | Handling grievances | Setting up grievance procedure, monitoring and recommending policy changes, based on analysis of grievances |
| Discipline | Responsibility for managing discipline | Advice on disciplinary rules, procedures and actions |
| Promotions | Final authority in performance-related decisions concerning promotions | Final authority in policy-related decisions concerning promotions; implementing reservation policy for scheduled castes, union agreements, etc. |

Unions expect the personnel management to bargain in good faith, establish equilibrium in power relations and implement agreements in letter and spirit. The government expects the personnel to implement its policies and meet statutory requirements. The role of the personnel department should bear relationship with the expectations and demands placed on them by these various client groups. Satisfying the multiple objectives of these diverse groups productively is a major challenge facing personnel executives.

## PERSONNEL ACTIVITIES

The number and nature of personnel activities seem to grow with the size of an organization, particularly of those which are imposed through legislation. For example, the following personnel activities are mandatory for organizations (or factories) employing at least the number of employees specified in brackets against each:

| | |
|---|---|
| Standing orders specifying working conditions, etc. | (100) |
| Provident Fund | ( 20) |
| Appointment of Labour Welfare Officer | (500) |
| Works Committee | (100) |
| Creche | ( 50 women workers) |

The attitude and expectations on the part of top management towards personnel function seem to influence significantly the role, size, scope, involvement and importance accorded to it in organizational decisions and tasks. An illustrative list of personnel activities is presented in Exhibit 1.2.

**EXHIBIT 1.2**

---

### An Illustrative List of Personnel Activities

| | |
|---|---|
| Absenteeism Control | Medical Services |
| | Motivation |
| | Organization Development |
| Bonus | Participative Management |
| | Performance Appraisal |
| Canteen | Potential Appraisal |
| Career Planning | Personnel Information System |
| Collective Bargaining | Personnel Research/Audit |
| Community Services | Placement |
| Counselling | Promotion Policy |
| | Public Relations |
| Discipline | |
| | Quality Circles |
| Education | Quality of work-life **programmes** |
| Employee Communications | |
| | Recruitment |
| Fringe Benefits | Redundancy Programmes |
| | Reward and Recognition Systems |
| Grievance Redressal | Retirement Benefits |

| | |
|---|---|
| Human Resource Development | Safety |
| House Journal | Selection |
| Human Resource Planning | Separation Schemes |
| Human Asset Accounting | |
| Human Resource Audit | Social Security |
| | Strikes |
| | Succession Planning |
| Incentives | Suggestion Schemes |
| Induction | |
| | Time Office |
| Job Analysis | Township |
| Job Design | Training |
| Job Descriptions | Transfer Policy |
| Job Evaluation | Transport |
| Job Specification | |
| | |
| Lay-offs | |
| Leave | |
| Leave-travel Concession | |
| Legal Aspects | |

## Personnel Policy and Procedure

Personnel Policy is a statement of what the organization wishes to do with regard to its employees in order to meet its objectives. It is a general guide to decision-making. Usually, the larger the size of an organization, the more the number of people who make decisions regarding how the employees are to be handled. The decisions may concern recruitment, promotions, transfers, appraisal, training, pay, benefits, leave and several other aspects. There is need for consistency and uniformity in all these matters in the interest of both the individual employee and the organization. Any variations or deviations in interpretation or implementation would mean setting a precedent, which influences policy and may be treated as policy itself.

For personnel policies to be effective they need to be implemented with a sense of objectivity, uniformly and consistently. Each policy should clearly state the purpose, and a procedure for implementation. The procedure should indicate (a) who has the authority to implement policy; (b) whether and who has the discretion; (c) the flow of paperwork in connection with action, and, (d) records to be maintained for monitoring and control.

Personnel policies are not the policies of the personnel department created by personnel executives in isolation. To begin with, legislation places restrictions on both the employer and the employees in formulating policies. For example, an organization may prefer annual earned leave to be availed by its employees for rest and relaxation to enable them to recuperate and be more productive. But legislation guarantees accumulation of such leave by employees up to 240 days. The air hostesses used to be thrown out of jobs on marriage till the Supreme Court ended this practice. Management philosophy, trade union practices, employee characteristics, social norms, financial position of the organization and a host of other factors can influence personnel policies in different ways. Tata Steel introduced a variety of welfare measures in the early part of this century, not because of pressure from unions or the state but because of a management philosophy guided by the enlightened paternal urge to take care of their employees.   On the other hand, in some organizations management, under pressure from unions may agree to grant overtime on a quota basis irrespective of the need for it.

Organizations can consult their counterparts or employer organizations for help in policy-making.   In addition, it is desirable if personnel policies evolve out of consultation and consensus among all levels of employees who are affected by policy administration.  Consultation and other participatory approaches in formulating policy reveal problems before adoption, offer a chance to explain management's viewpoint and set in motion processes which help gain company-wide acceptance of the policy.

The personnel department should take responsibility to compile and update formal personnel policies in the form of a manual or a handbook and communicate the same to all concerned. It should also promote understanding and compliance.   However, while policies and procedures have to be well-developed and widely disseminated, it is important to note that if there is too much emphasis on them, it can curb managerial initiative.   Periodic review and audit would ensure that policies are productive and facilitate rather than hinder organizational purposes.

## STRUCTURE OF THE PERSONNEL DEPARTMENT

When we refer to the structure of a sub-system in an organization, we are essentially talking about relatively stable relationship among the positions and groups of positions (units) that comprise the sub-system within the organization.   The structure is concerned with vertical differentiations (hierarchical levels of organization), authority, coordination and horizontal differentiations between organizational units—for example, between product or service lines, geographical areas, or skills.   The major problem that is characteristic of all organizations concerns the impact on organizations of the two strong and opposing forces that Max Weber described way back in 1922—the need for division of labour and specialization, and the need for centralized authority.

Broadly, we find three major forms in which the personnel is organized: (i) centralized, (ii) decentralized, and  (iii) matrix. These three forms are briefly discussed here:

### Centralized

The centralized staff in the personnel function is responsible for performing specialist functions such as policy formulation, human resource planning, recruitment, salary-administration, training and development, appraisals, personnel information system, etc.  This is the most common type of staffing in small, medium and even large units and single-product enterprises. It has certain advantages:

(i) The positions are filled by experts in the field.
(ii) It is possible to have consistency in policy and practice.
(iii) Economies of scale can be had by having one expert serving in multiple divisions.

Figure 1.1 shows typical centralized, staff specialist method of staffing and structuring the personnel department.

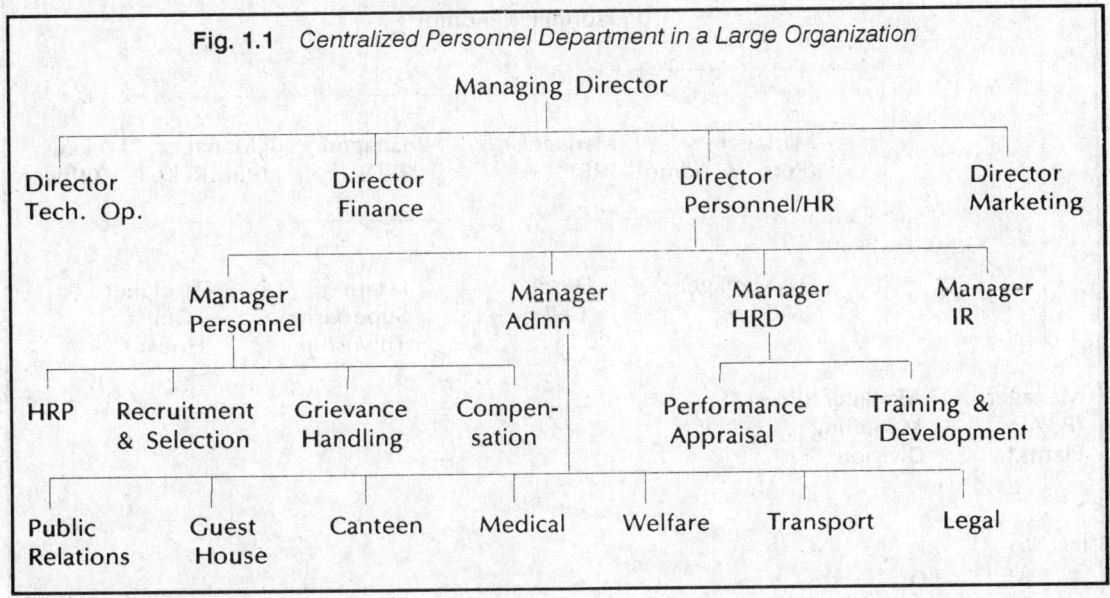

**Fig. 1.1**  *Centralized Personnel Department in a Large Organization*

## Decentralized

In some large organizations, the personnel function is decentralised among different functions/geographical areas/products. Whatever the form, no organization is either wholly centralized or decentralized. To an extent all have decentralized structures with some degree of centralization. As shown in Fig. 1.2 the organization structure of a multi-unit fertilizer cooperative is decentralized based both on function and geographical location. In the case of BHEL we observe there is decentralization based on product and geographical location. TELCO, Jamshedpur has a personnel department which is organized with a combination of centralization of certain specialized functions within personnel and decentralization, productwise.

There is a controversy about the appropriate organizational choices: Should an organization be structured according to product or function? Should all specialists in a given function be grouped under a common boss, regardless of differences in products they are involved in or should the various functional specialists working on a single product be grouped together under the same superior? It seems appropriate to suggest that both are feasible depending upon the organizational environment and the nature of the organization itself.

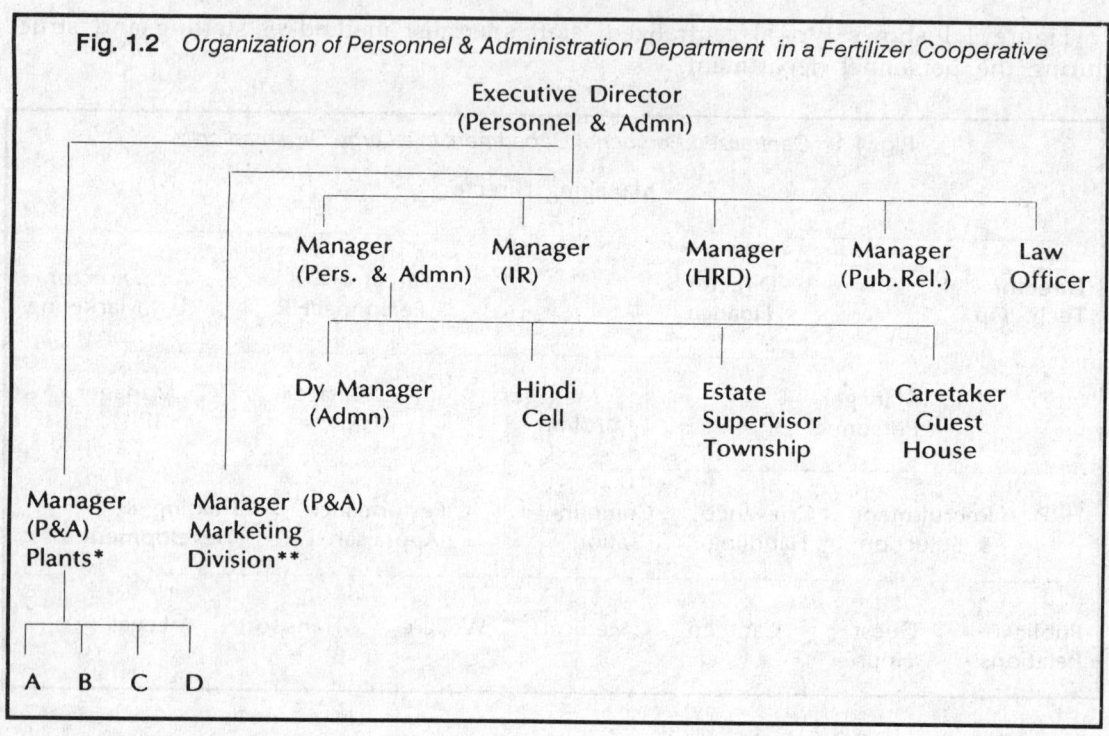

Fig. 1.2  *Organization of Personnel & Administration Department in a Fertilizer Cooperative*

\* Manager (P & A) of each plant reports to both the Executive Director (Personnel & Admn) at the Head Office and the General Manager in charge of the concerned plant.

\*\* Manager (P & A) of Marketing Division reports to both the Executive Director (Personnel & Admn) and the Marketing Director at the Head Office.

## Matrix Organization

Matrix organizational structure originated with the United States Aerospace programme of the 1960s and the aerospace industry's extraordinary and conflicting needs for system (for innovation) and order (for regulation and control). A matrix organization employs a multiple command system that also includes related support mechanisms and associated organizational cultures and behaviour pattern. A matrix organisation is not desirable unless (i) the organization must cope with two or more critical sectors (functions, products, services, areas); (ii) organizational tasks are uncertain, complex and highly interdependent; and, (iii) there are economies of scale. Figure 1.3 shows a typical matrix form of departmentation.

**Fig. 1.3** *Matrix Departmentation*

|  | VP R&D | VP Operating | VP Marketing | VP Finance | VP Personnel |
|---|---|---|---|---|---|
| Project A |  |  |  |  |  |
| Project B |  |  |  |  |  |
| Project C |  |  |  |  |  |
| Project D |  |  |  |  |  |

## SUMMARY

In this chapter we have attempted to present an overview of economic, demographic, socio-cultural, politico-legal and technological environment affecting the management of personnel in Indian organizations. We have observed that organizations are becoming large and complex with progressive industrialization and advent of new technologies. Over the years, government intervention, legal regulation and union pressures are also influencing the management of personnel in our organizations. We have also reviewed the changing role of personnel management in India from 1920s to date and observed the developments, shift in outlook and emphasis and transformation in the role and status of the function. It was noted that the personnel function which had an unnoticed beginning in the 1920s is likely to blossom into a profession when its outlook changes in the desired direction.

As of now, however, we have observed that personnel is not yet a profession as defined due to several reasons. There are no entry-level qualifications for the profession and doubts persist about the specific and unique expertise which personnel specialists possess, particularly in the wake of its ever-expanding role and developments within organizations, and the trend towards sub-functions seeking to become relatively more exclusive, autonomous disciplines. Personnel Management's professional association does not yet enjoy the same status as the professional associations in other fields like accounting, law, engineering or medicine. It is possible to set ethical standards and norms for the members of the profession, but there is, as yet, hardly any body to ensure their compliance.

The role and objectives of the personnel function should be considered in a client-centred perspective. The client groups include top management, line managers and employees besides customers, dealers, government unions and other public. The objectives are classified into four groups that include (i) societal (ii) organizational (iii) functional and (iv) personal. Striking a delicate balance between the multiple and conflicting objectives is critical to the effectiveness of the function.

The personnel manager's responsibility and authority have been described, personnel activities have been listed and the role of line managers and personnel staff in personnel functions have been delineated.

Three major forms of organization have been discussed while observing the structure of personnel department in an organization, (a) centralized, (b) decentralized, and (c) matrix structures.

---

## KEY WORDS

| | | |
|---|---|---|
| **Personnel** | : | A function commonly created as a separate unit/subsystem/department in medium and large organizations to facilitate the most effective use of people (employees) to achieve organizational and individual goals. Sometimes referred to as human resource management or employee relations. |
| **Pro-active Approach** | : | The tendency to initiate action in anticipation of challenges. |
| **Reactive Approach** | : | Taking action after the event. |
| **Line Managers** | : | Managers with authority to direct operations in their sphere of activity. |
| **Staff Authority** | : | Authority to advise, not direct, others. |
| **Functional Authority** | : | Functional authority allows staff specialists to make decisions in specified circumstances that are otherwise normally reserved for line managers. |
| **Matrix Organization** | : | An organization that employs multiple command systems. |

---

# COMPANY EXPERIENCE : NO GREATER REWARD*

Let me start on a note of modesty. If today I find myself where I am, there are obviously two reasons and two only. One is extreme good luck and the second is that I have been blessed with a deep love for other human beings, especially those less fortunate than I am. It is something that I was born with and which, in fact, has turned out to be my main interest in life. If there has been a reciprocal gesture on the part of other human beings towards me, it is but natural, because they must see in someone who feels for them a spark of affection which they reciprocate. It is really a simple human equation. One need not go into great depths of learning to understand that human relations are at the bottom of almost every conceivable facet of management.

It would be of interest to most people to know that Tata Steel has to its credit many firsts, not only in India but also in the world. It introduced the first 8-hour working day in 1912 before its acceptance in the USA, UK or Europe. It gave free medical aid in 1915; leave with pay, then unknown in England and America, in 1920; schooling for children in 1917; workers' provident fund schemes, unknown in England, in 1920; accident compensation in 1920; retiring gratuity in 1937 and profit-sharing bonus in 1934. The Company set up a Works Committee for handling grievances as early as 1919.

---

* This section is based on a speech by Russi H Mody in January 1981, when he was Vice-Chairman and Managing Director of the Tata Iron and Steel Company Limited. Subsequently Russi Mody succeeded J R D Tata as Chairman of the Company.

In spite of all this, however, Tata Steel had the biggest strike in its history in 1928. Now this is a paradox. We had working conditions which were well in advance of those prevailing in most other countries and yet, we had the biggest strike in our history, lasting for over three months. This was because we lacked human relations. Fortunately for us, that was the last strike we had and ever since then, there has been no confrontation between the Management and the Union for a period of over 50 years.

## Planting the Seed

In 1938, Mr J R D Tata became the Chairman of Tata Steel. I joined the company in 1939 as a young assistant. One soon got to hear that the labour leader, Prof. Abdul Bari, thought a great deal of Mr J R D Tata as a friend of labour. Prof. Bari recognized in him a person who saw that labour was not a commodity and that it needed a fair deal, which he was prepared to give.

Naturally, when Mr Tata made the first settlement with Prof. Bari which cost the company about Rs 2.5 crore in those days, most of his own colleagues on the Board thought that this sort of a settlement with the Union would lead to the ruination of the Company. But the seed of industrial harmony which Mr Tata planted with Prof. Bari survived and flourished under the care of Mr Michael John, who succeeded Prof. Bari after his death.

Between Mr Michael John and Mr J R D Tata there developed a rapport wherein each recognized in the other a thrust towards the same objective — an objective, incidentally, set by Jamshetji Tata himself many decades ago. This objective was that an industry should not be run merely for the sake of production and profit; that a worker's needs, his fulfilments and his basic necessities were as important as any other consideration in industry.

Once that rapport had been established, everything else became easy. That is not to say that there were no problems; problems abounded. But both sides recognized that the solution to those problems was not another strike, as happened in 1928, but dialogue, discussion, talk, give-and-take not only between Mr Michael John and Mr J R D Tata, but at all levels of management and labour.

This led to a situation where, soon after the War, Mr J R D Tata circulated a note to his colleagues in Tata Steel, which stated that since all kinds of activities of a technical nature required specialization, the handling of human beings also required some sort of specialization. This being so, the note recommended that a department should be created exclusively to handle the problems of human beings in the Company. So came into being in 1947 the Personnel Department of the Tata Iron and Steel Company.

## Turning Point

My own association with the Personnel Department started in the same year in unusual and slightly amusing circumstances. I was then the Deputy Superintendent (Coal Commercial) buying coal for the Company. I was stationed in Calcutta.

One afternoon, at the end of February 1947, I was working in my office when the *chaprasi* came and told me that *'Tata Sahib aur Dalal Sahib ne salam diya'*. "Send you greetings." Little did I imagine that this was to be a turning point in my career and that I was to leave the happy life of a commercial assistant and enter a field of adventure which, with hindsight, I can truly say I would not have missed for all the gold in Babylon. I entered the Chairman's room where that formidable administrator, Sir Ardeshir Dalal, was also present.

Mr Tata asked: "Russi, is it true that in the whole of Clive Street (now Netaji Subhas Road), a Union of Mercantile Employees has been formed and that your own Department of Coal is the only one in the whole of Clive Street that has not joined the Union?"

"As a matter of fact, it is true," I replied.

"Why?" he asked.

I blurted something about the employees being happy with my treatment of them and that they did not feel the necessity of forming a union.

Mr Tata said, "If that is so, I am forming a new department in Jamshedpur and I would like you to go and join it." And so, I went to Jamshedpur. On March 17, 1947, I found myself installed there as an Additional Labour Officer looking after the personnel functions in our mines and collieries.

*A Howling Mob*    Nothing very exciting happened until May 1, a date which is a memorable one for me. On that afternoon, I was walking back home after the day's work when I saw a lot of agitated officers and supervisors rushing out of the Plant, most of them shouting excitedly to me to stay away as there was some serious trouble inside the Plant. As one who had nothing to do with the Works — I was in charge of a colliery a hundred miles away — I ought to have stayed away. But youth, curiosity and a lack of discretion irresistibly propelled me towards the Plant. As I turned the corner round the Foundries, I suddenly found myself in the midst of a howling, raging crowd of men who had stopped work and were freely assaulting any supervisor they could lay their hands on.

The reason why I was not immediately dealt with in a similar manner I can only ascribe to the fact that I was not much known inside the Plant and my manner of dressing — in a white khadi shirt and shorts — further increased their doubts about my identity. Nevertheless, I was surrounded in a manner from which escape was impossible and I had to deal with the situation as best I could. In such circumstances, the first thing one thinks of is God and I doubt if the Almighty ever heard a louder voice seeking His help. I also realized that all my education and training at Harrow and Oxford were not going to be of any use in dealing with this situation. To this day I have not found a satisfactory explanation as to why things took the course they did but this is what happened.

Now, quite frankly, it was a question of survival. My Hindi, which is quite fluent now, was extremely poor at that time. I did not know what to say or do. Whatever it was, the people were shouting and screaming at me. So, in broken Hindi, I spoke to them as coherently as I could.

I asked those nearest to me: *Kya hai? Kya taqlif hai?* "What is it? What is the trouble?"

To my surprise, instead of attacking me, I found them responding to me. *'Sahib'*, they complained, *'yeh hai, woh hai'*. "Sir, it is this, it is that." They were telling me what their grievances were and I found myself automatically reacting to them with sympathy.

When the appropriate moment, I thought, had arrived, I ventured in a little further and said, *'Bait Jao na. Bait kar baat karo na'*. "Please sit down. Speak after sitting down." To my surprise, again, they sat down. In response to their complaints, all I could say was: "I will look into your grievances. I will personally look into them if some of you will come and talk to me." They said, "You will personally look into them?" I said "Yes". Gradually, the howling subsided, the tension eased and the men slowly withdrew from their state of frenzy. They were sitting before me keen to listen and act as I bid them. I still remember how my senior officers, who were all 'imposed' on the balcony of the building opposite, reacted with utter disbelief when later they came to know of what had happened. The men started explaining to me that throughout the period of the War (World War II) they had been oppressed. Now that they were going to be independent, they were going to have their own say in matters. I said, "All right, I am independent too, as you all are. Let us all get down together and talk about what is to be done."

Finally, after this had gone on for nearly an hour, I suggested, *'Abhi kam par chale jao na. Kal hum log baat karenge'*. "Now, please go to work. Tomorrow, we shall talk." Amazingly, they started moving out and returned to work.

***Three Sleepless Nights***    Now, to this day, I do not know the answer as to why this happened. Be that as it may, from that moment a rapport was established and for 34 years thereafter, I have received nothing but the utmost kindness and understanding from labour whenever I have had to deal with them.

The incident of May 1, 1947, was not an isolated one staged by the machine shops. It was obviously, a deep-seated plan on the part of labour in every department to stage such demonstrations and to assault their supervisors. Within 24 hours calls started coming to me to go to various departments to help out the supervisors and pacify the crowds. Obviously, the news had gone round that there was a crazy officer, who instead of running away from them was prepared to go and talk to them, and I remember not being allowed to lay my head on a pillow for three days and three nights.

After this incident, Management did the obvious thing. They took me away from personnel administration of the Mines and Collieries and gave me a room and a desk inside the Works. In other words, I was put in charge of the Personnel Department in the Works with a two-line directive from Sir Ardeshir Dalal that, whatever happened by way of labour trouble in the plant, I was to try and bring peace because no other officer was allowed to come inside the Works except myself. This I proceeded to do effectively with two disastrous consequences. First, I completely alienated the sympathy of the officers and supervisors towards the new Personnel Department and myself; secondly, in the process, I acquired a swollen head, the size of a zeppelin!

Power is a heady wine, and power over the masses even more so. Since this happened to me when I was only 28 years old, I completely lost my head and this created a great deal of difficulty for all concerned and not the least for myself. When peaceful times returned in the factory, my bosses, quite rightly and equally effectively, sat upon me and proceeded to cut me down to size.

**The Leap Forward**     However, there was sufficient exciting work to be done in the new Department and armed with an undated letter of resignation in my pocket, I set myself to these tasks with enthusiasm. One of the main areas of dispute was over a wage structure for which they had waited for many years and when it was finally produced it was not to their satisfaction and they made a big issue out of this. The basic fact was that during the war, they could not open their mouths and felt oppressed, and they were just waiting for an occasion to express their anger and frustration.

Anyhow, we settled down to run the Personnel Department with a purpose. Grievance Committees were already there as I had mentioned in the beginning, but these were not functioning properly. We formed Joint Committees on the basis of equal representation to them from both management and labour, and the Committees' task was to lay down all kinds of procedures, which did not exist before, to settle disputes.

None of us had ever read books on Personnel Management. In fact, the plethora of books that is now available on the subject was not, mercifully, written then. I must at this stage make a confession, which many find difficult to believe, that I have not till now read a single book on Personnel Management. A few chapters here and there, read under duress, provide all the knowledge I have gleaned from the scribes. But, then   lack of academic knowledge did not deter us from going about our task on an enthusiastic note.

## Handling Grievances

As a consequence of the events described above, I was made Chairman of the East and West Plant Joint Committees and we were faced with the task of clearing all the accumulations of 117 cases in one Committee and about 86 in the other. We decided that something had to be done about the backlog. I remember that one day I went to see the President of the Union, Mr Michael John, and put my difficulties before him with a suggestion that it would be nice if we were to start with a clean slate and that since most of the cases pending had been there for several months, if not years, perhaps the best practical solution would be for the management to concede 50%. There was much murmuring at this suggestion but ultimately common sense prevailed and this practical solution was applied. To the utter disbelief of the Management and the workers, in one week over 200 cases were "unanimously" decided!

Strangely enough, from then on, while we decided all cases on their merits, this principle of give-and-take permeated the thinking of the Committees, and in the next seven years there was only one case which could not be unanimously decided. This opened the eyes of both Management and the workers to the possibility of dealing effectively with grievances without the aid of outside agencies and in the last 34 years in Tata Steel not a single case has gone for arbitration or before a tribunal.

**Union's Contribution**     One of the major contributions that the union made in this kind of an atmosphere was on the subject of minimum qualifications. After the War, competition was on the horizon. We felt the necessity of departing from the age-old concept of seniority promotions. It is one of the things that beset all of us in industry. Now how to get out of it? Promotion by seniority had been established over the years. People who could not read two words in English had been made Foremen, General Foremen and even Assistant Superintendents.

We discussed the problem with Mr Michael John. Under different circumstances this problem might have led to a major confrontation in Tata Steel, but it was amicably settled by us.

A Joint Committee was set up. We drew up a schedule of minimum qualifications. Then the Union made a demand on us. "Now you open schools in polytechnics, where you can teach the existing workers the kind of course, degree courses, which we all have to do." We spent lakhs of rupees on this. But today we have, as a result of the foresight on the part of the Union and the responsibility that they displayed, a system whereby 99% of our promotions are given to technically qualified people. When you talk of appeasing the Union and being nice to them, can you imagine the inestimable benefit that accrued to the Company as a result of the Union being made to agree to a situation like this?

**Restoring Confidence**    Another very difficult task was to restore the confidence of the supervisors and officers shattered in the 1947 fracas. This was not easy and could not be done overnight. It required a great deal of tact and change of concepts on the part of all concerned. Ultimately a policy emerged in the Tata Iron and Steel Company that it would be best for the head of a department to also operate as his own personnel manager. Today, it is commonly accepted that the personnel function is an advisory one; it was not so in the late 40s and early 50s, and many were the battles fought on this concept of line versus staff responsibilities.

Over the last 30 years, Tata Steel has re-established the responsibility of line management. It is now accepted by all officers and supervisors that whereas their personnel function is advisory, their advice should normally be accepted or very good reasons should be furnished by them for not doing so.

**Reaching for the Top**    At a time when the newly formed Personnel Department was going great guns, the time came to shift me from Jamshedpur to the collieries. On my first visit to the collieries, I saw the miserable conditions under which the poor collier was working. I wrote a letter to our Chairman saying, "We are today the lowest in productivity of all except the Karam Chand Thapar Group." At that time the coal-fields were not nationalized and we were making a loss of Rs 50 lakh per year. In the letter I asked the Chairman for an expenditure of Rs 55 lakh over two years. I still remember the break-up. I wanted Rs. 12 lakh for making roads, about Rs 23 lakh for providing electricity to the workers' colony and Rs 20 lakh to supply drinking water in each of the colliery houses.

The Chairman (Mr J R D Tata) readily agreed. I am quite certain that nobody would have agreed to an expenditure of this magnitude in a division running on losses, but he did. He saw the point more clearly than any of us at that time. The net result of that was that after we had spent that money and made friends, shall I say, with our own people in the collieries, we started gaining in productivity and production.

Finally, we came to a stage when labour looked upon us almost with the same regard as they looked upon their own Union. Incidentally, today, we have the highest productivity in the coal-fields. And we achieved that, not because the other coal-fields were nationalized, but before the nationalization of the coal-fields, it was achieved because our workers got enthusiastic and wanted to work for us. They were looked after properly — their needs were met. We introduced helmets and boots at a time when they did not have them at the coal-fields. We got hell from our other colleagues, like the Indian Mining Association, for introducing these conveniences, but we went ahead and did so.

## Advantage: Employer

Now you will ask me: "Apart from all this, what is the kind of advantage that one gets?" I want to propound a theory. In our 'mai-baap' society of today, there is really no substitute for a good, enlightened manager. The poor Union leader, however strong he may be, is not your equal. He has to negotiate, he has to confront, he has to cajole both the Management and the workers.

Now you put yourself in the position of the worker. He goes to the Union, he waits for four or five months and finally he may get something. But he goes to the Managing Director who says, "Well, I think you are right. You take it." Here, the Union leader is at a great disadvantage. We are so accustomed to thinking of the Union leader as being on the offensive and ourselves being on the defensive. Actually, if you are an enlightened employer today, you are on the offensive and he is on the defensive. The worker will always look up towards good and enlightened leadership in management.

*Trial of Strength*     Let me give you some examples of what I mean. We were treating the colliery workers on a different footing in regard to the annual bonus from that applicable to our people at Jamshedpur. And one day my friend, Mr Kantibhai Mehta, a very fine, reasonable, responsible trade union leader, felt that he was not happy with the bonus that was given and, frankly, neither was I. I wanted the Colliery Division to enjoy parity with Jamshedpur, but for some reason or other my Managing Director did not think so. And so, Mr Mehta said, "I will have to ask my men to boycott the bonus."

I said, "Well, do that, but it will be equally my duty to send out a circular to the men explaining as to why they could not have the same bonus as that of Jamshedpur and requesting them to take the bonus. And if, by any chance, they listen to me and not you, don't come to me and say that I am trying to weaken the Union by this kind of action."

He said, "Fair enough." He told the men to boycott the bonus and I sent out a circular appealing to the men to accept it. Except for 19 people in the Accounts Department at Jamadoba Collieries' headquarters, 12,500 people accepted the bonus without a murmur.

Let me tell you another story. In the Company we have a very good ferro-manganese plant with a capacity for producing 30,000 tonnes a year. Our production never exceeded 1,800 to 2,000 tonnes a month against a normal production of 2,500 tonnes. I took charge of this plant in 1965.

On my first day, I asked my staff: "What are the grievances and what is the morale of the workers?" I asked, "How many people are there?" They said 450. "Start sending 50 at a time to see me in the Director's Bungalow." Never had the workers seen the inside of a Director's Bungalow.

*Boots, Helmets and Morale*   When the workers came there I made them sit down. I served them cold drinks and not one would touch his glass. They were scared. They had never been asked to see the Director-in-Charge of their operations in all these years. And I could not get a word out of them. I tried for 15 minutes, for 20 minutes, saying, *'Bolo kya taklif hai?'* "Tell me what is your difficulty." There was absolute silence. Somewhat luckily, one fellow spoke up. He said, *'Sahib, hum logon ko accha treatment nahi milta hai'*. "Sir, we do not get good treatment." *"Tum, log kya kism ka treatment mangte ho?"* "What kind of treatment do you people want?" I asked. The man said, "Sahib, we are working in front of the furnaces, and we don't even get boots." I said, *Boots nahi milta hai?"* "You do not get boots?" The manager was sitting there. I told him: "Give them 450 pairs of boots." Of course, I made a mental calculation as to how much it would cost, but that did not matter. Then, emboldened, another fellow said, *'Helmet nahi milta, sahib'*. I said, *'Helmet nahi milta?'* "You do not get helmets?" I turned to the manager and said, *'Helmet de do'*. "Give them helmets?" The poor manager was almost collapsing because if he had to get boots previously he would have to go through fifteen tiers before he could get a sanction. Here was a Director who was sanctioning them boots, helmets, aprons, gloves, all kinds of things.

The first batch of 50 went out dazed. The next batch of 50 came up and it took me only five minutes to get them to open their mouths. They asked for the same things. I said, "You have already got them!" Well, to cut a long story short, I saw all 450 of them. It might have cost us something like Rs 2 to Rs 3.5 lakh to provide for their requirements.

During the previous eight years, in which we had not operated to capacity, we had made a loss of Rs 8 crore. Within one month the production reached 2,200 tonnes, then the next month it reached 2,500 tonnes, the third month it rose to 3,000 tonnes and they have since kept an average of 3,000 tonnes with a record production of 3,400 tonnes without a single rupee being spent on additional equipment or anything.

*Dangers of Individualism*     There is, however, great danger in this. Here, I have to be a little immodest if you will forgive me. The danger lies in the fact that in all these instances there has been a personal equation. The word goes round in labour circles that "Mody is a friend of labour. Mody looks after us." But this is a dangerous thing.

What happens after Mody goes? Does the organization collapse? This is why it is very necessary that although, very occasionally, one may do this sort of thing, one should not do it all the time — even if you feel that you can do it. You may out-wit your Union, but in the long run you are outwitting yourself. You must not take advantage of this indiscriminately. One must build up the Union because that is what is going to, in the long run, deliver the goods — a strong centralized Union dealing with a good, enlightened Management. That concept should not be destroyed by any individual antics.

There have also been many occasions when I have had to be very tough with labour and I have never compromised on discipline. My experience, however, is that the men respond to strong leadership provided it is fair, just and objective. I have discharged many undesirable elements and I have succeeded in this only because basi-cally labour was with me and realized that what I was doing was for the general good of all concerned.

Now, no longer do I treat personnel management or industrial relations, as a *good to everybody* attitude. It has become a vital tool of Management towards higher produc-tion, higher productivity and getting the best out of my men.

Today, the stage has been reached — going back to Tata Steel again, and forget-ting Russi Mody for a while — where the men are so much with the Tata Iron and Steel Company that on the most important issue of nationalization, when it arose a couple of years ago, they were the ones who most strongly opposed nationalization along with us.

Can any company ask for a greater reward than this?

## QUESTIONS

1. Analyze Russi Mody's role as a personnel manager in the different situations described.
2. Discuss whether, in your opinion, Russi Mody:
   (i) adopted a pro-employee stand to build up his own personal image;
   (ii) had always tried to balance the interests of both the employees and the or-ganization;
   (iii) could have achieved what he did, if he did not have the top management sup-port? Give reasons.
3. How do you think Russi Mody got the support of top management?
4. In retrospect do you feel that there was any element of risk in Russi Mody's approach towards his role as personnel manager? Should every personnel manager emulate his example? Discuss pros and cons, if any and also the conditions necessary, both within the individual and in the context in which he is called upon to perform.

## REVIEW QUESTIONS

1. What is a profession? Is personnel a profession in India?
2. Outline the factors influencing personnel environment in India and discuss their im-plications.
3. Examine the changing role of personnel in India.
4. Visit a (i) manufacturing organization; (ii) a service organization like bank or hospi-tal; and (iii) a small scale enterprise. Examine how personnel activities are carried out.

# CASE : BILLY BISCUIT COMPANY

Billy Biscuit Company is a medium scale family-run company located in Eastern India. It employed 140 workers during the last two years. The company had strained industrial relations. When the workers went on strike the company declared a lockout. Four months later the workers' union and management resumed dialogue. The union agreed to cooperate with management provided the management lifts the lockout and abolishes the personnel department. The management agreed to both the demands.

Do you feel that even if the personnel department is abolished, personnel functions should still be carried out? Give reasons. If the answer is yes, discuss 'how' it is possible and who will have the responsibility for personnel activities in the organization?

## FURTHER READING

1. Fombrun, C, N M Toichy and M A Devanna, 1984. *Strategic Human Resource Management*, John Wiley & Sons: New York.

2. Rowland, K and G R Ferris, 1986. *Current Issues in Personnel Management*, Allan and Bacon: Boston.

3. Scheer, W E, 1985. *The Dartnell Personnel Administration Handbook*, Dartnell: Chicago.

4. Sharma, B R, 1974. *The Indian Industrial Worker*, Vikas: Bombay.

5. Sikula, A F and J F Mckenna, 1984. *The Management of Human Resources*, John Wiley & Sons: New York.

C H A P T E R  **2**

# Analyzing and Designing Jobs

---

**LEARNING OBJECTIVES**

After reading this chapter, you should be able to:
● Understand the meanings of the terms : job analysis, job description, job specification and job design  ● Appreciate the uses of job analysis information in activities relating to personnel management decisions
● Describe various methods used to collect job analysis information
● Familiarize yourself with the basic principles of job design  ● Develop awareness of the job redesign efforts made in the Indian context.

---

## JOB ANALYSIS

After having decided on the primary objectives of an organization, it is necessary to think of various activities that must be carried out to enable the organization to achieve its overall objectives. This breaking down of the objectives into manageable operations needs to be done in a manner that will ensure efficient utilization of resources — men, materials, machines and money — towards manufacturing goods or providing services of high quality.  This calls for a scientific and systematic analysis of various jobs that must be performed according to the laid down criteria and with maximum efficiency.  These jobs must fit together, coordinate and be directed towards the objectives of the organization.  It was immediately after the Industrial Revolution around 1900 that approaches to scientific analysis of jobs were developed by Frederick W Taylor and Gilbert, which have been widely used since then by manufacturing, commercial and service organizations throughout  the world.  Thus the study and understanding of jobs is an important part of any personnel programme.

Job analysis involves formal study of jobs.  It attempts to provide information on both the requirements of a job in terms of time for completion, necessary activities and the expected performance standards on the one hand, and also the specific technical and behavioural knowledge, skill and attitudes needed among the personnel to meet those job requirements on the other.

In this chapter the concept and process of job analysis and the contributions it has made to personnel programme and activities, as also the methods and techniques employed for job analysis will be discussed. The relationship of job analysis to design of jobs will be highlighted. Job analysis as the core of human resources management activities has been emphasized.

## The Uses of Job Analysis

Job analysis, through clearly defined and written job description and job specification, provides the basic information around which personnel functions can be carried out.

| | | |
|---|---|---|
| **Fig. 2.1** *Uses of Job Analysis* | | |
| Organization structure<br><br>• Responsibility<br><br>• Authority<br>• Accountability | Manpower planning<br><br>• Future job requirement<br><br>• Skill requirement | Recruitment, selection, placement<br>• Matching job requirement and skill |
| Labour relations<br>• Deviation from agreed job standards | JOB ANALYSIS | Orientation |
| Counselling<br>• Vocational guidance<br>• Rehabilitation<br>• Counselling | Job description    Job specification<br>• Factual statement of tasks, duties and responsibilities of a job    • Statement of human attributes, abilities, skill required to perform job | • What is expected? |
| | | Performance appraisal<br>• Performance standards<br>• Performance review |
| | | Career path planning<br>• Future prospects for movement along career paths |
| Engineering design and methods of improvement<br>Job design and matching of social and psychological requirements of employees technical system requirements<br>Job evaluation and rating<br>• Classification of jobs<br>• Guiding decisions on salary structures | Training and development<br>• Updating of skills<br>• Changing job requirements | |

It provides a fuller understanding of the specific requirements of jobs and personal attributes needed and thus helps in taking job-related personnel decisions. In order to use it as a source of additional input for decision making, job analysis needs to be carried out periodically, particularly in view of the changing nature of jobs necessitated by advancement in technology and variations in manpower characteristics. Not many organizations tend to use it in a systematic way for personnel-related decisions. Some of the uses of the job analysis process are shown in Fig. 2.1.

**Organization Structure and Design**     Job analysis helps in classifying job requirements and interrelationships among jobs. Responsibility, commensurate authority and accountability for various jobs can be specified so as to minimize duplication or overlap. Decisions regarding hierarchical positions and functional differentiation or integration could be taken on the basis of data obtained through this process for organizational efficiency.

*Manpower Planning*     Job analysis provides useful information for forecasting manpower requirements in terms of skills and expertise and in planning for transfers and promotion.

*Recruitment*     Information regarding the job in question is a prerequisite for recruitment decisions.

*Selection*     Methods of selection must be based on meaningful forecast of job performance. An understanding of what an employee is expected to do on the job is necessary for such a meaningful forecast.

*Placement*     A clear understanding of the requirements of a job and the abilities of a person to meet those requirements can help in taking placement decisions to ensure that specific jobs are assigned to those people who will be most productive.

*Orientation*     The orientation programmes could be geared towards helping the employee learn those tasks, activities and duties that are essential for doing a given job more effectively. A clear idea of what is required on a job provides clarity as to what is to be learnt.

*Performance Appraisal*     Job analysis provides understanding of critical parts of a job as well as what is expected of the job holder in those critical areas. Employee performance can thus be evaluated against known critical activities and standards.

*Career Path Planning*     Effective career path planning becomes possible only when employees have a clear idea of various opportunities in terms of career paths and jobs available to them. For both the organization and the individual, job analysis provides basic information necessary for career planning and development efforts.

*Training and Development*     Job analysis provides useful information for identification of training needs, design of training programmes and the evaluation of training effectiveness. All training activities are based on analysis of job requirements and personal skill requirements. Likewise employee development strategies like job rotation, transfers, higher responsibilities, can be based on these data.

*Job Evaluation*    Job analysis is a prerequisite for ranking of jobs in terms of their relative worth to the organization, to enable organizations to take decisions on salary structures.

*Labour Relations*    The information provided by job analysis is essential for both the management and the union before entering into negotiated agreements as well as for resolving grievances and jurisdictional disputes.

*Job Design*    Knowledge of job requirements, people requirements and individual capabilities obtained through job analysis provides basic information on which such job design decisions can be taken. This optimally meets the requirements of the technical efficiency with that of the social and personal requirements of the job holders.

*Engineering Design and Methods of Improvement*    Job analysis can also provide useful data to bring about improvements in the engineering design and work methods for higher efficiency and productivity.

*Safety*    In the course of carrying out job analysis, certain unsafe environmental and operational conditions or individual habits, if any, are discovered and thus may lead to safety improvements.

*Counselling*    Vocational guidance and rehabilitation counselling is facilitated by the information available on career choices and personal limitations.

## The Job Analysis Process

As stated earlier, to be meaningful and useful for personnel-related decision-making, job analysis must be carried more at frequent intervals than the practice in most organizations. Jobs in the past were considered to be static and were designed on the basis that they would not change. While the people working on those jobs were different, the jobs remained unchanged. It is now realized, that for higher efficiency and productivity, jobs must change according to the employees who carry them out. Some of the major reasons leading such change are:

*1. Technological Change*    The pace of change in technology necessitate changes in the nature of job as well as the skills required. Word processing has drastically changed the nature of secretarial jobs. Computerization and automation likewise give rise to new requirements of certain jobs while older requirements become redundant.

*2. Union–Management Agreements*    The agreements entered between management and the union can bring about change in the nature of job, duties and responsibilities. For example, under employees' participation scheme, the workers are encouraged to accept wider responsibilities.

**3. People**    Human beings are not robots; each employee brings with him his own strengths and weaknesses, his own style of handling a job and his own aptitude. There is a saying that the job is what the incumbent makes of it.

Thus, the job analysis process must take into account the changing nature of job on account of the factors listed above. Often, role analysis techniques (discussed later in the chapter) are used in dealing with the dynamic nature of job requirements.

**Steps in the Job Analysis Process**    The major steps to be followed in carrying out job analysis in an on-going organization are:

*1. Organization Analysis:*    The first step is to get an overall view of various jobs in the organization with a view to examining the linkages between jobs and the organizational objectives, interrelationships among jobs, and the contribution of various jobs towards achieving organizational efficiency and effectiveness. The organization chart and work flow or process charts constitute an important source of information for the purpose.

*2.Deciding on the uses of Job Analysis Information:*    Depending   on   organizational priorities and constraints, it is desirable to develop clarity regarding the possible uses of the information pertaining to job analysis. In the previous pages it has been already indicated that such information could be utilized for practically all personnel functions. Nevertheless, it is important to focus on a few priority activities in which the job analysis information could be used.

*3. Selection of Jobs for Analysis:*    Carrying out job analysis is a time-consuming and costly process. It is ,therefore, desirable to select a representative sample of jobs for purposes of analysis.

*4. Collection of Data:*    Data will have to be collected on the characteristics of job, the required behaviour and personal attributes needed to do the job effectively. Several techniques for job analysis are available. Care needs to be taken to use only such techniques which are acceptable and reliable in the existing situation within the organization. Various techniques of job analysis will be discussed under a separate heading.

*5. Preparation of Job Description:*    The information collected in the previous step is used in preparing a job description for the job highlighting major tasks, duties, and responsibilities for effective job performance.

*6. Preparation of Job Specification:*    Likewise, the information gathered in step (4) is used to prepare the job specification for a job highlighting the personal attributes required in terms of education, training, aptitude and experience to fulful the job description.

Job analysis thus carried out provides basic inputs to the design of jobs so that it is able to meet the requirements of both the organization (in terms of efficiency and productivity) as well as the employees (in terms of job satisfaction and need fulfilment). Developing appropriate job design is then the outcome of the job analysis process.

Following the steps outlined above provides the basis for carrying out job analysis exercise. It requires careful planning, and it is necessary for those having responsibility for job analysis to explain the rationale to affected employees as well as the management so that the necessary approval and cooperation can be obtained.

## Job Analysis: Methods of Data Collection

A variety of sources and methods are used for the collection of data relating to a job. None of them, however, is perfect and usually a combination of several methods is used for collecting data for job analysis. Before discussing various methods and their advantages and disadvantages, it is desirable to get an overview of the entire organization as mentioned earlier in this chapter.

The organization chart provides some basic understanding of the relationship between various departments and units, between line and staff functions, vertical levels representing decision and responsibility centres, and channels of communication and information flow. The chart spells out the formal requirements of the organization in these terms, even though it does not and cannot depict the informal arrangements that tend to develop when people work together. Yet another useful source of information is the process chart or work flow chart depicting the interconnections of various jobs in more specific terms. It represents the flow of activities pertaining to a job from input to output stage. These and similar other documents need to be consulted before beginning the use of other job analysis methods.

In order to collect certain core information relating to job analysis, a questionnaire called the *Job Analysis Information Format* (JAIF)* can be used. The JAIF can provide basic information for use of any job analysis method. Job incumbents are asked to complete the JAIF and on the basis of information obtained through this, decision regarding the use of various methods of data collection and further investigation can be taken. The JAIF has 17 items covering such areas as general purpose of the job, supervisory duties, work output, job duties, educational requirements of the job, experience needed to perform the job, skill required, equipments needed, physical and emotional demands, workplace location, environmental conditions, physical surroundings, health and safety.

The methods of data collection that are commonly used for job analysis are given below.

*Job Performance*    This method involves the analyst actually doing the job under study to get first-hand exposure to actual tasks, and physical, environmental and social demands of the job. This method can be used only in jobs where skill requirements are not high and, therefore, can be learnt quickly and easily. This method is not appropriate for jobs requiring extensive training.

---

* Henderson, R I, 1979. *Compensation Management*,   Reston: Virginia, pp 146–152.

*Observation*    The analyst observes, without getting directly involved in the job, the worker or a group engaged in doing the job. Observations are made on various tasks, activities, the pace at which tasks are carried out, and the way different activities are performed. This method is appropriate for jobs that involve manual, standardized, and short job cycle activities. The information thus obtained is recorded in a standard format.

There are, however, many aspects of a job involving mental processes and unforeseen circumstances which cannot be observed easily by an analyst.

*Interview*    This is a widely used method particularly in those jobs which do not lend themselves to either observation or actual performance of the job on the part of the analyst. It can also be used in conjunction with observation for seeking clarification on job-related aspects. The workers are, therefore, interviewed to collect data on various requirements of the job. It is desirable to use a standard format so as to focus the interview to the purpose of the analyst. Standardized interview schedule with job-related questions needs to be prepared carefully to enable the interviewer to be in control of the situation. Data thus collected from a number of workers can be compared to discern the common and critical aspects of a job.

One major problem with interviewing is that inaccurate information may be collected. If the purpose of interview is not clear, the worker may provide information to protect his own interest. Establishing rapport between analyst and worker is a prerequisite for effective use of this method.

*Critical Incidents*    Yet another way to obtain information on job requirements is to distinguish between effective or ineffective behaviours of the workers in the job. The workers are asked to describe several incidents based on their past experience related to a particular job. The incidents collected from individual employees are analyzed and categorized according to the general job areas they describe. The end result draws a fairly clear picture of actual job requirements.

This method is time-consuming and requires high level of skill on the part of the analyst to do the content analysis using the descriptive accounts presented by workers.

*Questionnaire*    This method involves developing structured questionnaires on different aspects of job-related tasks and behaviour such as coordinating, negotiating, manual and mental processes. Each task or behaviour is described in terms of characteristics such as frequency, significance, difficulty and relationship to overall performance. The questionnaires are administered to relevant employees and they are asked to give their ratings of these job dimensions. The ratings thus obtained are analyzed and a profile of actual job requirements is developed. Some of the standard questionnaires are the Comprehensive Occupational Data Analysis Programmes (CODAP), Position Analysis Questionnaire (PAQ) and Functional Job Analysis (FJA).

The Position Analysis Questionnaire (PAQ)* is a behaviour-oriented job analysis

---

* McCormick, E J, et al., 1972. "A Study of Job Characteristics and Job Dimensions Based on the Position Analysis Questionnaire (PAQ)", *Journal of Applied Psychology*, vol. 56, pp 347-368.

questionnaire consisting of 194 items that fall into the following categories:

1. *Information input*—where and how the worker gets the information to do his job.
2. *Mental processes*—the reasoning, planning, and decision-making involved in a job.
3. *Work Output*—physical activities as well as the tools or devices used.
4. *Relationship with other persons.*
5. *Job Context*—physical and social.
6. *Other job characteristics*—any other relevant characteristics not covered above.

Each of the items under the above categories is rated in terms of its importance to the job to be analyzed in terms of a 5-point scale:

DNA — Does not apply

1. Very minor
2. Low
3. Average
4. High
5. Extreme

For analyzing managerial jobs also, the following two structured questionnaires are available.

*Management Position Description Questionnaire (MPDQ)* [*] It is a 208 item behaviourally based instrument for describing, comparing, classifying and evaluating executive positions in terms of their content. The latest version of the MPDQ is classified into 10 parts:

1. General information
2. Decision making
3. Planning and organizing
4. Supervising and controlling
5. Consulting and innovating
6. Contact
7. Monitoring business indicators
8. Overall ratings
9. Know-how
10. Organization chart.

*Supervisory Task Description Questionnaire (STDQ)* [**] This questionnaire includes 100 job related activities of first-line supervisors in seven areas:

1. Working with subordinates
2. Organizing work of subordinates
3. Work planning and scheduling
4. Maintaining efficient quality and production
5. Maintaining safe and clean work areas
6. Maintaining equipment and machinery
7. Compiling records and reports.

---

*Rornow, W W and P R Pinto, 1976. "The Development of a Managerial Job Taxonomy: A System for Describing, Classifying, and Evaluating Executive Positions", *Journal of Applied Psychology*, vol. 61, pp. 410-418.

**Dowell, B E and Wexley, K N, 1978. "Development of a Work Behaviour Taxonomy for First Line Supervisors", *Journal of Applied Psychology*, vol. 63, pp. 563–572.

The questionnaire method enables the analyst to cover a large number of respondents in the shortest possible time and provides a breadth of coverage that is extremely difficult to obtain otherwise. Data obtained through this method can be quantified and processed by computer which opens up vast analytical possibilities.

The disadvantages of the questionnaire method are:

(i) developing standardized questionnaires is time-consuming and expensive.

(ii) direct rapport between analyst and respondent is not possible.

(iii) respondent's cooperation and motivation are not guaranteed due to impersonal approach.

## JOB DESCRIPTION

The data collected for job analysis provide the basis for preparing job description for each job. This functional description describes what the job entails. Although there is no standard format for a job description, it usually includes:

1. *Job title* — a title of the job.

2. *Job Summary* — a brief statement of what the job entails.

3. *Job activities* — a description of the tasks performed, material used and extent of supervision given or received.

4. *Working conditions and physical environment* — heat, light, noise level, hazards are described.

5. *Social environment* — Information on size of work group and interpersonal interactions required to perform the job.

## JOB SPECIFICATION

Another output of the job analysis process is the preparation of job specifications for different jobs in the organization. The job specification spells out the attributes of a person in terms of education, training, experience, abilities, skills and aptitude required to perform a particular job, requirements of which have already been indicated in the job description. For every job description it is desirable to have job specification so as to enable the organization to know what kind of persons are required to do particular jobs. The personal attributes can be classified under three categories:

(i) *Essential attributes* — abilities, skills and knowledge that a person must possess.

(ii) *Desirable attributes* — those attributes that one ought to possess.

(iii) *Contra-indicators* — attributes that will become a handicap to successful job performance.

There is a great deal of disagreement with regard to developing complete and correct job specification unlike the job description which provides more objective assessment of job requirements. The decision to specify minimum human requirements for a job is a difficult one as it involves considerable degree of subjectivity. There is a general feeling that organizations generally tend to establish relatively high requirements for formal education and training, resulting in a situation where highly qualified people end up doing jobs of routine nature. Particularly, in India, highly qualified personnel are recruited for jobs where their abilities, skills and knowledge are under-utilized.

Despite these problems, however, minimally acceptable human requirements need to be specified for various jobs and category of jobs. The format for job specification should include the following items:

1. Position title
2. Education/training
3. Experience
4. Knowledge
5. Abilities
6. Skills
7. Aptitude
8. Desirable attributes
9. Contra-indicators, if any.

## ROLE ANALYSIS

Job analysis as mentioned earlier is based on the assumption that jobs in an organization are relatively static and that it is possible to identify and predict critical job-related behaviours which leads to effective performance. In reality, job-related behaviour is guided by a number of factors in the situation which cannot easily be predicted. The situation in which a person works keeps changing and so does his behaviour. Job analysis, therefore, must be extended to take into account the dynamic behaviour of job-holders. A concept that enlarges the scope of job analysis is called *Role Analysis*.

**EXHIBIT 2.1**

---

**Position Title : Systems Manager**

Systems Manager will be responsible for the overall management of the Computer Centre and will assist the Head, Computer Centre in planning and management of various facilities at the Centre.

Specifically, his responsibilities include:

(a) Supervision of all the operational and maintenance requirements of the Centre.
(b) Interaction with the computer users.
(c) Regular performance monitoring and tuning of the system(s) available at the Centre.
(d) Software acquisition and installation.
(e) Software development and maintenance.
(f) Planning and conducting short-term courses primarily for the computer users.
(g) Planning and preparing relevant documentations for the computer users.
(h) Attending to any other duties/responsibilities as may be assigned by the authorities of the Institute and the Head of the Computer Centre.

The Systems Manager will lead a team of Software Engineers and Operational staff and he may be provided with accommodation on priority basis and on payment of license fee as per the rules of the Institute.

---

*Qualifications*
(a) M.E/M. Tech./B.E./B. Tech. in Computer Science or in any field of Engineering with good academic record.
OR
(b) M.Sc. in Computer Science/Mathematics/Physics with good academic record.
*Experience*
The candidate should have at least 10 years of relevant experience, out of which not less than 3 years should be in System Programming/design and at least 2 years must be in a supervisory position. Experience with a large time-sharing computing facilities is desirable.

**EXHIBIT 2.2**

**Job Title: Group  Personnel  Manager**
Looks after the personnel and  administration  affairs of a fast expanding and diversified group of companies.  The main role is to assist management in developing the group companies.  Work involves review of organization structures, systematic assessment of the corporate plans, manpower needs and managerial resources, and strengthening the organization by appropriate recruitment, job rotation and training. Upgradation of personnel policies and procedures and overseeing the routine personnel management functions are the other responsibilities. Works under the general supervision of the Managing Director, exercising independent judgement and initiative in carrying out tasks.
*Activities*
Participates in developing corporate plans and policies relating to human resources management.
Develops manpower plans within the framework of overall corporate plan.
Interacts with institutions and consultancy firms for recruitment and selection of personnel.
Reviews with top management organization structures of various groups and recommends changes, if any.
Coordinates with departmental heads in developing manpower development plans.
Provides expert opinion on the interrelation of company policies relating to recruitment of minority communities.
Initiates innovations in personnel management functions.

Role is a more dynamic concept as it takes into account the expectations that superiors, top management, subordinates, colleagues or peers, union and even the outside agencies have of the job holder and his performance. These expectations could at times contradictory to each other, resulting in a conflict situation. For example, management's expectations from a job holder may be contradictory to what the union expects him to do.  The job holder encounters these situations every day and in order to resolve these conflicts, he has to adopt innovative behaviour often.  Moreover, as the expectations of different groups of people keep on changing, the required behaviour of the job holder is also likely to undergo change.

Likewise, the management philosophy, organization climate and industrial relations climate also affect the actual role that a job holder is likely to perform.  For example, job description of supervisory jobs could be similar in two organizations, but the actual behavioural requirement is likely to be different depending on whether the management style is democratic or authoritarian.  In an organization with a democratic management style, the supervisor's required behaviour will be one of involving his workers in the decision-making process. Under an authoritarian management style, the supervisor would be required to keep the decision-making authority to himself, to give direction and to maintain a watch on the activities of his subordinates.

It is desirable, therefore, to supplement the job analysis process with role analysis to obtain a realistic picture of the requirements of a job as also the essential human attributes needed to perform the role.

## THE JOB DESIGN

One of the major purposes of carrying out job analysis exercise is to develop appropriate design of job for improved efficiency and productivity. Job analysis provides details of the tasks and activities to be carried out on a particular job as also the human characteristics required through examination of inter-relatedness of activities, combining them in manageable work units, using input-output analysis and matching them with required human skills and motivation in such a way so as to maximize productivity and human satisfaction. In recent years there has been significant advancement in our knowledge in this area and alternative designs of jobs are being introduced in practically all types of organizations throughout the world.

### Classical Approach to Designing Jobs

A systematic body of knowledge on the design of jobs is a product of the Industrial Revolution and the rise of large-scale economic enterprises. It was around 1900 that Frederick W Taylor developed what are commonly known as the Principles of Scientific Management which form the basis for designing jobs in most organizations. The primary emphasis of scientific management was on planning, standardizing, and improving human effort at the operative level in order to maximize output with minimum input. The principles on which job design is based can be stated as follows:

*Task Fragmentation*    In order to achieve technical efficiency, a task needs to be broken down into smaller operations.

*Technology Optimisation*    Through a scientific analysis of task, it is desirable to develop the best method for doing the task. This best method cannot be altered without sacrificing efficiency.

*Standardization of the Method*    The method so discovered is standardized through time and motion studies.

*Specialization*    Workers need to be selected to perform specific tasks thus leading to narrow specialization.

*Training*    Workers so selected should be trained in the most efficient method for performing the task. Cost and time for training are considerably reduced due to fragmentation of tasks into simple operation requiring low skill-level.

**Individual Responsibility**    Each worker is made responsible for a single operation forming part of the total task.  Thus one-man–one-job becomes the building block of the organization.

**Economic Incentive**    Having assigned responsibility of specialized and standardized operations, a system of economic incentive as reward for performance is developed.

The design of jobs based on principles mentioned above has its own implication for organizational efficiency and for human motivation, such as the following:

*(i) Narrow Specialization*    A worker performs only one or a couple of operations or duties.  Only limited potentials of workers are utilized.

*(ii) Routinization*    Due to fragmentation of task and narrow specialization, the same operation or duty has to be repeated again. This results in boredom and dissatisfaction.

*(iii) Reduction in Work Cycle*    The interval at which the same operation is repeated becomes less, leading to monotony.

*(iv) Techno-economic Criteria of Evaluation*    The design is based on the criterion of technical efficiency alone; human satisfaction and well being are not taken into account. Emphasis on economic rewards reduces a worker to the status of an economic man denying the existence of complex multiple needs.

The rational and task centred approach to job design has serious limitations in that the social and personal needs of human beings engaged in the task are not taken into account.  Adam Smith anticipated these consequences two centuries ago: "The man whose whole life is spent in performing a few simple operations... becomes as stupid and ignorant as it is possible for a human creature to become".[*] An in-depth study of the automobile workers by Kornhauser validates the prediction of Adam Smith as summarized below.

1. Large numbers of automobile workers manifest feelings, attitudes and behaviour that signify un-satisfactory life adjustments or mental health.  Their responses reveal feelings of inadequacy, low self-esteem, anxiety, hostility, dissatisfaction with life and low personal morale.

2. Mental health varies consistently with the level of jobs the workers perform. That is, the higher the occupation (in respect of skill and associated attributes of variety, responsibility and pay), the better is the average mental health.

3. By far the most influential attribute in determining job satisfaction and dissatisfaction is the opportunity the work offers–or fails to offer–for use of the worker's abilities and for associated feelings of interest, sense of accomplishment, personal growth, and self respect.[**]

In short, jobs designed on classical principles to maximize efficiency and to reduce cost lead to situations where hidden psychological costs are very high, particularly in

---

[*]  Smith, Adam. *An Inquiry into the Nature and Causes of the Wealth of Nations* (1776) quoted in R H Campbell, *et al.*(Eds),1976. Oxford University Press: London.

[**]  Kornhauser, A, 1965. *Mental Health of the Industrial Workers*, John Wiley & Sons: New York.

the present with heightened awareness, improved education and rising aspirations of the employees. If jobs fail to provide opportunities for human need satisfaction, a majority of employees become alienated and frustrated. The alienation and frustration of employees at organizational level get reflected in such behaviour as superficial attention to work, poor quality-consciousness, loss of interest in work, absenteeism, resistance to change and even sabotage. At individual level, it may result in physical illness, poor mental health, chronic depression and maladjustment to family and community life. The psychological and motivational costs of monotonous, unchallenging jobs may well exceed their presumed economic benefits.

## The Behavioural Approach : Job Redesign

The search for alternative ways of designing jobs to counter the dysfunctional consequences of designs based on traditional principles began with the developments in behavioural sciences and in the general systems theory. The first systematic attempt at redesigning jobs were successfully made in the coal mining industry in the UK and in the textile industry in India in the early 1950s.

Before we take up the experiences of organizations in India and abroad for discussion, it is worthwhile to understand the concept of job redesign. Since 1950s a number of terminologies like humanization of work, work redesign, work structuring, participative system design and the like have been used; all of which, however, can be subsumed under the concept and theory of what has come to be known as the *Quality of Working Life Movement*. In its ultimate analysis the Quality of Working Life (QWL) Movement aims at designing and developing *with* directly concerned people such work systems as are capable of optimizing the fulfilment of human needs and the demands that technologies (technical system of work) place on them are able to generate adaptive responses to environmental realities. We shall, for the sake of clarity, refer to the concept as job redesign in the present context.

The dominant approach to job redesign for individuals over the last decade has been the job characteristics theory of Hackman and Oldham.

The model representing the theories is shown graphically in Table 2.1.

This model is based on the assumption that three key psychological states of a job holder affect motivation and satisfaction on the job. The three states are:

*1. Experienced Meaningfulness* The degree to which the job holder experiences work as important, valuable, and worthwhile.

*2. Experienced Responsibility* The extent to which the job holder feels personally responsible and accountable for the results of the work performed.

*3. Knowledge of Results* The understanding that a job holder receives about how effectively he or she is performing the job.

When an employee experiences these three states on the job, he or she feels internal work motivation. Also, to the extent that these states are important to an employee, he or she feels the urge to perform well.

There are a number of key job core dimensions that lead to these psychological states. These are:

*1. Variety of Skill* This refers to the degree to which the job requires the person to do

Table 2.1   Job Characteristics Model*

| Implementing Concepts | Core Job Dimensions | Critical Psychological States | Personal and Work Outcomes |
| --- | --- | --- | --- |
| Combining tasks | Skill variety | Experienced meaningfulness | High internal work motivation |
| Forming natural work units | Task identity | | High quality work performance |
| Establishing client relationships | Task significance | Experienced responsibility for outcomes of the work | High satisfaction with the work |
| Vertical loading | Autonomy | | Low absenteeism and turnover |
| Opening feedback channels | Feedback | Knowledge of the actual results of the work activities | |

*    This model is based on: Hackman, J R and G R Oldham, 1980. *Work Redesign*, Addison-Wesley, Reading, Massachusetts. Also see: Hackman, JR, GR Oldham, R Janson and K Purdy, 1975, "A New Strategy for Job Enrichment", *California Management Review*, vol.17, p.58.

different things and involves the use of a number of different skills, abilities and talents.

2. *Identity of the Task*   This involves a complete module of work; the person can do the job from the beginning to end with visible outcomes.

3. *Significance of the Task*   This is concerned with the importance of the job.  Does it have a significant impact on others both internal and external to the organization?

4. *Autonomy*   This  refers to the  amount of freedom, independence and discretion the person has in areas such as scheduling the work, making decisions and determining how to do the job.

5. *Feedback*   This involves the degree to which the job provides the person with clear and direct information about job outcomes and performance.[*]

As can be discerned from the meanings of various job dimensions—skill variety, task identity and task significance—all contribute to a sense of meaningfulness. Autonomy is directly related to feelings of responsibility.   Feedback is related to knowledge of results.

Only people who strongly value and desire personal feelings of accomplishment and growth and who are satisfied with the organization's internal environment (pay, security, supervisors and co-workers) will respond positively to a job that is characterized by the five core dimensions.   Personal traits, characteristics and need patterns

* Nadler, D A, J R Hackman and E E Lawler, 1979.  *Managing Organizational Behaviour*. Little Brown: Boston, pp 81-82.

of the person holding the job, therefore, must be considered in redesigning jobs. If there is a fit between the person and the job, the personal and work outcome will be as follows:

- High internal work motivation
- High quality work performance
- High satisfaction with the work
- Low turnover and low absenteeism.

*Implementing Concepts*    The strategy for redesigning job involves the following principles.

(i) *Forming natural work units* — identifying basic work items and grouping them into natural categories.

(ii) *Combining tasks* — if possible, to form larger modules of work.

(iii) *Establishing client relationships* — identify who the client is, establishing the most direct contact possible and specifying criteria by which the client can evaluate the quality of the product or service he receives.

(iv) *Vertical loading* — closing the gap between planning, doing and controlling the work.

(v) *Opening feedback channels* — by establishing client relationships, placing quality control close to the worker and providing summaries of performance to the worker.

Redesign of jobs based on the above principles leads to formation of self-managing or semi-autonomous groups. Some characteristics of such groups are:

(i) They are *real*, meaning they are intact, identifiable social systems.

(ii) They are *work groups* that have to do a specified piece of work that results in product, service or decision whose acceptability is measurable.

(iii) They are *self-managing groups* whose members have the authority to manage their own task and interpersonal processes as they carry out their work.

## Job Diagnostic Survey

There are several ways that the above model can be used to diagnose the degree of task scope that a job possesses. For example, a manager could simply assess a particular job by clinically analyzing it according to the five core dimensions. Hackman et al., however, have developed a Job Diagnostic Survey (JDS)[*] questionnaire to analyze jobs. The questions on this survey yield a quantitative score that can be used to calculate an overall measure of *job scope*. The formula for this motivating potential score (MPS) is as follows:

$$\text{MPS} = \left[ \frac{\text{Skill Variety} + \text{Task Identity} + \text{Task Significance}}{3} \right] \times \text{Autonomy} \times \text{Feedback}$$

---

[*] Hackman, J R, et al, 1975. "A New Strategy for Job Enrichment." *California Management Review*, Summer, pp 57–71.

It is clear from the above formula that *autonomy* and *feedback* stand as the critical and most important dimensions. If score on either of them is 0; the MPS will also be 0 — indicating that the job is offering no motivating potential at all.

## JOB REDESIGN APPLIED : INDIAN EXPERIENCES

The experience in redesigning jobs based on the principles enunciated in the preceding pages is not a new one in India. As far back as the early 1950s, a pioneering effort was made in developing alternative job design in a textile manufacturing plant at Ahmedabad by Professor A K Rice of Tavistock Institute of Human Relations, London. This experiment happened to be the second of its kind; the first one being that of the coal mining industry in the UK. After the Ahmedabad experiment, it was not until mid 70s that the interest in this area was revived by behavioural scientists working at the National Labour Institute, New Delhi. The revival of interest in job redesign in India coincided with similar developments all over the world, particularly in Scandinavia, West Europe and the USA. Today job redesign which forms a part of *Quality of Work Life* improvement programme has become a significant movement in different parts of the world. The details of this movement and its implications to personnel function will be discussed later in the book in Chapter 11. Here it will suffice to provide examples of job redesign experiments in three different types of organisations in India.

# *THE AHMEDABAD TEXTILE MILL**

The company had installed automatic looms, in the early 50s, as part of its modernization programme. Industrial engineering procedure based on classical principles of job design were used in identifying 12 occupational roles and in assigning these roles to individual workers numbering a total of 29. The occupational roles and their distribution were: eight weavers, five battery fitters, three smash hands, two bobbin carriers, two gaters, one cloth carrier, two jobbers, two assistant jobbers, one feeler-motion fitter, one oiler, one sweeper, one humidification fitter. Each weaver thus tended 24 or 32 looms, each smash hand 75 looms. The other nine occupations were service and maintenance and each worker had either 112 or 224 looms.

Although the mill appeared to be superbly engineered, it failed to bring about improvement in quantity or quality of cloth woven even when compared with the old semi-automatic looms. Despite technological modernization and design of jobs based on industrial engineering, the productivity did not improve.

---

* Rice, A K, 1958. *Productivity and Social Organization: The Ahmedabad Experiment*, Tavistock Publications: London.

The diagnostic study carried out by Dr A K Rice to discern the causes of low productivity yielded following factors:

1. Close team work of all 12 occupations was required to maintain production, yet the way the work was designed prevented this team work. Each battery fitter was not a team unit, even though the nature of the process required it. The situation was even more confused with smash hands who tended 75 looms.

2. The eight weavers felt that they were not being adequately serviced by the different other functionaries. Each weaver came into contact with five-eighths of a battery fitter, three-eighths of a smash hand, one quarter of a gater and so on.

3. Since these activities were highly interdependent, a high degree of coordination was required to keep going. This co-ordination was not possible due to the distribution of fragmented operations among various individuals

4. The existing work-machine assignments produced organizational groupings and interaction patterns which disturbed continuity of production.

5. There was a tendency for each group or individual to blame others for poor performance.

6. Highly fragmented jobs created a confused pattern of inter-relationship among the workers and between the workers and the supervisor.

The diagnostic study showed that there was a need to redesign the organization of work in such a way that it would meet both the technical system requirements of the task as well as social system requirements of the workers. To start with, 12 occupational roles were combined into four groups of seven each. Each team of seven workers was made responsible for the operation and maintenance of a group of 64 looms—a geographic rather than a functional division of the weaving room which produced regular interaction among individuals whose jobs were interrelated. Instead of the various jobs being fractioned, members of the group would do each other's work with an overall group leader. Departmental duties were common to all the teams and one person was in charge of that function for the entire loomshed. *The ratio of looms per worker was increased from 7.7 to 9.1.*

As a result of these changes, efficiency rose from an average of 80% to an average of 95% after 60 working days and the average damage per cent dropped from 32% to 20%. In those parts of the weaving shed where job design remained unchanged, efficiency dropped to 70%, finally rising again to 80, and damage remained at 32%.

The breakdown of production tasks into component operations, and the performance of the components by different workers, was found to be common in modern industrial planning. Less common was the re-examination of a number of complementary component operations with the aim of reinstituting a larger and more satisfying task. In the original form of work organization in the automatic loom, shed tasks and occupational roles had been broken down to such an extent that the workers were no more than an aggregate of individuals, with confused jobs and personal relationships and no adequate means of knowing where they stood in relation to the work of the shed, to each other and to supervision. The new organization created small work groups, each responsible for its own control and for a comprehensible contribution to the work of the shed as a whole.

# ENGINEERING INDUSTRY*

During the mid 70s a pilot project on job redesign was started at the BHEL plant located at Hardwar. Following intensive interaction with the management, the trade unions and the supervisory staff, Block V where 25 workmen were engaged in fabrication of the upper part of the condenser unit, was selected for the pilot experiment. Some of the criteria for selection of this work unit were its compact character, reasonable layout and the favourable attitude of the manager and the shop floor trade union leaders. Moreover the productivity in the shop was low (appx. 30% in May 1975). The break up of the 25 workers in terms of their assigned jobs was 9 fitters, 3 fettlers, 3 welders, 2 gas cutters, 1 crane operator, 2 riggers, 2 helpers, and 3 workmen involved in material supplies.

The workers participated in a series of meetings with both internal and external consultants and agreed that there was a need to redesign the work. Diagnosis of the existing work system with their help revealed the following bottlenecks that came in the way of improving efficiency:

1. Each worker was concerned exclusively with his own trade. None of them identified himself with the product.

2. There was invariably forced idle time because when a particular worker was engaged at a given location, another who was required to work in close proximity had to wait until the first worker had finished his job.

3. There was uneven demand of the services of the materials supplies group, the crane operator and the riggers.

To initiate action on job redesign, the workers decided to set up a task force consisting of representatives of each category of workers together with the supervisor. Membership of the task force was to be on rotational basis except in the case of two workers with leadership skills and the supervisor. The task force consisted of eight members. An Industrial Engineer was associated with the task force as a Consultant. The Manager in charge of the shop could also participate in the task force deliberations if he wished. The task before this group was to evolve an alternative system of work which would improve the workers' motivation as well as productivity.

The task force in association with the rest of the workers came up with the following decisions:

1. Formation of Direct Production Group consisting of 1 welder, 3 fitters and 1 fettler with responsibility for the complete task.

2. Doing one another's job by undergoing on-the-job training.

3. Crane operators and riggers to learn each other's skills.

4. Gas cutters, helpers, and material supplies group to be integrated into the new work system at a later stage.

The above reorganization led to several benefits; a welder now started working as a fitter and training in other trades was given to fitters, fettlers, gas cutters and others.

---

* De, N R, 1979. *India: New Forms of Work Organization*, vol. 2, International Labour Organization: Geneva.

In September 1975, the workers, based on the confidence generated in them through the new work system, attempted further redesign of their job and decided that the workforce should be distributed in two shifts: Shift one consisting of five fitters, five welders, one gas cutter and one fettler and shift two comprising four fitters, four welders, one gas cutter and one fettler.

In addition, there would be crane operators in both the shifts. Each shift group became integrated and self-contained. It was decided that one shift would fabricate the right side of the upper part of the condenser unit, the other shift would do the same with the left side.

The above reorganization led to the following advantages:

1.  Productivity rose from 30% in May 1975 to over 75% in February 1976.
2.  One-man-one-job concept was replaced by multiple skill acquisition.
3.  Individual system of working gave way to team work.
4.  Groups were self-managed, the traditional supervisory functions of work allocations, coordination, monitoring and control being performed by the groups.
5.  Identification with the total product and concern for quality became a reality.
6.  Personal idle time (wasted in gossiping, loitering, and in unauthorized absence from workplace) was dropped considerably.
7.  Workers' supervisor and the manager showed a high degree of work commitment.

# POST OFFICE*

At the initiative of the Director, Postal Training and other senior officers of the Post and Telegraph department, Chaura Maidan Post Office at Shimla was selected for introduction of the new concept of job redesign in mid 70s. This post office has 43 full-time employees of which two were active trade union leaders. As a first step, job satisfaction survey was conducted among the employees to gain an insight into the perceived causes of satisfaction and dissatisfaction with work. The findings of the survey were:

1.  Clerks and postmen felt that superior authorities' interest in their welfare and job satisfaction was inadequate.
2.  Higher authorities were not receptive enough to the needs of the workers.
3.  The workers were not consulted on decisions affecting them.
4.  Most of the workers felt that they were doing the job as they had no alternative means of earning a living.

In effect the survey revealed that the workers experienced no satisfaction either with the work content or work climate.

The technical system of work including work flow and inter-relationships was studied jointly with the employees. The study showed that the work space was inadequate

---

* *Ibid.*

and congested; the procedure was typically bureaucratic, the one-man–one-job principle was rigidly adhered to, each counter was providing only a single service resulting in a situation where one customer would have to visit several counters depending on his needs and would, therefore, have to stand in long queues. Apart from the delay, this was a major cause of irritation among the public leading to the negative image of the postal service. As the physical conditions of work were relatively poor, no job redesign effort could be undertaken unless this problem was resolved. The management provided additional space and also brought about improvement in the working conditions.

Subsequently it was decided jointly by the management and the employees to redesign the system of work in selected areas of operations. The delivery section was chosen for this purpose. This section had three delivery clerks, one head postman and 14 postmen. The main task of delivery section is the collection and delivery of mail including valuable articles such as money orders and registered and insured articles. This section, thus, had an identifiable input and output and all the activities pertaining to collection and delivery of different types of articles could be combined together to make it a whole task. It was decided that the delivery personnel would work as a group instead of individually and that they would be responsible collectively for the total task. The group further decided to have a group leader appointed by rotation every fortnight so as to provide an opportunity to every postman to become a group leader. The group leader was chosen mainly to provide liaison between the group and the sub-postmaster.

The group started functioning satisfactorily. The postman would bring mail from post boxes located on different beats, deface the postage stamps on letters and parcels and close bags for the railway mail service. With the new system both postmen and clerks started going beyond their original work assignments. For example, if on a particular day preliminary or detailed sorting work was taking too much time, additional members would join in to expedite the work. Similarly, for accountable items such as registered letters and money orders, if the delivery clerks were unable to cope with the pressure of preparing necessary documents, the postmen themselves would volunteer their assistance.

## SUMMARY

Job analysis is the process of obtaining information about requirements of tasks and human attributes needed to meet those requirements. The immediate outputs of job analysis are job description and job specification. Job analysis is central to human resource management system and the data generated through this process can be utilized for all personnel functions. The methods of data collection for job analysis include job performance, observation, interview, critical incidents and standardized questionnaires. Usually a combination of methods is used for analyzing jobs. Job analysis needs to be supplemented with the more dynamic concept of *role analysis* which takes into consideration changing requirements of jobs and provides a realistic picture of the way employees carry out their jobs.

Job analysis provides useful data for designing jobs for improved efficiency. There are broadly two approaches to designing jobs: the classical and the behavioural approach. The classical approach based on scientific management and industrial engineering principles lays emphasis on designing jobs for technical efficiency. Social and psychological needs of human beings are not taken into account. As a result, employees become alienated and frustrated, which gets reflected in their poor mental health and poor organizational performance. The behavioural approach used to redesign jobs emphasizes both the technical and human requirements for achieving optimum efficiency. Jobs are enriched to provide skill variety, task identity, task significance, autonomy and feedback. Semi-autonomous groups around natural work units are formed which are self-regulatory in nature. Job redesign as a part of the plan to improve the quality of working life has become a world-wide movement. In India also efforts in this direction have also been made. Three cases from different types of Indian organizations where jobs were designed on behavioural principles have been discussed.

## KEY WORDS

| | | |
|---|---|---|
| **Job Analysis** | : | Process of obtaining information about the tasks to be done on the job, and the personal characteristics like education, specialized training and experience necessary to carry them out. It consists of both job description (task requirements and responsibilities) and job satisfaction (personal attributes). |
| **Job Description** | : | Description of factual statement of the duties and responsibilities of a specific job. In brief, it should tell *what* is to be done, *how* it is to be done and *why* it is to be done. |
| **Job Specification** | : | Provides information on the human attributes in terms of education, skills, aptitudes and experience necessary to perform a job effectively. |
| **Task** | : | A distinct work activity carried out for a distinct purpose. Stamping an envelope or typing a letter are examples of tasks. |
| **Duty** | : | A large part of the work comprising a number of tasks performed by an individual. For example, one of the duties of a personnel officer is to conduct job satisfaction survey. This duty will include the following tasks: designing survey questions, distributing questionnaires to respondents, tabulating data, etc. |
| **Position** | : | One or more duties performed by an individual in an organization at a given time such as director of personnel. |
| **Job** | : | A group of positions similar in their significant duties such as system analysts, computer programmers, etc. |
| **Job Family** | : | A group of two or more jobs that have similar job specifications or contain parallel work tasks, for example, sales jobs and production jobs. |
| **Job Evaluation** | : | A systematic process of determining the worth of a job in relation to other jobs. The purpose is to determine the appropriate rate of pay. It follows the job analysis process which provides the basic data for comparison and evaluation. |
| **Job Classification** | : | A grouping of jobs on some specified basis for selected characteristics such as the kind of work or pay. For example, skilled, semi-skilled, unskilled, class I, II, III, IV employees. |
| **Autonomy** | : | The degree to which the job provides opportunities to the job holder to exercise his discretion and independent judgement in deciding how, when and at what place the job is to be carried out. |

| | | |
|---|---|---|
| **Feedback** | : | The degree to which a job holder is able to get direct and immediate information on his performance on the job. |
| **Job Design** | : | Groupings of tasks and activities in such a way that both the technical efficiency criteria and the socio-psychological requirements of job holders are met. |
| **Job Characteristics Model** | : | A model of designing jobs based on the view that three psychological states toward a job affect a person's motivation and satisfaction level. These states are experienced meaningfulness, experienced responsibility and knowledge of results. A job's skill variety, identity and task significance contribute to meaningfulness; and feedback is related to the knowledge of results. |
| **Skill Variety** | : | The degree to which the job provides an opportunity to carry out a variety of different activities, thereby allowing the job holder to use his multiple skills and talents on the job. |
| **Task Identity** | : | The degree to which the job requires completion of a whole and identifiable piece of work with visible outcome. |
| **Task Significance** | : | The degree to which the job has a substantial impact on the lives of other people in the organization or the community as a whole. |

## REVIEW QUESTIONS

1.  Identify job description and job specification. What are the distinguishing features of the two?
2.  In what ways, could the job analysis data be of use to operating managers? How would you convince them of the usefulness of job analysis process?
3.  Based on the analysis of the three cases that you have read, identify common features that characterize the job redesign experiments.
4.  Do you think jobs in Indian organisations need to be redesigned? Identify forces, both internal and external, to organisations that necessitate redesigning of jobs.
5.  As a personnel specialist what specific steps would you suggest for introducing job redesign on experimental basis in an organization?

## FURTHER READING

1.  International Labour Officer, 1979. *New forms of Work Organization*, vol.2, ILO: Geneva.
2.  Hackman, J R and G R Oldham, 1980. *Work Redesign*, Addison-Wesley: Reading, Massachusetts.
3.  Child, J, 1984. *Organization: Guide to Problems and Practice*, 2nd edn, Harper and Row: London.
4.  Davis, L and J Taylor, 1979. *The Design of Jobs*, 2nd edn, Goodyear, 1st edn, Penguin: London, 1972.

# Human Resource Planning

**LEARNING OBJECTIVES**

After reading this chapter, you should be able to:
Examine the purpose and process of Human Resource Planning (HRP);
● Study the methods and techniques of forecasting demand and supply
and identifying human resource requirements; ● Understand the types of
action plans and approaches to monitoring and control; and ● Review
the HRP practices and concerns.

Human Resource Planning (HRP) may be defined as a strategy for the acquisition, utilization, improvement and preservation of an enterprise's human resources. It is the management activity aimed at coordinating the requirements for and the availability of different types of employees. This involves ensuring that the firm has enough of the right kind of people at the right time and also adjusting the requirements to the available supply.

## Reasons for Current Interest

Major reasons for the present emphasis on manpower planning include the following.

*1. Employment–Unemployment Situation*  Though in general the number of educated unemployed is on the rise, there is an acute shortage of a variety of skills. This emphasizes the need for more effective recruitment and retaining people.

*2. Technological Changes*  The changes in production technologies, marketing methods and management techniques have been extensive and rapid. Their effect has been profound on job contents and contexts. These changes can cause problems relating to redundancies, retraining and redeployment. All these contribute to the need to plan human resource needs intensively and systematically.

**3. Organizational Change**     In a turbulent environment marked by cyclical fluctuations and discontinuities, the nature and pace of changes in organizational environment, activities and structures affect human resource requirements and require strategic consideration.

**4. Demographic Changes**     The changing profile of the work force in terms of age, sex, literacy, technical inputs and social background have implications for human resource planning.

**5. Skill Shortages**     Government control and changes in legislation with regard to affirmative action for the disadvantaged groups, working conditions and hours of work, restrictions on women and child employment, casual and contract labour, etc. have stimulated the organizations to become involved in systematic human resource planing.

**6. Legislative Controls**     The days of executive fiat and *hire and fire* policies have passed. Now legislation makes it difficult to reduce the size of an organization quickly and cheaply.  It is easy to increase but difficult to reduce the numbers employed because of recent changes in labour law relating to lay-offs and closures.  Those responsible for managing human resources must look far ahead and attempt to foresee human resource position.

**7. Impact of Pressure Groups**     Pressure groups such as unions, politicians and persons displaced from land by location of giant enterprises have been raising contradictory pressures on enterprise management in areas such as internal recruitment and promotions, preference to employees' children, displaced persons, sons of soil, etc.

**8. Systems Concept**     The spread of systems thinking and the advent of microcomputer as part of the on-going revolution in information technology emphasizes planning and adopting newer ways of handling voluminous personnel records.

**9. Lead Time**     A longer lead time is necessary for the selection process and for training and development of the employees, to handle new knowledge and skills successfully.

---

## HUMAN RESOURCE PLANNING (HRP)
## FOR ECONOMIC DEVELOPMENT

---

There is a growing awareness, since 1950s, about the critical role of human resources in the economic development of a nation.  Human capital formation is acknowledged as one of the most potent sources in contributing directly and significantly to economic growth.*  In developed countries like the USA studies revealed and have

* Thurow, L C, 1947. *Investment in Human Capital*, Wadsworth: California; G S Becker, *Human Capital*, New York: National Bureau of Economic Research, 1964; T W Schultz, 1961. "Investment in Human Capital", *American Economic Review*, March.

attempted to quantify the extent of contribution of education and development of human resources as a major source of economic growth. * In most developing countries the development of human resources has been regarded as one amongst many objectives of long-term economic growth.   As a result even the objectives of economic planning and the priorities thereof began to be shifted away from purely growth-oriented development strategies to those that recognize and partly remedy the past neglect of such social sectors like  population planning, health, education, housing, social security and other social services.  The following have been the prime concerns of governments in developing countries.

- How to cope with the phenomenal explosion in population?
- How to provide productive employment to the already unemployed and to those who are entering the labour market?
- What supplementary programmes to initiate for specific target groups (rural/urban poor, socially disadvantaged groups like the scheduled castes/tribes, backward classes, minorities, women, children, physically handicapped, etc.) for employment creation, income generation and poverty alleviation?
- What pro-active measures to take up to meet the skill shortages so that there is no problem in realizing plan targets due to shortage in critical  skills at various levels and in various trades/disciplines?
- How to upgrade technical, administrative and managerial skills in different sectors of the economy to sustain and improve productivity and further the pace of economic development?
- How to cope with the growing imbalances in the supply and demand side of human resources in an uncertain and turbulent environment within and outside the country in an increasingly interdependent world?

## HRP at Macrolevel

The broad framework for HRP at macrolevel would encompass all these and other concerns, dealing with both the supply and the demand side of the problems.   It should cover not only quantitative aspects, but also qualitative factors.  The objectives of HRP in India, as in most other developing countries at the macrolevel, should thus encompass all aspects of human resource development, from population planning on the one hand to investments in health, education, housing and other social welfare services on the other.**

The four major components of human resource planning based on environmental analysis and adjustment are:
- Population planning Employment planning
- Educational planning
- Other aspects of social and human development

The Government of India has spelt out the human resources planning objectives at

---

*Denison, 1960. *Sources of Economic Growth in the USA*, The Brookings Institute: Washington.

**Rashid Amjad, 1987. *Human Resource Planning: The Asian Experience*, ILO/ARTEP: New Delhi, p  3.

the macrolevel in successive five-year economic plans. The prime concern, throughout, has been to find a solution to the problem of unemployment and the poverty that goes with it. The key issues involved relate to questions on the rate and pattern of growth. A data base is created to facilitate the formulation of sound policies and programmes. The decennial census conducted by the office of Registrar General constitutes the most comprehensive source of population statistics while the quinquennial labour force survey conducted by the National Sample Survey Organization (NSSO) serves as the most important source of labour force statistics. The Annual Survey of Industries (ASI) also furnishes vital data on employment trends in industry. In earlier plans through the Fourth Plan (1968–73), the employment content of Plan schemes was estimated directly for each scheme. *Indirect* employment effects were added and total employment potential calculated.[*] At the state, district and project levels, such procedures continue till date. In 1960s, the Institute of Applied Manpower Research was sponsored by the Planning Commission to help conduct studies covering a wide range of subjects to estimate the manpower requirements of various plan projects. The Institute has a wealth of studies and considerable expertise. In 1970, the Committee of Experts on Unemployment Estimates (*Dantwala Committee*) of the Planning Commission made detailed recommendations on measuring unemployment on the basis of different activity status categories, taking into account such distinguishing characteristics as seasonality, region, rural-urban residence, status and class of workers, age and sex, industry, occupation and educational qualification.[**] The revised International Standards on Employment and Unemployment Statistics recommended at the 13th International Conference of Labour Statisticians in 1982 were very similar to those recommended by the Dantwala Committee.[***] Yet, when it comes to actual measurement, much of the employment data is unusable.[****] There are three principal sources of data on the labour force: The decennial census, NSS data and the Employment Exchanges. The first (census) is a census of employment status, the second (NSS) an estimate of labour participation rate and the third (Employment Exchanges) is based on registration. The three types of data are not comparable and each has its own limitations in terms of obsolescence and accuracy, among others. The gravity of the unemployment situation led the government to initiate, from time to time a variety of special employment schemes such as the National Rural Employment Programme (NREP), Minimum Needs Programme, National Scheme of Training Rural Youth for Self-Employment (TRYSEM), Integrated Rural Development Programme (IRDP) and the Self-Employment Scheme for Educated Unemployed Youth (SEEUY).

As part of the decentralized strategy for human resources planning and employment generation, state planning boards and district-level manpower planning generation

---

[*] Alagh, Y K, 1987. "Employment and Structural Change in Indian Economy", in Rashid Amjad (Ed.): *Human Resource Planning: Asian Experience,* op.cit., pp 285–303.

[**] Planning Commission, 1970. *Report of the Committee of Experts on Unemployment Statistics,* Govt. of India: New Delhi.

[***] Alagh, Y K p. 287.

[****] Venkata Ratnam, C S, 1986. "Unemployable Figures", *The Financial Express,* May 31.

councils have been set up.  These councils are assisted by the District Employment Exchange, District Industries Centre, District Agriculture Office, Lead Bank, University Employment and Guidance Bureau, Special Employment Exchanges for major public sector projects as also those for handicapped, professionals, etc. in preparing a portfolio of opportunities for salaried, self and wage employment. The employment exchanges have three broad functions (i) registration and placement of job seekers; (ii) rendering vocational training and career advice services; and (iii) collection and dissemination of manpower data.

Along with measures for generating employment in the successive plans, attention was paid to provide a substantial infrastructure for education and technical training. Skill formation has also been provided for in various beneficiary-oriented programmes. Apprenticeship Act was enacted to induce the corporate sector to take part in the process of skill formation.  The major concerns are still on how to substantially bring about improvements in education, training, values, knowledge, skills and attitudes relevant to the needs of the society and its development tasks.  Special measures are also required to deal with the paradox of unemployment and skill shortages in certain disciplines/sectors, persistent problem of migration and the regulation of overseas employment to minimize their exploitation and also to deal with the negative effects of possible brain drain,  A variety of legislative and administrative measures have taken place at national, state and district levels.

Thus it is seen that the broad framework, contents and processes involved in HRP at macrolevel are indeed complex.  The complexity is further compounded by the rapid changes in *environment* in the  many senses of the term.  The approach to HRP at macrolevel has therefore to be a dynamic process.  It is indeed difficult to make any objective evaluation of the success of efforts in this context.  While India can boast of having the third largest pool of scientific and technical personnel, the technological lag in its economy is striking.  The country still has critical shortages in certain skills even as a large number of those trained/educated in even related disciplines remain unemployed.  There is the irony of doctors without patients and patients without doctors!  These are some of the issues that become critical in matching the supply and demand of human resources.

## HRP at Microlevel

The objectives of human resource planning  at the *microlevel* are to ensure that the organization:

(i) obtains and retains the quantity and quality of human resources it needs at the right time and place; and

(ii) makes optimum utilization of these resources.

## CORPORATE PLANNING AND THE HRP PROCESS

Human resource planning constitutes an integral part of corporate plan and serves the organizational purposes in more ways than one.  For example, it helps organizations to (i) capitalize on the strengths of their human resources; (ii) determine recruitment levels; (iii) anticipate redundancies; (iv) determine optimum training levels; (v) serve as a basis for management development programmes; (vi) cost manpower for new projects; (vii) assist productivity bargaining; (viii) assess future requirements; (ix) study the cost of overheads and value of service functions; and (x) decide whether certain activities need to be subcontracted.

Human resources planning influences corporate strategy and is in turn influenced by it. The HRP process may incorporate all the stages shown in Fig. 3.1. The planning process may not always give exact forecasts, and to be effective it should be a continuous process with provision for control and review.

The human resource plan is a part of the corporate plan. Without it there can be no manpower plan for human resources. If there are several imponderables and unpredictables in the corporate plan, there will be difficulties in HRP. Whether or not the HRP meets the requirements and is in tune with reality depends on clarity of goals and the validity of the stated assumptions. The other important point is the time frame in defining the *future*. In HRP the future can be classified into three periods: (i) the short-range or immediate future; (ii) the mid-range; and (iii) the long-range future, none of which can be spelt out in terms of a set number of days, months or years. The *immediate future* may refer to current situation and experiences and may even concern issues such as overtime and replacements. If there has been previous planning for human resource such plans can serve as a guide in the immediate future. If not, a beginning should be made at once.

The *mid-range* future has a different time span in various companies. It can be as short as a few months or as long as several years. Most would agree upon 2–3 years' period as a mid-range.

The *long-range* plan could be five years, while 10 to 15 years span could be used for a perspective plan. Long range plans must be made on the basis of various trends in the economy and in the labour market, and on long-term trends of production in the company. Long-range plans are general rather than specific, flexible rather than rigid.

Nevertheless, a plan can be extremely useful in identifying factors and trends that need to be reckoned with for early warning on possible problems. The long lead time provides the opportunity and resilience to meet exigencies and make necessary adjustments. More complete plans can be had as time slowly brings the long-range into short-range.

The first step in the HRP process is the establishment of a planning horizon. One should know the period for which the plan will apply. Then, the specific corporate objectives and strategies should be clear. Based on these, estimates or projections for demand and supply of human resources can be made using the approach and methods suggested in the next unit. The difference between the estimates of demand for and supply of human resources is often referred to as the *human resource gap*, and one of the main components of the human resource strategy is to formulate plans for closing such gaps–perhaps by recruitment and training (if the demand is positive, i.e. demand exceeds supply) or by planned redundancy (if the gap is negative).

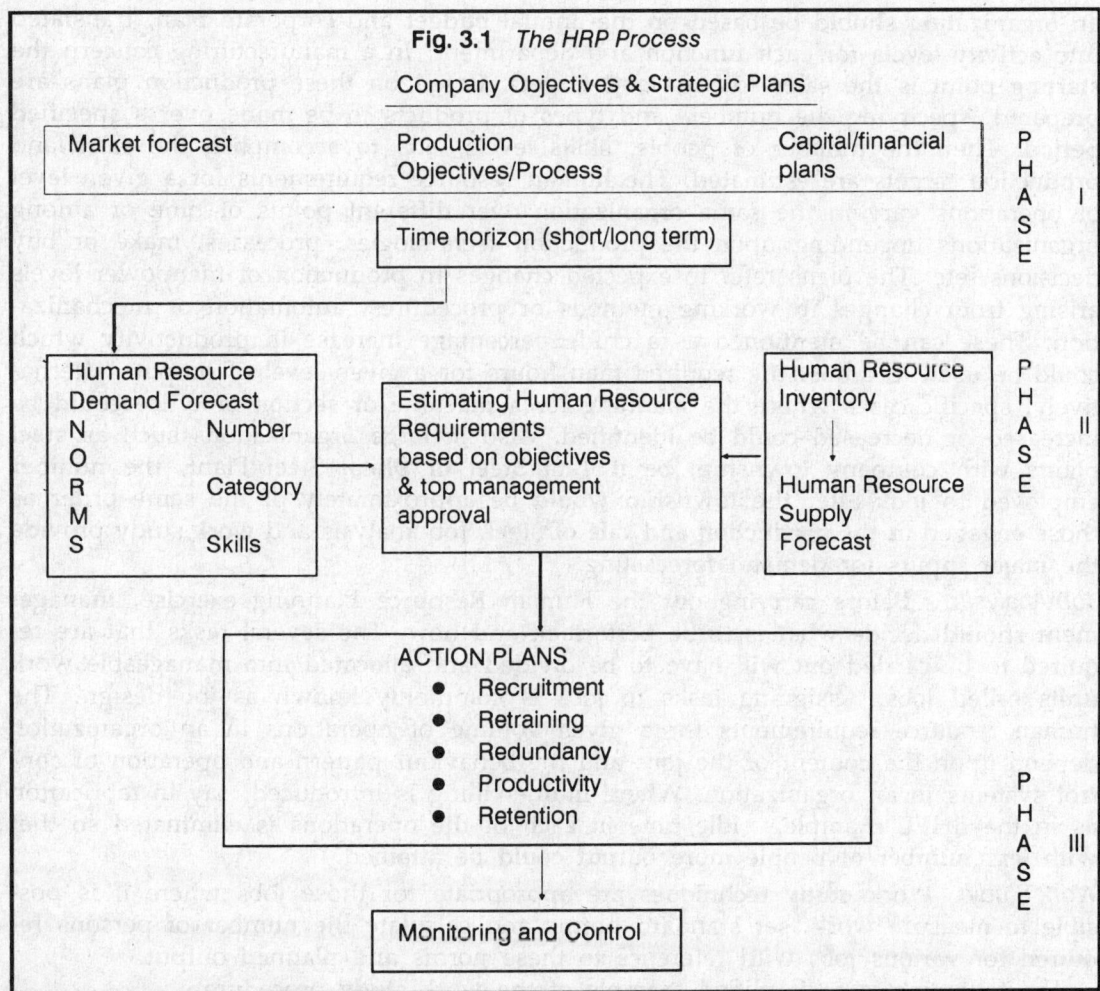

**Fig. 3.1** *The HRP Process*

Company Objectives & Strategic Plans

| Market forecast | Production Objectives/Process | Capital/financial plans |

Time horizon (short/long term)

Human Resource Demand Forecast
NORMS
N — Number
O
R — Category
M
S — Skills

Estimating Human Resource Requirements based on objectives & top management approval

Human Resource Inventory
↓
Human Resource Supply Forecast

ACTION PLANS
● Recruitment
● Retraining
● Redundancy
● Productivity
● Retention

Monitoring and Control

PHASE I
PHASE II
PHASE III

## Major HRP Activities

HRP entails the following five areas of activity:
1. Demand forecasting
2. Supply forecasting
3. Determining human resource requirements
4. Action planning
5. Monitoring and control

Though these activities are listed separately, they are interrelated and often overlap. The purposes, methods and techniques of these six activities are briefly discussed here.

***Demand Forecasting***     Demand Forecasting refers to the process estimating the future need of human resources in the context of corporate and functional plans and forecasts of future activity levels of the organization. Demand for human resources in an organization should be based on the annual budget and corporate plan, translated into activity levels for each function and department. In a manufacturing concern the starting point is the sales forecast and targets. Based on these production plans are prepared, specifying the numbers and types of products to be made over a specified period. Then the number of people, skills levels, etc. to accomplish the sales and production targets are estimated. The human resource requirements for a given level of operations vary in the same organization over different points of time or among organizations depending upon the production technologies, processes, make or buy decisions, etc. The plans refer to expected changes in production or manpower levels arising from changes in working methods or procedures, automation or mechanization. These can be mentioned as a crude percentage increase in productivity which could be used to adjust the required man hours for a given level of output. Alternatively, specific cases where the manning for a machine or section or office could be increased or decreased could be identified. Also in large organizations such as steel plants with company township, be it Tata Steel or Bhilai Steel Plant, the number employed to look after the township would be approximately of the same order as those engaged in the production and sale of steel. Job analysis and work study provide the major inputs for demand forecasting.

*Job Analysis*[*]    Before carrying out the Human Resource Planning exercise, management should decide what is to be performed and how. The several tasks that are required to be carried out will have to be divided and allocated into manageable work units called jobs. Assigning tasks to jobs is commonly known as job design. The human resource requirements for a given volume of operations in an organization depend upon the content of the jobs and the behaviour pattern and operation of control systems in an organization. Where multi-skilling is introduced, say in fabrication as in the BHEL example,[**] idle time in each of the operations is eliminated so that with less number of people more output could be attained.

*Work Study*    Work study techniques are appropriate for those jobs where it is possible to measure work, set standard norms and calculate the number of persons required for various jobs with reference to these norms and planned output.

The following is a simplified example of the work study procedure.

*Example:*

| | |
|---|---|
| Planned output for the year | 10000 units |
| Standard hours per unit | 3 hours |
| Planned hours required | 30000 hours |
| Productive hours per person year | 1500 hours |
| (Allowing for absenteeism, idle time,etc.) | |
| No. of workers required | 20 workers |

If the span of control is 10, two supervisors will be required to supervise the work of 20 workers.

Since work study techniques are more appropriate for direct production workers than for any other category of employees, usually these are used in conjunction with other techniques.

---

[*] This aspect was discussed at length in Chapter 2.

[**] *Ibid.*

There are three methods for demand forecasting which are briefly explained here.

*Managerial Judgement*   Under this method, experienced managers prepare guidelines for departmental managers. Such guidelines which have the approval of top management, indicate broad assumptions about future activity levels which will affect their departments. Targets are set and desirable changes in flow of work and job design are also indicated where considered necessary. Taking cue from these, the departmental managers prepare forecasts with help from personnel, O & M, or work study specialists. Meanwhile, the personnel department also may, in conjunction with other departments in the organization, prepare a forecast of the company-wide demand for human resources. Later the two sets of forecasts could be reconciled and reviewed by a committee consisting of functional heads to arrive at a final forecast.

The subjective element of this method is its weakness as also its strength. The weakness can be somewhat overcome by checking subjective assumptions with data from O & M, work study exercises, etc. The value of the information about intangible factors like informal group norms and their effects on estimates and output cannot be gauged so well by employing any other method.

*Simple Statistical Models*   The most common method is ratio-trend analysis. In its simplest form, it refers to ratios between say, the number of direct and indirect workers or the number of workers and supervisors and so on. Future ratios are forecast based on time series extrapolation, after making some allowances for the changes that are likely to occur in future. Then the number of employees required for different groups/skill levels, etc. are calculated.

For use of mathematical models for HRP, time series statistical data is necessary. Besides, it becomes necessary to identify and describe a number of variables affecting human resource requirements in a mathematical formula. These variables could be investment, sales, etc. The process is complex and suitable only to large organizations.

*Mathematical Models*   A model is a standard or a representation, generally in miniature, to show the structure or serve as a copy of something. Models may be descriptive, representing present or past patterns or they may be normative, representing possible future patterns. Descriptive models aid comprehending complex data on personnel flows/movements. This is attempted through mathematical techniques that present a simplified and abstract view of complex and often contradictory empirical data on personnel flows, surpluses and shortages relative to needs. Future needs may be forecast through application of past patterns in projections by use of probabilities and correlations as also by making appropriate assumptions. The normative models of *proper* or *adequate* staffing are usually influenced by such subjective elements as experience, assumptions and philosophy guiding managerial decision-making. Models are used mainly to generate a series of alternative scenarios so that managers may select the forecast they consider most apt for their needs.

Based on certain assumptions concerning possible changes in the future, models may be developed to show how an organization looks like in terms of its staffing pattern. The modelling techniques which seek to project organization change include succession analysis, probabilistic analysis (referred to also as *Markov* analysis of personnel flows based on probability theory) and regression analysis. Simulation analysis is another variant of modelling change in organization where alternative patterns are generated by modifying the assumptions and variables.

*Probabilistic Models:*    In succession planning the unit of analysis is the data concerning the individual. In probabilistic model the unit of analysis is data concerning groups of employees, classified according to organizational units, job categories, locations, levels, grades, etc. Here the probability of employees moving from one classification to another or out of the organization is considered. A matrix or table of personnel flows is determined at specified intervals of future time. While personnel policies, practices and past trends concerning promotions, transfers, separations, etc. provide a useful basis in the forecast exercise, the projections are influenced more by the assumptions that managers make. The most popular technique in this category is called the *Markov analysis*. Here simple arithmetical calculations are made to indicate possible movements from job category A to B to C and so on from one point of time to another. Such calculations are repeated for all jobs/categories/levels for successive periods. The sequences of transitions depicted in the matrix are called *Markov Chains*. The process involves certain mathematical properties such as the strict independence of the job categories, constant transition probabilities and a number of forecasting cycles. Considering the uncertainties in ever-changing business context and the inevitable influence of subjective elements in decision-making processes, the forecasts are to be treated as merely probabilistic.

Computerized simulation models based on stochastic processes have also been developed. Among them, the *Minnesota Manpower Management Simulation* model which seeks to represent the role of important personnel decisions, the consequences of personnel performance measures and accomplishment of corporate goals merit special mention.

The implications of normal attrition and personnel policies concerning internal promotions, transfers, career development, etc. could also be gauged by building these variables into the models.[*]

*Regression Models*    Regression analysis is used to measure the relationship between one or more independent variables to explain a dependent variable. In HRP regression analysis can be used to correlate personnel requirements with output, revenue, etc. As in trend-ratio and time-series analyses, the analysis is based more on historical patterns. The real value of regression analysis in HRP is in generating alternative scenarios in personnel needs. It is important to bear in mind that the relationships are not always linear and the purpose of the analysis is not to present the management with precise quantitative forecasts.

*Optimization Models*    Some models seek to present optimal or the best or minimal costs, minimal employee turnover, desired degree of blend in employee/skill mix, etc. Mathematical techniques such as linear, nonlinear and dynamic programming are among the optimization modes used in HRP also. Goal programming which is a refinement of linear programme, can also be used in HRP if the purpose is to examine the

---

[*] See Walker, J W, 1980. *Human Resource Planning*, McGraw-Hill: New York, pp 99-122.

discrepancies between forecasted results and identified targets and suggest optimum goals that are attainable in given circumstances and time perspective.

**Supply Forecasting**    Every organization will have two major sources of supply of human resources: internal and external. In unionized firms, agreements up to certain job levels may determine the ratio of internal and external sources of supply. Also, as shown in Fig. 3.2. manpower flows in and out of an organization due to a variety of reasons. Policies affecting each of these aspects need to be reviewed regularly to assess their possible effects on human resource supplies.

*Internal Sources*   Proper HRP and information systems enable the organization to know the profile of the employees in terms of age, sex, education, training, experience, job level, performance and potential.

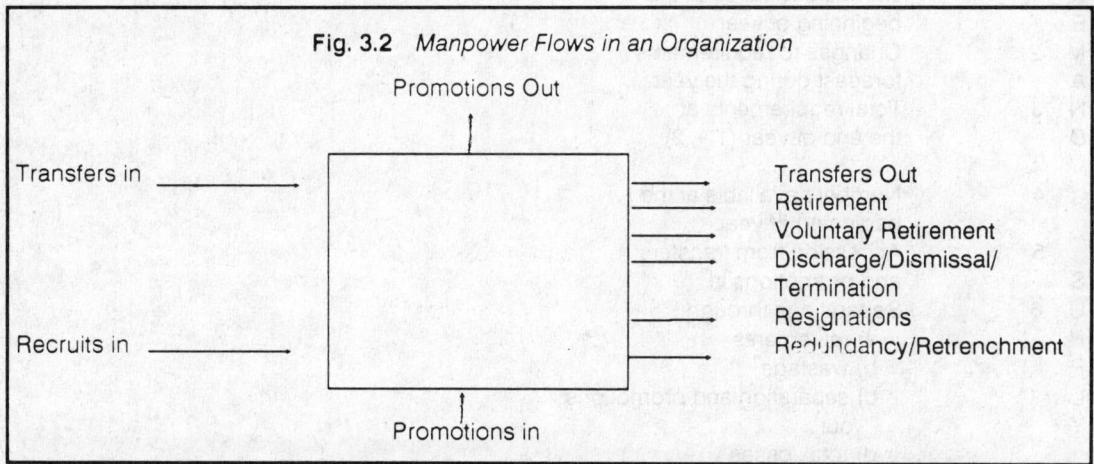

**Fig. 3.2**  *Manpower Flows in an Organization*

Promotions Out

Transfers in _____

Transfers Out
Retirement
Voluntary Retirement
Discharge/Dismissal/
Termination
Resignations
Redundancy/Retrenchment

Recruits in _____

Promotions in

Manpower requirements arise out of organizational growth or diversification or because of the movement of the employees on account of transfer, promotion, job rotation, voluntary retirement, resignation, retirement, dismissal, discharge or death. In either case, as and when vacancies arise, organizations can match the skill and level requirements with the profile of the employees and meet the requirements. While some of the internal changes and external supply could be predicted (such as growth opportunities, transfer and promotions, retirements, etc.), others are not so easy to predict. But past experience and historical data may be of some help. The companies which have systematized personnel records and information systems and which have well-established career and succession plans find it easier to project internal sources of supply relatively accurately.

*External Sources*   When the company grows rapidly, diversifies into newer areas of operations or when it is not able to find the people internally to fill the vacancies, it has to resort to outside recruitment. To the extent a firm is able to anticipate its outside recruitment needs and scans the possible sources of supply with a feel of the labour market, its problems in recruiting the right number with appropriate skills at the required time would become easier.

***Determining Human Resource Requirements***      Human resource requirements are determined by relating the supply to the demand forecasts and identifying deficits or surpluses of human resources that will exist in the future.   Table 3.1 shows how demand and supply forecasts can be scheduled over a period of five years.   The reconciliation of demand and supply forecasts give us the numbers of people to be recruited or made redundant as the case may be.   This forms the basis for the action programmes in HRP.

**Table 3.1    Determining Human Resource Requirements**

|  |  |  | Year | | | | |
|---|---|---|---|---|---|---|---|
|  |  |  | 1 | 2 | 3 | 4 | 5 |
| D | 1. | Numbers required at the beginning of year |  |  |  |  |  |
| E |  |  |  |  |  |  |  |
| M | 2. | Changes to requirements forecast during the year |  |  |  |  |  |
| A |  |  |  |  |  |  |  |
| N | 3. | Total requirements at the end of year (1 + 2) |  |  |  |  |  |
| D |  |  |  |  |  |  |  |
|  | 4. | Numbers available at the beginning of year |  |  |  |  |  |
|  | 5. | Accession from transfers and promotions in |  |  |  |  |  |
| S |  |  |  |  |  |  |  |
| U | 6. | Separations through: |  |  |  |  |  |
| P |  | a) retirements |  |  |  |  |  |
| P |  | b) wastage |  |  |  |  |  |
| L |  | c) separation and promotions out |  |  |  |  |  |
| Y |  | d) total losses |  |  |  |  |  |
|  | 7. | Total available at the end of year (4+5+6) |  |  |  |  |  |
| R | 8. | Deficit or surplus : (3 – 7) |  |  |  |  |  |
| E | 9. | Losses of those recruited during the year |  |  |  |  |  |
| Q |  |  |  |  |  |  |  |
| U |  |  |  |  |  |  |  |
| I | 10. | Additional numbers required during the year (8 + 9) |  |  |  |  |  |
| R |  |  |  |  |  |  |  |
| E |  |  |  |  |  |  |  |
| M |  |  |  |  |  |  |  |
| E |  |  |  |  |  |  |  |
| N |  |  |  |  |  |  |  |
| T |  |  |  |  |  |  |  |

***Action Planning***      The human resource requirements identified along the procdure shown in Table 3.1   need to be considered within a strategic framework. Organizations operate in a changing environment, so  manpower structures also do not remain static.  Review of activities and roles of persons at different levels and O & M studies may provide useful insights and opportunities to modify assumptions about manpower structures, job design, etc. and change the requirement estimates.  Changes in production methods, union agreements on productivity, off-loading maintenance, sub-contracting, etc. are some of the strategic decisions that help organizations to significantly alter their human resource needs without affecting the volume of business.  Once the human resource requirements are studied and analyzed amongst the strategic options like those mentioned,  the following action plans could be drawn up.

1. The *recruitment plan*, which will set out:
(i)    the number and type of people required and when they are needed;
(ii)   any special problems in recruiting the right people and how they are to be dealt with; and
(iii)  the recruitment programme.

2. The *redeployment  plan*, which will set out programmes for transferring or retraining existing employees for new jobs.

3. The *redundancy plan*, which will indicate:
(i)    Who is redundant, where and when;
(ii)   the plans for retraining, where this is possible; and
(iii)  alternative programmes for voluntary separation (golden hand- shake), retrenchment, lay-off, etc.

4. The *training plan*, which will show:
(i)    The number of trainees or apprentices required and the programme for recruiting or training them;
(ii)   the number of existing staff who need training or retraining and the training programme; and
(iii)  the new courses to be developed or the changes to be made in existing courses.

5. The *productivity plan* which will set out programmes for improving employee productivity or reducing employee costs through:
(i)    Work simplification through O & M studies;
(ii)   mechanization and automation;
(iii)  productivity bargaining;
(iv)   incentives and profit-sharing schemes;
(v)    job redesign; and
(vi)   training and re-fresher training.

6. The *retention plan* to reduce avoidable wastage by review of reasons for employee turnover. Additional information can be obtained through exit interviews and necessary changes initiated in:
(i)    Compensation policies and programmes;
(ii)   induction and training;
(iii)  changes in work requirements; and
(iv)   improvements in working conditions.

In each of these areas it is necessary to estimate the cost and weigh them against possible benefits.

**Monitoring and Control**    While assessing future requirements, the estimates also depend upon the human resource policy assumptions in the organization. Corporate strategy can influence manpower strategy and *vice versa*. Here we may consider three approaches: zero budgeting, ideal and realistic.

*Zero budgeting*, as the name implies, is an approach in which one forces unit/division managers to justify their total operation from zero. The objective is to encourage managers to seriously think about their current activities. Given the restrictions posed by law and unions, the practicality of this approach for ongoing organizations in HRP is doubtful.

Mainly new units can start thinking about HRP in terms of what might constitute an *ideal* approach. Any decisions on sub-contracting, off-loading functions like maintenance, production technology, etc. may depend on the perceived notions of what constitutes *ideal* for the organization. What is considered ideal by the management from the firm's short-term view may, at times, force ethical dimensions.

Organizations can proceed with a *realistic* approach using the existing information. A company which operates on a three-year planning cycle may record manpower levels in subunits or divisions in such a way that it is easy to monitor and hold managers responsible (see Table 3.2). Organizations which choose to supplement human resource plans with other business parameters and manpower ratios (for example, gross value added per employee, capital employed per employee, turnover per employee), have to be wary about the fact that the future may not follow the past and adjustments may have to be made for variations.

**Table 3.2    Monitoring Manpower Levels**

| Item | Current Year | Forecast Year 1 | Forecast Year 2 |
|---|---|---|---|
| Stock as on 1 January | | | |
| Manpower increases | | | |
| • Business Activity | | | |
| • Capital Expenditure | | | |
| • Takeover/merger | | | |
| Manpower decreases | | | |
| • Business activity | | | |
| • Capital expenditure | | | |
| • Divestment | | | |
| • Productivity improvement | | | |

## HRP Practices

A recent survey* of HRP practices in 45 companies covering a cross-section of the manufacturing industry (12 in public sector and 32 in private sector) has shown that all organizations, either in a fragmentary sporadic way or in totality, carried out functions which were associated with HRP. A majority of the companies were performing many HRP activities without the support of corporate plans. These were mostly

* Krishnaswamy, K N, 1985. *Manpower Planning Practices in Indian Manufacturing Organization*, *ASCI Journal of Management*, vol. 15, no. 1, September, pp 47–76.

smaller companies.

In forecasting human resource requirements, several approaches were adopted by managements of large organizations. Less than half the number of companies utilized systematic HR inventories. Special skills and age structure were not emphasized in them. About one-eighth of the organizations, however, reported using computers for HRP. Manpower audit was systematic in only one-fifth of the total number of organizations studied and these were mostly larger ones. Smaller organizations reviewed mostly when there was a change in the level of activity. Involvement of line management was more in planning for new incumbents than in analyzing employee turnover. Casual employment and lay-offs to adjust work force in an organization was not so much affected by its size as by its technology and input conditions.

The larger companies kept employee turnover information category-wise. The smaller ones were not doing it mainly because the number in most of the categories tended to be very small and keeping statistics like averages for small groups was not very meaningful. The participation of top management, industrial engineering department and operating division was more common for HR forecasting than for HR audit or exit interviews.

A larger proportion of bigger companies recruited systematically young employees on the basis of plans. This was done at the lowest levels of hierarchy for each category like workers, technical supervisors and managers. Career planning was an nascent function of HRP in the Indian manufacturing organizations. Only 4% of them had systematic strong career planning systems. Individual job descriptions for the worker-category were maintained in almost all the organizations. Only in 20% of the companies, job descriptions for executives and technical personnel were maintained. The difference in HRP practices between the public and private sector organizations did not appear to be considerable, but the public sector organizations seemed to have developed better HRP procedures.

The available evidence from the survey is not adequate to suggest that better HRP procedures lead to better human resource planning. While surplus manpower is a chronic problem with public sector, tight manning is characteristic of most private sector organizations.

The National Institute of Personnel Management expressed concern in a series of national seminars in 1988, about personnel professionals spending "more time on planned manpower reductions than on manpower planning". This becomes inevitable human resource considerations did not receive adequate attention in strategic business discussions. The proposed merger of the two air-lines did not take place because in the first instance, it was attempted without regard to human resource implications. A major port which went in for mechanical ore-handling plant recruited fresh candidates from technical institutes and polytechnics and two years later, found that they had a problem of surplus manpower. When the port management sought the cooperation of the union, the union asked the management as to why it did not take inventory of existing resources at the time of recruiting people for the mechanical ore-handling plant. If this had been attempted, it would have provided career opportunities to those who were underemployed and eased the problem of surplus manpower. In another case at a public sector paper unit located in eastern India, it was assumed during the feasibility study, that it would not be difficult to meet the manpower requirements.   After the plant was set up, it was realized that despite large unemployment situation locally there was an acute shortage of relevant skills.   In yet another case, a multinational pharmaceutical company located in Bombay diversified into cosmetics and detergents.   Since the new division did not become a profit centre even after three years, the company decided to wind up the division.   The mass retrenchment/termination that ensued, landed the organization in public controversy and legal squabbles.   There could be many more examples.   But the lessons are obvious. All organizational decisions have human resource implications.   If we overlook these in the beginning the problems loom large at a later stage.

Most Indian organizations do not have adequate records and information on human resources.   Several of those who have them, do not have proper retrieval systems. There are understandable difficulties in resolving the issues and complexities in design, definition and creation of computerised personnel information systems for effective HRP and utilization.   Even the current technologies and knowledge in this respect is not put to use optimally.   This is a strategic disadvantage.

## SUMMARY

Human Resource Planning forms an integral part of the strategic corporate planning process. There are several valid reasons for the current interest in the subject.   As we have seen in Chapter 1, the effectiveness of all organizations is contingent upon the behaviour and performance of human resources.   In this chapter we have briefly discussed the objectives and purposes of HRP which point to the key role of HRP in giving the firm the strategic competitive edge.   Participation of top management, line managers, O & M, work study and personnel specialists in the HRP process would not only create better understanding but also ensure support for the plan.   The HRP activities were considered in this chapter in an integrated manner.   We have focussed on the simpler, less complex methods and techniques to forecast supply and demand and estimate human resource requirements based on corporate plans, company objectives, inventory of current resources and top management policy.   The various action plans — recruitment, retraining/redeployment, redundancy, productivity and retention — were considered in an integrated framework along with the need for their monitoring and control.   We have also reviewed the findings of a recent survey of HRP in 45 firms in India besides pointing to the pitfalls in neglecting human resource implications in strategic corporate decisions.

## KEY WORDS

| | | |
|---|---|---|
| **Human Resource Information System** | : | Information on individual employees designed to equip the human resource specialists with personnel information required (personal data). |
| **Human Resource Planning** | : | The process that helps to provide adequate human resources to achieve future organizational objectives.   It includes forecasting demand and supply and action to bridge the gap between the two. It also covers strategies for the acquisition, utilization, improvement and preservation of a firm's human resources (HRP and manpower planning are treated as synonyms). |

| Human Resource Strategy | : | Activities concerning the contribution of human resources to an organization. |
| Manpower | : | Human resource of an organization. |
| Markov Analysis | : | An approach to forecast the internal supply of human resources tracking past patterns of personnel movements. |

# COMPANY EXPERIENCE: PLANNING FOR MANPOWER IN A NEW ENTERPRISE*

M/s Bhamba Associates Ltd had been in the textiles business for quite sometime. As the fortunes of the textile industry dwindled and a general recession set in, Bhambas decided to review their business philosophy and the programme of diversification. After considerable deliberations they came to realize that their survival depends only on diversification.

Keeping in view the trend of industrial and economic growth in the country, they came to the conclusion that sugar industry could offer them some opportunity for survival and growth. It could also offer scope for the absorption of redundant manpower in the textile units. While the technical and technological aspects of planning, designing and building of new units were assigned to the technical experts, the job of manpower planning was entrusted to the General Manager (Personnel and Management Services). Management Services group comprised the following functions:

(i) Manpower planning
(ii) Industrial engineering
(iii) Economic studies

The General Manager (P & MS) examined the tentative phased plan of diversification and the program decided for putting up new sugar units in different parts of the country. This was necessary as manpower planning is an important part of the overall corporate planning of an organization and cannot be developed as a supportive or parallel activity. Keeping in view the plan of expansion, it was decided to chalk out the manpower plan for the new units.

The General Manager (P & MS) called a meeting of the functional heads like Manager (Manpower Planning) and Manager (Industrial Engg.), Deputy Chief (Long-range Planning) and Economic Analyst to have a brainstorming session to chalk out strategy. During the course of discussion it became clear that the process of manpower planning would have to be undertaken in the following context:

i) Stages of manpower planning
ii) Phases of manpower planning

---

* This is a condensed version of a case study prepared by Mr V M Budhiraja. It will provide an insight into the operational aspects of HRP. Reproduced from *Personnel Today*, Oct.–Dec. 1984, pp. 3–4 and 24–25 with the permission of the publisher.

It was, therefore, decided to elaborate these two factors in their operative dimensions so as to proceed further.   The *stages of manpower planning* were thus divided into the following stages. (a) Conception, (b) Feasibility,   (c)  Construction, (d) Commissioning and  (e)  Operation.

As regards *phases of manpower planning* the various important landmarks were determined as listed here. (a)  Survey,   (b) Source identification, (c)  Recruitment, (d) Placement,   (e) Induction, (f)  Maintenance  and (g)  Separation.

After having identified these areas, it was decided to allocate studies to different functional heads like Manager,(IE) and Manager, (MPP).

The Manager (IE)  was asked to study the detailed project report with a view to identifying the following aspects.

1.   Technology of the plant
2.   Nature and type of equipments to be used
3.   Capacity of the plant
4.   Actual process of production
5.   Pattern of operation and material flow
6.   Organization of work and grouping of units and activities

The Manager (MPP) was asked to study the following areas.

1.   Norms prescribed by the manpower consultants in the sugar industry at different stages.
2.   Actual manpower available in the sugar industry as a whole and in the various units depending on their technology and sophistication.
3.   Choice to be made with regard to manpower planning studies in the units through consultants, internal resources or institutes or other external agencies.
4.   Internal agencies to be associated with the process of manpower planning at different stages and phases namely, industrial engineering, manpower planning, Training and Management development, personnel and line management.
5. .   Methodology of manpower planning.

Having outlined the scope of study on a broad scale, the experts were asked to crystallize their ideas further and spell out the precise details and line of action for the study.   Accordingly Manager (IE) furnished the following guidelines.

*Conception Stage*   The Manager (IE) informed that at the conception stage the dimensions of manpower are mainly macro- in nature and only a general idea is provided about the scale of manpower required.   One has to conceptualize mainly in terms of broad numbers, main areas of specialization and the deployment pattern in similar industries and units.

*Feasibility Stage*   At this stage the magnitude of manpower is spelt out in more detail and a broad assessment is made in terms of not only numbers but also specialization, vocational composition and the pattern of manpower; usually available in other units of similar size for designing, building, operating and maintaining the plant. However, transplantation of other unit practices need to be punctuated by local situation in the manpower context for suitable adaptation.

*Construction Stage*     Orientation to manpower exercise has to be mainly aligned to the construction activity, and the numbers and levels have to be determined in terms of the various specialities like civil, mechanical, electrical and instrumentation engineering as required by the organizational plan and the structure envisaged.

*Commissioning Stage*     For the purpose of manpower planning is this stage normally gets merged with the operational stage and the pattern of manning has to be worked out in the context of the requirements for different functions like production, services and auxiliary activities. The Manager (IE) also made a study of the detailed project report to ascertain the technology of the plant, nature and type of equipment and the capacity of the units normally in operation in the country as also the process of production envisaged for the units. These studies showed that the sugar factories could be grouped in terms of capacity per day as under.

Up to 1200 TCD

1251 to 1800 TCD

1801 to 2500 TCD

2501 and above TCD

*TCD - Daily Cane Crushing capacity*

He also identified certain other ratios like capital output, employment output, wages/net value and other technical factors. These ratios were then taken as the broad parameters for determining the magnitude of manpower for the various factories.

**Norms for Manpower:**     Manager (MPP) came out with the results of his studies and furnished the following data:

As per Manager (MPP) the manpower norms prescribed in the western countries for sugar units of the capacity varying from 1000 to 4000 tons were as under:

| Plant Capacity | Number of men | |
| --- | --- | --- |
| | Conventional | Modern |
| 1000 tons | 240 | 149 |
| 4000 tons | 353 | 220 |

He also pointed out that for a few projects of 1250 TCD capacity, a normative figure of 583 men has been assessed by the National Federation of Co-operative Sugar Factories, India (NFCS). He also furnished data in respect of other parameters like:

1. Occupational structure of the employees,
2. department-wise employment, and
3. educational level of the employees in the various sugar plants.

On the basis of the information collected by the Manager (MPP), it was seen that mainly two agencies, i.e. consultants or specialists from various organizations make out detailed assessment of manpower requirements for the sugar plants. These experts also spell out other details of the operative dimensions of manpower. He then suggested the manpower planning methodology to be adopted for their plant as follows:

1. The number of men will have to be assessed in terms of level, specialization and departments.
2. Source of employment would need to be identified including surplus manpower available with the textile units.

3.  The assessment will have to be made with regard to the scope for:
    (a) Pre-employment training
    (b) Apprentice training
    (c) On-the-job training and retraining for skill conversion of manpower as indicated at Sl. no. (2) above.
4.  Data will have to be collected with regard to the manpower status in the region in terms of education, vocational exposure, training facilities available, aptitude of people for a particular job, social inhibitions relating to vocation and employment, culture of the community and the value systems.
5.  Source of training available within the categories, i.e. professional, highly skilled, skilled and semi-skilled would have to be trained.

**Recommendation of Manager (Manpower Planning):**    Having brought these factors to the notice of the GM (P&MS), he furnished his recommendations with regard to the following:

1.  Market Intelligence — regarding level of education, nature of training, employment level, labour mobility, work habits, wage levels, wage differentials etc.
2.  Sources of recruitment.
3.  Mode of selection and placement.
4.  Legislative and company policy constraints governing the mode of recruitment and placement.
5.  The level and manner of induction and job specifications in terms of education and expertise prescribed at the entry level.
6.  Manpower policies to be worked out in the area of maintenance, acculturization, social organization, promotion, motivation, transfers, grievance handling, welfare measures, etc.
7.  Various schemes for separation of employees from organization factors like voluntary separation, involuntary separation, pre-retirement training, post-retirement planning and other related matters.

He further stated that the operative manpower plan would incorporate the following:

1.  Organization plan – keeping in view the latest ideas regarding reduced decision-making levels, improved span of control and supervisory effectiveness
2.  Departmentation scheme
3.  Encadrement and Line of Promotion—incorporating multiple trades, curtailment of insurance, work force and job mobility
4.  Manning tables
5.  Duty posts
6.  Policy on allowances
7.  Exact numbers of people required on the basis of education levels, functions and cadres.
8.  Number of people required on the basis of full time, temporary and overtime; the manpower composition given the seasonal nature of the industry.
9.  From the existing pattern of deployment of manpower in nearly 40 units in

states like Andhra Pradesh, Uttar Pradesh, Maharashtra and Bihar, the following ratios were assessed among different categories of manpower.

| | | |
|---|---|---|
| Officer to supervisor | — | 2.7 |
| Officer to clerical | — | 7.78 |
| Supervisor to worker | — | 27.7 |
| Supervisor to Skilled/semi-skilled worker | — | 11.22 |
| Skilled/Semi-skilled worker to unskilled worker | — | 1.46 |

10. The various categories of staff in three broad areas, i.e. production, maintenance and administration on the basis of deployment in the plants as indicated in Sl.no. 8 above would be as follows:

*Production*
Pan in-charge
Panman
Panmate
Laboratory chemist
Asstt centrifugal mate
Evaporator mate

*Maintenance*
Fitter
Turner
Welder
Electrician
Moulder
Wireman
Blacksmith
Carpenter

*Administration*

Clerical — Section officers, assistants and clerks

Secretarial — Private secretary, confidential assistants and stenographers

Service staff — Daftary, messengers, watchmen, sweepers and caretakers

Miscellaneous — Doctors and para-medical staff in the hospital, teaching staff in the education department, estate and maintenance staff for the township and security and fire personnel

11. Education-wise nearly 5% of the work force (officers and employees) had ITI certificate level or higher qualifications, 10% had non-technical qualifications above matriculation level and the remaining 85% comprised either non-matriculate or illiterates despite the fact that sugar industry had a fairly sophisticated technology.

Based on the guidelines furnished by both the Manager (IE) and Manager (MPP), the professionals at lower levels were assigned the details of working out a comprehensive manpower plan for the various sugar plants which had to come up in course of time. Depending on the size of the units, manpower availability, level of education, level of productivity, environmental culture with regard to supervisory practices, discipline and aptitude for work, the manpower was assessed at 500 to 800 for different units. This plan was forwarded to the GM (P & MS) who in turn had detailed discussions with the various professionals at different levels and after suitable modifications presented the final study to the management for consideration.

## REVIEW QUESTIONS

1.   Discuss the purposes and process of human resource planning.
2.   Examine the reasons for the current interest in human resource planning.   Discuss company experiences.
3.   Review the major activities of human resource planning.
4.   The scope of human resource planning extends beyond identifying the number of people required.   Discuss different types of action plans based on human resource planning exercise in an organization.

EXERCISE 1

Take up the case of any organization (the one where you work or the one with which you have some acquaintance).   Discuss with key persons in personnel and other functions and prepare a brief write up (not more than 1000 words) outlining its

- profile
- objectives and corporate plans
- human resource planning practices, and
- key issues in human resource planning/strategies.

EXERCISE 2

Choose an organization where you work or have previously worked or the one with which you have some acquaintance.   Assume that you have been given a personal computer and told to create a Human Resource Information System (HRIS).   Identify and prepare an inventory of the types/nature of information that you need to put into your system for being used for the kind and variety of action plans suggested in the text.

## FURTHER READING

1.   Bennison, M and J Casson, 1983.   *The Manpower Planning Handbook*. McGraw-Hill: London.

2.   Gautam, V, 1988. *Comparative Manpower Planning Practices*, National Publishing House: New Delhi.

3.   Krishnaswamy, K N, 1985.   "Manpower Planning Practices in Indian Manufacturing Organizations", *ASCI Journal of Management*, vol. 15, no. 1, Sept., pp 47–76.

4.   Mozina, S, 1984.   *Guide to Planning for Manpower Development*, ICPE : Ljubljana (Yugoslavia).

5.   Walker, J W, 1980. *Human Resource Planning*, McGraw-Hill: New York.

# CHAPTER 4

# Recruitment, Selection, Placement, Induction, Internal Mobility and Separations

**Learning Objectives**

After going through this chapter you should be able to:
Understand the concepts: underlying recruitment, selection, placement, induction, internal mobility and separations;  • Familiarize yourself with the purpose, process and special problems of recruitment and selection;  • Deve -lop awareness about different sources of recruitment and various types of selection tests;  • Appreciate the importance of placement and induction; and,  • Review the key issues in transfers and promotions (which together account for internal mobility) and aspects relating to separations.

All organizations are basically human organizations. They need people to carry out the organizational mission, goals or activities. Every organization needs to recruit people. The recruitment policy should, therefore, address itself to the key question: what are the personnel/human resource requirements of the organization in terms of number, skills, levels, etc. to meet present and future needs of production and technical and other changes planned or anticipated in the next few years?

The Indian labour market is characterized by an apparent abundancy of labour. Unemployment is growing, yet there are critical skill shortages which are frequently aggravated by overseas migration of skilled personnel. The inadequacies of the education system result in the general and growing problem of non-availability of suitably trained work force. With too many people chasing limited number of jobs, there are social and political pressures tampering with and influencing selection decisions. Rapid social and technological changes are making not only forecasting human resource requirements difficult, but rendering a variety of human skills and jobs redundant. The skill shortages are putting a premium on employees. These have implications for evolving newer and effective strategies to replace and/or retain people as the case may be. In this chapter, we shall consider aspects relating to recruitment, selection, placement, induction, internal mobility and separation.

## RECRUITMENT

To recruit means to enlist, replenish or reinforce. It refers to the process of bringing together prospective employees and employer with a view to stimulate and encourage the former to apply for a job with the latter. The purpose of recruitment is to prepare an inventory of people who meet the criteria laid down in job specifications so that the organization may choose those who are found most suitable for the positions vacant.

## Process of Recruitment

Recruitment begins by specifying the human resource requirements, initiating activities and actions to identify the possible sources from where they can be met, communicating the information about the jobs, terms and conditions and prospects they offer, and enthuse people who meet the requirements to respond to the invitation (at factory gate, word of mouth, campus interview, etc.) by applying for job(s). Thereafter, the selection process begins with the initial screening of applications and applicants.

  Job analysis would have already provided the basis for job specification (see Chapter 2 for details) in terms of qualities, qualifications, experience and abilities. Human resource planning (see Chapter 3) provides the basis to arrive at decisions concerning the number, levels and timing of recruitment.

## Sources of Recruitment

The human resource requirements can be met from internal or external sources.

*The Internal Sources*    They include those who are already on the pay-roll of the organization and those who served the organization in the past (but quit voluntarily or due to retrenchment) and would to return if the organization likes to re-employ. There is merit in looking for internal resources since they provide opportunities for better deployment and utilization of existing human resources through planned placements and transfers or to motivate people through planned promotions and career development where vacancies exist in higher grades. The law provides preferences to retrenched employees when vacancies arise in future.

*External Sources*    Organizations may look for people outside it. Entry level jobs are usually filled by new entrants from outside. Also in the following circumstances organizations may resort to outside sources, (a) when suitably qualified people are not available; (b) when the organization feels it is necessary to inject new blood into it for fresh ideas, initiatives, etc; (c) when it is diversifying into new avenues; and (d) when it is merging with another organization.

## Methods of Recruitment

The methods of recruitment may include one or more of the following: (a) Internal; (b) Direct; (c) Indirect; and (d) Third-party.

*Internal Method*     This is a practice of filling vacancies from within through transfers and promotions.  All transfer decisions are usually taken by management and communicated to those concerned.  In the case of promotions, however, information about the vacancies is communicated through internal advertisement or circulation and applications are invited from eligible candidates who wish to be considered for the positions.  Alternatively, organizations may prepare seniority or seniority-cum-merit lists and consider the eligible candidates for internal promotions.

Some organizations keep *badli* lists or a central pool of persons from which vacancies can be filled for manual jobs.  Such people may be listed out for different jobs according to which they are best suited.  Any person who remains on such rolls for 240 days or more is treated, in the eyes of law, as a permanent employee, and is therefore, entitled to all relevant benefits including Provident Fund, Gratuity and retrenchment compensation under section 25F of the Industrial Disputes Act.  Though the system thus appears to be costly, it has its benefits in that : (a) continuous supply of labour is assured; (b) work is not affected due to the problem of absenteeism; (c) there is no problem of fresh induction; and (d) it is possible to train the people in multi-skills.

*Direct Method*     These include campus interviews and keeping a live register of job seekers.  Usually used for jobs requiring technical or professional skills, organizations may visit ITI's, IITs, IIMs and colleges and universities and recruit persons for various jobs.  Usually under this method, information about jobs and profile of persons available for jobs is exchanged and preliminary screening is done. The short-listed candidates is then subjected to the remainder of the selection process.

Some organizations maintain live registers/records of job applicants and refer to them as and when the need arises.  Usually in all such cases, preliminary screening is completed by examining the application form filled by the candidate and/or preliminary interviews.

*Indirect Method*     These include advertisement in the print media, radio, television,trade, professional and technical journals, etc.  It is appropriate to clearly state the responsibilities and requirements along with definite hints about the compensation, prospects, etc.

This method is appropriate where there is plentiful supply of talent which is geographically or otherwise spread out and when the purpose of the organization is to reach out to a larger target group.  However, it is not always possible to get key professionals or those with rare skills through this method.

*Third-party Method*    They include reference to Employment Exchange, which is a statutory requirement for the jobs/organizations to which the Employment Exchanges (Compulsory Notification) Act applies. Special Employment Exchanges have been set up in different places for displaced persons, ex-military personnel, physically handicapped, professionals, etc.  For highly skilled or technical jobs, University Employment Bureaux and the Council of Scientific and Industrial Research have also been set up. There are several difficulties in developing such services efficiently and organizations successfully contested such  rulings by filing cases in courts when they were asked to select *only* from among those sponsored by the employment exchanges.

Head-hunting services, consultancy firms, professional societies and temporary help agencies are among the newer sources of third-party help in recruitment, some of which use computerized data bases. Traditionally, in India the following methods were used, some of which were discredited due to their abuse.

- Casual labour presenting itself at the factory gate on a day-to-day basis and offering for employment;
- Hiring through labour contractors, maistries etc.
- Spreading information about jobs through word of mouth including friends and relatives, present employees, etc.

The Royal Commission on Labour  has frowned upon the system of recruitment through labour contractors and contract labour was statutorily abolished in certain jobs.  However, in recent times new forms of sub-contracting, franchising, home-work and contractual norms of work are emerging for which protection from unions and statutes is still a far cry.  Some of the legal and political restraints limiting the sources of recruitment are discussed briefly in the following.

## Legal and Political Considerations

The Constitution provides for the following as the Fundamental Rights of a citizen:

"*Article 16(1)*: There shall be equality of opportunity for all citizens in matters relating to employment or appointment to any office under the State."

"*Article 16(2)*:  No citizen shall, on ground only of religion, race, caste, sex, descent, place of birth, residence or any of them, be ineligible for or discriminated against in respect of any employment or office under the State."

"*Article 16(3)*: Nothing in this article shall prevent Parliament from making any law prescribing, in regard to a class or classes of employment or appointment to an office (under the government of, or any local or other authority within a state or union territory), any requirement as to residence within that state or union territory prior to such employment or appointment.

The Constitution ensures, in the Directive Principles of State Policy, certain safeguards for Scheduled Castes, Scheduled Tribes and other weaker sections.  Except in cases which are covered by *Article 46* of the Constitution, there can be no discrimination in the matter of employment anywhere in the country for any citizen.

"*Article 46*: The State shall promote with special care the educational and economic interests of the weaker sections of the people, and in particular, of the Scheduled

Castes and Scheduled Tribes, and shall protect them from social injustice and all forms of exploitation.

The Directive Principles of State Policy also envisage certain restrictions on the employment of women and children, even as they envisage equal right to men and women to have adequate means of livelihood. *Articles 39* and *41* list certain principles to be followed by the State.

"*Article 39*: The State shall, in particular, direct its policy towards securing;

(a) that the citizens, men and women equally have the right to an adequate means of livelihood;

(e) that the health and strength of workers, men and women, and the tender age of children are not abused and that citizens are not forced by economic necessity to enter avocations unsuited to their age or strength;

(f) that childhood and youth are protected against exploitation and against moral and material abandonment;"

"*Article 41*: the State shall, within the limits of its own economic capacity and development, make effective provision for securing the right to work, to education and to public assistance in cases of unemployment, and in other cases of undeserved want."

The Fundamental Rights are justiceable while the Directive Principles are not justiceable. In other words, a citizen can sue over denial of Fundamental Rights but not for non accrual of benefits under the Directive Principles of State Policy.

In pursuance of the ideals envisaged in the Constitution and the objectives of planned economic development under successive plans, several legislations have been enacted. The following are among the major *legislations* which impinge upon recruitment policies and practices of organizations:

**Child Labour (Prohibition and Regulation) Act, 1986**    This Act, which replaces the Employment of Children Act, 1938, seeks to prohibit the engagement of children below 14 years of age in certain employments and to regulate the conditions of work of children in certain other employments. Penalties on employers who contravene the provisions include fine and imprisonment.

**The Employment Exchanges (Compulsory Notification of Vacancies) Act, 1959**    The Act requires all employers to notify the vacancies (with certain exemptions) occurring in their establishments to the prescribed employment exchanges before they are filled. The Act covers all establishments in public sector and non-agricultural establishments employing 25 or more workers in the private sector. Employers are also required to furnish quarterly return in respect of their staff strength, vacancies and shortages and a biennial return showing occupational distribution of their employees. While notification of vacancies is compulsory, selection need not be confined only to those who are forwarded by the concerned Employment Exchanges.

**The Apprentices Act, 1961**    The Act seeks to provide for the regulation and control of training of apprentices and for matters connected therewith. The Act provides for a machinery to lay down syllabi and prescribe period of training, reciprocal obligations for apprentices and employers, etc. The responsibility for engagement of apprentices lies solely with the employer. An apprentice is not a *workman* but where there is a condition in the apprenticeship contract, that the apprentice shall, after successful completion of his apprenticeship training, serve the employer, the employer shall, on such completion be bound to offer suitable employment to the apprentice.

The Apprentice Rules, 1962, formulated under the Act, were amended in 1986 prescribing revised rates of compensation for apprenticeship as also for failure on the part of the employer to carry out the terms and conditions of the contract.

**The Contract Labour (Regulation and Abolition) Act, 1970**     This Act seeks to regulate the employment of contract labour in certain establishments and to provide for its abolition in certain circumstances. The Act applies to every establishment/contractor employing 20 or more persons.

**Bonded Labour System (Abolition) Act, 1976**     This Act seeks to provide for the abolition of bonded labour system with a view to preventing the economic and physical exploitation of the weaker sections of the people. The *bonded labour system* means any system of forced or partly forced labour which a debtor enters, or is presumed to have entered into with the creditor to the effect that in consideration of the advance and/or interest on the advance by him or his lineal ascendants or descendants he and/or any or all of the members of his family would fully or partly forfeit right of employment or other means of livelihood and the right to sell his labour or product of his labour for a specified or unspecified period.

**The Inter-state Migrant Workmen (Regulation of Employment and Conditions of Service) Act, 1979**     This Act seeks to safeguard the interests of the workmen who are recruited by contractors from one state for service in an establishment situated in another state and to guard against the exploitation of such workmen by the contractors.

**The Factories Act, 1948, the Mines Act, 1952, etc.**     Certain legislations, like the Factories Act and the Mines Act prohibit employment of women (in night work, underground work, etc.) and children (below 14 years of age) in certain types of jobs. The International Labour Organization is reviewing the conventions/recommendations prescribing the ban of employment of women in night work, underground work, etc as they have restricted the employment opportunities for women.

**Reservations for Special Groups**     In pursuance of the constitutional provisions, statutory reservations and relaxed norms have been provided in education and employment to candidates belonging to Scheduled Castes and Scheduled Tribes in central and state services including departmental undertakings, government corporations, local bodies and other quasi-government organizations. Most state governments have issued policy directives extending the reservations to notified backward communities also.

Over the years, the concept of reservation in education and employment has been extended to other categories as measures to tackle social problems or to pursue socio-political objectives. Such categories include: physically handicapped and disabled persons, women, ex-service persons, sportsmen, etc.

In the case of physically handicapped and the ex-servicemen special rehabilitation arrangements have been made to find suitable employment opportunities to the concerned.

**Sons-of-the-Soil**     The question of preference to local population in the matter of employment has become more complex today than ever before.  In Andhra Pradesh and Maharashtra, the pre-independence era practice of *mulki* qualification, i.e. the qualification being domicile for a period of at least, say, 15 years continues till date. The National Commission on Labour suggested that the solution to the problem of *sons-of-the-soil* has to be sought in terms of the primacy of common citizenship, geographic and economic feasibility of locating industrial units on the one hand and local aspirations on the other.  The Government of India recognized the main elements of the arguments on behalf of the sons of the soil and laid down certain principles in the matter of recruitment to its public sector projects (Exhibit 4.1), whose implementation, however, is left to the undertakings themselves.

**Displaced Persons**     Whenever major projects are set up, large tracts of land are acquired for the purpose, displacing several hundred households in each case.  Payment of compensation for land was at one time considered a sufficient discharge of obligation towards persons who are dispossessed of land. This alone does not solve the question of earning  livelihood.  Therefore, it is argued that young persons from families whose lands are acquired should be provided opportunity for training (between the time the land is transferred to the hands of new owners and an industrial unit is set up) and for employments likely to be created in new units set up on these lands.  The National Commission on Labour made the following suggestions.

(a) Young persons from families whose lands are acquired for industrial use should be provided training opportunities for employments likely to be created in new units set up on these lands;

(b) To remove unjustified apprehension among local candidates, the following steps should be taken to supervise implementation of the  Government of India directive on recruitment in public sector projects:

(i) While recruiting unskilled employees, first preference should be given to persons displaced from the areas acquired for the project; next should be preferred those who have been living within the vicinity.

(ii) Selection of persons to posts in lower scales should not be left entirely to the head of the units.  It should be through a recruitment committee with a nominee of the Government of the State within which the unit is located as a member of the committee.

(iii) In the case of middle-level technicians where recruitment has to be on an all-India basis, a member of the State Government should officiate on the Board of the Directors.

(iv) Apart from the report sent to the concerned ministry at the Centre, the undertaking should send a statement to the State Government at regular intervals, preferably every quarter, about the latest employment and recruitment position.

Although the Commission has suggested these steps for employment in the public sector, they feel that the above should apply equally to recruitment in the private sector, though the mechanism to regulate recruitment in the private sector will necessarily differ from that in the public sector.

**EXHIBIT 4.1**

---

### Note on Recruitment Policy in the Public Sector Projects
(Laid on the table of the Lok Sabha on 14-4-1961)

1.    There is technically no restriction in the matter of recruitment to these units on the areas from which the employees come.  It will be of advantage to the units in various directions, if persons who come from areas near about the place of location of the project secure appointment to posts in the lower scales. In the case of unskilled workers, even without any special effort they are generally drawn from the locality where the project is situated. Every effort should be made in such requirements to give preference to persons displaced the areas acquired for the project especially or Scheduled Castes and Scheduled Tribes (e.g. *Adivasis*). Next should be preferred those who, even if they come from some distance, have been or are about to be retrenched from other government undertakings.

2.    In the case of skilled workers, clerks and other non-technical staff whose scales are comparatively low, so long as the basic qualifications and experience are forthcoming, preference should be given in the order of priority mentioned in the previous paragraph.

3.    In the case of the middle level technical and non-technical posts, having higher starting salaries equivalent to the Class-I junior scale of the Government of India (Rs 350–850), recruitment should be made on an all-India basis, merit and qualifications being the principal criteria.  Complaints have sometimes been made in the past that local candidates do not receive a fair deal.  Special care should be taken to ensure that there is no reasonable ground for any such complaint.

4.    In the case of higher non-technical posts, e.g. top general management, finance and accounts, sales, purchase, stores, transport, personnel management and welfare and town administration, carrying a salary of Rs 600 and above, candidates available in the Industrial Management Pool should first be considered, failing such candidates, there should be advertisement on all-India basis.  This does not, however, preclude considering candidates who may have applied on their own or may have been retrenched from other government projects, etc.

5.    For the higher technical posts, the best qualified persons will have to be recruited, either by advertisement on an all-India basis or by personal contact.

6.    All vacancies of the kind referred to in paras 1 and 2 should be communicated to the Employment Exchanges close to the project.  Advertisements, which are made in the papers should be in local languages and in the local newspapers.  Such advertisements should specially mention that preference would be given to persons who are registered in Employment Exchanges.  All the applications received along with the list sent by the Employment Exchange should be screened and appointments made by Selection Committees specially set up for the purpose by each unit.  These Selection Committees should include representatives from the State Government or their nominees.

7.    The Selection Committees set up for recruitment to all other medium-level or higher technical or non-technical posts should include at least one representative of the State Government, preferably a State Government official who is on the Board of Directors.

8.    Representation for local interests in the shape of a State Government nominee, etc. as detailed above should also be provided for in any standing committees that may exist for the purpose and not confined to only special ad hoc committees.

9.    Where the exigencies of work require the making of urgent ad hoc appointments, it will be open to the Managing Director to make such appointments and then inform the Selection or Standing Committees.

10.    The above principles may be kept in view by Boards of directors and Managing directors/Chairmen of public sector projects while making recruitments to posts within their projects.

# SELECTION

To select means to choose. Selection is a part of the recruitment function. It is the process of choosing people by obtaining and assessing information about the applicants (age, qualification, experience and qualities) with a view to matching these with the job requirements and picking up the most suitable candidates. The choices are made by elimination of the unsuitable at successive stages of the selection process.

## Purpose of Selection

What is the purpose of selection? The purpose is to pick up the most suitable person who would match the requirements of the job and the organization best. As one chief executive observed, "If you make a wrong selection in recruiting the Maintenance Engineer your maintenance may suffer for over 30 years". The emphasis in selection is, therefore, on the optimal match between the person and the job. Now the question arises as to which is the dependent variable? Person or job. Some organizations emphasize on selecting *the Right Person for the Right Job*. Here the job is usually considered constant (though jobs and job contexts do undergo changes over time) and the person is sought to be fitted into the job. Creative and innovative organizations, instead, seek to find *the Right Job for the Right Person*. They select key professionals who can knit together and leave the structuring of the tasks to themselves.

A secondary objective in selection could be to choose the best person available. However, there could be a real problem with such an objective if the job is not appropriate for the person concerned. It may become difficult for organizations to retain their best people in jobs that do not offer opportunities for them to harness their potential; instead, they may lead to problems of monotony, boredom and frustration among individuals and increased turnover of staff for the organization.

For the selection process to remain dynamic and purposive  organizations need to continually focus attention and understand the chemistry between people and jobs.

## Criteria of Selection

Selection decisions are usually based on how an applicant is rated (rather, predicted) in terms of the likelihood of success on the job. The  information used is found in the application blanks, performance in one or more tests and the interview(s).

The criteria of selection needs to be critical to the job. The key job dimensions identified in job analysis and job description (discussed in Chapter 2) provide the basis for determining relevant criteria.

Frequently educational qualifications, technical skills and achievements are used as the basis for selection. But is there a statistical relationship between such requirements and job performance? It appears that certain job requirements can be measured more easily and accurately than certain others (Table 4.1). The core job skills like sensory motor skills and manipulative skills and achievement can be measured relatively more than one's aptitude, interest and personality traits.

A recent survey of the criteria for selection in managerial recruitment in 50 companies (Table 4.2) notes that integrity, loyalty, initiative/drive/resourcefulness and intelligence/mental alertness are the key attributes influencing the selection of managerial employees. All these attributes being subjective are hard to assess accurately, yet are widely attempted. Perhaps it is so because managements and employers in India have relatively less pressure to defend the criteria. A cursory review of court decisions on selection issues suggests that more and more selection decisions are questioned when they concern promotions rather than first appointment in an organization; the reason may be that the adverse impact of decisions of the organization to the employee is hard to establish in the latter case.

## The Selection Process

The selection process begins with the job specification. The more clearly and precisely it is done the less would be the number of qualified applicants. Suppose the purpose is to select management trainees. If the qualification prescribed is MBA, the number of applicants may be in hundreds. If the qualification is graduation in any discipline, the number of applicants may be in thousands. Of course, the reputation of the firm, the job content, compensation package, location, etc. also influence the response to any recruitment drive. But job specification does plays an important role in deciding the quantity and quality of response from prospective applicants. It also makes it easy to ward off or limit pressures from less qualified persons.

**Table 4.1    Relative Accuracy in Tests**

| Human Requirements | Typical Jobs | Job Requirements | Test Accuracy |
|---|---|---|---|
| Sensory motor | Bus driver Labourer | Eye-hand coordination | High degree |
| Manipulative | Machinist | Fingers, operates, cordinates | |
| Achievement | Technician | Information, knowledge, technical experience, procedure | |
| Aptitude | Engineer | Perceive, interpret, analyze, integrate | |
| Interests | Buyer | Preferences, discriminate | |
| Personality Traits | Therapist | Patience, cooperative, empathy | |
| | | | Low Degree |

Table 4.2    Selection Criteria for Managerial Recruitment: The Top Ten
Attributes

| Top Management | Middle Management | Lower Management |
|---|---|---|
| Integrity | Integrity | Integrity |
| Leadership | Loyalty | Energy |
| Maturity | Job knowledge and skills | Loyalty |
| Initiative,drive and resourcefulness | Initiative, drive and resourcefulness | Relevant qualifications: education, industriousness, litelligence and mental alertness |
| Loyalty | Maturity | |
| Organizational skills | Energy level | |
| | Leadership | Initiative,drive and resourcefulness |
| Communication | Communication | |
| Confidence and selfreliance | Intelligence and mental alertness | Manner and attitude |
| Intelligence and mental alertness | Relevant qualification/ education | Perseverance, motivation and ambition |

*Source:* Deepak Kumar Verma and Nandu Rajadhyaksha, 1986.  "Selection Criteria for Managerial Recruitment: A Survey of 50 companies," *Business India*, 20 Oct.–2 Nov., pp 87–88.

The selection process covers the period from the job specification and initial contact with the applicant to his final acceptance or rejection.  The successive stages in the selection process (Fig. 4.1) are referred to as hurdles that the applicants should cross.  Not all selection processes, however, include all these stages.  The complexity of the selection process usually increases with the increase in the skill level and job level (responsibility and accountability) of the position for which selection is being made.  The sequencing of the hurdles also may vary from job to job and organization to organization.

When a market research firm is recruiting research investigators on temporary basis for a specific assignment it may ask the candidates to appear for interview along with written application forms in the next two days following the date of advertisement and make job offers immediately after the interview without any other tests or references.  The Union Public Service Commission's selection process for civil services consists of screening of applications, preliminary objective test, written test, viva voce and physical examination and references.  Several industrial/business organizations follow the process described in Fig. 4.1, with minor variations, for selecting management trainees.

***Initial Screening***    The initial screening and/or preliminary interview is done to limit the costs of selection by letting only suitable candidates go through the further stages in selection.  At this stage, usually a junior executive either screens all enquiries for positions against specified norms (in terms of age, qualifications and experience)

**Fig. 4.1** *The Selection Process*

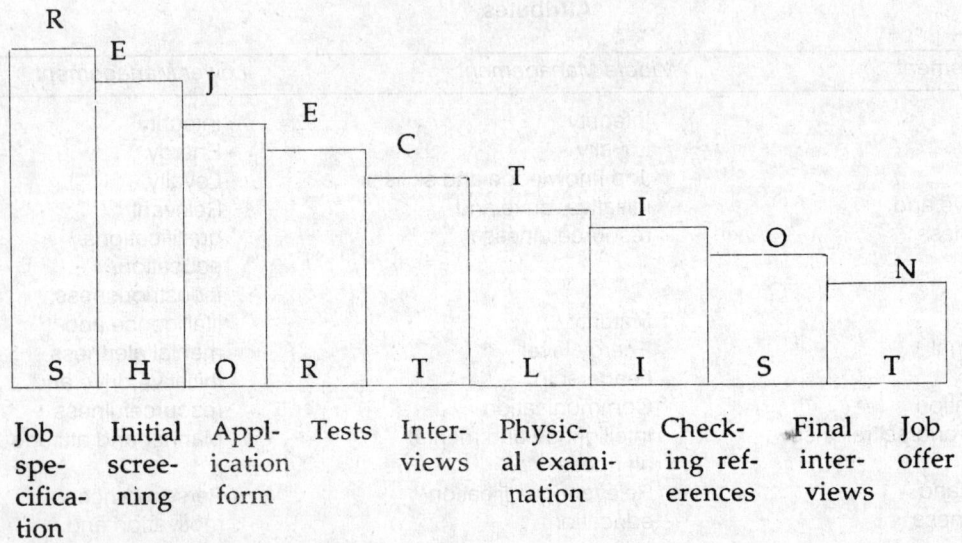

| Job spe-cifica-tion | Initial scree-ning | Appl-ication form | Tests | Inter-views | Physic-al exami-nation | Check-ing ref-erences | Final inter-views | Job offer |

through preliminary interview where information is exchanged about the job, the applicant and the mutual expectations of the individual and the organization. If the organization finds the candidate suitable, an application form, prescribed for the purpose, is given to these candidates to fill in and submit.

*Application Form* The application form is usually designed to obtain information on various aspects of the applicant's social, demographic, academic and work-related background and references. The forms may vary for different positions. Some organizations may not have any form specially designed and instead, ask the candidates to write applications on a plain sheet.

It is important to determine what kind of information can and needs to be asked. It is equally important to know that asking for certain types of information relating to race, caste, religion and place of birth may be regarded as evidence of possible discrimination in the selection process.

The application form should provide for all the basic information an organization needs to determine whether a candidate can be considered for the position he is applying for as also to provide the inputs to start the interview. It also serves as the basis to screen and reject candidates if they do not meet the eligibility criteria relating to qualifications, experience, etc.

**Tests** A test is a sample of an aspect of an individual's behaviour, performance or attitude. It also provides a systematic basis for comparing the behaviour, performance or attitude of two or more persons. Tests serve as a screening device and provide supplementary inputs in selection decisions. Their value lies in the fact that they serve as additional predictors intended to make selection decisions more apt and accurate.

*Intelligence Tests* These are tests to measure one's intellect or qualities of understanding. They are also referred to as tests of mental ability. The traits of intelligence measured include: reasoning , verbal and non-verbal fluency, comprehension, numerical, memory and spatial relations ability.    Binet-Simon; Stanford-Binet and Weshler-Bellevue Scale are some examples of standard intelligence tests.    Such tests are used for admission into MBA programmes, recruitment in Banks and a host of other organizations.

The major criticism against these tests is that they tend to discriminate  against rural people and minorities.    Also, since most of these tests are administered in English, the results may be more influenced by one's command over language (particularly the lack of it) rather than one's intelligence.

*Aptitude tests*    Aptitude refers to one's natural propensity or talent or ability to acquire a particular skill. While intelligence is a general trait, aptitude refers to a more specific capacity or potential.  It could relate to mechanical dexterity, clerical, linguistic, musical, academic, etc.

Most aptitude tests are so standardized that they are not specific to any particular job.  However, they are general enough to be used in different job situations.  OTIS Employment Test, and Wesman Personal Classification Test are examples of general aptitude tests. Certain types of aptitude tests called psychomotor tests measure hand and eye coordination and manipulative skills.  The MacQuarrie Test for Mechanical Ability and the O'connor Finger and Tweezer Dexterity Tests are examples of psychomotor tests. There are other types of aptitude tests to measure personal (how to decide for themselves appropriately in time) and interpersonal (social relations) competence.

*Achievement tests*    These are proficiency tests to measure one's skill or acquired knowledge. The paper and pencil tests may seek to test a person's knowledge about a particular subject.  But there is no guarantee that a person who knows most also performs best. Work sample tests or performance tests using actual task and working conditions (than simulated one's) provide standardized measures of behaviour to assess the ability to perform than merely the ability to know. Work sample tests are most appropriate for testing abilities in such skills as typing, stenography and technical trades. Work sample tests bear demonstrable relationship between test content and job performance.

*PIP tests*    PIP tests are those which seek to measure one's *personality, interests and preferences*.  These tests are designed to understand the relationship between any one of these and certain types of jobs.

Tests of one's personality traits or characteristics are sometimes referred to as *personality inventories*. These tests help evaluate characteristics such as maturity, sociability, objectivity, etc. Unlike tests, however, inventories do not have right or wrong answers. Personality inventories aid in selection decisions and are used for associating certain set of traits with salespersons and  certain others, say, research and development personnel.  Minnesota Multiphasic Personality Inventory and California Psychological Inventory are examples of personality inventories.

Interest tests are inventories of likes and dislikes of people towards occupations, hobbies, etc.  These tests help indicate which occupations (e.g. artistic, literary, technical, scientific, etc) are more in tune with a person's interests.    Strong Vocational

Interest Blank and Kuder Preference Records are examples of interest tests. These tests do not, however, help in predicting on the job performance. Besides, they leave room for faking and the underlying assumptions in the tests could be belied.

Preference tests seek to match employee prefernces with job and organizational characteristics. Hackman and Oldham's Job Diagnostic Survey is an example of a preference test. The Job Diagnostic Survey indicates how people differ in their preferences for accomplishment, discretion, meaningfulness, contingency, etc. in their jobs.

*Projective tests*    These tests expect the candidates to interpret problems or situations. Responses to stimuli will be based on the individual's values, beliefs and motives. Thematic Apperception Test and Rorschach Ink Blot Test are examples of projective tests. In Thematic Apperception Test a photograph is shown to the candidate who is then asked to interpret it. The test administrator will draw inferences about the candidate's values, beliefs and motives from an analysis of such interpretation. The main criticism against such tests is that they could be unscientific and reveal the personality of the test designer/administrator more than the candidate/applicant.

*Other tests*    A vide variety of other tests also are used, though less frequently and in rare instances. These include polygraphy (literally means many pens), graphology (handwriting analysis), non-verbal communication tests (gestures, body movement, eye-contact, etc) and lie-detector tests. Most of these tests, with the possible exception of non-verbal communication tests, are designed more to identify the negative aspects in the personality, behaviour and attitudes of a person. In the Indian context, it was found in a handful of cases, employers who have an ardent zeal for having their management practices rooted in 'our tradition and culture', use horoscope, face reading and palmistry (hand-reading). They contend that if the person is destined to succeed he should be selected so that 'he will not only do good to himself but also to the organization'. They add that traditionally marital alliances are made this way; so we can select our employees the same way and expect them to have a life- long association with us". But, these kinds of tests are indeed very exceptional and rather unusual by the  general standards.

The following could be considered as the thumb rules of selection tests:

(a)    Tests are to be used as a screening device.

(b)    Tests scores are not precise measures. Use tests as supplements than on stand alone basis. Each  test can be assigned a weightage.

(c)    Norms have to be developed for each test; and their validity and reliability for a given purpose is to be established before they are used.

(d)    Tests are better at predicting failure than success.

(e)    Tests should be designed, administered, assessed and interpreted only by trained and competent persons.

# Interview

Interview is an oral examination of candidates for employment. No selection process is complete without one or more interviews. Interview is the most common and core method of both obtaining information from job-seekers, and decision-making on their suitability or otherwise. Organizations may seek to make their selection process as objective as possible. But, interview, which is an essential element of the process, by and large, still remains subjective.

Interviews usually take place at two crucial stages in the selection process, i.e. at the beginning and in the end. Interviews can differ in terms of their focus and format. Usually several individuals interview one applicant. This is called *panel interview*. Such panels usually consist of representatives from personnel and concerned operating units/line functions. In this method, usually, applicants get screened from one stage to another, at least in the initial stages. The interviews can be structured or unstructured, general or in-depth. Some times where the job requires the job holder to remain calm and composed under pressure, the candidates are intentionally subjected to stresses and strains in the interview by asking some annoying or embarrassing questions. This type of interview is called the *stress interview*.

Interviewing is both an art and a science. The effectiveness of the interview as a screening device can be improved by taking care of certain aspects like the following:

1. The interview should be based on a checklist of what to look for in a candidate. Such a checklist could be based on proper job analysis. Each critical attribute which the interview seeks to evaluate may be assigned a specific weightage.

2. It is desirable to prepare a specific set of guidelines for the interview.

3. The interviewers need to be trained to evaluate performance in the interview objectively. Also, all interviewers need to develop common understanding about the criteria measures, their purposes and weightages.

4. The interviewers may use past behaviour to predict future behaviours and obtain additional information to attempt such linkages more meaningfully.

5. There should be proper coordination between the initial and succeeding interviews.

6. The interview (even stress interview) should be conducted in a relaxed physical setting.

## Background Investigation

The background investigation in selection process may include verification of references from past teachers, employers or public men; police verification; and, medical examination.

The purpose of background investigation is to gather additional information about the mental faculties, behaviour and physical health. In the USA, the Civil Rights Act prescribes limits and procedures for disclosure of information to protect individual liberty and privacy. In India similar provisions do not exist at the moment. Typically, the selection process in civil service and public sector employment involved routing of applications through present employer, reference verification, police verification and medical examination. Private sector firms do not expect the applications to be routed through present employer. They also do not normally make use of police verification though for certain top managerial positions, discrete enquiries in professional circles and or through private investigators are resorted to, though seldom.

Background verification is sought to guard oneself against possible falsification by applicants. But given the acute skill shortages and competitive pirating strategies of employers it is possible for some of them to give a clean chit to those whom they wish to get rid of and be unfair to those whom they are not prepared to lose. Therefore, employers in private sector generally find that they get more accurate information when they track the actual past performance than when they merely ask for references reflecting one's opinion about the candidate.

Medical and physical examinations are usually resorted to by employers as part of the selection process mainly to:

- determine whether the applicant has the physical ability to carry on the duties and responsibilities effectively;
- ascertain whether the applicant has a record of health problems which can potentially affect his behaviour and performance on the job adversely;
- know whether the applicant is more sensitive to certain aspects of work-place environment such as chemicals.

For the above reasons, the medical and physical examinations are considered to provide significant inputs, which are fair and valid, for selection decisions.

## PLACEMENT

Placement refers to assigning rank and responsibility to an individual, identifying him with a particular job. If the person adjusts himself to the job and continues to perform as per expectations, it might mean that the candidate is properly placed. However, if the candidate is seen to have problems in adjusting himself to the job, the supervisor must find out whether the person is properly placed as per the latter's aptitude and potential. Usually, placement problems arise out of wrong selection or improper placement or both. Therefore, organizations need to constantly review cases of employees performing below expectations/potential and employee related problems such as turnover, absenteeism, accidents and assess how far they are related to inappropriate placement decisions and remedy the situation without delay.

## INDUCTION

Induction refers to the introduction of a person to the job and the organization. The purpose is to make the employee feel at home and develop a sense of pride in the organization and commitment to the job. The induction process is also envisaged to indoctrinate, orient, acclimatize and acculturate the person to the job and the organization.

The basic thrust of induction training during the first one or few weeks after a person joins service in the organization is to:

- introduce the person to the people with whom he works;
- make him aware of the general company policies that apply to him as also the specific work situation and requirements;
- answer any questions and clarify any doubts that the person may have about the job and the organization; and
- provide on-the-job instructions, check back periodically how the person is doing and offer help, if required.

While the personnel staff may provide general orientation relating to organization, the immediate supervisor should take the responsibility for specific orientation relating to the job and work-unit members.  The follow-up orientation is to be coordinated by both the personnel department and the supervisor with a view mainly to obtain feedback and provide guidance and counselling as required.

Proper induction would enable the employee to get off to a good a start and to develop his overall effectiveness on the job and enhance his potential.

## INTERNAL MOBILITY

Employees may be required to move within an organization, laterally or vertically (see Fig 3.2 in Chapter 3) for a variety of reasons which include:
- satisfying the needs of the organization and the individual;
- maximizing  the effectiveness of the person to the organization;
- make adjustment in placement based on further feedback about aptitudes and potential as also to fill vacancies or meet shortages and redundancies;
- effect changes in jobs and organization structures responding to the changing environment and business needs;
- provide for individual and organization development as also career and succession planning; and
- reinforce discipline and making organizational rewards, etc. contingent on performance.

Internal mobility may be in the form of transfer, promotion and demotion, each of which are briefly discussed here.  Separations also cause internal mobility in a way which will be discussed separately later.

## Transfer

A transfer is a lateral movement within the same grade, from one job to another.  A transfer may result in changes in duties and responsibilities, supervisory and working conditions, but not necessarily salary.

Transfers may be made for reasons such as:
- Correcting misplacement
- Filling vacancies internally
- Meeting skill shortages/job redundancies
- Dealing with problem employees
- Facilitating superior-peer adjustment
- Providing a chance for wider experience
- Job rotation as part of career development
- Accommodating personal needs and conveniences of the individual
- Reward or punishment
- Change working conditions (e.g. manual to mechanical   operations)
- Humanitarian/compassionate ground (transfer to one's native place to  enable the  person  to  look after the sick or old parents).

Transfers could be temporary and ad hoc when they are made to meet emergencies.  They may be regular and planned as part of training, development, career and succession planning activities.  Transfer decisions may be perceived as negative or positive depending upon an individual's personal preferences, needs and aspirations. An organization may consider transfer from a regional office to the head office as a reward since it enables the person to broaden his knowledge and experience; but the individual concerned may feel otherwise if it means breaking his ties with the people and community. Some may consider posting in the chief executive's secretariat as a prestigious assignment, others may look down upon it as an avoidable headache!

Nowadays several organizations are facing stiff opposition from trade unions against transfers which sometimes are used as an instrument for victimization by management. Labour courts set aside transfer orders if the affected employee can prove that the transfer was part of management strategy to victimize him for trade union activities. Some organizations have agreements with unions for unionized staff providing for transfers only when they are accompanied by promotion while others (like the public sector firm, Minerals and Metals Trading Corporation) have agreements creating two cadres of Local Officers and All India Officers; promotions to and within the former cadre are less accelerated than in the latter, but do not entail transfer.

Whether transfers are planned or ad hoc, employees and their families face certain practical difficulties particularly when a transfer means change in location:
- Timing of the transfer
- Housing/accommodation
- School/college admission of children
- Working spouse/dependent family
- Relocation/hardship expenses.

Transfer is a major motivation tool available with any management. Organizations need to develop proactive measures to deal with practical difficulties that affect individuals at the time of transfer. They need to have a humane perspective while developing transfer policies.

## Promotions

Promotion is the advancement of an employee from one job level to a higher one, with increase in salary. It should also usually result in changes in duties and higher level/degree of responsibility, status and value. Sometimes the job itself may be upgraded (e.g., steno to secretary) to a higher level of skill, responsibilities and pay.

It is considered good personnel policy to fill vacancies in a higher job through promotions from within. Such promotions provide an inducement and motivation to the employees, removes feelings of stagnation and frustration and inculcates a sense of growing up with the organization reinforcing common goals between the individual and the organization.

The criteria for promotion decisions may include the following, though the crux of the issue centres around the dilemma over seniority versus merit:
- Performance—length of service (seniority) or merit and ability
- Educational/technical qualifications
- Assessment of potential
- Career and succession plan
- Organization chart based vacancies
- Motivational strategies—job enlargement

- Spacing of the promotion and career span of the individual
- Training

The promotion policy should seek to optimize the interests of the organizations as well as the needs and aspirations of the individual employee. Over the years, organizational practices and pressures from trade unions and industrial jurisprudence produced the following types of broad options in promotion policies:

- Time scale promotion (Based merely on seniority)
- Merit promotion (Based mainly on merit)
- Merit-cum-seniority (Striking a balance between merit and seniority)
- Adhocism (No policy, only adhocism based on expediency)

The National Commission on Labour reviewed the subject and suggested that promotion policies for unionized employees may be evolved by the management in consultation with the recognized union where it exists. The National Commission on Labour has suggested that as a general rule, particularly among the operative and clerical categories in the lower rungs, seniority should be the basis for promotion. In respect of middle management, technical, supervisory and administrative personnel, seniority-cum-merit should be the criterion. For higher managerial, technical and administrative positions, merit alone should be the guiding factor.

If the National Commission on Labour seems to have oversimplified the issue, it is probably because of the lack of proper criteria, known standards, measures and weightages to assess merit objectively enough. Also the pressures to respect seniority are fairly strong not only from trade unions of blue collar and clerical workers, but also from very senior officers belonging to defence services, judiciary and civil services, to name a few. While considering promotions to secretary level even from among those belonging to the Indian Administrative Service, the batch to which a candidate belongs has become a moot point since it reflects his seniority. In the past, on several occasions very senior defence officers and judges have resigned in protest, on the ground that they were superseded by their juniors.

Evidently, both seniority and merit must be taken into consideration. The promotion policy laying down the criteria, standards, measures, weightages and the process and procedure for evaluation and communication must be specified and explained clearly so that all concerned have proper understanding of the subject. It is also appropriate to communicate the rationale of promotion decisions to those who were superseded even though their seniority was considered.

A good promotion policy may include the following:[*]

- Encouragement of promotion within the organization, instead of looking outside to fill vacancies in higher posts;
- An understanding that ability as well as seniority will be taken into account in making promotions;
- Drawing up an organization chart to make clear to all the ladder of promotion. Where there is a job analysis and a planned wage policy, such a chart is quite easy to prepare;
- Making it clear to all concerned who may initiate and handle cases of promo-

---

[*] Sur, M, et al., (Eds), 1970. *Personnel Management in India*, Asia Publishing House: Bombay, pp 231–232.

tion. Though departmental heads may initiate promotion, the final approval should lie with top management, after the personnel department has been asked to check whether any repercussion is likely to result from the proposed promotion;

- All promotions should be for a trial period, in case the promoted person is not found capable of handling the job. Normally during this trial period he draws the pay of the higher post, but it should be clearly understood that if "he does not make the grade" he will be reverted to his former post and his former pay scale".

Usually trade unions argue that they should have a say in promotions. It is desirable to involve the recognized union, where it exists, in formulating the promotions policy. But implementing it is a managerial function. If management develops an objective scheme for promotion it can minimize conflict and controversies over promotion decisions.* Systematic records of employee performance and potential review, regular and prompt feedback, coaching and counselling will enhance the prospects for the acceptability of promotion decisions.

## Demotions

Demotion is the opposite of promotion. It is a downward movement from one job level to another preceding it, leading to a reduction in rank, status, pay and responsibility. Demotions become necessary when:

- a promotee is not able to meet the demands of the new job;
- adverse business conditions lead to downsizing of the organization which can then decide to lay off some and downgrade other jobs; and
- it is viewed as a disciplinary measure.

Demotions should be:

- effected during the trial period after promotion, if the cause of demotion is poor performance. However, the candidates should be given a fair opportunity to improve and be offered training and counselling, before a final decision is taken;
- reversed and *status quo ante* restored once business conditions improve in case demotions are a result of adverse business conditions;
- normally not resorted to as a disciplinary measure.

Demoting an employee is not an easy matter and calls for tact and diplomacy. Perhaps it is easy to dismiss than to demote. In both the cases the person's interests and pride will be hurt, but in the latter case, since the person still continues his association with the organization he may avenge by hurting the interests of the organization.

## SEPARATIONS

Employees may move out of the organization or be separated for a variety of reasons

---

* Gupta, B P, 1986. *Industrial Relations: Some Aspects*, PHD Chamber of Commerce and Industry: New Delhi (see Chapter 21 on Promotion for a review of some judicial pronouncements on the subject, pp 170–174).

like retirement, resignation, suspension, discharge, dismissal; redundancy, retrenchment and outplacement. These are discussed here very briefly.

## Death, Retirement and Resignation

Some employees may die in service. Such deaths may be caused by accidents or other reasons. Where the death occurs due to occupational hazards, the provisions of Workmen's Compensation Act apply. Organizations may additionally have insurance and family-benefit schemes. Several organizations also have a policy of offering employment to the spouse/child/or dependant of an employee who dies in service.

Typically all employment contracts stipulate the age of superannuation. Employees retire from service on attaining the age of superannuation. Some organizations may have a policy to reappoint professionals and others who possess rare skills for a limited duration at a time. All contractual appointments terminate after the expiry of the period of contract. The normal retirement benefits such as provident fund, pension and gratuity as applicable accrue and become payable to the employee on retirement. Some organizations (e.g. Tata Steel and some public sector oil companies) extend certain employee benefits like medical facilities to the employees and their families even after retirement. Usually the retiring employees are bid farewell appropriately with a party, gift and a mention in the house journal.

Organizations are also providing liberal incentives for people to leave before reaching the age of superannuation when they are faced with the situation of surplus staff. Employees may opt to retire voluntarily to avail the benefits of such schemes and possibly pursue a second career or self-employment. Such a scheme is referred to as *voluntary retirement* or the *golden handshake scheme*. Most such schemes have not evoked the desired response from organizational point of view. Several complain that not withstanding the limits they put and the care they exercise *good people are leaving*. Also, unless they address themselves to the basic question of overstaffing, the problem may recur after a few years.

Resignation refers to a situation where an employee takes or is made to take the initiative to leave the job. Resignation may be voluntary or involuntary. A person may leave the job if he is discontented with it or any other aspect of the organization or when he gets a better job elsewhere.

Resignation is considered involuntary when the employer advises the employee to resign or face disciplinary action. However, in disciplinary cases, it is better to follow the due process of domestic enquiry than to shorten the process and accept the *forced* resignation. Otherwise the affected employee can subsequently go to the union and/or court and assert that the resignation was obtained under duress, even if there was no duress.

Where the incidence of separation is high due to resignation, it is appropriate for the organizations to know the reasons through holding exit interviews. Exit interviews are interviews that employers hold with the employees leaving the organization for obtaining information regarding reasons for their leaving. If more people are leaving due to dissatisfaction with organizational factors such as pay, supervision, company policies and working conditions or low morale and motivation, the organization would do well to take immediate measures to remedy the situation so that such departures do not reach the proportion of an exodus.

In recent times, more than ever before, organizations are finding it difficult to retain people. The cost of replacement is becoming prohibitively high. Exit interviews and similar types of feedback will help an organization to take proactive measures to reduce employee turnover and by creating more congenial work environment.

## Suspension, Discharge and Dismissal

Suspension means prohibiting an employee from attending work, stopping him from performing the duties assigned to him and withholding the remuneration payable to him. Suspension is not termination of services of an employee, but may in some cases, eventually lead to it.

An employee may be suspended as a matter of punishment for a specified period in accordance with the provisions in the standing orders. Suspension may be procedural when the employer feels that the delinquent employee be kept away from work pending enquiry into his alleged misconduct so that he will not tamper with evidence or the enquiry itself. Procedural suspension is usually resorted to only in major or repetitive acts of misconduct (see Chapter 12).

Dismissal is termination of the services of an employee for misconduct. Discharge also means termination from service of an employee, but not necessarily as a punitive measure. The Industrial Employment (Standing Orders) Act, 1946, the Industrial Disputes Act, 1947 and the extensive interpretation of the principles of natural justice in various judgements by labour courts, industrial tribunals, high courts and the Supreme Court considerably abridged the employer's right to discharge and dismiss employees covered by the relevant legislation. Section 11A of the Industrial Disputes Act empowers labour courts and tribunals to set aside or modify the orders of discharge and dismissal and direct reinstatement of employees or grant any other relief if they feel that the principles of social and natural justice are violated or that the punishment given is disproportionate to the offence committed. Section 33 of the Industrial Disputes Act provides that if an employee is to be dismissed or discharged, and he is a party to a dispute which is pending before any conciliation, arbitration or adjudication authority, management should obtain prior permission of the concerned authority before it orders discharge or dismissal.

## Redundancy, Retrenchment and Outplacement

Employees may become surplus with the introduction of new technology, automation, modernization, rationalization, loss of market for the product, etc. The surplus employees may be laid off or retrenched. Lay-off of employees refers to the failure, refusal or inability of an employer to provide employment due to factors beyond his control such as shortage of inputs and infrastructure, break-down of machinery, etc. Lay-off does not mean termination of service, but leads to a temporary denial of employment. Retrenchment means the termination by the employer of the services of an employee for reasons other than punishment but does not include retirement or termination for reasons of ill-health. The 15th Indian Labour Conference, 1957, declared that there shall be no retrenchment on account of automation and rationalization.  Chapters V-A and V-B of the Industrial Disputes Act, 1947, introduced in 1953 and 1976 respectively, seek to regulate retrenchment and lay-off of employees in organizations employing 100 or more persons.  The legal provisions stipulate employers' obligations to give advance notice (one month or equivalent wages), pay compensation (15 days average pay for each completed year of service) and follow the prescribed procedure (first-in-last-out principle to be followed, and a notice to be served to the appropriate government).  Employers should give preference to retrenched employees if they advertise for re-employment against future vacancies.

When labour becomes surplus, some organizations seek to provide them training in marketable skills and actively assist them in finding a job elsewhere.  *Outplacement* refers to such activities.  Erstwhile multinational firms like the ESSO Refinery have, in 1960s gone beyond training and verbal encouragement and provided them assistance like paid leave, reimbursement of travel charges for selection tests/interviews, waiving bond requirements if any and lien on jobs for a limited period so that the employees may return to their previous jobs if they do not like or cannot adjust themselves with the new employer.  Employers reason that though this too entails some investment, the benefits outstrip the costs.  There is no need to resort to hasty retrenchment.  So, the morale of the people will be high.  Those who leave may go in for better jobs in terms of pay, skill, prospectus, etc. and so the organizations retain their goodwill.  The intangible benefits of positive feelings and outcomes and their effects on the rest of the employees are incalculable.

## SUMMARY

In this chapter we have considered the aspects relating to recruitment, selection, placement, induction, internal mobility and separations.  Objectives determine the choice of sources, future employee profile and the process and methods of selection.  Several legal and political considerations also influence recruitment and selection.  The entire effort could be person or job- and organization-centred.  The effort should ideally be to achieve a balance between the two for the optimal fit between the job and the person.  Recruitment and selection are integrally related to other subsystems in organizational human resource management.  This is evident from the numerous cross references made in this chapter to the key role of job analysis and job specification (Chapter 2), HRP (Chapter 3), career and succession planning (Chapter 6) and employee relations (Chapter 12) among others.

The purpose of recruitment and selection could be to attract, employ and retain those who can succeed in their jobs.  But  as we note, the ingredients of success being many and some difficult to measure objectively and effectively.  Various methods and techniques were examined.  But finally however scientific the method and professional the approach is, the subjective human element still rules.  Therefore, one may constantly look at validating the reliability of the criteria and methods employed to recruit and select employees. Then, it is not enough to just recruit and select *good* people.  They need to be properly placed and inducted into the organization.

Over time, employees move within and out-side organizations.  The employee movement within the organization, *internal mobility*, takes the form of transfers, promotions and demotions.  We have considered the need to be clear about the purpose, process and the rationale for spelling out appropriate policies on these aspects which need to be deftly handled.  Employees move out of the organization for a variety of reasons.  We have briefly discussed the need for review and feedback about employee separations and employee turnover to keep it within limits. We also noted that several legal provisions and judicial pronouncements restrain and regulate employer from forcing indiscriminate separations.

## KEY WORDS

| | | |
|---|---|---|
| **Recruitment** | : | Seeking or obtaining recruits to replenish or to fill up deficiencies (or vacancies). It refers to the entire process and set of activities involved in bringing together prospective employees and employer with a view to obtain (and employing) those who meet the requirements of the job best. |
| **Selection** | : | Choosing or picking up the suitable candidates by rejecting or excluding the unsuitable. |
| **Placement** | : | Assigning rank and responsibility to an individual and so identifying him with a particular job. |
| **Induction** | : | Introduction of a person to the job and the organization. |
| **Transfer** | : | A lateral movement within the same grade, from one job to another. |
| **Promotion** | : | Advancement of an employee from one job level to a higher one, with increase in salary. |
| **Demotion** | : | Downward movement from one job-level to another preceding it, leading to a reduction in rank, status, pay and responsibility. |
| **Retirement** | : | Termination of service on reaching the age of superannuation. |
| **Resignation** | : | Termination of service by an employee by serving a notice on the employer. |
| **Retrenchment** | : | Termination of service of an employee by the employer for reasons other than punishment but not including retirement or termination for ill-health. |
| **Lay-off** | : | The failure, refusal or inability of the employer to provide employment due to factors beyond his control such as shortage of inputs and infrastructure, break-down of machinery, etc. |

## REVIEW QUESTIONS

1. Outline the legal and political considerations in recruitment.
2. Describe different types of tests, their uses and limitations.
3. What could be the basis to identify the criteria for selection? How can its validity and reliability be established?
4. Distinguish between:
    (a) Recruitment and selection
    (b) Placement and induction
    (c) Transfer and pomotion
    (d) Discharge and dismissal
5. Write notes on
    (a) What should be the elements of a promotion policy
    (b) The purpose of background verification.
6. Comment on the recruitment policy in public sector as shown in Exhibit 4.1.

# CASE I: PRESSURE POLITICS*

ABC is a public sector undertaking having all-India sales set-up. It deals with consumer products. It had advertised for appointment to the posts of sales representative/sales engineer for its marketing set-up. After preliminary scrutiny, a few candidates were called for personal interview. One such candidate, Mr X, was a civil engineer. In the interview, the Selection Committee found that Mr X was not suitable to the post advertised. However, the selection committee enquired whether Mr X was prepared to work in any other capacity. Mr X replied in the affirmative. Mr X was offered the job of a depot supervisor as recommended by the selection committee.

Mr X accepted the appointment letter as depot supervisor without any reservation. He was posted to Delhi Depot. When Mr X was asked to fill in the company forms concerning employment formalities, he sought further information from the company in this respect. Later Mr X brought pressure on the Management of the company through the Ministry for a transfer from Depot Supervisor to a position of an engineer. Mr X had formally submitted a representation to the Management listing his various grievances. Management took some time to decide where Mr X could be posted. Finally, it was decided to post him at Bombay to look after the construction of residential units of the company since he was a civil engineer. Mr X, simultaneously took up the matter with a Member of Parliament who in turn had written a letter to the minister concerned stating that Mr X was a victim of a partisan attitude. Having applied for the position of sales representative/sales engineer he was offered appointment as depot supervisor only, which carried much less power and prestige. Though the pay scales of the depot supervisor and sales representative/sales engineer are the same, positions in sales establishment are perceived to carry much glamour and prestige. The sales representative/engineer is required to travel far and wide, and build up contact with public. He is given car allowance and works in neat surroundings independently. The depot supervisor on the other hand, holds a stationary job and has to supervise the work of blue-collar workmen in depots. Further the career progression of sales representative/sales engineer in the company is faster than that of depot supervisor.

Owing to the pressures, the Management finally served a transfer order on Mr X to Bombay. Mr X made a representation that he should not be transferred to Bombay and that he should be posted as sales engineer at Delhi itself. Further he represented that on enquiry from officers of the company he came to know that sales representatives were also called sales supervisors and thinking that there was no difference between sales supervisor and depot supervisor, he had accepted the post of depot supervisor. In the meanwhile, complaints were received from Delhi Depot about the indiscipline of Mr X. It appeared that Mr X was not performing his duties, openly flouting orders of his superiors and spending time entirely towards preparing and submitting petitions. Mr X had started building up a case by writing letters to

---

* Case prepared by Dr P L Rao and edited by Dr C S Venkata Ratnam.

the management asking them to furnish him details of pay and perks for several positions in the organization. The company replied that it was not its policy to furnish such information. Within six months of his joining the services there was sufficient correspondence built up on this case and, therefore, the management has to write to the employee that no further correspondence would be entertained on his purported grievance which had already been sufficiently clarified. While his indiscipline continued unabated, Mr X was attending Delhi Depot even on Sundays and started claiming allowances and compensatory off without doing any work concerning his job. The indiscipline and misbehaviour of Mr X was brought to the notice of top management and the regional management had asked it to take suitable action. After reviewing the position, the Management had extended the probationary period of Mr X by six months.

Mr X continued to write letters to the management seeking for such information as organizational charts, duty charts of various officers, terms and conditions of service for sales engineers, sales representatives, depot supervisors, etc. The indiscipline of Mr X had increased and he started misbehaving with his subordinates, peers and superiors. He started questioning the authority and powers of his superiors, and even refused to receive official communications by hand. The company had replied to the minister's enquiries about Mr X, explaining the case of Mr X in detail. In view of his unsatisfactory performance, the probationary period of Mr X was extended for a further period of six months. Mr X was informed of his deficiencies and warned in writing that if there was no improvement in his job performance, his services would be terminated. Having found no improvement in his performance, his services were finally terminated after the expiry of the second extended period of probation. Mr X made a representation to the Ministry that he was badly treated by the management of a public sector undertaking and great injustice was done in terminating his services when he put forth his grievances for redressal. The Ministry sought comments on his representation. The Management of the company had sent a detailed report on Mr X. The Ministry was satisfied with the action taken by the Management on Mr X.

Again after a few months, Mr X brought pressure on the Minister concerned through a Member of Parliament requesting that Mr X may be given yet another chance. The minister verbally asked the management of the company to consider giving another chance to Mr X for a year. Thus, after a break of one year, Mr X was again issued fresh appointment letter as a civil engineer in the projects in the salary group 'A', i.e. the same as applicable to depot supervisor. While accepting the offer of appointment, Mr X again made a representation that he should be taken in Salary group 'B' which is one grade higher than 'A'. The request was rejected by the management. Mr X also took up with the management some claims which were due to him during his previous employment. He wrote to the Member of Parliament about his claims who in turn had taken up the matter with the company through the Ministry. This clearly indicates that Mr X had influence in the Ministry through a powerful group of Members of Parliament. After a lot of correspondence, the company finally conceded all his monetary dues pertaining to his previous employment. Every time Mr X wrote a letter to the Ministry, it was promptly forwarded by the Ministry to the company for detailed comments.

Even during his re-employment, the job performance of Mr X was not satisfactory. Therefore, the company, after reviewing his performance appraisals terminated his services on completion of one year of re-appointment. Mr X promptly took up the matter with the minister concerned through Members of Parliament. Simultaneously, he managed to raise various questions in the Parliament through the Members of Parliament on the recruitment of depot supervisors, sales representatives and sales engineers of the company. Every time a reply was given by the company to the Parliament, different questions were framed and more information was sought through Parliament by way of starred and unstarred questions (it may be noted that while a reply to unstarred question is placed on the table of Parliament, a starred question attracts supplementaries to the main question by way of further clarification to be answered by the minister). While this tussle in the Parliament continued for three years, enquiries from the Ministry on various aspects of recruitment and service conditions of the company continue to pour in which were promptly replied with full details.

## QUESTIONS

1. Was it proper on the part of the company to offer a job to Mr X other than the post for which interviews were held?
2. Was it proper for the company to transfer Mr X from depot supervisor at Delhi to civil engineer at Bombay in a civil project?
3. Does Mr X have a right to question the mode of selection and method of compensation paid to various posts at entry-level in the company?
4. Was it prudent on the part of the company to offer re-appointment to Mr X after his termination of service in the first instance, due to unsatisfactory services.
5. How far can the administrative ministry intervene in day-to-day matters while overseeing the activities of the companies under its administrative control?

# CASE II: DISSATISFIED GRADUATE ENGINEERS*

The Mild Steel Company, established in January 1965, employed 500 workers and a large number of technical and clerical staff. The company had its units at various places and and its sales offices were scattered throughout the country. Each unit was headed by a director. The corporate policies were formulated by the Board of directors.

For a long time, the company had no well defined recruitment policy. Several employees without any professional background were elevated to the post of managers. Some of them were not even graduates. Subsequently, when these persons demanded promotion, the management conceded their demands by promoting them to even

* Steel Authority of India Ltd, 1989. *Managerial Experiences in Focus: Second Volume of Cases*, New Delhi, pp 133–134 (Reproduced with permission from the publishers).

higher posts. But in recent years, with the changing economic conditions, growing competition, and consequent marketing difficulties, the management felt that qualified young engineering graduates would be best suited for the front line executive posts. In their opinion such young people would not only bring more vitality to the organization but they would also have necessary scientific bent of mind to conduct the operations of the various key positions in an efficient manner. If properly trained, the management concluded, the young engineers would be able to put the entire organization on a sound footing after a few years when they reach higher positions. The management further contemplated mechanization of certain operations with the help of these young graduates.

Before recruiting the young graduates, the management decided to put a qualification embargo on the old-timers so that the inadequately qualified managers would never have a chance to rise in the organizational hierarchy.

The company advertised in all leading newspapers inviting applications from First Class Engineering graduates for appointment as Junior Executives. The selected candidates were to get an all-inclusive salary of Rs 1,600 per month. The candidates were required to serve in any part of India and were to be put on probation for one year, after which they could be confirmed in their posts. Nearly 300 candidates responded to the advertisement. Fifty candidates were selected after a written examination and an interview. The selected candidates were imparted intensive theoretical and practical training for one-and-a half years and were placed in various shops.

The management started watching the functioning of the various shops that were run by the young and qualified executives. But they found no improvement. Meanwhile, discontent was growing in the *old timers*. They protested that their promotion opportunities were blocked by the management's new recruitment policy. On the other hand, the new executives complained that there was no job satisfaction. The management was very perturbed when 27 of the new executives submitted their resignations one after another. At the time of resignation some of them had already completed their probationary period. The management also learnt that the remaining graduate engineers were also in search of better prospects elsewhere.

The Chief Personnel Manager of the company conducted an *exit interview* of the graduate engineers and discovered the following grievances:

1. They were not deriving any satisfaction from their jobs. They were also not in a position to utilize their special knowledge and training to the fullest extent.
2. Their working conditions were not satisfactory.
3. The work environment was not congenial.
4. They did not want to put up with unfair practices and pressure tactics.
5. There was no challenge in the job and future prospects were completely bleak.
6. The management–workers relation was very unhealthy. The entire atmosphere was charged with doubt, suspicion, apathy, and misunderstanding.
7. The senior officers did not give any importance to them and their suggestions.

The management called for a conference of the senior executives to review the company's policies of selection, recruitment, training and induction.

Discuss the key issues and suggest possible corrective action.

# CASE III: KHAN DIDN'T MAKE IT*

Heavy Instruments Limited was a large undertaking employing a manpower of 50,000. The main production unit consisted of several large departments in operations and maintenance. The company had eleven layers in the non-executive level.

Vacancies were filled through one of the following methods:

1.  Direct recruitment from the open market.
2.  Promotion of eligible employees as per lines of promotion through the departmental promotion committee.
3.  Internal circulars confined to the employees working in particular department or alternatively through internal circulars open to all the employees of the unit as per the conditions of eligibility.

If there was a vacancy in a grade, a departmental promotion committee was constituted for promoting the eligible person from the next lower grade in the same line in promotion. The committee consisted of the departmental head and an officer from the Personnel Department. The minimum eligibility period for promotion from one grade to another was three years.

If there was an urgent need to fill up a vacancy and the persons in the next lower grade were not eligible for promotion due to non- fulfillment of the minimum eligibility period or otherwise, internal circulars were issued inviting applications from the persons belonging to the same department.

If even then eligible persons were not found, the coverage of the internal circular was extended to all the departments of the unit for filling up the vacancy.

For promotion, seniority-cum-merit was the criteria. In the case of internal circulars, however, merit was the only criteria for selection. In the case of a tie, the senior-most candidate was selected.

In one of the maintenance departments at one time there were four vacancies for the post of Crane Operators in Grade I. There were many operators in the next lower grade, i.e., Grade II, but none of them had completed the minimum eligibility period. The head of that department felt that these vacancies should be filled up urgently and recommended that an internal circular be issued.

Then the Personnel Department issued an internal circular in March 1983 inviting applications from candidates who had completed two years in the Grade II level within that department. As per the policy the selection was to be done through a two-stage screening process consisting of technical efficiency test and an interview. The technical efficiency test was conducted by a committee consisting of representatives from the concerned department, Training Department, and Personnel Department.

In the present case, the operators were required to operate the same equipment which they were operating in Grade II because even after their selection and absorption as Grade I operators they would be required to operate the same equipment.

Five applications were received. The senior-most among the five was Khan whose past performance was satisfactory. Satisfactory rating was given to such persons

* *ibid.*, pp 137–138.

whose performance was just tolerable; it did not debar them from promotion. The interview and the technical efficiency test was conducted in May 1983. Khan failed in the test, and the junior-most person among the five topped the list.

For various reasons, the list of the selected candidates was not officially notified for three months. In the middle of July the five operators stopped work and obstructed the work of others for 16 hours in protest against the delay.

Then the selection order of the four candidates was notified and Khan's name did not figure in that. Khan intervened saying that he was dropped because he belonged to a particular union and the other four were selected because all of them belonged to another union. Khan's union also backed him and insisted that the selection was biased. The industrial relations situation in the department gradually started deteriorating.

## QUESTIONS

1.  Discuss the key issues. Explain how the matter could have been handled?
2.  At this stage of the problem, what kind of options does the management have to deal with it? What steps should management initiate?

## FURTHER READING

1.  American Psychological Association (Division of Industrial Organizational Psychology), 1980. *Principles for the validation and use of Personnel Selection Procedures*, 2nd edn, Washington, DC.

2.  Bureau of Public Enterprises and Standing Conference of Public Enterprises, 1985. *Government Policy for the Management of Public Enterprises*, vols I & II, New Delhi.

3.  Famularo, J J, (Ed-in-Chief), 1986. *Handbook of Human Resources Administration*, 2nd edn, McGraw-Hill: New York.

4.  Government of India (1969). *Report of the National Commission on Labour*, New Delhi (Ch. 7: Recruitment, pp 67-79 and Ch. 8: Training, Induction and Workers' Education, pp 80-94).

5.  Lawson II, J W, 1984. *How to Develop a Personnel Policy Manual*, Dartnell: Chicago.

6.  Sur, M, *et al.*, 1970. *Personnel Management in India*, IIPM and Asia Publishing House, Bombay (Ch. 17: Recruitment, Selection, Induction and Promotion, pp 217-234).

7.  Scheer, W E, 1985. *The Dartnell Personnel Administration Handbook*, 3rd edn, Dartnell: Chicago.

8.  Taylor, B, and G Lippitt, 1983. *Management Development and Training Handbook* (Chs 11 and 12), McGraw-Hill: London.

# CHAPTER 5

# Performance Appraisal

## LEARNING OBJECTIVES

After going through this chapter, you should be able to:
Gain familiarity with the concept, tools and techniques and other issues in performance appraisal; • Understand the purpose and uses of performance and potential appraisal; • Develop awareness about effective feedback and counselling; and, • Determine the characteristics of an effective performance appraisal system.

Performance appraisal is an important component of the information and control system. People are selected and recruited for effective job performance in the organization. Therefore, it is necessary for organizations to develop performance analysis and review systems which:

- Define the specific job criteria against which performance will be measured;
- objectively and accurately measure past job performance;
- determine rewards based on performance;
- develop programmes (including feedback and job contexts) to enhance performance in the current job and prepare and realize the potential for future responsibilities.

## Objectives of Performance Appraisal

The objectives of performance appraisal could be either for evaluation (judgemental) or development (helping).

The evaluation objectives include:

- Provision of feedback to subordinates to know where they stand;
- developing valid data for personnel decisions concerning placement, pay, promotion, punishment, etc.

The developmental objectives include:

- diagnosing individual and organizational strengths and weaknesses;
- counselling, coaching, career planning and motivation of subordinates; and,

- developing positive superior–subordinate relations.

Sometimes, the objectives of evaluation and development could be in conflict. When performance is expected to meet the evaluation objectives, superiors may have to make difficult judgements. When the evaluation is communicated and the immediate consequences to subordinates are adverse, the superior–subordinate relations can become strained. At that stage the superior plays the role of a helper to meet the developmental objectives of appraisal. The different communication processes required to accomplish the conflicting objectives pose difficult problems for superiors. This dilemma raises issues concerning the appraisal process. It is suggested that uncoupling the twin objectives and dealing with them separately could be a better alternative.

Whatever be the objectives, any performance appraisal system should seek to address itself to the following five aspects that concern almost every employee in every organization:

- Tell me what you expect from me
- Give me opportunity to perform
- Let me know how well I am getting on
- Give me guidance where I need it
- Reward me according to my contribution

## Uses of Performance Appraisal

Performance appraisal system can be put to several uses covering the entire spectrum of personnel/human resource functions in an organization. The illustrative list of uses of performance appraisal to promote a variety of management objectives includes:

- Systematic efforts to tone up performance based on performance results, appropriate feedback and corrective actions
- input for an array of personnel decisions such as placement, transfer, promotion and reward
- to identify individuals with high potential
- to develop career and succession planning
- to analyze training and development needs
- to take decisions on termination
- human resource planning
- for diagnosing individual and organizational problems
- to validate selection and recruitment tests and procedures.

By making effective use of the performance appraisal system, an organization may seek to:

- Improve productivity
- Promote internal control through timely detection and feedback on actual performance
- create a positive work environment
- stimulate, recognize and reward achievements
- provide objective measures of performance
- furnish information for other human resource sub-systems.

While the potential uses of the performance appraisal system are many, very few organizations seem to make effective use of the system. When it is disused, it becomes a ritual; when it is infrequently used, employees voice concern about the possible abuse. Therefore, it becomes imperative that organizations are clear about the aims and outcomes of appraisal, take responsibility to evolve objective parameters to analyze and review performance, and initiate appropriate follow-up actions to ensure that the performance data is used to the best advantage of both the individual and the organization.

## PERFORMANCE APPRAISAL SYSTEM

Performance appraisal system in any organization depends substantially on five factors—concept, criteria, context, culture and contingency. Each of these aspects are briefly considered here.

*Concept*     The performance dimensions are several. They include duties, responsibilities, behaviour and traits. For each of the relevant dimensions and sub-dimensions thereof standard will have to be fixed based on past performance, industrial engineering principles or any other base. Relative weightages have to be assigned to each of these in turn. Performance appraisal involves at least two persons/parties: the appraiser (who does the appraisal) and the appraisee (whose performance is being appraised). The appraisee should know the following aspects of performance appraisal: what, why, how, when, and by whom? In the context of performance appraisal, the appraisee expects the following from the appraiser:

| *Appraisee expects* | *Appraiser should* |
| --- | --- |
| • to know what his duties and responsibilities are | • prepare job descriptions |
| • to know what is expected of him and whether the expectations are *reasonable* enough | • facilitate appraisee to set goals/targets |
| • to know how he is doing | • analyze results with appraisee |
| • to have appraiser's help, if need be | • advise, guide, coach and counsel |
| • rewards to be commensurate with performance | • reward for good results |

Proper appreciation of the mutuality and reciprocity in the roles is vital for clarity about the concept of performance. This has indeed been highlighted in the recent examples of *Memorandum of Understanding* which is a framework instrument to analyze the performance of chief executives of public sector organizations in India.

*Criteria*     Several performance measures such as output, quality, punctuality, cost control contribution, job knowledge, discretion, initiative, team work, resourcefulness, honesty, and leadership qualities are usually reckoned as some of the criteria against which performance is assessed. These words often carry multiple meanings. For example resourcefulness should be normally attributed to job context, but some may intentionally or otherwise consider resourcefulness in attending to the personal chores of the superior (e.g. obtaining a ration card!).

In most cases criteria setting involves a combination of personal data (e.g. good or bad work habits as perceived by the superior), output data (quantity than costs and quality) and judgemental data (e.g., about knowledge of the job, ability to get along with peers). However judicious one would like to be, there would often be a problem with *perceived* subjectivity (whether real or not) which needs to be dealt with carefully. Additional care needs to be taken in assigning and communicating weights to different factors, identifying standards for comparison and fixing responsibility. There is also the dilemma over relative weightage to processes (activities) and outcomes (results).

*Context*    The top management philosophy values and belief system in the organization influence the notions about people in the organization (Theory X or Theory Y type assumptions, for instance) and the type of control, motivation and communication systems. Those who do not hold positive attitude about the work culture, habits or competence of their subordinates may tend to perpetuate a system of management control based on direction and control while others who have positive notions about the subordinates may like to introduce management systems based on consensus and control. In the former case, targets are handed down and appraisal is *done* to the individuals. In the latter case, goals are fixed through discussion and mutual agreement and appraisal would in effect be carried out as a joint review with a problem-solving approach.

*Culture*    The culture of people in general seem to effect appraisal system. Studies and commentaries on Indian organizations seem to point to a pattern where the loyalties of employees is more to the people than to the tasks or to organizations; people are power-centred in the sense that those in authority would like to influence their subordinates and subordinates in their own interest are willing to accept a *dependency* syndrome. Where these observations hold good, there is every danger that performance appraisal turns out to be more *personal* than system or organization oriented.

*Contingency*    The most important aspect of any information and control mechanism in any organization is the use it is put to and how? Unless there is a systematic effort to link performance appraisal to other sub-systems of human resource management such that all personnel decisions use the performance appraisal data as a critical input, it becomes difficult to impart seriousness into the system. The result would be apathy on the point of both the appraiser and the appraisee to the entire process, which eventually would become a mere ritual. Therefore it is important for organizations to say and show that organizational rewards are contingent upon performance.

## Appraisal Techniques

Different techniques are used for performance appraisal. They include:

*Appraisal by Objectives*    Some organizations introduce goal-setting as part of the appraisal process. The objectives for the evaluation period (usually 12 months) are determined through joint discussion and negotiation between the superior and subordinate. This system is followed even in organizations which do not have a formal programme of 'Management by Objectives'. Invariably, in many organizations where the objectives are predetermined, Key Performance Areas (KPAs) or Key Result Areas (KRAs), are also decided in advance through joint effort. The evaluation is done in terms of the degree of achievement and non-achievement of objectives/KPAs/KRAs. In several cases the objectives are written down at the beginning of the period by the ratee who gives his own evaluation in the self-assessment section. The ratee is also allowed to state exceptional conditions/situations, if any, which may have contributed to significant deviations from the objectives set at the beginning.

Usually in most organizations, most of the appraisal is done in a descriptive form, with specific mention about output, costs, and time schedules where applicable. The descriptive analysis is supplemented in some cases with a rating on a 4, 5 or 9 point scale. Organizations generally limit applying this technique to managerial employees.

**Confidential Report**     This is a traditional form of performance appraisal, found in most government organizations. A confidential report is a report on the subordinate by the immediate superior and covers a limited range of aspects like the candidate's strengths, weaknesses, major achievements or failures and information on some personality traits and behavioural aspects. The confidential report system is usually a descriptive one and permits a lot of subjectivity. In recent years, due to the intervention of courts and pressure from trade unions, a negative confidential report is required to be communicated to the ratee and if the ratee disagrees, there should be a noting on the format to that affect.

The confidential report system is widely used for a variety of personnel decisions, particularly transfers and promotions.

**Trait Appraisal**     Individual traits are being currently used by most organizations as performance dimensions. Commonly used individual traits include several distinguishing characteristics firmly anchored in human behaviour that manifest themselves on the job and influence performance. These characteristics include the following listed below.

| | |
|---|---|
| Ability for sustained hard work | Drive |
| Acceptance of responsibility | Effort |
| Adaptability | Efficiency |
| Analytical ability | Honesty |
| Appearance | Industriousness |
| Attendance | Initiative |
| Attitude towards criticism | Integrity |
| Capacity to train | Intelligence |
| Commitment to task | Judgement |
| Communication | Leadership |
| Conduct | Loyalty |
| Confidence | Motivation |

| Cooperation | Perseverance |
| Cost consciousness | Personality |
| Courtesy | Planning |
| Creativity | Punctuality |
| Crisis management | Resourcefulness |
| Decision-making | Self-control |
| Delegation | Sense of responsibility |
| Dependability | Sincerity |
| Discipline | Tactfulness |

The problem with these traits and others is that they often relate more to people than to jobs. How well they relate to job performance is hard to say. Also, the rater can freely interpret them thus making them highly susceptible to subjectivity. In the USA and elsewhere federal legislation and court rulings questioned the credibility of traits in evaluating job performance. The causal relationship between traits and performance is yet to be firmly established. However, some effort is made to identify relevant employee traits that can be described in behavioural terms through a process of job content analysis and workplace behaviour. For example:

• *Honesty (trait)*: Employee can be trusted and does not lie, steal or deceive.
• *Honesty (job-related behaviour)*: Employee does not use company property for personal use. Where trait-based job-related behaviour can be identified and described without ambiguity, there is little problem in perception, understanding and interpretation. Therefore, organizations which would like to continue to follow trait appraisal would do well to develop job or workplace behaviour that is trait-based than merely seek to measure, say, integrity on a five-point scale.

*Rating Scales*     These are techniques where performance is measured through assigning numbers (0 to 4, 1 to 5 or 1 to 9), alphabets (A to D or E) or words which are descriptive adjectives (e.g., outstanding, very good, good, fair, poor) to items or events to describe differences. Most rating scales are *forced choice methods* since the differences have to be indicated in terms of one or the other of options given.

There are problems in observing and accounting for variations in performance through the rating period and also the effects of external influences on demonstrated performance which make it difficult to select the appropriate interval on a scale. In some cases, the descriptions used may not be precise or adequate to make proper selection. In all rating scales, most organizations are finding it useful to have an extra column to record N.A. (not applicable) or N.O. (Not observed) or any other comment as appropriate.

*Ranking Techniques*     Ranking techniques encourage superior or peers to rank-order all their subordinates or peers as the case may be. This is a form of comparative measurement. Three major ranking techniques are currently in vogue in many organizations:

*Simple or straight ranking* This technique provides for an ordinal scoring; first, second, third and so on. This technique requires the rater to rank from the best to the poorest all the subordinates in the same work unit doing the same job. Here the ranking is usually confined to one factor, i.e. overall performance or effectiveness. This technique is simple. However, it is difficult to assign relative ranking to those at the bottom and ratees may perceive this as a zero-sum game, one wins and the other loses. If raters are allowed to rank two or more ratees equally, the negative aspects of zero-sum game can be avoided.

*Forced distribution ranking* This is ranking technique where raters are required to allocate a certain percentage of ratees to certain categories (e.g., superior, above average, average, etc.) or percentiles (e.g. Top 10%, Bottom 20%, etc). Both the number of categories and percentage of employees to be allotted to each category are a function of the performance appraisal design and format. The technique serves a useful function if the purpose is to relatively rank members of the same work unit by assigning different categories or positions (e.g. top, middle and bottom) but it is difficult to obtain accurate relative standings of members of different work units by different raters.

*Paired-comparison* This technique requires the rater to appraise which of the two employees is superior, instead of having to rank-order all the employees in the same work unit doing the same job. This is widely used when one is comparing a small number of people. The rater compares an employee with every other individually as shown in the following diagram. Usually the overall ability to perform is reckoned.

| ROW\COLUMN | A | B | C | D | E | F |
|---|---|---|---|---|---|---|
| A | | | | | | |
| B | x | | | | | |
| C | x | x | | | | |
| D | x | x | x | | | |
| E | x | x | x | x | | |
| F | x | x | x | x | x | |
| G | x | x | x | x | x | x |

The number of comparisons to be made for a given number of comparison items (or persons) is indicated in the following formula:

$\dfrac{N (N-1)}{2}$ , when N = the number of persons to be compared

Comparing 7 persons, $\dfrac{7 (7-1)}{2}$ = 21 comparisons

Comparing 15 persons, $\dfrac{15 (15-1)}{2}$ = 105 comparisons

It is seen that when the number of persons is roughly doubled, the number of comparisons to be made rose by a factor of five. Therefore, it is better to divide the work group into smaller sub-groups and restrict paired comparisons to members within the sub-group.

The final ranking is determined by the number of times that an individual is judged better than the others.

*Narrative or Descriptive Methods*     The ongoing search for newer and better techniques of appraising employees performance led to several descriptive methods. These include the essay and the critical incident methods, among others. Both these methods require the rater to provide a written description of employees performance, but differ as discussed below.

*The Essay method*     In this method, the rater describes the ratee in terms of several broad categories such as the person's strengths and weaknesses, major achievements and failures, potential, training and development needs and overall performance. The success of the essay method depends on the writing skills and the analytical ability of the rater. It is time consuming. Processing the essays for decision-making purposes would be difficult.

This method is recommended for assessing very senior managerial staff and other categories where the numbers involved is small.

*The Critical incident method*     This method requires the rater to maintain a record of major observations of what he feels are work behaviours critical to the difference between success and failure. It provides information based on systematic observation of actual job performance.

This is time-consuming and cumbersome. Also quoting incidents after considerable time lapse may evoke emotions and problems. The main advantage of this method is that it is defensible from the raters point of view.

*Behaviourally Anchored Rating Scales (BARS)*     These are descriptions of various degrees of behaviour relating to an aspect of performance dimension. The performance dimensions are derived and described from an analysis of job content and work behaviour. The behaviours are described for a set of intervals ranging from the most negative to most positive. Considering the complex range of behaviours that occur and the difficulties in relating them to different levels of performance, BARS is considered a rather difficult, cumbersome and expensive method to develop.

## Raters

A rater is the one who appraises. The raters could be any one or more of the following:

*Appraisee*     The appraisee (ratee) can be his own appraiser (rater). This is possible in organizations where 'self-appraisal' is an important component of the performance appraisal system. The purpose is to help an employee to review and control his own performance and to initiate efforts for self-development. In such systems, where the superior's assessment is at variance with appraisee's own assessment, the substantive aspects merit discussion by the two concerned or a review by the superior's superior.

*Superior*     Normally in hierarchical organizations the immediate superior would rate the performance of his subordinates.

*Subordinate*    The subordinate could be asked to rate the performance of his superior. This is, however, seldom practiced.

The teacher–student relationship is *not* similar to the one between a superior and subordinate. Still, it is useful to mention that in some academic institutions the students or participants evaluate the performance of the concerned faculty.

The students learning is influenced by the teachers style and therefore feed-back from the former to the latter will help the latter to adapt teaching styles. In a similar vein, as subordinates performance is also a function of the nature and quality of supervision, it is appropriate for the subordinates to give their feedback to their superiors.

*Peers*    Peers or colleagues can rate each other's performance. This is considered useful particularly in work situations where team work matters most. This may be useful while considering promotions from within or when some one within the group is to be assigned a leadership position in the group. However, it is important to be wary about the effects of group dynamics and group solidarity in producing wrong choices.

*Clients/users*    Particularly in service oriented organizations, the clients and users are asked to rate the employees with whom they interact most and those who render them services. Some organizations (e.g. Modi Xerox and Chola Sheraton) have been linking at least one component of compensation to the ratings given to their employees by the clients/users.

*Managers/Specialists of other units*    Specially in jobs which require interfunctional departmental cooperation, the managers of different units are asked to rate the employees with whom they interact. The purpose is broadly similar to the one when rating is solicited from clients/users. The difference here is that the clients/users will be from within the organizations. This is important to reinforce the profit centre concept without sacrificing the service aspect.

*Consultants*    Outside consultants may be involved in rating employees. This is not generally recommended except in rare cases when the organization has difficulties in rating senior managers who are to be assigned very senior positions.

*Top Management*    Top management rates those who report directly to them. It may also intervene to rate senior executives from different functions/departments/units where it finds that such intervention is desired to ensure homogeneity in criteria and uniformity in appraisal.

## Rater Concerns

Generally raters (here, we are mainly concerned with superiors in their role as appraisers) are found to have the following concerns which may affect their rating. If superiors are rated also for their ability to appraise the performance of their subordinates, it may serve as a check.

**Desire to be Accepted**     "If I rate my subordinate's performance as poor how am I going to get his cooperation?  After all, both of us have to work together for long and, I cannot afford to strain the relation."

**Concern with Self-protection**     "If I rate him well he will rate me well and not create any problem for me".  But sooner than later results should speak and the organizational systems should not tolerate such compromises.

**He is like me**     Affiliation with those holding similar views make it difficult for raters to be objective.

**Fear of playing God**     "He will lose his job if I rate him again  as a poor performer."  "He will not be called even for an interview by the Departmental Promotion Committee if I rate him as 'C'".  Such concerns tend to make raters to be lenient.

**Lack of skills**     Raters may lack prior education, training, experience or skills.  So they may be less sure of their ability to rate.

## Typical Rater Errors

Rater concerns of the type described above result in various kinds of errors.  Some typical errors are discussed here.

**First impressions**     Raters may identify some specific qualities or features of the ratee and quickly form an overall impression about him.  The identified qualities and features may not provide adequate base for appraisal.

**Stereotyping**     Stereotyping is a standard mental picture that an individual holds about a person because of that person's sex, caste, age, physical characteristics or other features.  Stereotyping results in an oversimplified view of the individual and may blur the raters perception and assessment of the person's performance on the job.

**Halo Effect**     Basing the entire appraisal on the basis of one perceived positive quality, feature or trait in an individual.  Affiliation with views may result in a higher rating than is warranted.  He too sits late in the evening.  So he must be working hard!"

**Horn Effect**     Basing the evaluation on the basis of one negative quality or feature perceived.  This results in an overall lower rating than may be warranted.  "He does not shave regularly.  He must be lazy at work too!".

*Central Tendency*     Most appraisal forms require the rater to justify if assessment is outstanding or very poor.  So, a rater may say to himself: "Better rate most people as average so that I do not have to justify or clarify".

*Strict or Lenient Rating*     Depending upon the rater's own standards, value system, and or physical and mental make-up at the time of appraisal, ratees may be rated very strictly or very leniently.  Such rating usually does not carry any reference to actual performance of the person or bear any resemblance to how similar performance is rated elsewhere in the organization.

*Latest Behaviour*     Rating is influenced by the most recent behaviour ignoring the commonly demonstrated behaviours during the entire appraisal period.

*Spillover Effect*     Allowing past performance to influence how present performance is evaluated.  "The person who has done good work in the distant past is assured to be okay at present also."

## Improving the Accuracy of Ratings

The rater concerns and errors can be minimized by:
(i)     Developing well-defined performance factors and criteria.
(ii)    Focusing attention on behaviour over which the ratee has greatest control.
(iii)   Improving familiarity of the raters with the observed behaviour.
(iv)    Insisting that raters document behaviours to help improve recall.
(v)     Preparing a check-list to obtain and review job-performance related information.
(vi)    Conscious efforts to minimize personal biases.
(vii)   Imparting accountability for ratings and review.
(viii)  Arranging for rater feedback.
(ix)    Tieing up ratings with actual performance of units under raters control.
(x)     Arranging training to raters covering, among others, each of the above aspects.

## Review

Performance appraisal systems need to have a mechanism for review.  The following safeguards may be provided for the purpose:
(i)     Provide for review by raters seniors or by a committee.  Appraisal by a committee is favoured to provide interfunctional/divisional consistency.
(ii)    Raters should be asked to provide specific examples or tangible proof.
(iii)   Personnel department may scrutinize appraisal data using statistical or other methods to compare results of operations with appraisal rating and also to see whether raters are unusually strict or lenient.
(iv)    Communicate appraisal.  Discuss differences and record dissent.
(v)     Provide for an appeal system.

# ASSESSING POTENTIAL

Assessing potential is different from appraising performance. Potential refers to the abilities present but not currently utilized or the ability to discharge higher responsibilities in future roles. Performance refers to one's behaviour, skills, abilities in meeting the requirements on the job which one currently holds.

Potentials can be assessed by:
- Reviewing present performance
- Analyzing personality traits, management skills, etc.
- Relooking at past experience
- Considering age and qualifications
- Exploring one's unused knowledge/skills

## Appraisal Interview and Feed-back

*Focused Objective*     The appraisal interview is a part of the effort for a face-to-face review of the subordinates performance. Performance appraisal has multiple objectives. But appraisal interview should have a focused objective.

*Participative Problem Solving Approach*     The interview should focus on the mutual benefit of the employee and the organization. It may seek to:

(a)  improve job performance through identifying problems in a participative, problem-solving perspective;

(b)  foster the competence and growth and development of the persons in their jobs by measuring up the expectations and enhancing one's potential; and,

(c)  exchange valuable information for career planning.

*Importance of job performance*     Appraisal interviews serve the purpose if the employees realize that their survival (in present jobs) and growth (promotions) are contingent upon their performance on the job and they sense and feel reasonable opportunities exist for desired job improvements through their own efforts, as also complementary efforts from the supervisor and the organization in terms of appropriate coaching, placement and training.

*Appropriateness of timing and location*     Ideally, performance appraisal interviews should consist of continuous informal reviews, guidance, coaching and counselling as the need arises and occasional, formal interviews. The formal interviews could be monthly, quarterly, bi-annual or annual. It is preferable to schedule formal interviews more than once   particularly in cases where raters change, ratees are transferred to new assignments, major changes occur in ratee's job assignments or work environment to reduce the adverse effects of accumulating unexpected information.

The location should be a relaxed setting, providing for privacy and creating an environment of warmth, friendship and equality rather than reinforce feelings of hierarchical authority and power.

*Agreement on context and process*    Both the rater and the ratee should agree on the content and process. Presenting unanticipated or unexpected information would affect the interaction. Where there is proper and systematic documentation of job performance/behaviours and continuous informal reviews, it becomes easy to agree on the content. Usually, an appraisal interview may cover the following aspects: (a) job assignments/targets; (b) demonstrable efforts and outcomes and standards and measures used for the purpose; (c) utilization of resources/opportunities; (d) review of major contributions/shortcomings affecting job performance; (e) identification and analysis of problems; (f) rating of performance; and, (g) developing a future plan of action for improving job performance.

*Split roles*    The rater typically is required to play the role of a judge (evaluation) and mentor and helper (coaching and counselling) for improvement in job performance and career growth and development. Where the performance rating is poor, enacting the split roles becomes particularly ticklish. The ratee may now be emotionally tuned-off to hear anything that is not directly related to the rating. There is a danger, then, that the credibility of one of the two divergent roles suffers. Therefore it is suggested that the interview process be divided into two distinct sessions: one for reviewing or assessing performance and the other for counselling and improving performance.

*The approach*    The approaches in performance interview may be directive or non-directive. When the approach is directive, the interview will proceed in a *matter of fact* fashion where specific questions are raised and definite responses are sought. The rater may use a checklist of standard questions. Though this approach is easy it may not be effective because it makes it hard to identify and analyse job related problems and develop workable solutions. The ratee usually becomes defensive or offensive in responding to *blunt* questions. The directive approach may also be referred to as tell and sell method because the rater takes the initiative throughout the interview in reviewing ratee's performance, identifying problems and suggesting solutions or corrective actions the ratee should take. The non-directive approach makes use of broad, open-ended questions and seeks to draw the ratee to discuss his perceptions or problems affecting his performance. It requires the rater to be very good at asking questions and listening, besides other skills, such as patience, empathy and appropriate verbal and non-verbal communication skills. The non-directive method may be referred to as *tell and listen* method. Here the rater emphasizes more on listening to ratee's reasons for his performance.

It would be appropriate to combine both the approaches. The rater may identify key areas and develop a list of general questions to review the ratee's performance. But the interview essentially adopts a problem-solving method whereby the ratee identifies performance problems, and lists actions needed to improve his performance.

*Orientation*    The inter and intra-personal orientation of the rater and ratee may act as gateways or barriers to effective interviewing. A trusting behaviour with positive beliefs, values and expectations about the ratee's abilities and behaviour may lead to empathy and understanding and enable the rater to treat the ratee in good esteem and confidence. A non-trusting behaviour may reinforce negative feelings and produce suboptimal performance. Personal differences (relating to social background, work habits, etc.), game playing behaviour (tendency to skirt the issue, being tricky, etc.), physical and emotional disturbances, assessing present performance based on past experience, etc., may serve as barriers to effective interviewing.

**Exchanging feedback**    The purpose of any performance interview is to obtain and give feedback about performance and exchange facts and mutual perceptions about the reasons leading to them. The feedback will be effective and credible when it is specific, rather than general, descriptive rather than evaluative, consistent, open, timely, accurate, balanced and fair. It should help the recipient in checking accuracy with others through relevant examples to enable him to do what is logically expected upon receiving it. Feedback should be given with verifiable data, soliciting additional information to get clearer perspective. Then it promotes interpersonal trust, openness and understanding. Similarly, receptivity to feedback increases self-awareness and understanding in processing the data and reinforces a feeling of mutuality.

**Conduct of interview**    There are four critical phases in an interview—*rapport building* at the opening phase, *exploration* and *action planning* during the course of the interview and *summarizing* at the conclusion phase.

At the rapport building phase the rater should establish a climate of acceptance, warmth, openness and understanding. He should care to listen to the ratee's problems and feelings with empathy and genuine concern.

At the exploratory and action planning phases, the rater should adopt participative problem solving approach and help the ratee to know for himself with the help of documented records and data to the extent possible, diagnose the reasons, and come up with an action plan to improve the performance. The rater may help the ratee by raising appropriate questions to understand the problems.

Finally, in the concluding phase, it is appropriate to summarize what happened, what has been agreed to, what needs to be done and how to ensure that what is to be done is done. The rater should not adopt any threatening postures. He should distinguish between internal (self/family) and external (work related) pressures as also between causes and effects of ratee's behaviour. The focus should be on how the rater and ratee may, together, endeavour to improve performance.

## DESIGN OF AN EFFECTIVE APPRAISAL SYSTEM

It is useful to focus on aspects such as the following so that the appraisal system can be effective:

    (i)    Appraisal objectives and uses should be specific, clear, relevant, timely, adequate, open and fair. It should be adequately and appropriately linked with the other subsystems of human resource management and capable of being put to use in a manner beneficial to the individual employee and the organization.

(ii)   It should be an ongoing process of managing performance with the employee actively participating and supervisor playing the role of coach and developer.

(iii)  The information generated should be tailored to the needs of the organization, performance requirements and norms of behaviour.

(iv)  Recognize individual differences in system design.  Identify the needs of ratees in terms of feedback, mobility, self-esteem, confidence, openness, etc.

(v)   The overall purpose should be developmental than judgemental.  Evaluation and development should be uncoupled to take care of the problem of split roles as discussed earlier.  Also, it is important to separate evaluation of performance and potential.

Finally, an appraisal system can be considered effective if it can answer all the five questions that were raised while discussing appraisal objectives earlier.

# Company Experience: Performance Appraisal System in an International Donor Organization

The agency has a formal mechanism of appraising performance of its employees.  It has a special administrative order which lays down the mechanism of appraising performance of its employees from time to time. This order has been revised as and when warranted.

Formal appraisal system concerns all the employees and almost all decisions relating to personnel are made on the basis of appraisal reports.  The performance evaluation in the organization is briefly described as under:

## Responsibilities

**Personnel Office**    (a) Develops, interprets and administers policies and procedures for evaluating performance of all categories of employees.

(b) Plans, prepares and conducts training courses and periodically holds group training sessions to assure that all participants are thoroughly familiar with Personnel Evaluation Report (PER).

**Employees**    The employee should request clarification from the supervisor of any work requirements which are not clearly understood.  The employee advises the supervisor of any facts or circumstances which should be taken into consideration in evaluating performance and should accept, in a constructive spirit and manner, evaluations of and suggestions for the improvement of work performance.  The employee is urged to comment on performance, adequacy of supervision or other aspects that are important to the employee.

**Rating Officer**    The person who is responsible for the work of and gives the assignments to the employee and:

(a) Makes clear to the employee the duties of the position and the requirements for satisfactory performance at the beginning of the rating period;

(b) Discusses strengths, weaknesses and ways to improve performance at the end of the rating period and at other times, as necessary;

(c) Gives recognition to superior performance;

(d) Counsels or takes appropriate action if employee performance is below standard.

**Reviewing Officer**    The supervisor of the Rating Officer is the Reviewing Officer. He prepares the required statement of Personnel Evaluation Report for professional staff specifying:

(a) The thoroughness, objectivity, soundness and compliance with evaluation instructions of the PER;

(b) whether the employee has received  adequate supervision and guidance;

(c) whether the rating appears unduly harsh or lenient; and

(d) whether the Reviewing Officer concurs with the contents of the report.

## Types of Reports

**Annual Evaluation**    At least 30 days prior to the due date for grade increase, the Personnel Officer forwards the prescribed Form, (Exh. 5.1) and Performance Evaluation Report to each Rating Officer. The supervisor should complete the evaluation report and forward them to the Reviewing Officer, if applicable, for review and signature.  The employee's rating is then discussed with him by the rating officer, and a copy of PER given to the employee.  The completed PER in original must reach the Personnel Office at least 10 days prior to the due date for grade increase for appropriate action.

**Special Evaluation**    Special PER's are required under the following circumstances unless a current rating was prepared within the preceding three months.

(a) Departure, change or transfer of Rating Officer;

(b) Transfer or reassignment of  employee to another position;

(c) Sixty days after an unsatisfactory rating;

(d) Completion of 90 days from date of joining on duty.

## Transmittal and Record

PER's are either hand carried by authorized personnel or transmitted in a sealed envelope.

The Personnel Officer files the original of the completed PER in the employee's personal file.

## Evaluation of Performance

**Performance Rating**    All factors must be rated unless in the judgement of the Rating Officer certain factors are not applicable.  Where a factor cannot be rated the Rating Officer should write N/A or Not Observed, as applicable.

**EXHIBIT 5.1**

| PERFORMANCE EVALUATION REPORT | REGULAR REPORT [] PROBATIONARY REPORT [] INTERIM REPORT (State Reason) [] | |
|---|---|---|
| NAME OF EMPLOYEE RATED | GRADE | TITLE |
| | POSITION NUMBER: | |
| POST AND ORGANIZATION | PERIOD COVERED BY REPORT From: To: | DATE PREPARED |
| TIME IN PRESENT JOB | TIME UNDER PRESENT SUPERVISOR | |

**I. DUTIES PERFORMED**

List the principal tasks performed during the rating period; these should be discussed with the Rated Employee at the beginning of the rating period. Indicate if rated employee has supervisory responsibilities.

**II. EVALUATION OF PERFORMANCE**

| A. PERFORMANCE FACTORS (Mark NA, Not Applicable or (NO, Not Observed if appropriate below) | FAILS TO MEET NORMAL REQUIREMENTS | MEETS NORMAL REQUIREMENTS | EXCEEDS NORMAL REQUIRE- MENTS | GREATLY EXCEEDS NORMAL REQUIRE- MENTS |
|---|---|---|---|---|
| Productivity | ( ) | ( ) | ( ) | ( ) |
| Thoroughness and accuracy | ( ) | ( ) | ( ) | ( ) |
| Dependability | ( ) | ( ) | ( ) | ( ) |
| Ability to work with colleagues and supervisors | ( ) | ( ) | ( ) | ( ) |
| English language skills | ( ) | ( ) | ( ) | ( ) |
| Job knowledge and skills | ( ) | ( ) | ( ) | ( ) |
| Initiative and resourcefulness | ( ) | ( ) | ( ) | ( ) |
| Judgement | ( ) | ( ) | ( ) | ( ) |
| Effectiveness in organizing own work | ( ) | ( ) | ( ) | ( ) |
| Creativity and originality | ( ) | ( ) | ( ) | ( ) |
| Oral communication | ( ) | ( ) | ( ) | ( ) |
| Written communication | ( ) | ( ) | ( ) | ( ) |
| Decisiveness | ( ) | ( ) | ( ) | ( ) |
| Ability to instruct and train supervised employees | ( ) | ( ) | ( ) | ( ) |
| Managerial effectiveness | ( ) | ( ) | ( ) | ( ) |
| Analytical ability | ( ) | ( ) | ( ) | ( ) |
| Effectiveness in outside contacts | ( ) | ( ) | ( ) | ( ) |

*Overall Rating*    The Rating Officer places an 'X' in the block which most accurately reflects the rated employee's general level of performance. The overall rating should be consistent with the rating assigned to individual factors.

*Superior or Outstanding Rating*    An overall *superior* or *outstanding* rating requires a detailed justification on the reverse side of the form. This justification is important because it reflects the degree of achievement by the employee and also his capacity to assume greater responsibility.

*Unsatisfactory Rating*    (i) When "fails to meet the normal requirements" is assigned to one or more individual factors, but the overall rating is marked *satisfactory* or superior, the Rating Officer must provide justification for the overall rating on the reverse of the PER.

(ii) An employee is rated unsatisfactory only after the Rating Officer has given the employee a written warning 90 days prior to the report and an opportunity to demonstrate improvement in performance. The written warning should state:

(a) Which job requirements the employee is failing to perform satisfactorily; and

(b) What efforts will be made to help the employee improve unsatisfactory performance;

(iii) An unsatisfactory rating must be justified on the reverse of the PER by stating:

(a) The cause for written warning; and

(b) The efforts made to help the employee improve during the 90 days period.

(iv) Upon receipt of an unsatisfactory evaluation, the Personnel Office issues a letter of warning to the employee advising that unless work performance improves sufficiently to meet an overall "satisfactory" rating within the next 60 days, notice of proposed separation will be initiated. At the end of the 60 day period, an interim PER is prepared by the supervisor and forwarded to the Personnel Officer. If the performance has improved and the employee has been given an overall "satisfactory" rating, no further action is taken. If the employee performance has not improved, the employee is separated. Employees whose overall efficiency ratings are "unsatisfactory" are not eligible for periodic step increases in the grade.

## Appeal

There is a provision of appeal. The overall rating in the PER may be appealed after discussion with the Rating and Reviewing Officers. If employee is not satisfied with the report of the Rating Officer and Reviewing Officers, he can submit a written appeal to the Personnel Office within 7 days upon receipt of PER. This appeal must indicate why the employee disagrees with the rating received. The Personnel Officer reviews the facts and then convenes an Appeal Panel consisting of four employees of the organization appointed by its Chief Executive Officer.

The Appeal Panel, on review requests that the rated employee and the Rating and Reviewing Officers appear before the panel. After hearing both positions, the panel independently discusses the merits of the case and votes to either  grant or reject the appeal. The panel transmits the decision in writing to the rated employee through the Rating and Reviewing Officer with a copy to the personnel office. The Personnel Officer will effect any change on the PER. Concurring documents are filed in the employee's personal folder.

**EXHIBIT 5.2**

---

**ABC Company**
**ANNUAL PERFORMANCE APPRAISAL**

OF

SHRI/SMT./KUM. _____

DESIGNATION _____

EMPLOYEE NO. _____

GRADE _____

DEPARTMENT _____

LOCATION _____

YEAR  199

---

**Personal Data**

| NAME | EMP. NO | DESIGNATION | | DEPARTMENT |
|------|---------|-------------|---|-----------|

SHRI/SMT./KUM.

| DATE OF BIRTH | SALARY GRADE | INITIAL EMPLOYMENT DATE | DATE OF APPOINT-MENT TO THE PRESENT POST |
|---------------|--------------|-------------------------|------------------------------------------|

QUALIFICATIONS

**ASSIGNMENTS HELD IN THE PRESENT GRADE**

| DESIGNATION | DURATION | LOCATION/DEPTT./SECTION |
|-------------|----------|-------------------------|
| | | |
| | | |
| | | |
| | | |

GUIDELINES FOR ASSESSORS

This form is designed to help executives appraise each employee, his work performance and potential abilities. It helps the corporation in placement, transfer, promotion and training of its officers.

To serve these important purposes the report must be prepared in a careful and thorough manner. Here are some suggestions:

1. The manner in which this report is completed by you is a direct reflection of the value and importance you attach to evaluate your subordinates and appraise their performance. This aspect of your performance as a supervisor/manager will be taken cognizance of when your supervisor evaluates your performance.

2. Base your assessment on the direct knowledge and performance of the work that the employee has done during the period under review.

3. Consider only one item at a time and rate only in relation to the requirements of the employee's job level.

4. Extreme ratings on either side of the scale should be supported by justification under the "Related Remarks" column, at the end of Part I.

5. Make sure that a strong or a weak quality under one attribute does not cloud your judgment of his standing on the rest.

6. Have the rating reflect typical 'Normal' performance; avoid being influenced by recent instances of success or failure which are not typical.

7. Do not rate any item which is not applicable or which you have had no opportunity to judge.

## Annual Performance Appraisal Part I

| | [] | [] | [] | [] | [] |
|---|---|---|---|---|---|
| **1. VOLUME OF WORK** <br> Amount of acceptable work produced; consistency and regularity of output. | Output of work exceptionally high and much more than required of the job | Generally high output of acceptable work | Produces volume of work required in the job | Output inadequate | Output far below the job requirement |
| **2. QUALITY OF WORK** <br> Thoroughness, accuracy and general excellence of output; extent of work free from errors; consistency of work under varying conditions. | Consistently thorough and accurate in his work under all conditions | Generally does a thorough and accurate job; work needs minimum correction | Produces work of acceptable quality | Work barely upto mark; needs to be checked | Work consistently below required standard. Makes no effort to improve |
| **3. COST CONSCIOUSNESS** <br> Efforts towards optimum utilisation of available resources and elimination of waste | Always makes optimum utilisation of resources. | Generally makes optimum utilisation | Utilises resources well and reduces | Aware of effecting economy but | Wasteful in his work and totally un- |

|  | | | | |
|---|---|---|---|---|
| | Constantly tried to reduce costs and eliminate waste | of waste resources; is conscious of elimination of waste | makes no special efforts; | aware and uninterested in cost reduction |
| **4. JOB KNOWLEDGE** (Functional) <br> [] | [] | [] | [] | [] |
| | Excellent knowledge of his job | Very good knowledge of his job | Adequate knowledge of his job and keen to learn | Knowledge of job not upto what is required but tries to learn | Knowledge of job much below what is required. Makes no effort to learn |
| **5. JOB KNOWLEDGE** (Inter-functional/departmental; company/industry role) <br> [] | [] | [] | [] | [] |
| | Excellent knowledge | Very good knowledge | Adequate knowledge | Knowledge not upto the required mark | Knowledge much below what is required |
| **6. TIME SCHEDULE** <br> [] | [] | [] | [] | [] |
| | Excellent ability to complete assignments ahead of schedule | Normally completes a plan of action on schedule | Completes assignments in reasonable time | Completes assignments after frequent delays | Lacks ability and desire to complete assignments within time schedule |
| **7. PLANNING AND ORGANIZING** <br> Ability for anticipating work needs for arranging work in logical order & devising efficient methods to attain predetermined plans <br> [] | [] | [] | [] | [] |
| | Exceptional ability to anticipate future work needs ahead of time and works in a logical order to meet plan | Normally anticipates work needs and is able to prepare a plan of action; generally good in arranging work load at meet plan | Is systematic and methodical | Ability to plan and organise is marginal | Very unsystematic and unmethodical in his work. Does no planning at all |

| 8. CONTROL | [] | [] | [] | [] | [] |
|---|---|---|---|---|---|
| Ability to monitor planned activities to ensure performance in line with plans; extent of corrective action when required | Effectively develops and maintains monitoring systems and takes prompt deviations are perceived | Successfully maintains monitoring systems, takes corrective action when deviations occur | Generally able to satisfact-orily relate progress vis-a-vis planned activities | Monito-ring of planned activities marginal | Has no monitoring mechanism of any type to assess progress of planned activities. Shows no interest |
| 9. LEADERSHIP | [] | [] | [] | [] | [] |
| Ability to make positive impact on the team and inspire and influence them | Commands respect by virtue of own capabilities. Always successful in developing enthusiasm and team spirit | Develops high degree of enthusiasm and team spirit | Generally maintains enthusiasm and team spirit | Only marginally able to inspire and influence the team. Relies more on authority of the position | Does not inspire the team and is unable to create en-thusiasm. Heavily relies on the authority of the posi-tion |
| 10. COMMUNICATION | [] | [] | [] | [] | [] |
| Skilled and desires to share available information with all concerned. (Upward and downward) | Excellent clarity of thought and expression; uses all channels of communica-tion. Keeps all concerned well informed | Shares information with all concerned. Very good in expression | Reasonably clear in expression. Keeps people informed | Has desire to share informa-tion but does not put in practice | Does not share per-tinent and relevant in-formation with con-cerned people. Keeps things to himself |
| 11. INITIATIVE | [] | [] | [] | [] | [] |
| Ability to be self-reliant and move forward on a task without outside direction | Always self-reliant; exceptionally good at applying mind to getting the job done. Is a self-starter. | Never waits to be told for getting things done and overcomes obstacles indepen-dently. | Reasonably good at thinking out things indepen-dently. Requires instructions occasionally. | Requires much help and instruc-tions while doing things | Always re-quires to be told. Does not apply mind to get things done. |

| | [] | [] | [] | [] | [] |
|---|---|---|---|---|---|
| **12. DEPENDABILITY**<br>Reliability to perform and complete assigned task within scheduled time; extent of follow-up required | Always completes work well ahead of time. Needs no follow-up. | Generally completes work ahead of time; needs occasional follow-up. | Usually completes his work in time. Requires only normal follow-up. | Frequently not able to complete work in time. Requires follow-up. | Never completes work in time; requires constant follow-up. |

| | [] | [] | [] | [] | [] |
|---|---|---|---|---|---|
| **13. PROBLEM ANALYSIS & DECISION MAKING**<br>Ability to identify problems, analyse alternative courses of action and decide on the best action. | Excellent analytical ability; always takes sound decisions even on complex problems. | Good analytical ability; always makes sound decisions pertaining to his job area. | Makes sound decisions pertaining to his job area. | Decisions frequently not sound due to faulty analysis. | Lacks analytical ability; takes no decisions. |

| | [] | [] | [] | [] | [] |
|---|---|---|---|---|---|
| **14. TRAINING AND DEVELOPMENT OF SUBORDINATES**<br>Efforts towards on the job-trg; & support in providing opportunities to subordinates for devt & growth. (Mark NA if having no subordinates) | Continuously guides, trains and encourages subordinates; always tries to promote the growth and development of subordinates | Generally guides and trains subordinates; is conscious of promoting their growth and development. | Generally interested in training and development of the subordinates. | Desires to train subordinates but does not make sufficient effort. | Is neither interested in imparting on the job training nor in developing subordinates. |

| | [] | [] | [] | [] | [] |
|---|---|---|---|---|---|
| **15. RELATIONS WITH COLLEAGUES/ SUBORDINATES**<br>Degree of coordination and co-operation with colleagues. | Very co-operative, respected and liked by colleagues. | Co-operative; good relations with colleagues. | Relations with colleagues cordial. | Occasionally creates friction in dealing with colleagues. | Non-cooperative and cannot function in group. |

| 16. WILLINGNESS TO ACCEPT RESPONSIBILITY | [] | [] | [] | [] | [] |
|---|---|---|---|---|---|
| This relates to the employee's willingness to accept and seek additional responsibility. | Eager to increase usefulness; actively seeks responsibility. | Most of the times seeks responsibility. | Accepts but does not seek responsibility. | Rarely accepts responsibility. | Tries to evade responsibility. |
| 17. ADAPTABILITY TO CHANGE/RECEPTIVITY TO NEW IDEAS | [] | [] | [] | [] | [] |
| This relates to the employee's capacity to adjust to change & also his receptivity to new ideas/suggestions & his cooperation in implementing them. | Very high | High | Reasonable | Low | Very low |

| 18. COURAGE OF CONVICTION | [] | | [] | | [] | | [] | | [] |
|---|---|---|---|---|---|---|---|---|---|
| This related to courage of conviction to express one's beliefs and value. (This does not mean stubbornness or refusal to actively support a decision after considering all facts and points of view but which may not be in line with the officer's views.) | | | | | | | [] High | | [] Low |

| 19. INTEGRITY | | | | [] Above board | [] Doubtful (if so give comments below) |
|---|---|---|---|---|---|
| SUMMARY APPRAISAL | [] | [] | [] | [] | [] |
| | Outstanding | Very Good | Satisfactory | Fair | Unsatisfactory |
| | Exceptional overall performance. Distinctly stands out compared to others. | Overall performance of high standard. Better than the majority. Performance beyond normal requirements. | Satisfactory overall performance. Meets the job requirements. | Performance barely adequate. Requires improvement in certain areas as per report. | Performance. In adequate and well below acceptable standards. |
| RELATED REMARKS | | | | | |

| SIGNATURE OF THE COUNTERSIGNING OFFICER | SIGNATURE OF THE REVIEWING OFFICER | SIGNATURE OF THE REPORTING OFFICER |
|---|---|---|
| NAME | NAME | NAME |
| DESIGNATION | DESIGNATION | DESIGNATION |
| DATE | DATE | DATE |

**EXHIBIT 5.5**

<table>
<tr><td colspan="2"> Annual Performance Appraisal Part II<br>ASSESSMENT OF POTENTIAL </td></tr>
<tr><td>1. IS THE OFFICER FIT FOR SHOULDERING HIGHER RESPONSIBILITIES?</td><td>[] READY NOW [] READY IN     [] CANNOT JUDGE NOW<br>                DUE COURSE</td></tr>
<tr><td>2. MOBILITY<br>This related to acceptance of responsibility at different locations/deptts;</td><td>(i) INTRA UNIT [] HIGH      [] LOW<br><br><br>(ii) INTER UNIT [] HIGH      [] LOW</td></tr>
<tr><td colspan="2">3. AREAS WHERE HE/SHE HAS DONE WELL<br>(i) FUNCTIONAL ........................<br>(ii) MANAGERIAL ........................</td></tr>
<tr><td colspan="2">4. AREAS WHERE HE/SHE NEEDS HELP<br>(i) FUNCTIONAL ........................<br>(ii) MANAGERIAL ........................<br>REMARKS OF THE REPORTING OFFICER:<br><br><br>                                                  Signature<br>                                                  (Reporting Officer)</td></tr>
<tr><td colspan="2">REMARKS OF THE REVIEWING OFFICER:<br><br><br>                                                  Signature<br>                                                  (Reviewing Officer)</td></tr>
<tr><td colspan="2">REMARKS OF THE COUNTERSIGNING OFFICER:<br><br><br>                                                  Signature<br>                                                  (Countersigning Officer)</td></tr>
</table>

## Annual Performance Appraisal Part III

### JOB ROTATION AND DEVELOPMENT PLAN

**1. DOES THE OFFICER FEEL HE IS IN THE RIGHT JOB, CONSIDERING HIS QUALIFICATIONS, EXPERIENCE AND APTITUDE?**

| VIEWS OF THE OFFICER: | VIEWS OF THE REPORTING OFFICER: |
|---|---|
| | |

**2. IF THE OFFICER FEELS HE NEEDS A CHANGE, WHAT TYPE OF ASSIGNMENT DOES HE PREFER?**

| VIEWS OF THE OFFICER: | VIEWS OF THE REPORTING OFFICER: |
|---|---|
| | |

**3. DO YOU THINK THIS OFFICER SHOULD BE GIVEN ROTATIONAL ASSIGNMENT IN HIS/HER OWN DEPARTMENT OR ANY OTHER DEPARTMENT AND IF SO HOW SOON SHOULD THIS ROTATION TAKE PLACE?**

VIEWS OF THE REPORTING OFFICER

Signature of the Reporting Officer

COMMENTS OF THE REVIEWING OFFICER

Signature of the Reviewing Officer

**4. DATE OF DISCUSSION WITH OFFICER:**
(to be mentioned by Reporting Officer)

## Training Needs Part IV

| NAME SHRI/SMT./KUM. | EMPLOYEE NO. | DESIGNATION |
|---|---|---|
| SALARY GRADE          PRESENT LOCATION | | DEPARTMENT |

**1. TRAINING PROGRAMME ATTENDED BY THE OFFICER IN THE LAST FIVE YEARS.**
(To be completed by Training Dept)

| S. No. | NAME OF THE PROGRAMME | YEAR | DURATION | LOCATION |
|---|---|---|---|---|
| 1 | | | | |
| 2 | | | | |
| 3 | | | | |
| 4 | | | | |
| 5 | | | | |

6

7

2. Considering the officer's areas of strengths and the areas where improvement is needed, what specific training would you recommend?

(These recommendations should be proposed in consultation with the Officer and keeping in view his own perception of the training needed by him. This may not be restricted to only courses or programmes being conducted by the Training Centre).

There are two types of training needs: namely 'Staple/Functional' training which is required by him to do his job well and 'Developmental training' which would be useful for his further development (so that he can shoulder higher responsibilities in due course of time). The nominations for external training programmes can be proposed where in-company training programmes are not available, and keeping the organisational needs in view.

| S No | STAPLE/FUNCTIONAL COURSE | S No | DEVELOPMENTAL COURSE |
|------|--------------------------|------|----------------------|
| 1 |  | 1 |  |
| 2 |  | 2 |  |
| 3 |  | 3 |  |

DATE OF DISCUSSION OF TRAINING NEEDS:

NAME:

DESIGNATION:

------------------------

SIGNATURE OF REPORTING OFFICER

NOTE: To be filled in duplicate — one copy will be retained along with the CR in the Personnel Deptt and the other copy will be sent to the Trg Dept for further action.

**EXHIBIT 5.3**

### X Y Z International

#### PERFORMANCE EVALUATION REPORT

(Before filling out the report, please read the Steps for Completing the Performance Evaluation Form given at the end of the Form)

**PART 1 - To be completed by the Personnel Officer**

NAME (LAST, FIRST, MIDDLE)      TITLE OF POST      GRADE      AT THIS GRADE SINCE

TYPE OF APPOINTMENT      GRADE OF POST      IN THIS POST SINCE      CODE NUMBER

DUTY STATION      DIVISION/SECTION/UNIT      PERIOD COVERED BY REPORT FROM      TO

**PART 2 - To be completed by Immediate Supervisor**

2.1  At the beginning of the reporting period, plan with the staff member the assignments to be undertaken during the period, the accomplishment of which will form the basis of the next performance evaluation.  The initials of the staff member indicate that the plan has been established in consultation with the staff member.

Staff member's initials and date: _____      _____

2.2 (To be completed by the immediate supervisor in consultation with the staff member.) Please list any additions, changes or deletions to the above assignments during the reporting period. The initials of the staff member indicate that revisions to the plan have been made in consultation with the staff member.
Staff member's initials and date: _____       _____

PART 3 - To be completed after the performance evaluation discussion
3.1 (To be completed by staff member.) For each assignment in Part 2, describe what you achieved during the year. If some were not achieved or only partially achieved, explain why.
3.2 (To be completed by staff member.) List any additional accomplishments which you feel deserve mention.
3.3 (To be completed by immediate supervisor.) Evaluate the staff member's accomplishments as stated above.
PART 4 - To be completed by immediate supervisor
Comment on the following:
4.1 *Competence* (Application of professional/technical knowledge, skills and experience)
4.2 *Other* (Please specify other attributes which contributed significantly to the staff member's performance, such as initiative, judgment, sense of responsibility, team work)
4.3 *Performance as a supervisor* APPLICABLE ONLY FOR SUPERVISORS (Ability to motivate, develop, guide and evaluate the work of others)
PART 5 - Signature and review
5.1 (To be completed by the staff member.) Comment if you wish on Parts 2, 3 and 4, and on the quality of performance-related discussions during the year.
I have no comment. _____
5.2 (To be completed by the supervisor.) Comment if you wish on the staff member's comments in 5.1.
Signature and date: _____       Name and Title:
_____
5.3 (Review and comments by second reporting officer.) State also how well you are acquainted with the staff member's work.
Signature and date: _____       Name and Title:
_____
5.4 (Signature by staff member.) Your signature does not indicate agreement with the report, but only that you have seen it and received a copy. You may submit a written explanation or rebuttal within one month of receipt of this report under the terms of the relevant administrative instruction. Please indicate if you intend to do so.
Signature and date: _____       _____
STEPS FOR COMPLETING THE PERFORMANCE EVALUATION REPORT FORM
1. Read or review the guidelines carefully BEFORE beginning to complete the PER form.
2. The appropriate personnel or administrative officer completes Part 1 prior to the start of the staff member's reporting period.
3. The supervisor, in consultation with the staff member's performance plan in 2.1 at the beginning of the reporting period.
4. The supervisor sets down the staff member's performance plan in 2.1 at the beginning of the reporting period.
5. The supervisor, in consultation with the staff member during the reporting period, sets down in 2.2 any additions, changes or deletions which have been made to 2.1.
6. The staff member and supervisor have a performance evaluation discussion at the end of the reporting period. The staff member then completes 3.1 and 3.2.
7. The supervisor then completes 3.3 and all of Part 4.

8. The staff member then completes 5.1.
9. The supervisor then completes 5.2.
10. The second reporting officer then completes 5.3.
11. The staff member then signs in 5.4.
12. The supervisor should make an appointment with the staff member during the first month of the new reporting period to set the next performance plan.

## SUMMARY

Performance appraisal is an important component of management information and control system. We have seen that its objectives and uses could be several. An appraisal system should tell the person what us expected of him, give him an opportunity to perform, provide feedback, guidance and support and establish personnel policies concerning rewards, training, career development, etc., which are contingent upon one's performance. We have also noted that besides these, the clarity of the concept, criteria used, the culture and context of the organization also influence appraisal.

The major appraisal techniques include appraisal by objectives, confidential report, trait appraisal, rating scales, ranking methods, narrative or descriptive methods and behaviourally anchored rating scales. Each method works best in a different context with its own strengths and weaknesses.

The raters could be any of the following: superior, subordinate, peers, clients/users, managers or specialists of other units, consultants and top management. We have noted that the rater concerns and errors are many. Still there are several ways to improve the accuracy of ratings. It is appropriate to have review and appeal system.

Assessment of potential is different from appraisal of performance. The interview and feedback play an important role in performance appraisal which need special skills and orientation. Finally we have considered the major aspects which influence the design of an effective appraisal system and described policies and formats of their organizations.

## KEY-WORDS

| | | |
|---|---|---|
| **Behaviourally Anchored Rating Scales (BARS)** | : | These are descriptions of various degrees of behaviour relating to an aspect of performance dimension derived and described from an anlysis of job content and work behaviour. |
| **Halo effect** | : | Basing the entire appraisal on the basis of one perceived positive quality, feature or trait in an individual. |
| **Horn effect** | : | Basing the evaluation on the basis of one negative quality or feature perceived. |
| **Ranking techniques** | : | These are comparative measurement techniques where superiors or peers rank-order their subordinates or peers as the case may be. Usually, ranking is confined to one factor, i.e., overall performance or effectiveness. |
| **Rating scales** | : | These are techniques where performance is measured through assigning numbers, alphabets or words which are linked to descriptive adjectives for items or events to describe differences. |
| **Stereotyping** | : | It is a standard mental picture that an individual holds about a person because of that person's sex, caste, age, physical characteristics or other features. |

## REVIEW QUESTIONS

1. Discuss the objectives and uses of performance appraisal.

2. Review any five appraisal techniques and comment on their pros and cons.

3. Comment on the appraisal formats exhibited in this Chapter. Discuss whether they meet the information requirements to objectively appraise performance of employees. Explain what needs to be done to improve the objectivity.

4. Is feedback to rater the same as the one to the ratee? Explain the similarities and dissimilarities in their purposes and processes.

5. What are the major concerns and errors of the raters? How can they be overcome?

6. Describe the characteristics of an effective performance appraisal system.

## EXERCISES

1. Examine whether you can develop completely objective system to appraise the performance of a salesman. Describe the system. See whether and how far similar system can be extended to appraise the performance of a person holding a staff function like Assistant Manager (Provident Fund) on the basis of identification of key result areas (KRA), Performance criteria, Standards, Measures, Weightages, etc. If possible, describe the system. If not, give reasons. (The results of this exercise can be shared by the participant with those of others which can form the basis for discussion).

2. State how you would like your job performance to be assessed, in the job that you held recently or hold currently. Discuss with your supervisor (or in the class with other participants) and share the respective viewpoints.

## FURTHER READING

1. Basu, M K, 1988. *Managerial Performance Appraisal in India*, Vision Books: New Delhi.

2. Bolar, M, 1978. *Performance Appraisal: Readings, Case Studies and a Survey of Practices*, Vikas: New Delhi.

3. Dayal, I, 1976. *Cultural Factors in Designing Performance Appraisal Systems*, *Vikalpa* vol. 1, no. 2, pp 59–68.

4. McGregor, D, 1972. "An Uneasy Look at Performance Appraisal," *Harvard Business Review*.

5. Anderson, R I, 1984. *Performance Appraisal*, 2nd edn, Reston: Virginia.

6. Rao, T V and Pareek V, 1978. *Performance Appraisal: Manuals*. Learning Systems: New Delhi.

7. Rao, T V, 1985. *Performance Appraisal*, Vikas: New Delhi.

8. Mairer, N R F, 1973. *Psychology in Industrial Organizations*, 4th edn, Houghton Mifflin: Boston.

# Career and Succession Planning

Career and succession planning of employees carried out systematically and regularly provides valuable information on the extent of current and potential utilization of human resources and is an important input to manpower planning process. In the following pages the emergent need for career planning and the concepts of individual career and organizational career systems will be discussed. A description of steps involved in the career planning process aimed at integrating the individual needs and aspirations with organizational requirements will be presented. The concept and process of succession planning will be briefly described followed by a discussion on career management and development. For an insight with the practical aspects, career path of officers of Indian Administrative Services is presented as an illustration.

## NEED FOR CAREER PLANNING

The ability of an organization to ensure optimum utilization of its human resources depends on the extent to which it is able to meet the multiplicity of needs and aspirations of its employees. Organizations have, however, their own requirements and constraints which limit their capacity to meet the unique individual expectations. The changing expectations of employees and limits imposed by organizational constraints usually create a situation of conflict. If this conflict is not resolved properly, the organization will not be able to get the best out of its employees. Career planning provides a set of tools and techniques for productive resolution of this conflict between the individual and the organization.

The relationship between an individual and an organization could be long-term or short-term depending upon whether the employment relationship is life-long (i.e. till superannuation) or not. Where the individual feels that an organization is not able to meet his career aspirations he has the option to continue in employment or switch organizations. While exercising the latter option, an individual would do well to take the following precautions:

- Be discreet in selecting the field of employment and employer. In terms of where one wants to be ultimately, does this move help? Should one accept some short-term trade-offs for long- term benefits (e.g. low paying jobs with better opportunities for training and exercise of one's skills and discretion)?
- Examine whether one is adequately familiar with opportunities the present organization provides.
- Introspect current performance, strengths and weaknesses to see for oneself whether one is being merely ambitious or whether one has outlived one's utility in the organization presently employed
- Plan one's exit so that one is leaving at one's convenience than of the organization.
- Leave the organization on a cordial note.

Individuals need to consciously and continuously examine what they themselves ought to be doing for their own career development rather than merely wait for something to happen.

Organizations on their part, should invest time and effort to improve aspects relating to job text and context and in planning and guiding people for careers. They would do well to take into account the individual career development objectives in performance planning and review and personnel decisions. Companies which provide fair and reasonable opportunities for satisfying careers will be able to attract, retain and motivate committed and industrious work force. In recent years, with the slow, but steady increase in the proportion of women employees particularly in technical and managerial jobs, career planning has become more complex than before. Now individuals and organizations are required to recognize and cope with the challenging problems of dual careers, i.e. careers for the couple, than just one of the spouses. The dual-career couple need to manage not only their jobs and careers but also their family responsibilities and, therefore, require and demand (a) flexible working hours, (b) special counselling, (c) supportive, humane, personnel policies to facilitate swift transfers and relocations, and (d) outplacement assistance. The problems are more complex if the dual-career couple do not work for the same organization.

Organizations which care to focus on individuals in helping the latter to plan and manage their careers better pay specific attention to the following aspects.

***Induction***    Orienting the employee to acculture and acclimatize the individual to the organization. Induction training becomes crucial in this regard.

***Mentoring***    A mentor is a teacher, advisor, guide, friend, philosopher and confidante. Organizations should actively promote mentor relationships and provide adequate time for the mentor and the new entrants to meet, interact, understand and develop a sense of trust and confidence in each other. The mentor will then be able to guide the new entrant and act as a sounding board for dealing with work-related problems. Proper mentor relationships help reduce stresses and strains of new entrants, increase the chances of their survival and success in the organization.

## THE CONCEPT OF A CAREER

*Career* is viewed as a sequence of positions occupied by a person during the course of his lifetime. This is the *objective* career. Career may also be viewed as an amalgam of changes in values, attitudes and motivation that occur as a person grows older. This is called the *subjective* career. In both the perspectives the focus is on the individual. The implicit assumption in any discussion on the subject is the belief that the individual can make a difference to influence his destiny over time, and can adjust in ways that would help him to enhance and optimize the potential for his own career development. Career planning is important because it would help the individual to explore, choose and strive to derive satisfaction with one's career objectives.

While artists, professionals and creative personnel may deal independently with their own careers, the careers of those employed by someone else do not leave much scope for their own individual pursuits.

### Career Anchors

Most individuals develop an idea—a mental image—of what career they would like to pursue quite early in life. However, all of us may not be aware of the direction in which we would like to move. The urge to take up a certain type of career is governed by the basic drives acquired during the socialization process. These basic drives are called the *career anchors*, some of which are as follows.

| | | |
|---|---|---|
| 1. Managerial competence | : | Career providing opportunities for higher responsibility, decision-making, control and influence |
| 2. Technical competence | : | Providing for professional satisfaction, continuous learning and updating one's expertise in a technical or functional area |
| 3. Security | : | Ensuring security of career through compliance with organization's prescriptions |
| 4. Creativity | : | Enterpreneurial and innovative opportunities |
| 5. Autonomy | : | A career that provides freedom of action and independence |

As individuals differ in their career anchors, it is important to identify the basic drives of individual employees.

## Stages of Growth and Career

Yet another factor that influences our career choice is the stage of growth and development towards maturity and old age—as can be seen from Table 6.1.

**Table 6.1**

| Stages of Growth | Primary Role Definition | Career Implications |
| --- | --- | --- |
| 1. Infancy | Dependent child | Growth |
| 2. Adolescence | Assertion of independence | Exploratory |
| 3. Adult | Establishing one's family of procreation | Establishment |
| 4. Middle Age | Concern for children's career | Maintenance |
| 5. Old Age | Personal security | Decline |

As it is obvious from Table 6.1, transition from one stage of life to another has its own implications to our career. As an infant, an individual channelizes his energies in ensuring his growth and development through education; as an adolescent he explores various career anchors; as an adult he establishes himself in the career of his choice; as middle aged person he consolidates, stabilizes and maintains his achievement in the career and as an old person interest in the career declines and he tends to withdraw.

While the stages of growth of an individual in general have implications for career advancement needs, one on joining an organization passes through a series of stages involving important career issues. These can be broadly categorized as follows:

(i) *Early career issues*:
- Locating one's area of contribution
- learning how to fit into the organization
- becoming productive
- seeing a desirable future for oneself in the career.

(ii) *Mid-career issues*:
- locating one's career anchor and building one's career around it
- specializing or generalizing

(iii) *Late career issues*:
- becoming a mentor
- using one's experience and wisdom
- letting go and retiring

The issues confronted by individuals in various stages of their career must be resolved by appropriate actions and decisions on the part of the organization so as to create conditions conducive to optimum utilization of the human potential.

# Career System in Organizations

Like individuals, organizations also have their own career paths and requirements. For the individual the objective of a successful career is influenced by some of the factors mentioned above. Some employees may look forward to leading a decent life style, while others may like to reach the top of the hierarchy on the occupational scale or aspire to be in a position to do what they like to do, rather than what is determined by the organization. In some cases, the career aspirations and orientation may be toned down or moderated by concern for happy social and family life. However, a serious trade off between one's career and the family life may be quite unacceptable for some.

For the organization, individual career needs and aspirations usually become relevant only to the extent they can be integrated into the requirements of the organization. Rarely, if ever, organizations build activities around individuals. The organization's own life cycle and its position vis-a-vis business cycle effects largely determine the extent and kind of career opportunities it can create and sustain. Growing and diversifying firms may offer more and wider choices while stagnant and decaying firms may cause even the existing opportunities to shrink or even dry up. Personnel policies, beliefs and value systems also limit or open up career opportunities for people at different levels. For example, some organizations do not encourage people who join as workers to move beyond supervisory levels, while a few others would take pride in making opportunities available to everyone. In some organizations people reach a plateau when they reach 40 to 45 years of age, while in other organizations career opportunities remain open virtually till the day of superannuation.

Career systems in organizations can be classified according to (i) scope (ii) limitations on entrance and (iii) orientation for reward and status.

*Scope*     Some organizations limit the scope of movement of employees from one function to another. While in others, movement of people among various functions, departments and jurisdiction is encouraged. The former may be called *specialist career system* while the latter *organizational career system*. The debate between the proponents of the specialist and generalist career systems is too well known to be discussed here.

*Limitations on Entrance*     In some organizations, like the government and public sector undertakings, recruitment of new employees is restricted at the entry level only. Upper level positions are filled in entirely from within and lateral entry is discouraged. This is called *Closed Career System*. In the *Open Career System*, entrance is permitted at any or all levels. The private sector organizations usually prefer open career systems.

*Orientation to Reward and Status*     The career systems can be *job-oriented or status oriented*. In the job-oriented career system, employees are rewarded on the basis of their merit and performance. Job assignment and promotion decisions are taken strictly on the basis of proven competence. In the status-oriented career system, on the other hand, it is seniority and length of service that determine the reward and promotability.

## Career Paths

Organizations identify and communicate characteristic career paths that employees tend to follow. Career paths represent logical and possible sequences of positions that could be held, based on what and how people perform in an organization. Career paths represent real career progression possibilities, both lateral and upward. These are, of course, tentative and flexible and may change over time. The skills, knowledge and other attributes required to perform effectively at each position along the paths and how they can be acquired must be specified.

Development of a career system, comprising of individual career paths also becomes necessary. This involves (a) analyzing jobs to determine similarities and dissimilarities among them, (b) grouping jobs with similar behavioural requirements into job families, and (c) identifying career paths within and among job families, and (d) integrating the overall network of career paths into a single career system.

## Promotion Policies

Career planning, thus, will need to be balanced and dovetailed with the appropriate criteria for promotional decisions. There can be several permutations and combinations of merit-seniority spectrum shown in Fig. 6.1.

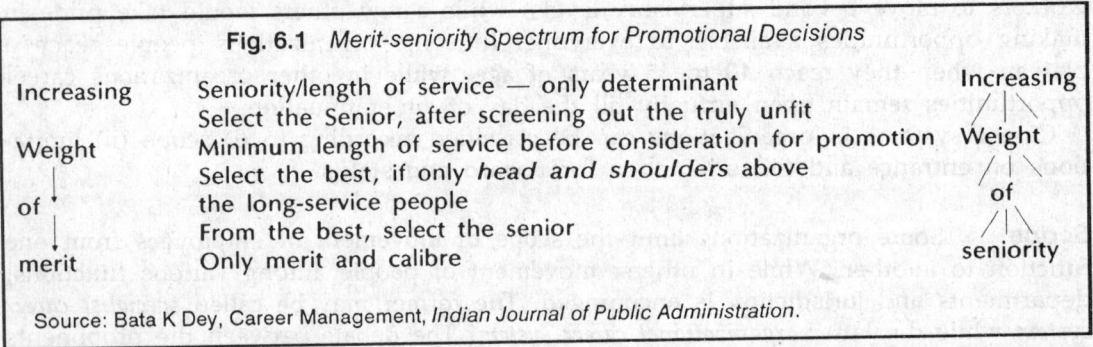

**Fig. 6.1** *Merit-seniority Spectrum for Promotional Decisions*

| Increasing | Seniority/length of service — only determinant | Increasing |
| | Select the Senior, after screening out the truly unfit | |
| Weight | Minimum length of service before consideration for promotion | Weight |
| | Select the best, if only *head and shoulders* above | |
| of | the long-service people | of |
| | From the best, select the senior | |
| merit | Only merit and calibre | seniority |

Source: Bata K Dey, Career Management, *Indian Journal of Public Administration*.

Though in a competitive world, organizations would like to emphasize merit, most have not been able to develop and implement objective parameters and systems to assess merit. Also, in respect of unionized employees (even managers are unionized in some cases) collective bargaining lay down the norms and quotas which influence promotion policies.

## CAREER PLANNING PROCESS

It is obvious from the foregoing analysis that individuals differ a great deal in terms of their career orientation. The career orientation is influenced by the preference for a particular career anchor, the life-cycle stage one is in and individual differences in values, goals, priorities and aspirations. Organizations also differ in terms of the career paths and opportunities that they can provide given the reality of their internal and external environments. The career systems available in organizations also depend on their value system, growth potential, goals and priorities. The difference between what the employees look for in terms of their career progression and what career growth opportunities the organization is able to provide, gives rise to a situation of potential conflict between the individual aspiration and organizational opportunities. If the conflict is allowed to persist, the employees will experience dissatisfaction and withdraw from being actively engaged in the productive pursuits. They might even choose the option of leaving the organization. In either case, the organization is not able to optimally utilize the potential contributions of its employees towards the achievement of its goals.

The possibility of conflict between the individual and organization objectives calls for career planning efforts which can help identify areas of conflict and initiate such actions as necessary to resolve the conflict. Career planning, thus, involves matching of rewards and incentives offered by the career path and career structure with hopes and aspirations of different categories of employees regarding their own concept of progression. A general approach to career planning would involve the following steps:

(i) Analysis of the characteristics of the *rewards and incentives* offered by the prevailing career system needs to be done and made known to employees. Many individuals may not be aware of their own career progression paths as such information may be confined to only a select group of managers.

(ii) Analysis of the characteristics of the *hopes and aspirations* of different categories of employees including identification of their career anchors must be done through objective assessment. Most organizations assume the career aspirations of individual employees which need not be in tune with the reality. The individuals may not have a clear idea of their short and long-term career and life goals, and may not be aware of their aspirations and career anchors.

(iii) Mechanisms for identifying *congruence* between individual career aspirations and organisational career systems must be developed so as to enable the organization to discuss cases of mismatch or incongruence. On the basis of above analyses, it will be necessary to compare and identify specific areas of match and mismatch for different category of employees.

(iv) Alternative strategies for dealing with *mismatch* will have to be formulated. Some of the strategies adopted by several organizations include the following:

(a) Changes in the career system by creating new career paths, new incentives, new rewards, by providing challenges through job redesign opportunities for lateral movement and the like.

(b) change in the employees' hopes and aspirations by creating new needs, new goals, new aspirations or by helping the employees to scale down goals and aspirations that are unrealistic or unattainable for one reason or the other.

(c) seek new basis of integration, compromise or other forms of mutual change on the part of both employees and organization through problem-solving, negotiations or other devices.

A framework of career planning process aimed at integrating individual and organizational needs is presented in Fig. 6.2.

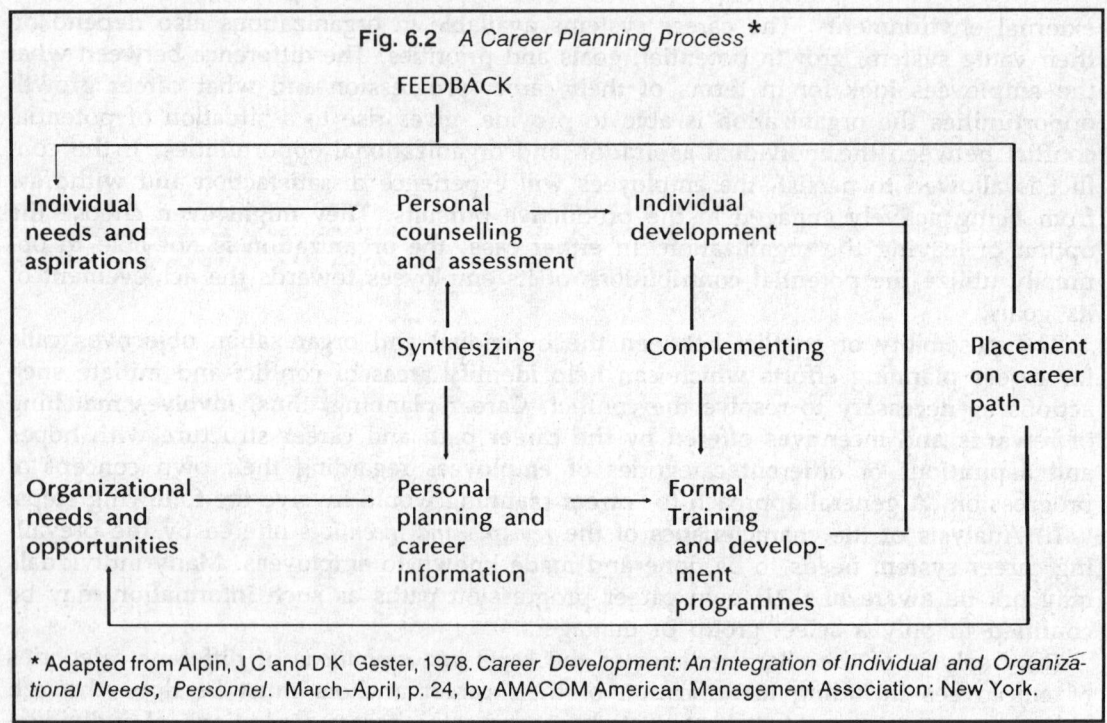

Fig. 6.2   *A Career Planning Process**

* Adapted from Alpin, J C and D K Gester, 1978. *Career Development: An Integration of Individual and Organizational Needs, Personnel.* March–April, p. 24, by AMACOM American Management Association: New York.

## SUCCESSION PLANNING

The continued existence of an organization over time requires a succession of persons to fill key positions. The purpose of succession planning is to identify and develop people to replace current incumbents in key positions for a variety of reasons: superannuation, resignation, promotion, growth, diversification, creation of new positions, realigning responsibilities, etc.

Succession can be from within or from without the organization. Succession by people from within gives a shared feeling among employees that they can grow as the organization grows. Therefore, organizations need to encourage the growth and development of its employees. They should look inward to identify potential and make efforts to groom people for higher and varied responsibilities. More so when they are growing steadily and their future corporate plans do not differ significantly from those in the past. In some professionally run large organizations (be they in public or private sector or subsidiaries of multinationals) managers and supervisors in every department are usually asked to identify three or four best candidates to replace them in their jobs should the need arise. However, organizations may find it necessary to search for outside talent in certain circumstances such as the following: when qualified and competent people are not available internally, when it is planning to launch major expansion or diversification programmes requiring new ideas, etc. Complete dependence on internal sources may cause stagnation for the organization. Similarly complete dependence on outside talent may cause stagnation in the career prospects of the individuals within the organization which may, in turn, generate a sense of frustration.

## Individual Career Planning

Succession planning would be effective when individual needs and aspirations are integrated with organizational needs and opportunities, synthesizing personnel counselling and assessment with personnel planning and career information and complementing individual development efforts with formal training and development programmes. This requires development of individual career plans by the process described in Fig. 6.2.

## Performance Review and Potential Identification

Performance review and analysis should result in constructive feedback, performance recognition and appraisal of potential. Potential, per se, is usually not formally and explicitly communicated mainly for one reason: there may be a time gap between the time employee potential is identified and harnessed in an organization. In the intervening period there may be changes in the individual or the organization situation whereby the potential or the opportunities to harness the potential may change. Also, the organizations would not like individuals to grow complacent on being told about their potential. Nonetheless, to help individuals know and understand for themselves who they are, how they are seen what their options are and how they can best accomplish their goals is good organizational strategy. Discerning analysis of the nature of assignments, placements, and recognition would help people to gauge the implicit message.

## CAREER MANAGEMENT

Career management involves both organizational actions and individual initiatives to ensure that when the career plans developed by the organizational requirements and individual aspirations undergo unanticipated changes, they are managed appropriately on a continuing basis. Figure 6.3 describes various components and processes of a career management model.

As can be seen from the model, organizational career planning and individual career planning must be integrated by designing individual career paths, creating developmental strategies and providing career counselling. These actions in turn lead to career development plans involving implementation of career plans, publicising job vacancies, appraising employee performance, off the job experience and evaluating career progression.

## CAREER DEVELOPMENT

A properly designed career development programme should address itself to the following activities.

## Career Need Assessment

The organization should provide assistance to employees in assessing their own internal career needs. A number of evaluation instruments to test aptitude, abilities, attitude, etc. are available which provide a fair idea of the career needs of people. Life planning workbooks can be used to help employees to gain an insight into the life goals they want to pursue and aspire to achieve. Many employees may not be aware of what they really want in their lives and what they want to be. For career development purposes it is necessary for employees to develop goal clarity.

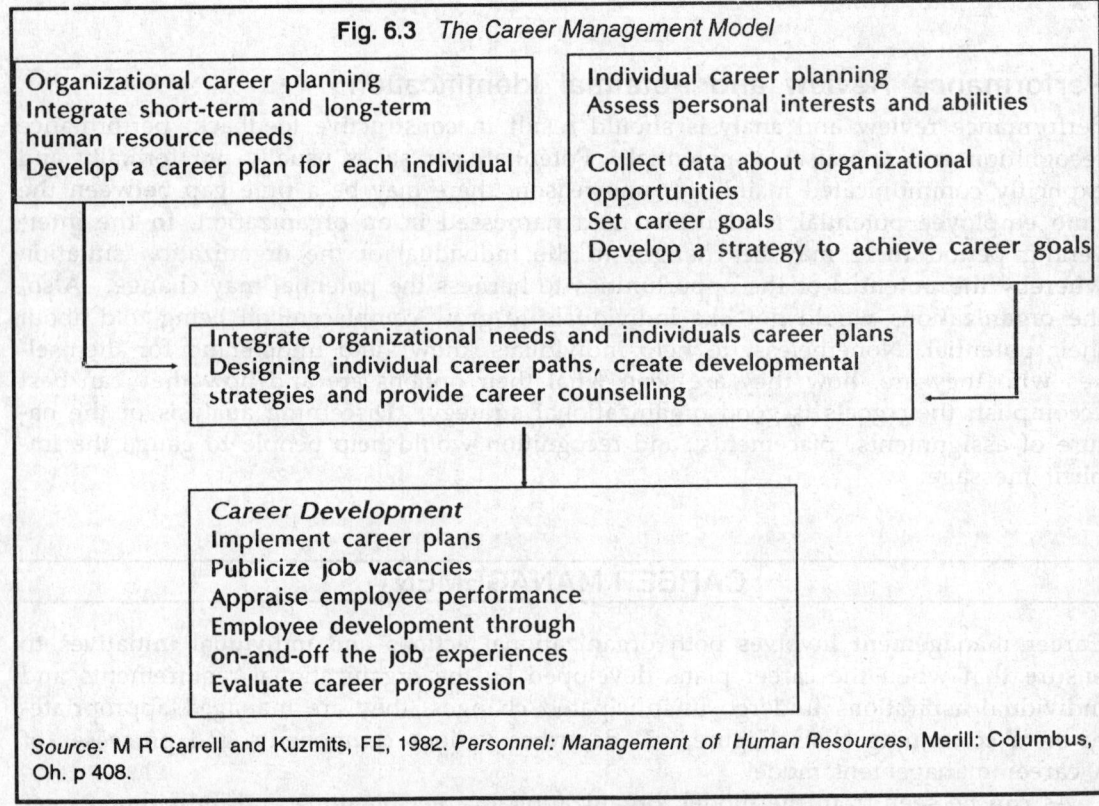

**Fig. 6.3** *The Career Management Model*

Organizational career planning
Integrate short-term and long-term human resource needs
Develop a career plan for each individual

Individual career planning
Assess personal interests and abilities

Collect data about organizational opportunities
Set career goals
Develop a strategy to achieve career goals

Integrate organizational needs and individuals career plans
Designing individual career paths, create developmental strategies and provide career counselling

*Career Development*
Implement career plans
Publicize job vacancies
Appraise employee performance
Employee development through on-and-off the job experiences
Evaluate career progression

*Source:* M R Carrell and Kuzmits, FE, 1982. *Personnel: Management of Human Resources*, Merill: Columbus, Oh. p 408.

In recent years, formal assessment workshops have become quite popular as methods for assisting executives in developing goal clarity and in choosing life goals in formulating strategies for achieving those goals and in developing concrete plans of action in that regard. These assessment workshops are conducted by specialists for executives of different organizations. In a nonthreatening learning environment executives explore their strengths and weaknesses, develop self awareness and plan for their future career growth. A wide variety of pedagogical tools and techniques such as psychological tests, simulation of real life situations, in-depth interviews, etc. are utilized for helping executives in the exploration of their existing potential and future career goals.

## Career Opportunities

The organization must develop and publicize the available career opportunities for employees. Career opportunities can best be known through job analysis and job design efforts. Job description, job specification and particularly job redesign will throw several possibilities of employee movement and provide several lines of advancement for them. Having discerned the career opportunities that can be made available, it is important to publish them in a booklet form which can be made available to employees. Such a booklet will provide necessary information on the basis of which individual employees can plan their own career movement and progression.

## Need–Opportunity Alignment

The next step in the career development programme involves aligning of employees needs and abilities with available career opportunities. The organization must design such developmental programmes as will help the employees integrate their development needs with organizational opportunities. The development programmes in this context are seen as relevant not for today's job, but for the future job. Preparing the person for prospective roles is imperative if the person is to be effective in those roles/positions. Some of the developmental programmes used by organizations are explained below.

*Individualized development techniques*    A number of techniques like special assignment, sabbaticals, under-study programmes, supervisory coaching, planned job rotation, and job enrichment can be used depending on the specific requirements and existing organizational constraints.

*Performance Appraisal*    Performance appraisal system can provide an objective assessment of not only the current performance standards of employees but also provide insight into their potentials. A well designed performance appraisal system can become a powerful mechanism for aligning the employees needs and aspirations with the organizational requirements and goals in the present as well as future contexts.

*Management by Objectives*    Management by objectives is one of the planned change strategies which emphasises goal setting, action planning, and self monitoring by individual employees. The employees are encouraged to set personal development objectives and develop action plans for achieving them within the framework of their own roles in organization. Through continuous monitoring, attempt is made to integrate the individual objectives with those of the organization.

*Career Counselling*    Career counselling can be provided either by superiors or by professionals specialized in career guidance to employees with a view to assisting them to develop awareness of their strengths and weaknesses, to elimnate unrealistic expectations, and appreciate the constraints existing in the organization in terms of availability of career opportunities. It can help employees deal with feelings of frustration arising out of unrealistic expectation, and help to set realistic career goals, and formulate concrete plans of action for achieving those goals.

*Recording and Tracking Career Moves*　　As indicated earlier, meaningful career planning and development efforts should be carried out on a continuing basis to take care of the changing expectations of both the individual and the organization. It is important, therefore, to maintain a record of career movements of employees and to monitor their progress towards the predetermined career goals. This will enable the personnel specialists to discover discrepancies and to adopt corrective measures at an early stage.

In case appropriate career opportunities are not available for some employees, the organization may assist those in finding suitable positions externally, rather than allowing their dissatisfaction to grow disproportionately. Such an approach will necessitate active involvement of employees in jointly planning and following up the career development programmes.

Career development programmes will be successful, if it is ensured that (a) employees believe that their supervisors care for their career development, (b) there is awareness about the individual strengths and weaknesses and an appreciation of organizational constraints, (c) career plans are developed with necessary support systems to provide a fair and equal opportunity to all concerned within and among different job families. The key support systems include communication and information sharing about career plans, career paths, job vacancies, etc. employee performance review and planning, potential appraisal and internal staffing decisions including those concerning seniority, merit, etc.training and development, and evaluation of career progression.

**EXHIBIT 6.1**

---

**Career Path in the IAS**

*1st year* (Junior scale)
(a) Junior sub-divisional charge under close supervision
(b) Subordinate office charge in collectorate under close supervision
(c) Posts of close contact with elected bodies up to sub-divisional level.

2–4 years
(a) (i) Magistracy in cities and metropolitan areas
    (ii) Second-level posts involving coordination of district development department in the field
(b) (i) Senior sub-division charge
    (ii) Independent office charge in collectorate

*5th year* (Senior Scale)
(a) Regional developmental department head
(b) District charge
(c) State Secretariat (US/DS) in department operating programmes

*6th year*
Training (4 months)

*7-9 Years*
(a) District charge
(b) (3 years) Central Secretariat (US) in department operating programmes of Home/Finance (3 years).
(c) District charge

---

*10-11 Years* (Training Abroad and Study Leave, etc.)
(a) District charge
(b) Public sector undertaking at state level
(c) Head of medium-sized State departments
(d) State Secretariat, Planning, Finance, Personnel and Programme Operating Departments
(e) Central Secretariat—Home, Finance, Planning Commission, Programme Operating Ministries.
*12-16  Years* (Secondment to Select Grade/Teaching/Institutions.)
(a) Major charge as department Head under State government
(b) District charge
(c) Public sector undertaking at the Centre
(d) State Secretariat
(e) Central government (Field/Secretariat)
*17-27 Years*
(a) Start of Supertime Scale
(b) Commissioner in the State/Joint Secretary in the Centre
(c) Additional Secretary to the Government of India
*30th Year* Secretary to the Government.

Source: Dey, BK, "Career Management", *Indian Journal of Public Administration*

---

# SUMMARY

*Career planning* as a process of integrating the employees' needs and aspirations with organizational requirements has assumed far greater importance today in view of the need for organizations to attract, retain and utilize the potential of the technical specialists and professional managers. A wide variety of career opportunities encompassing both lateral and vertical movement of personnel will have to be provided in order to accommodate the unique individual requirements in terms of changing career anchors and the stages of growth. A systematic approach to career planning would entail assessment of career needs of employees, creation of career opportunities in the organization and adoption of various strategies for career management and career development. Career development programmes require both individual and organizational actions, some of which have been discussed above. Active involvement of employees in planning their own career as also the willingness on the part of organizations to develop more flexible management policies and practices. The design of work, performance analysis, reward and recognition system and promotion and career advancement systems are necessary conditions for making career and succession planning an important tool for harnessing the human potential.

---

# KEY WORDS

| | | |
|---|---|---|
| **Career** | : | A sequence of positions occupied by a person during the course of his lifetime. |
| **Career Anchor** | : | The basic drives acquired by an individual during the socialisation process which urge him to take up a career of a certain type. |
| **Career Paths** | : | The logical and possible sequences of positions that could be held by an individual based on what and how people perform  in an organization. |

Career Planning          :    The process or activities offered by the organization to individuals to identify strengths, weaknesses, specific goals and jobs they would like to reach/occupy.

Career Development      :    It refers to a set of programmes designed to match an employee's needs, abilities and goals with current or future opportunities within the organization.

Career Management      :    It refers to a set of activities and actions, involving both the individual employee and the organization, designed to cope with the changes in career plans caused by organizational requirements and individual needs and aspirations, whether foreseen or not.

Succession Planning     :    It refers to the process or activities connected with the succession of persons to fill key positions in the organization hierarchy as vacancies arise.

---

## REVIEW QUESTIONS

1.    Discuss the concept of a career and explain the career planning process.
2.    Explain the need for career planning from the point of view of an
        (i) individual employee
        (ii) organization
3.    What is meant by career development? What are the roles of the individual and the organization in developing and managing an individual employee's career.
4.    Write notes on :
        (i) Career on anchors and career paths
        (ii) Succession planning

## FURTHER READING

1.    Monappa, A, *Human Resource Planning and Career Planning*, IIM: Ahmedabad (Mimeo).

2.    Deegan II, A X, 1986. *Succession Planning: Key to Corporate Excellence*, John Wiley & Sons: New York.

3.    Taylor, Bernard  and G Lippitt, 1983. *Management Development and Training Handbook*, 2nd edn, McGraw-Hill: London.

4.    Schein, E H, 1978. *Career Dynamics: Matching Individual and Organizational Needs*, Addison-Wesley: Reading, Massachussetts.

# Training and Development

**LEARNING OBJECTIVES**

After going through this chapter, you should be able to:
• Appreciate the need for adopting an integrated approach to training and development in pursuit of organizational objectives. • Familiarize yourself with various approaches to and techniques of assessment of training needs. • Understand the relevance of a wide variety of training methods and techniques to specific learning objectives. • Describe the steps involved in designing training programmes. • Develop awareness of the importance and techniques of evaluation of training and development efforts.

The effectiveness of career planning in an organization system will largely depend on the extent to which training and development opportunities are made available to employees to enable them to realize their growth potential and to make contributions towards achievement of organizational objectives. Training and development activities are the main mechanisms through which individual's goals and aspirations can be integrated with organizational goals and requirements. Such an integration can be achieved only when training and development efforts are linked with the organizational requirements and are carried out in a systematic manner throughout the organization.

In this chapter, an attempt will be made to establish the linkage between the training and development activities and the organizational objectives and purposes. The emphasis will be on training as one of the tools for employee development. The steps involved in adopting systematic approach to training such as training need assessment, setting of training objectives, design of training, and evaluation of the outcome and consequences of training will be described in brief. A case from Indian company will be presented as an illustration of the systematic way training activities can be carried out and their linkages established with the organizational requirements.

## NEED FOR TRAINING AND DEVELOPMENT

Before discussing the conditions necessitating training and development activities, it would be relevant to differentiate between the terms *Training* and *Development* particularly in the context of industrial and service organizations. The objective of training is to develop specific and useful knowledge, skills and techniques. It is intended to prepare people to carry out pre-determined tasks in well defined job contexts. Training is basically a task oriented activity aimed at improving performance in current or future jobs. The term management training connotes equipping managers with such knowledge, skills and techniques as are relevant to managerial tasks and functions.

Development encompasses the whole complex process by which employees as individuals learn, grow, improve their abilities to perform a wide variety of roles within and outside organizations and acquire socially desirable attitudes and values. Management development is aimed at improving one's abilities to perform professional management tasks. It involves learning on the job through experience. Participation in formal training or educational programmes is an integral part of overall management development. Several other approaches like job rotation, placement, job enrichment, task forces constituted around specific problem areas, participation in continuing education programmes like distance education, etc can be used to promote management development. Management development, like any form of personnel development, is a highly individual matter; it is essentially self-development.

The need for training and development of employees on a continuing basis in organized sectors of human activity is no longer a matter of debate. The need has been recognized as an essential activity not only of management in public and private sectors but also of trade unions, academic institutions, professional bodies and the various departments and agencies of the government.

Some of the conditions that have led to the awareness of the importance of training and development activities in organizations in the post-1960 period in India are:

- (i) Suboptimal performance of organizations in public, government and private sectors.
- (ii) The ever-increasing gap between planning and implementation of projects.
- (iii) Technological change necessitating acquisition of new skills.
- (iv) Qualitative change in the form of professionalisation of managerial staff and workmen.
- (v) Increased uncertainties and complexities in the environment necessitating flexible and adaptive responses.
- (vi) Need for individuals and organizations to grow at rapid pace.
- (vii) To meet challenges of global competition.
- (viii) To harness the human potential and give expression to their creative urges. Arising out of the above, the main areas in which training is provided are:

*(i) Knowledge:*　　The training in this area aims at helping the trainee learn to understand and to remember facts, information and principles.

*(ii) Technical skills:* The trainee is taught physical acts or actions like operating a machine, working with a computer, using mathematical models to take decisions, etc.

*(iii) Social skills:* The employees are provided opportunities to acquire and sharpen such behavioural and human relations skills as are necessary for improved interpersonal relationship, better team work and effective leadership.

*(iv) Techniques:* This involves teaching of application of knowledge and skill to dynamic situations.

*(v) Attitudes:* This involves attitudinal change towards increased work commitment and a positive orientation towards the organization and society. The basis of attitudes, and the knowledge and skill with which to change them have to be carefully diagnosed.

*(vi) Experience:* It cannot be taught in the classroom. It is the result of practicing the use of knowledge, skills, techniques and attitudes over a period of time in different work situations.

Most organizations depending on their specific developmental requirements at various levels in the organizations tend to assign priority to one or the other areas above for training purposes. Usually a well designed training programme aims at facilitating learning in practically all the areas, the emphasis, however, may differ based on the specific requirement of tasks and people.

Although in many cases need for training has been realized; infrastructure created; financial support provided; yet the benefits of training are not reflected to the desired extent in the overall improvement in the current state or preparedness for future challenges. Training to be meaningful, therefore, must be integrated into the overall human resource development strategies of organizations. Such an integration can be achieved only when training activities are carried out in a systematic manner. A systematic and integrated approach to training should consist of various interrelated components as shown in Fig. 7.1.

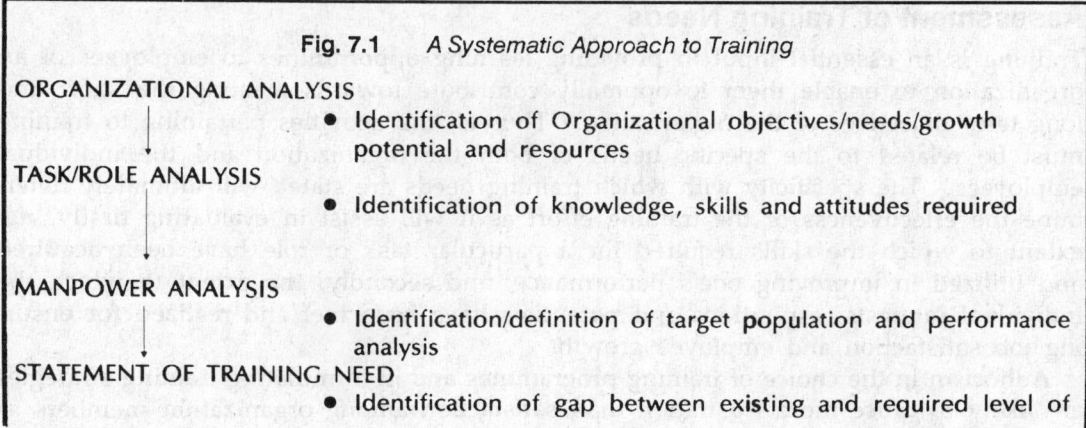

**Fig. 7.1** *A Systematic Approach to Training*

ORGANIZATIONAL ANALYSIS
- Identification of Organizational objectives/needs/growth potential and resources

TASK/ROLE ANALYSIS
- Identification of knowledge, skills and attitudes required

MANPOWER ANALYSIS
- Identification/definition of target population and performance analysis

STATEMENT OF TRAINING NEED
- Identification of gap between existing and required level of

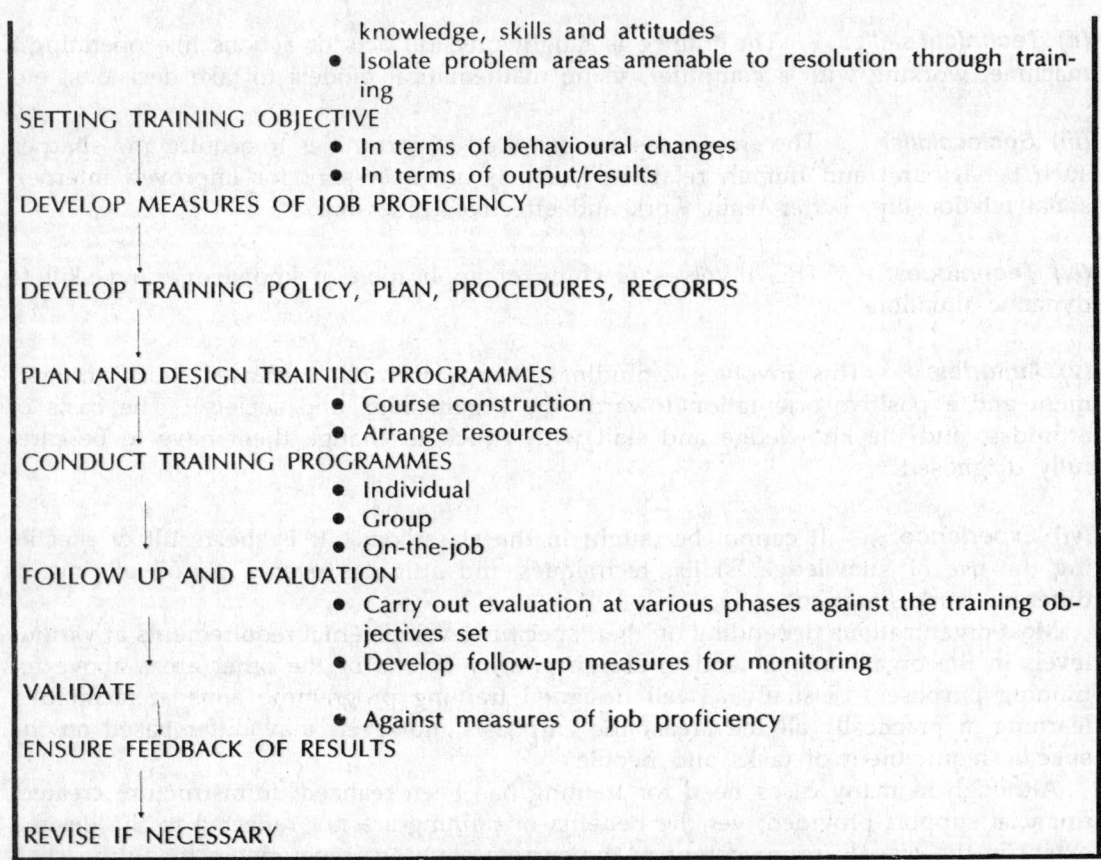

knowledge, skills and attitudes
- Isolate problem areas amenable to resolution through training

SETTING TRAINING OBJECTIVE
- In terms of behavioural changes
- In terms of output/results

DEVELOP MEASURES OF JOB PROFICIENCY

DEVELOP TRAINING POLICY, PLAN, PROCEDURES, RECORDS

PLAN AND DESIGN TRAINING PROGRAMMES
- Course construction
- Arrange resources

CONDUCT TRAINING PROGRAMMES
- Individual
- Group
- On-the-job

FOLLOW UP AND EVALUATION
- Carry out evaluation at various phases against the training objectives set
- Develop follow-up measures for monitoring

VALIDATE
- Against measures of job proficiency

ENSURE FEEDBACK OF RESULTS

REVISE IF NECESSARY

As can be seen from Fig. 7.1., all training activities must begin with organizational analysis and must ultimately contribute to solving organizational problems identified in the process of carrying out the analysis. The main phases involved in the systematic approach to training will be discussed in the following pages.

## Assessment of Training Needs

Training is an essential input in providing learning opportunities to employees of an organization to enable them to optimally contribute towards meeting the short and long term objectives of the organization. Thus all the activities pertaining to training must be related to the specific needs of both the organization and the individual employees. The specificity with which training needs are stated will ultimately determine the effectiveness of the training effort as it will assist in evaluating firstly, the extent to which the skills required for a particular task or role have been acquired and utilized in improving one's performance; and secondly, the extent to which the individual interests, aspirations and potentials have been met and realized for ensuring job satisfaction and employee growth.

Adhocism in the choice of training programmes and in formulating training strategies are likely to cause more frustration than satisfaction among organization members as they may not be able to utilize their newly acquired learning on their jobs. There is the need, therefore, to develop realistic plans for training and development of employees, execute them and follow them up with continuous monitoring and evaluation. The first phase in the planning process is the identification of specific training and development needs which involves the following.

**Organization Analysis**    This involves a study of the entire organization in terms of its objectives, its resources, the allocation and utilization of these resources for achievement of objectives, and its interaction patterns with the relevant socio-economic and technological environments. The training philosophy for the entire organization can be developed through this process. In more specific terms, the Organization  Analysis includes the following steps:

*(i) Analysis of Objectives*    Analysis of organization's objectives provides a clear understanding of both short and long-term objectives as well as the priorities that are accorded to various objectives. Specific goals and strategies should be stated for various divisions, departments and sections of the organization as a means of achieving the long-term priority objectives. Continuous review of objectives and their subsequent modification in the context of the  changing environment need to be undertaken at regular intervals. Also, it is necessary to translate general objectives into detailed and specific operational targets.

*(ii) Resource Utilization Analysis*    Having analyzed the objectives, the second step involves evaluating the process of allocation of various human and physical resources and the extent of their efficient utilization in meeting the specific operational targets across the organization. Various efficiency indices can be derived to determine the adequacy of specific work flows, so that detailed examination of the inputs and outputs of the total system is possible. The focus should be on the contribution that human resources make towards these indices.

*(iii) Environmental Scanning*    This involves analysis of the enterprise as an organization or a subsystem operating in a distinct socio-cultural, economic and political environment. This enables the organization to influence certain aspects of its environment and to accept other parts as given constraints which cannot easily be controlled.

*(iv) Organization Climate Analysis*    The climate of an organization is a reflection of its members' attitudes toward various aspects of work, supervision, company procedures, goals and objectives and membership in the organization.

The prevailing organizational climate, especially the attitude towards employee development, determines the training programme's success. Lack of management support for the objectives of a particular training programme reduces or eliminates its potential for serving the organization. Often, training must be supported by other actions in the organization such as job enrichment, change in style of supervision, etc. to bring about desired changes. Another important consideration, particularly in management development, is an enterprise's need to project requirement trends during the careers of its current management force.

**Task/Role Analysis**    This involves a careful study of jobs within an organization in a further effort to define the specific content of training. It requires an orderly, systematic collection of data about the job, role or position; and its purpose is to spell out, in as much detail as possible, what tasks constitute the job, how they are to be performed and what behaviour; skills, knowledge, and attitudes, the job holder must have to perform certain specified tasks.

In the collection of job information for the purpose of formulating training programmes, particular attention must be paid to performance standards required of employees, the tasks in which they will be engaged, the methods they will use on the job, and, most important, the way they have learned these methods.

Many different ways of collecting job information are available, such as: Questionnaires, interviews, personnel records, observation, business and production reports, tests, etc.

*Manpower Analysis*    The focus of this analysis is on the individual in a given job, rather than on the job itself.   Three basic issues are involved in a manpower analysis for training purposes.   First, through appropriate observation, supervisory evaluation, and diagnostic testing we need to determine whether performance is substandard and training is needed.   Second, we need to know whether current employees are capable of being trained, and the specific areas in which training is required.   Finally, we need to ask whether current employees with substandard performances can improve their work through appropriate training or should be transferred to make room for those who can already do the job.   Other alternatives to training like modifications in the job or new equipments or processes should also be considered as solutions.

Job knowledge tests, work samples, diagnostic psychological tests, and performance reports provide the kind of information needed to choose from the above alternatives.

If the training programme is to remain relevant and viable, then the three kinds of analyses described above must be carried on continuously.   Training programmes should be reviewed constantly and revised in the light of changes in a company's resources, objectives, internal climate, and external environment.   Further, these analyses should be integrated in a carefully designed and executed research programme.

## TRAINING OBJECTIVES AND STRATEGIES

Having identified the training needs based on the various analyses discussed above, the next logical steps are to set training objectives in concrete terms and to decide on the  training strategies to be adopted to meet these objectives.  The training needs basically highlight the gap between the existing and desired repertoire of knowledge, attitude and skills at individual, group and organizational level to enable the employees to contribute towards the realization of organizational objectives at optimum efficiency.  The training effort, thus will have to aim at filling in this gap by clearly stating the objectives in quantitative and qualitative terms to be achieved through training.  Such an exercise will also enable the training specialists to evaluate, monitor and measure the extent to which stated objectives have been met through training intervention. As the training objectives are related to organizational objectives, the involvement of the top management will be necessary to ensure that the two sets of objectives are integrated.

It will be desirable to use the following *criteria* in setting training objectives:

(i) Specific requirements of individuals and organizations so as to achieve integration of the two.

(ii) Roles and tasks to be carried out by the target group.

(iii) Relationship with other positions vertically and horizontally and technological imperatives.

(iv) Relevance, applicability and compatibility of training to work situations.

(v) Training as a means of bringing about a change in behaviour back on the job.

(vi) Behaviour including activities that can be observed, measured and/or recorded.

(vii) The expected change in behaviour must be useful, closely related to and subject to maintenance in the work environment.

More specifically the following *steps* could be involved in setting training objectives:

(i) Identification of the behaviour where change is required.

(ii) Nature and size of the group to be trained in terms of prior training, situational factors, formal education.

(iii) Existing behaviour defined in terms of ratio, frequency, quality of interaction and supervision, routineness and repetitiveness, innovations, omissions, error, etc.

(iv) Desired behaviour aimed at improving the existing condition stated preferably in quantitative terms such as ratio, frequency of occurrence, reporting by exceptions, self-monitoring mechanisms etc.

(v) Operational results to be achieved through training stated in terms of increase in efficiency and effectiveness criteria such as productivity, cost, down time, turnover, time for innovations and creativity.

(vi) Indicators to be used in determining changes from existing to the desired level in terms of ratio and frequency.

Depending on the objectives set, the next step is to decide on the *strategy* of training involving the following:

(i) Classification of objectives in terms of purposes:
   (a) Corrective objectives
   (b) Maintenance/status-quo objectives
   (c) Problem solving objectives, and
   (d) Innovative objectives.

(ii) Classification of objectives in terms of levels of learning:
   (a) Skills of motor responses, memorization and simple conditioning;
   (b) Adaptation level where one is gaining knowledge or adapting to a simple environment;
   (c) Interpersonal understanding and skill;
   (d) Values of individuals and groups.

(iii) On-the-job or off-the job training.

(iv) Inhouse or external training.

(v) Individual or group training.

(vi) Horizontal, vertical or diagonal/mixed group.

(vii) Changes required, if any, in the existing work roles, organizational relationships, work system requirements, process of supervision and alternative structures.

# TRAINING METHODS AND TECHNIQUES

In order to achieve the training objectives successfully, it is essential that a careful choice is made from amongst a variety of pedagogical tools, techniques and training methods available for facilitating learning. Training methods and techniques can be used interchangeably as tools for enabling adult learners acquire desired knowledge, sharpen behavioural and performance skills and develop appropriate attitudes.

While exercising choice on selection of methods, it is important to keep in mind certain practical ideas that have emerged from adult education research. In helping adults learn the trainer ought to use the adults' own resources brought into the learning situation. Some training issues worth considering are:

(i)    The adult learners have reservoir of experience which can contribute a great deal to the learning situation. It is our experience which helps us to define our 'identity' and shape our value system. Therefore, if we find ourselves in a situation where our experience is ignored, minimized or devalued, we feel rejected as a person and assume passive role.

(ii)   The process of growth to adulthood entails movement towards becoming more autonomous, self-directing and self-controlling. As a result, as learners we feel uncomfortable when placed in a dependent role with tight external control. One way to encourage more self-direction in learning is to give the responsibility for working out solutions to problems to the trainees themselves. The trainer serves as a resource to their problem-solving process.

(iii)  The adult learners feel comfortable in a situation where they can acquire such knowledge, skills and attitudes as will help them resolve their current issues, concerns and problems at work or home. The relevance of learning in terms of its applicability in the immediate environment is of paramount concern to adult learners.

(iv)   The adult learners are likely to pay more attention to those aspects of learning which will help them advance their career and personal life goals. Thus, in a training situation if they discover that *they don't know what they need to know*, it provides a climate most conducive to learning on their part.

The characteristics of adult learners mentioned above make it imperative to select such training techniques as will allow them to:

(i)    participate in setting learning goals and get actively involved in the learning process;

(ii)   contribute to the learning of others through sharing of experiences;

(iii)  reflect on their experiences with a view to discerning aspects of learning that have been helpful to them and those which have blocked their growth potential;

(iv)   establish relationships between the new knowledge and the work experience and to explore their interconnectedness;

(v)    raise their own problems and concerns and initiate search for alternative solutions within the framework of the content being discussed, and

(vi)   experiment freely with new ideas, approaches and feelings in a non-threatening situation devoid of the risks of the real life situation with a view to assessin͘ the impact of learning in here-and-now situation.

## Training Techniques

In keeping with the principles of adult learning, a number of training techniques have been developed and made use of in achieving different training objectives. Some of the widely used techniques are briefly discussed below.

*(i) Job Instructions Training (JIT)*     The job  instruction training is a form of individual instruction by supervisors and is similar to coaching . The technique is appropriate for acquisition or improvement of motor skills  and routine and repetitive operations.  The JIT involves the following four steps:

(a)   preparing the trainee in terms of existing skill on the job, securing his interest and attention;

(b)   presenting the Job operations in terms of what the trainee is required to do;

(c)   applying and trying out the instruction; and

(d)   following up the training.

*(ii) Coaching*     Coaching is again on-the-job training of individual by the supervisor in the area of specifically defined tasks. This technique is more appropriate for orientation of new employee and for helping disadvantaged employees to learn specific jobs.   The supervisor must have interpersonal competence and be able to establish helping relationship with the trainee.

*(iii) Programmed  Learning*     A form of individual study, the programmed learning is more suited to meeting the behavioural objectives and when non-motor skill or knowledge is to be learned by a large number of trainees.  The trainer monitors trainees' independent progress through the programme. This method is governed by the principle of positive reinforcement developed by B F Skinner and allows the trainee to learn through a series of small steps in phases and at his own pace.

*(iv) Job Rotation/Enlargement/Enrichment*     As already discussed in previous chapters, job rotation, job enlargement and job enrichment are the forms of on-the-job individual training with emphasis on providing the trainee experience in various types of jobs, locations and departments. These techniques are more appropriate for developing multiskilling, operational flexibility, providing satisfaction from routine jobs and broadening of overall perspective.

*(v) Lecture*     Lecture is by far the most widely used technique of training involving speaking to large number of trainees usually from prepared notes. This is more appropriate in situations where same information is required to be shared to a large audience and where there is no time for more participative method. There are at least two variations of this method, talk and discussion, which allow some participation of the trainees.   Talk involves encouraging trainees to raise questions thus maintaining interest in the topic. In discussion, knowledge, ideas and opinions are freely exchanged

among the trainees and the trainer.

*(vi) Conference*    The conference method is used to help employees develop problem-solving skills. Group discussions and Meetings are the two common techniques often made use of in organizations. The chairman or the trainer leads discussion, involves trainees in attempting to solve problems and in arriving at decisions. The conference leader must have the necessary skill to lead the discussion in a meaningful way without losing sight of the topic or theme. The conference method or group discussion effects changes in the participants through modification of their experiences due to sharing and reshaping of their views, thinking and attitudes.

*(vii) Laboratory Training*    Laboratory training, often called sensitivity training or T-Group, is based on the principles of group dynamics and is widely used as a tool for inculcating team spirit amongst employees. Both unstructured experience and structured exercises are provided to the participants to help them increase their self-awareness, develop interpersonal competence and sharpen skills to work in teams as effective members and leaders. The trainer must be professionally trained to lead the groups.

*(viii) Role Playing*    Role playing is used in helping trainees to diagnose human relations problems, to develop insight through indepth analysis of problems relating to human interaction and to acquire skills in interpersonal communication with particular emphasis on empathy and listening. A simulated situation is created in which trainees act out the thoughts and behaviour of persons in particular roles in the organization. Roles are often played spontaneously and unrehearsed.

*(ix) Case Study*    The case study method involves diagnostic and problem solving study of usually a written description of some event or set of circumstances on organizational problems providing relevant details. The method is appropriate for developing analytical and problem solving orientation and skill, providing practice in applying management concepts, tools and techniques and enhancing awareness of the management concepts and processes. The method is relevant for developing organizational, conceptual and functional skills among top and senior level executives.

*(x) In-Basket*    In-Basket or In-Tray technique involves simulation of a series of decisions a trainee might have to make in real life. The trainee is presented with pack of papers and files in a tray containing administrative problems and are asked to take decisions within specified time limit. The decisions taken by several trainees are recorded and compared with one another. Learning occurs as trainees reflect and evaluate the decisions taken on priorities, customer's complaint, superior's demand, irrelevant information and the like.

   In addition to the above, other training techniques worth mentioning are *Management games*—simulation of real life business world, *Workshops*—addressed to specific themes wherein a variety of techniques described above are used, *Project/Action Learning*—on specific organizational problems, *Critical Incident technique*—for gathering and analysing facts, and *Brain Storming* – a method for generating original, creative ideas on difficult and complex problems.

As stated earlier, choice of a technique depends on a number of factors some of which are as follows:

(i)   Profile of the trainer, the participants, the socio-cultural milieu and the organizational culture and practices
(ii)  The nature and type of training objectives
(iii) The content and subject area
(iv)  Time and infrastructural support
(v)   Principles of adult learning.

Table. 7.1   Choice of Relevant Method

| Skills | Appropriate Method |
|---|---|
| Selecting pertinent data | Critical incident |
| Diagnosing problems | Case study |
| Communication | Role playing |
| Team working | Laboratory method |
| Information sharing | Lecture |

Table. 7.1. provides an illustrative list of appropriate methods to be chosen for imparting specific skills to trainees.

## DESIGN AND ORGANIZATION OF TRAINING

A systematic approach to training requires a great deal of design effort such that the training needs are identified, the objectives set and the training methods selected are fully integrated and coherent. In designing training programmes, some of the following steps are to be followed.

## Developing Appropriate Strategies

In order to achieve the training objectives already set, appropriate strategies will have to be selected which will also partly determine the choice of training methods. For example, various objectives could be categorized under the following training strategies.

(a)   Common skills approach
(b)   The manager as an individual
(c)   The manager as a member of team
(d)   The manager and the organization
(e)   The manager and the environment

There are certain human relations skills like communication skill which are common to all employees irrespective of their functions and positions. The training programme will have to be designed in such a way that it can cater to the diverse background of a large number of employees. In terms of the choice of training methods, participative techniques like role plays and structured exercises will be more appropriate as these can be used regardless of the diversity in the target population. Whereas in the case of (d) above, the organization development strategies with emphasis on job content and organizational processes will have to be adopted. A wide variety of methods such as case study, simulation, and group discussion may be more appropriate.

## Deciding the Content

The general training objectives need to be broken down into various components such as knowledge, skill, attitude, and understanding. For each constituent, specific contents are decided, appropriate methods chosen and time frame specified. It is useful to work out in detail the specification for each constituent part called *event* or *block* in terms of

(a)  General objective
(b)  Specific objectives
(c)  Content
(d)  Method
(e)  Teaching aid needed
(f)  Time required
(g)  Evaluation
(h)  Resource persons.

## Developing Training Packages

Based on an analysis of each constituent segment of the objectives, a number of training packages can be developed to provide the organization with various alternative ways of achieving the objectives. For example, for meeting the objective of helping middle managers acquire human relations skill the following training packages could be suggested: Package 1— One week full time residential programme, Package 2— One week full time non-residential programme, Package 3—Two week part-time non-residential after working hours and the like. Through the analysis already done of the content, method, resources, facilities, and time required; it will be possible as also advisable to work out budget for each of the packages so as to enable the decision makers to choose an appropriate package.

Such a training package should also contain a detailed syllabus with proper sequencing of content and themes, consistency in their arrangement, and an appropriate mix of training methods. A major part of the syllabus can be planned with greater precision than others, and decision in this regard must be taken in advance. It is usually helpful to keep some part of the syllabus flexible so that unpredictable events or unique requirements of a particular group of participants can be accommodated in the training programme without losing sight of the original thrust.

## EVALUATION OF TRAINING

In order to assess the extent to which training programmes have achieved the purposes for which they were designed, it is necessary to evaluate various activities that have culminated in the implementation of the training package. Such an evaluation exercise would provide relevant information not only about the effectiveness of training but also about the future design of other training programmes. It is through the process of evaluation that training specialists can monitor the training programme and update, modify and innovate in future training programmes. The evaluation of the outcome and consequence of training also provides useful data on the basis of which relevance of training and its integration with other functions of management can be established.

Table 7.2 provides a broad framework of evaluation in terms of types, levels and methods, of activities pertaining to training and their effect on individual and the organization. Ideally it is desirable to carry out evaluation studies in a comprehensive manner. However, it may not always be feasible in practice to do so because of organizational constraints arising out of inadequate infrastructure, absence of clear training policy and unwillingness on the part of the decision makers to make use of feedback which may necessitate changes in personnel policies, performance appraisal system and even organizational processes. It is therefore, imperative that given the framework, the training specialist together with decision makers should make a choice as to the kind of evaluation to be carried out which could be gainfully utilized within the existing constraints of the organization.

**Table 7.2   Framework for Evaluation of Training**

| Types of Evaluation | Levels of Evaluation/Objective | Methods of Evaluation |
| --- | --- | --- |
| 1. *Context Evaluation* Obtaining & using Information about the current operational context i.e., individual difficulties, organization deficiencies - i.e., Training Need Assessment as basis for decision. To what extent are training courses related to job requirement? | 1. *Pre-training* | (i) Same as the ones used in assessment of training needs |
| 2. *Input Evaluation* Determining & using facts/ opinions about human/ material resources for training – to decide training method or types of training – inventory of outside training programmes. | - do - | (i)  Same as the ones used in design and organization of training |
| 3. *Process Evaluation* Monitoring training as it is in | 2. *Reactions Level* Opinions/attitudes about trainer, | (i) Observation by trainer unsystematic/random |

progress—continuous examination of administrative arrangements and feedback from trainees.

4.*Outcome Evaluation*
Measuring effects of training on the relation to his job.

presentation, usefulness, involvement.

3. *Learning Level*
Acquisition of knowledge, skills and attitudes, capable of translating into behaviour in training situation.

4. *Job Behaviour Level*
Changed behaviour back on the job

(ii) Rating Scales for each session or theme
– Analyze, present to trainees and discuss.
iii) Questionnaires/Interviews
(i)  Knowledge learning, factual and intellectual understanding
–programmed instruction
–multiple-choice questions administered at the beginning of training and end of session
–Examinations of academic type, written and/or oral.
(ii) Skill learning, technical and social
–practical tests to demonstrate skill administered at the beginning & at end.
(iii) Attitude Learning
–attitude scales
–Semantic Differential scales:
7 or 5 point scales stretching between pairs of adjectives with opposite meaning administered at the beginning and end of training.
(i)  Systematic, observation
(ii) Activity sampling – percentage of time spent by trainee on different aspects of his job.
- observer diaries, continuous record of his activities
(iii) Self diaries
(iv) Observation of specific Incidents, e.g., interviewing skills.
(v)  Self recording of specific incidents: devising tailor made evaluation instruments through which the trainee can himself

record details of the way in which he performs certain tasks.

(vi) Appraisal by superiors: asking questions such as, "Can you describe any specific incidents in which the employee demonstrated improvement in knowledge/skill/attitude ?"

(vii) Self-appraisal, used in conjunction with appraisal by others.

5. *Consequence Evaluation*
Measuring effects of training on overall efficiency of department/organization.

5. *Functioning Level*
Efficiency of the firm, effect on other's behaviour, cost reduction, etc.

(i) Productivity/efficiency of trainee's department

(ii) Morale of subordinate's expressed by absence rates; labour turn over rates or incidence of industrial disputes. Any index of functioning which is related to the training objective can be used.

(iii) Control Groups compare performance of similar employees who have not undergone training.

## COMPANY EXPERIENCE : TRAINING AND DEVELOPMENT IN A MULTINATIONAL PHARMACEUTICAL COMPANY IN INDIA

### The Environment

In the management by objectives environment in which they have been operating in the company during the last decade or so, the managers have broadly attempted to classify their needs into two categories, namely, (a) organizational and (b) individual. Their philosophy has been to mesh the organization and the individual to the extent possible. The consequent objective in the design of training programme has been to improve the performance of the managers and operatives to accelerate organizational performance. The monitoring system is shown in the following:

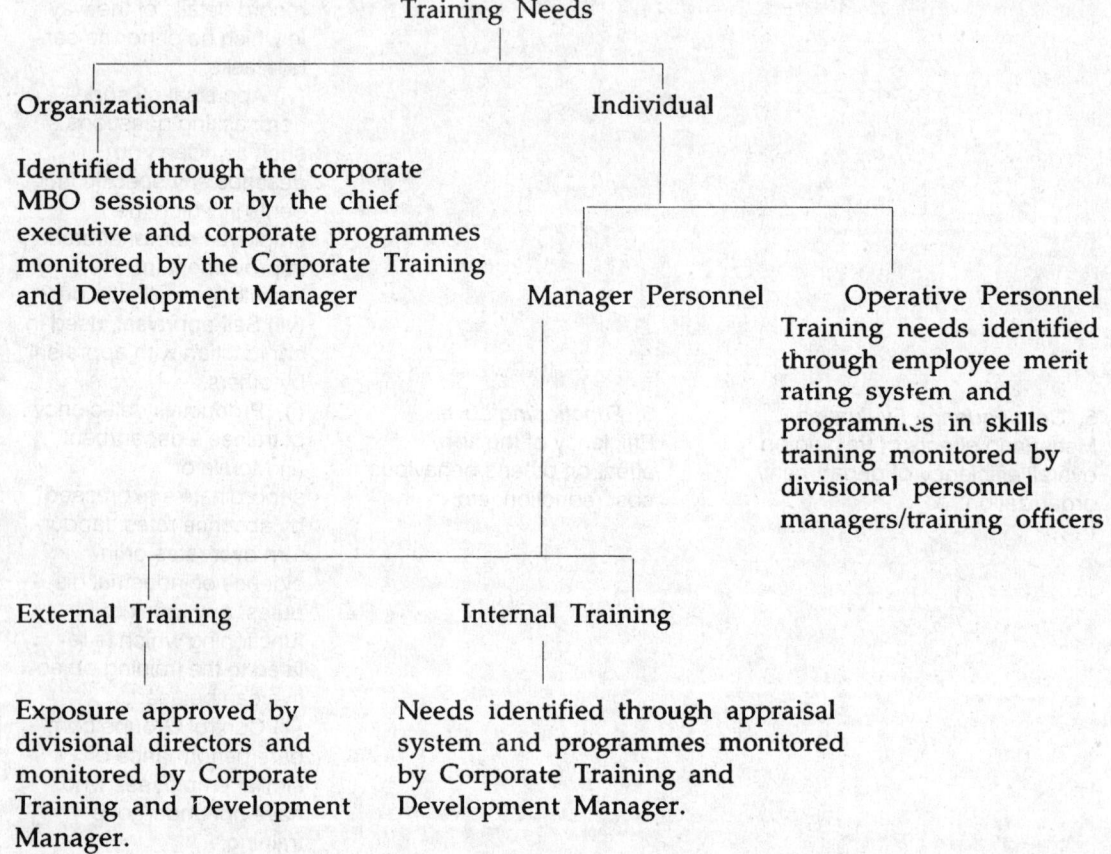

## Sources of Identification

The sources for identifying the needs in the two areas are distinctly different.

*Organizational*    The organizational needs generally flow from corporate MBO sessions in which only top management participate.  The members of the board identify the areas which are critical and important to the company's operations and in which the managerial component of the organizations needs to be actively involved for the acquisition of necessary knowledge and skills in working toward common objectives of the organization.

The sole objective of these forums is to highlight the areas of concern to every component  of the organization and improve perception and understanding for building up a cohesive work force.  It also helps in evolving uniform and standard practices across the organization in many key areas.  Generally, the responsibility for designing and organising such forums rests with the corporate training and development manager (CTDM), who liaises with the chief executive or the corporate personnel director.

*Individual Needs*    The main role of training and development is in this area, which is of prime importance to the company. Their philosophy of individual training and development is firmly entrenched in the belief that no improvement in organizational performance can ever be achieved unless they update the knowledge and skills of their people to meet the rapidly changing technical and administrative environment in which they operate. The identification of training needs basically flow from the appraisal system which in this organization is MBO based.

The appraisee assesses his own needs in the context of his performance on the current job. The process is, therefore, of *self-assessment* – the appraiser remains purely a catalyst and counsellor and eventually supporter and follower of the programme which has been mutually agreed within a pre-defined period of time. The training needs relate purely to the current job and not to the future job.

## The Process

The process of identifying the training needs at the time of the appraisal interview is briefly a five stage one:
   (i)    The appraisee himself identifies the needs in advance and records them.
   (ii)   The appraiser discusses with the appraisee the needs in the context of the gap in the appraisee's performance on the current job, recognising the factors that have impeded his performance.
   (iii)  A broad agreement on the *needs* is arrived at by both.
   (iv)   An agreed action plan is recorded by the appraiser in each of the segments.
   (v)    A period within which the plan would be operational and completed is also mutually agreed and recorded.

All the individual forms completed are then despatched to the corporate personnel division.

## Role of the Chief Training and Development Manager

In the office of the CTDM, each form is thoroughly scrutinized and the training needs of various departments are noted. The process that takes place after that comprises the following stages:
   (a)  A statement incorporating the needs of a given department or division is sent to the director-in-charge.
   (b) At a mutually convenient time these are discussed with each director/manager by the CTDM and priorities are mutually agreed on. A tentative time schedule is also drawn up for each programme.
   (c) When needs are not quite clear, a dialogue is arranged between the appraiser and the appraisee by the CTDM.

Finally, after discussion with every director of the company, a corporate training plan is formulated and in a very broad form, sent to the managing director for approval. The plan includes a budgeted provision of expenditure for each divisional and corporate programme.

## Design of the Programmes

In this process, the topics to be covered, the periodicity of a programme, whether residential or non-residential, the number of participants in which programme and the identification of internal and external faculties are some of the important points that are examined.  The CTDM designs a broad framework of each programme and discusses it thoroughly with the functional managers before finally seeking approval of the director-in-charge.  At times, the appraisees are also consulted in seeking clarification of some of their requirements.

Generally participation in external course is discouraged.  But if training is required in those functional or other areas where the company does not have the required skill and competence or if it is felt that interaction of personnel with his counterparts in other industrial organisations is necessary so that the participant acquires new knowledge and functional expertise external courses are supported.

The role of the CTDM in all internal development programmes is an intricate one. In several specifically designed programmes, he holds the responsibility of pinpointing the problem areas identified by the group and preparing a suitable action plan.

A report is also prepared by him for the managing director and divisional directors to keep them informed and to request them to follow up at the divisional MBO review sessions.

## Some Constraints

Where a large number of personnel identify their needs through the appraisal system it becomes almost impossible to cover all the appraisees in a period of one year.  The priorities regarding inclusion of specific personnel in the pre-identified training programmes rest solely with the divisional directors.

Those members of staff who are not covered by the proposed annual training plan are generally informed about their non-inclusion.

## Programmes for the Operative Personnel

These programmes are purely those which pertain to the development of *technical skills* for the new technology.  The training broadly covers, processes, methods, safety, etc. and the instructional methods vary in content.  Audio-visual techniques are used where language barriers exist.

The design and monitoring of these programmes are undertaken by the personnel manager or training officer of the concerned division.  The needs are identified through the employee rating form which has provision for recording the training needs.  Basically these needs are identified by the immediate superiors and not by the workmen concerned, although a dialogue exists between the two.

---

### SUMMARY

Training and development activities to be meaningful must be integrated with the overall human resource development strategy of an organization.  Training is an important tool for employee development and has assumed great importance due to unprecedented rate of change in the internal and external environments of organizations. The purpose of training is to effect change in the behaviour of employees so as to enable them to meet the current and future requirements of their tasks and roles.

Training as an instrument of behaviour change must be carried out in a systematic manner. The various phases involved in the systematic use of training for developmental purposes have been described in brief. A carefully designed training programme must take into account all the phases beginning from organizational analysis through design and organization of training programme to evaluation of effect of training on the individual, his performance in the job and overall efficiency of the department and organization on a whole. The evaluation studies provide data on the basis of which the personnel specialist can ascertain the extent to which problems identified during the organization analysis phase have been solved. The data thus generated can also be used for modifying the objectives, content, methodology and administrative arrangements so as to make the training programme more relevant and meaningful.

## KEY WORDS

| | | |
|---|---|---|
| **Attitude** | : | It refers to the orientation of an individual in terms of settled mode of thinking or behaviour. |
| **Skill** | : | It refers to expertness, practical ability, or facility in an action, or in doing or to do something. |
| **Job Instruction Training (JIT)** | : | The Job Instruction Training is a form of individual instruction by supervisors and is similar to coaching. |
| **Programmed Learning** | : | This is a form of individual study where the trainee learns through a series of small steps using the principle of positive reinforcement developed by B.F.Skinner. |
| **Laboratory Training** | : | Laboratory training, often called sensitivity training or T-Group, is based on the principles of group dynamics and is widely used as a tool for inculcating team spirit amongst employees. |
| **Role Play** | : | A simulated situation is created in which trainees act out the thoughts and behaviour of persons in particular roles in the organization. Roles are often played spontaneously or unrehearsed. |
| **Case Study** | : | It refers to diagnostic and problem solving study of usually a written description of some event or set of circumstances on organizational problems providing relevant details. |
| **In-basket** | : | In-Basket or In-Tray technique refers to simulation of a series of decisions a trainee might have to make in real life, sifting through a pack of papers and files containing administrative problems. |

## REVIEW QUESTIONS

1. Discuss the need for training and development. Describe how training needs are assessed.
2. Outline training objectives, strategies and methods.
3. Design the broad framework of a training package for graduate engineer trainees in a

large, multiplant engineering firm.  Suggest aspects relating to its organization.

4.  Discuss the linkages of training with other aspects (or sub- systems) of human resource management in an organization.

5.  Can training be evaluated?  Why?  How?

# CASE : HINDUSTAN CHEMICALS LTD

The Hindustan Chemicals Ltd (HCL) is a public sector firm engaged in petrochemical business.  It employs about 1,600 most of whom are well-qualified, fairly young (average age 32) and typically have an urban background.  HCL has retained one reputed consulting and training organization each to impart training in supervisory skills for their junior managers, human resource management programme with emphasis on organization analysis and behaviour modification skills for middle managers and advanced management programmes for senior managers.  HCL wanted to train all managerial employees over a period of 12 to 15 months in batches of 20 per month at junior and middle levels and 20 senior managers in once every two months.

IAM, a renowned management institute was assigned the responsibility to cover middle managers.

A couple of months after the start of the training intervention, the top management learnt of a growing tendency on the part of some of the employees on night shift to sleep while on duty.  Since it was a tightly manned petro-chemical complex any negligence or dereliction of duty in certain critical areas could be potentially hazardous and extremely risky.  Therefore, the Director (Personnel) and a couple of members of the top management team went around the plant one night, without any prior information to the plant people about their visit.  They caught red handed, four persons sleeping on duty, recorded evidence and proceeded with taking steps to initiate disciplinary action the following day.  When the charge sheets were being prepared, trade union leaders descended on the scene, persuaded the top management to be lenient, as an exception in this case, to the concerned persons.  The union leaders also assured that they would advise their members not to sleep while on duty.  In the interest of maintaining good industrial relations, the top management did not pursue the cases.

This gesture on the part of the top management was perceived as a sign of their weakness by the officers' association and its members.  They protested to top management whether they (the latter) would be equally considerate in cases involving them (the managers).  The workers felt that so long as there is no problem in the plant, management would be considerate enough.  With the result, the incidence of sleeping on night duty began to grow.  Top management became alarmed.  The Personnel Department was asked to advise all line managers, particularly shift in-changes in night duty to keep a vigil on those who have a tendency to sleep and report cases of persons who are found guilty of sleeping on duty.  The circular did not register any impact on the middle and junior managers.  Instead, they derisively laughed and ignored the circulars. They also felt that "the top management's perception of industrial relations dynamics at the plant is very different from that of junior and middle level managers."

Seeing no improvement in the situation, the top management asked IAM to include a module on Handling Indiscipline with role play sessions on 'How to conduct Domestic Enquiry'. The Programme Coordinator readily agreed to the suggestion because he felt that in doing so he was making it tailor-made to the needs of the organization.

When the module was first offered to the fifth batch of middle managers, the participants wondered why this subject was additionally introduced. They wanted to know why it did not form an integral part of the programme from the beginning itself and whether the need for including the topic was felt by their colleagues who attended the programme in the previous batches or by the top management. When they learnt that it was at the latter's instance, they stoutly protested in chorus and said, "We know the importance of Discipline. In fact, with growing violence our physical security is often threatened due to sabotage, violence and vandalism by a handful of unruly elements. Discipline, therefore is not merely an organization need, but also a personal need for us whereas for the top management it is a bargainable aspect of shop-floor industrial relations. What we need is not training but proof that top management means what it says. We demand that the top management supports and sustains the actions we initiate in maintaining discipline. We will be able to have confidence in top management if it shows us the way by first initiating actions on the cases they themselves have booked."

Such restiveness affected the receptivity in what was on the agenda in the training schedule for that afternoon. But the trainees became intensely involved the following day when they were doing the organization analysis in small groups. Most participants wondered what happened to the suggestion their predecessors made while presenting the findings of their group discussions on organization analysis before some members of the top management team on the last day of every programme held thus far. One participant asked: our colleagues gave their feedback to the top management. We understand the latter agreed on most points. But we see no evidence of follow-up of any kind." A second one argued with the programme coordinator, "Why are you asking us to give vent to our feelings? Do you realize that our top management is merely using you and the other faculty as a buffer?" A third one queried, "You quoted Kurt Lewin on the first day and observed that behaviour is a function of personality and situation. Now tell us whether top management is merely wanting to change our personality but does not want to change the situation. We do not know whether discussion on aspects concerning their personality should remain a taboo since projection will not help us."

Discuss the key issues in this case. Identify the lessons for developing training strategies. What remedial steps would you suggest in this case?

## FURTHER READING

1.   Craig, R L (Ed.), 1976. *Training and Development Handbook: A Guide to Human Resource Development*, 2nd edn., McGraw-Hill: New York.

2. Dayal, I, 1989. *Management Training in Organizations: Text, Cases and Simulated Exercises*, Prentice-Hall of India: New Delhi.

3. Jack, P J, 1990. *Handbook of Training Evaluation and Measurement Methods*, Kogan Page: Houston, Texas.

4. Lynton, R P and U Pareek, 1990. *Training for Development* (2nd edn.), Vistaar Publications: New Delhi.

5. Turrell, M, 1980. *Training Analysis: A Guide to Recognizing Training Needs*, Macdonald and Evans: Plymouth.

6. Virmani, B R and P Seth, 1986. *Evaluating Management Training and Development*, Vision Books: New Delhi.

# Pay and Benefits

**LEARNING OBJECTIVES**

After going through this chapter you should be able to:
- Understand the macro, (public policy), micro (enterprise/company level) and theoretical considerations in pay and employee benefit programmes;
- Be familiar with the concepts, methods and prerequisites of job evaluation, and the role of pay surveys in pay determination;  • Obtain an oveview of the procedure for evolving pay structure, and the methods of payment components of pay structures;  • Review Incentive schemes/payment by results systems; and,  • Examine the key considerations in fringe benefits and current approaches to fringe benefits.

Pay and benefits constitute an important element in human resource management. A number of considerations like theoretical, public policy and legal framework, company objectives, labour market situation, pressures from unions and competition, etc. impinge upon policies and programmes concerning pay and benefits. Job evaluation and pay surveys provide the basis for a systematic approach to the subject. The pay structures need to be evolved carefully to provide for meaningful wage differentials and salary progression. Certain parts of the components of the pay structure bear no relation to performance. Therefore organizations are finding the need to develop various incentive schemes and payment-by-results systems. Employee benefits began on a voluntary note at employers' instance. Today involuntarism has set in its place, with many benefits becoming entitlements either because of legislation or wage settlements, competitive pressures and the need to attract and retain the right people. Organizations are searching for means to find innovative approaches which give the desired flexibility and provide a measure of harmonization that contributes to positive attitudes and better performance besides making pay and benefits administration simple, fair and equitable.

## Theoretical Considerations

A number of economists have propounded theories which assert the following:

- That the natural price for labour is the subsistence-level wage. Higher wages will, over time, increase labour supply and bring down wage levels. The reverse also could happen. For, if wages fall below subsistence level, people will die of disease and malnutrition which will lead to a diminition in the supply of labour (Divid Ricardo's *Subsistence Theory of Wages*).

- That there is a predetermined fund (surplus income) which decides the wages. It pays to increase the fund through collective efforts than to ask for a higher share in the existing fund through legislation or otherwise (Adam Smith's *Wage Fund Theory*).

- That workers will never receive full compensation and that wages constitute an inadequate payment for the surplus value created by the workers for employer (Karl Marx's *Surplus Theory of Wages*).

- That state has to manipulate the allocation of income to wage-earners to restore full employment (J M Keynes *General Theory of Employment, Interest and Money* – it is not a theory of wages as such).

- That cheap labour would be a basis for comparative cost advantage in international trade (comparative costs theory – this is also not a theory of wages as such).

All these wage theories suffer from several limitations and are generally irrelevant for the determination of wages at enterprise level.[*]

Since 1930s a number of behavioural scientists have tried to examine relationship between work rewards and work motivation by focusing attention on the objectives of the reward system, the content of the reward and the process of rewarding. The reward system, it is indicated, should be evaluated to determine if the objectives are accomplished. The objectives could be several and may include attraction, retention and motivation of people with right knowledge, skills, attitude and experience who could be committed to excellence in every sense of the term.

Several theories of motivation focused on the *content* part, i.e. what it is that initiates, energizes, and sustains individual behaviour.[**] Frederick Herzberg's Two-Factor Theory (see Chapter 10) suggests that rewards affect work behaviour in substantially different ways depending upon whether they are intrinsic rewards (motivators/satisfiers) or extrinsic rewards (hygiene factors dis-satisfiers). Intrinsic rewards are those that are built into or inherent in the job such as recognition, responsibility, accomplishment and autonomy. Employees gain or experience these rewards as they perform their jobs. Extrinsic rewards are external to the job and include such aspects like pay, benefits, working conditions, job security, etc. These are external to or separate from the task.

The intrinsic rewards do not seek to compensate an employee for services/effort or

---

[*] It is not proposed either to describe or evaluate the theories at any length. See A K Das Gupta, 1976. *A Theory of Wage Policy*, Oxford University Press: New Delhi.

[**] This section has drawn from the work of R N Kanungo and Manuel Mendonca, 1987. *Work Rewards and Management of Human Resources, Indian Management*, April, pp 8–19.

output but focus on developing a positive dispensation to one's role and tasks in the organization that contribute to superior performance. The extrinsic rewards, largely form part of a compensation system and some of these have become intrinsic, as entitlements once given, cannot be easily withdrawn. Since all employees may not want enriched jobs, unions may take the position that management should focus on providing extrinsic rewards like good pay, better working conditions and a wide range of benefits.

But the intrinsic-extrinsic theory is flawed on various accounts such as the difficulty in distinguishing between satisfiers and dissatisfiers and what constitute intrinsic and extrinsic rewards. Therefore, it was felt appropriate to focus on the *process* than merely the *content*. The process theories seek to explain how the individual work behaviour is started, energized, directed, sustained and stopped. Of the several process theories, the various forms of *expectancy* theories have analyzed observable work behaviour, identified the elements critical to work motivation and suggested the following four constructs which seem to explain and predict the relationships involved – ability, contingency, valued and equitable rewards and saliency. They note that the motivating power of rewards does not reside in the rewards themselves, but in a process which meets the perceptions and expectations of the employees as well as the needs of the organization. An employee will perform at a given level if he believes that a series of conditions exist and organizations would do well to ensure that these conditions are met (see Table 8.1).

#### Table 8.1   Work Behaviour and Incentives

| Sl No | Conditions | Organizational Incentives |
|-------|------------|---------------------------|
| 1. | The employee must have the skill/ability to perform at desired level (If the employee does not have the skill or ability how can a reward help?) | Ensure this through proper recruitment, placement and training |
| 2. | Rewards should be contingent upon performance, i.e. directly linked to results | Provide performance-based pay/promotion systems |
| 3. | The rewards should be valued and equitable. | Design and administer rewards which are instrumental in satisfying employee need(s). They should be objective, rational and non-arbitrary. |
| 4. | Reward must be salient in the sense that it should be uppermost in the mind of the employee. | Survey employee needs and build the reward system around employee needs. |

## Public Policy and Legal Framework

Most modern societies profess to be welfare states. Laissez faire conditions no longer prevail. The State actively intervenes, sets the tone, directs and sets conditions which govern, among other things, the wage and salary administration policies. The Constitution, employers and unions, legislatures and courts actively influence public policy. The tone and tenor of public policy on wages/salaries in post-independent India have been set out in the Industrial Truce Resolution (1947), Industrial Policy Resolution (1948), the Constitution, successive plan documents, ministerial speeches, etc.

We shall briefly review the key public policy considerations, wage concepts, legal framework and instruments.

*Key Considerations*     The key considerations in Public Policy concerning wages/salaries in India may be identified as following:

(a) To end exploitation and provide remuneration to capital and labour such that "while in the interests of the consumers and the primary producers excessive profits should be prevented by suitable measures of taxation and otherwise, both will share the product of their common effort after making provision for payment of fair wages to labour, a fair return on capital employed in the industry and reasonable reserves for the maintenance and expansion of the undertaking" (Industrial Policy Resolution, 1947)

(b) to fix statutory minimum wages in selected industries and promote fair wage agreements in the more organized industries (Industrial Policy Resolution, 1948)

(c) to ensure equal pay for equal work (Constitution of India)

(d) to provide for wage differentials

(e) to regulate wages and salaries to eliminate/reduce undue disparities

(f) to link remuneration to productivity

(g) to compensate for the rise in cost of living

(h) to determine fair wages over and above minimum wages with due regard to (i) the productivity of labour; (ii) the prevailing level of wages; (iii) the level of national income and distribution; and (iv) the place of industry in the economy of the country

(i) the capacity to pay.  However, the Supreme Court ruled that 'an employer who cannot pay minimum wages has no right to exist.' The capacity to pay becomes a subject of consideration to determine fair wages over and above minimum wages

(j) the basic needs of labour.  (The 15th session of Indian Labour Conference held in 1957 suggested that the minimum wages be need-based)

(k) to secure a living wage for workers (*Article 43*, which is a part of the Directive Principles of State Policy of the Constitution).

*Wage Concepts*     The Committee on Fair Wages (1948) and the 15th session of the Indian Labour Conference (1957) propounded certain wage concepts such as minimum wage, living wage, fair wage and the need-based minimum wage. The Committee on Fair Wages defined the first three (distinct) levels of wages while the need-based minimum wage was defined by the 15th session of the Indian Labour Conference. These definitions are considered here.

*Minimum Wage*   A minimum wage must provide not merely for the bare sustenance of life but for the preservation of the efficiency of the worker by providing some measure of education, medical requirements and amenities.

*Living Wage*   It represents a standard of living which is provided not merely for a bare physical sustenance but decency, protection against ill-health, requirements of essential social needs and some insurance against the more important misfortunes including old age.

*Fair Wage*   While the lower limit of the fair wage must obviously be the minimum wage, the upper limit is equally set by what may broadly be called the capacity of industry to pay.  Between these two limits the actual wage would depend on (i) the productivity of labour, the prevailing rates of wages, (iii) the level of national income and distribution, and (iv) the place of the industry in the economy of the country.

*Need-based Minimum Wage*   The minimum wage should be need-based and "should ensure the minimum human needs of the industrial worker, irrespective of any other consideration."

The basis for calculating the Need-based Minimum Wage is as following:

(i) The standard working-class family should be taken to consist of three consumption units for one earner; the earnings of women, children and adolescents should be disregarded; (ii) minimum food requirements should be calculated on the basis of a net intake of 2,700 calories, as recommended by Dr Aykroyd, for an average Indian adult of moderate activity; (iii) clothing requirements should be estimated at a per capita consumption of 18 yards per annum which would give for the average worker's family of four, a total of 72 yards; (iv) in respect of housing, the norm should be the minimum rent charged by the government in any area for houses provided under the subsidized Industrial Housing Scheme for low-income groups; and, (v) Fuel, lighting and other miscellaneous items of expenditure should constitute 20% of the total minimum wage." The Minimum Wages Act, 1948 did not define the minimum wage. Courts and employers go by the definition given by the Committee on Fair Wages while trade unions would like to consider the need-based minimum wage concept.

The Pay Commissions appointed by the Government of India to consider the question of revision of wages/salaries of Central Government employees did not accept the need-based minimum wage formula because of budgetary implications, unemployment and low wage levels in agriculture, etc. The Third and the Fourth Pay Commissions conceded, directly or otherwise, that except in large organized private and public sector enterprises the actual wage levels fall short of the need-based minimum wage as per the formula recommended by the 15th Indian Labour Conference.

Time and again, the trade unions argued, in vain, for a national wage policy.  The National Labour Commission considered it neither feasible nor desirable, but recommended regional minima.

*(i) Nominal/Money Wage*   The earnings in cash or its equivalence.

*(ii) Real Wage*   Money wages discounted by the cost of living index to denote the purchasing power of the wages.

Since the Second World War the gap between nominal wages and real wage has started declining. Where the rate of neutralization for rise in cost of living is less than 100%, the real wages tend to decline. A steep decline usually leads to industrial unrest, particularly when the affected workers are unionized.

*(iii) National Minimum Wage*   A uniform minimum wage for the country as a whole.

The National Commission on Labour (1969) and the Study  Group on Wages, Incomes and Prices (1978) considered among other things, the question of a national minimum wage. The former found it neither feasible nor desirable while the latter recommended but it was not endorsed by the Government. It is generally reccognized that fixation of minimum wage by the State may be impracticable and also not in the interest of the workers.

From time to time there have been demands for a national wage policy. However, the efforts in this direction did not bear fruits because it usually meant some regulation. And without a check on prices and incomes it was considered infeasible to check wages.

**Legal Framework**    The legal framework for the payment of wages/salaries is governed mainly by four legislations besides the guidelines for managerial remuneration. These are briefly discussed here.

*The Payment of Wages Act, 1936*    The main purpose of the Act is to ensure regular and prompt payment of wages and to prevent the exploitation of wage earner by prohibiting arbitrary fines and deductions from his wages.   It also stipulates the rate of payment for overtime work and penal deductions for participation in illegal strikes (eight days' wages can be deducted for one day's participation in illegal strike). The Act is applicable to all those employed in factories/establishments declared as factories under Section 85 of the Factories Act, 1948, etc. and drawing less than Rs 1,600 per month.

*The Minimum Wages Act, 1948*    This Act requires the appropriate government, Central or State, as the case may be, to fix minimum rates of wages payable to employees in any employment specified in Part I or Part II of the Schedules appended to the Act and any employment subsequently added to either part of the Schedule.

The Act does not define minimum wages. The definition given by the Fair Wages Committee, 1948 is considered for legal interpretation.  The appropriate government notifies the industries/trades covered by the Act, set up a tripartite machinery (including representatives of employers, unions and government) to prescribe rates for different classes/categories/trades/employments/localities/adults, adolescents, children and apprentices. The minimum wages can be fixed by hour, day, month or such other large period.

The Act symbolizes the fulfilment of 1928 ILO convention on the subject.  Courts held that minimum wages be paid irrespective of the employer's capacity to pay.

The real purpose of the Act is to prevent exploitation of labour through the payment of unduly low wages.  However, the minimum wages prescribed do not enable the person to come even up to the poverty level officially determined from time to time.   Even so, the employers grouse that often the wage rates bear little relation to the rule of the market and the law of demand and supply.  There is widespread criticism about several inadequacies in the implementation of the legislation.

**The Payment of Bonus Act, 1965**    The main purpose of the Act is to provide for the payment of bonus to persons employed in certain establishments and for matters connected therewith.  The Act extends to all factories as defined in Section 2(m) of the Factories Act, 1948 and to all other establishments in which 20 or more persons are employed on any day during an accounting year.

The Act provides for a minimum (8 1/3% of pay) and maximum (20% of pay) bonus and for negotiations on bonus. The minimum bonus is payable, subject to certain exemptions specified in the Act, irrespective of profit/loss.

The Act is supposed to reduce industrial conflict on account of bonus but this objective has not generally been achieved in most years since 1965.

*The Equal Remuneration Act, 1976*      The main object of this Act is to provide for the payment of equal remuneration to men and women workers engaged in same or similar work. The Act stipulates stringent punishments for contravention of the provisions of the Act.

*Regulation of Managerial Remuneration*      The regulation of managerial remuneration is a special feature of company law in India.   Section 198 of the Companies Act provides for an overall ceiling of 11% of the net profits as the maximum managerial remuneration that can be paid by a company in any financial year.   Within the ceiling there are sub-ceilings as per Section 309, on remuneration payable to managing director or wholetime director (up to 5% of profits if one, and 10% if more than one managing director and/or wholetime directors).   Ceilings are prescribed for directors etc. under different situations.   Section 637AA inserted by the Companies (Amendment) Act, 1974, further empowered the Central Government to adopt administrative guidelines and ceilings within statutory limits in respect of salary, commission and perquisites.

A comparative statement of these ceilings from 1969 to date is shown in Table 8.2. It is seen that the remuneration (particularly pay and commission) was steeply reduced during 1978–83, and considerably stepped up since 1987.

Several arguments have been made in support of the regulation of managerial remuneration.   Some of these include the following:

(i) The per capita income is low and a large proportion of India's population has remained poor over time;

(ii) high salaries encourage conspicuous consumption which have undesirable socio-economic effects;

(iii) the public policy seeks to reduce income disparities. Several Committees noted that the differences in chief executive's remuneration between Public Sector (including nationalized banks) and Private Sector is 1:3 and between civil servants and private sector chiefs it is 1:4.

(iv)safeguard the interests of consumers and public, including minority shareholders; and,

(v) avoid unfair competition in managerial remuneration to attract talent which may have undesirable impact on the social welfare sectors of the economy.

The 1969 guidelines were challenged before the Gujarat High Court in *Citibank's case*.   The High Court held that the guidelines were illegal and ultra vires the statutory provisions.   The 1978 guidelines, as modified in 1979 were also struck down by the Delhi High Court in case of *M/s Mahindra & Mahindra Co. Ltd v. Union of India*.   On an appeal filed by the government the Supreme Court  granted interim stay and liberty to the Central Government to operate these guidelines only in respect of those companies, which consent to the fixation of remuneration as per these guidelines and to keep in abeyance proposals of those who object to such fixation. The same ruling holds good for 1983 and 1987 guidelines also. Whatever be the rationale and extent of regulation, in actual practice ironically it appears that there is no statutory limit for managerial remuneration. If companies are willing to bear the tax on the disallowed portion of the pay, it is not necessary to have any government approval, unless the executive desires a seat on the board of directors. A change in designation from Director to Vice-President was enough to come out of statutory restraints on remuneration. In the process, however, company boards may be deprived of professionals. The fact that the remuneration of the chief executives in public sector continues to be only a third of that of their counterparts in private sector has implications for flow of talent from one sector to another, though at that level remuneration alone may not be the driving force.

**Table 8.2   Ceilings on Managerial Remuneration**

|  | Prior to 1969 Rs | 1969–78 Rs | 1978–83 Rs | 1983–87 Rs | 1987 Rs |
|---|---|---|---|---|---|
| Salary | 1,80,000 | 90,000 | 60,000 | 90,000 | 1,80,000 |
| Commission |  | 45,000 | 12,000 | 45,000 | 90,000 |
| Perks |  | 30,000 | 60,000 | 88,000 | 1,35,000 |
| Total | 1,80,000 + perks | 1,65,000 | 1,32,000 | 2,23,000 | 4,05,000 |

## Institutions

Who decides the wages to be paid to different categories of employees? Within the framework of public policy, labour market situation and enterprise strategy, practices vary and include the following.

*Employer*   Traditionally the employer unilaterally fixed wages till unions, government, courts and tribunals began to intervene. Even now in newly set-up organizations, for managerial cadres in most private sector organizations and much of the unorganized sector are not effectively covered by minimum wage legislation, the employer unilaterally decides wages/compensation package. But for 'protected' workmen covered by the Industrial Disputes Act, this method of wage determination has become archaic and irrelevant in today's context.

*Legislation*   In industries/regions and occupations which are notified under the Minimum Wages Act, minimum wages are determined as per the procedure prescribed under the law. The Minimum Wages Act provides for tripartite (representatives of government, employees and trade unions) consultation for the purpose. The implementation of Minimum Wages Act is considered to be generally ineffective.

***Collective Bargaining***     Wages are usually determined in business and industrial organizations through bipartite negotiations between representative/recognized union(s) and employer(s) at plant, enterprise, industry or industry-cum-region levels.  Such agreements are usually valid for a period of three to four years.  Industry-cum-region agreements are common in textiles and engineering.  Nationwide industry settlements are common in such core industries like coal, steel, banks and ports and docks.  In public sector the Bureau of Public Enterprises (BPE) issues guidelines specifying the norms and limits of wage settlements.  Collective bargaining survives in India despite the lack of conducive legal framework, the difficulties in identifying the representative/recognized union and the conferment of industrial relations rights on minority unions.

***Third Party (including judiciary)***     Industrial Disputes Act, 1947, provides for settlement of all labour disputes, including wage disputes, through conciliation, arbitration and adjudication.  Labour courts, industrial tribunals and higher judicial bodies also decide wages after hearing both the parties and their decisions are binding on the parties.  Adjudication has been one of the more common methods of wage settlement compared to conciliation and arbitration.

***Wage Boards***     Government of India sets up Wage Boards on industry wise basis to decide pay and benefits.  Over 20 wage boards were set up during 1957–66.  Thereafter, the wage boards were set up once for ports and docks and more than once for sugar, working journalists and non-working journalists.  The wage boards adopt time-consuming procedures and their awards are usually contested by parties.  Generally wage boards are not popular either with the unions or the employer.

***Pay Commissions***     The government employees, also known as public employees include civil servants (the white-collar employees who run the bureaucracy), quasi-industrial employees (railways, post and telegraph, civil defence, civil aviation and the like), and industrial employees in factories and workshops operating in the public sector like the locomotives, aircraft, fertilizers, etc.  The pay and benefits of these government employees decided by Pay Commissions appointed by the appropriate (central or state, as the case may be) government.  So far the Central Government has appointed four Pay Commissions.

The disputes arising out of Pay Commission awards and their implementation are decided by commissions of inquiry, adjudication by tribunals and The Joint Consultative Machinery (JCM).

## Company Compensation Policy

Compensation policies need to be established in every enterprise taking the following aspects into consideration, besides due regard to the provisions of public policy, job evaluation and collective bargaining.

***Attraction and Retention***     Usually an enterprise endeavours to recruit and retain the best people available. One of the ways of attracting and retaining the best and the brightest is to pay more than what they would get anywhere else for similar skills and levels. Some firms endeavour to be *wage leaders*. This deliberate corporate strategy may create a situation of *wage islands* which pose problems from societal point of view.

Unlimited wage disparities cause distortions in the economy. Still, enterprises with prime concern for micro consideration may adopt this strategy subject to governmental restraints on account of national wage/income policies. Multinationals operating in developing countries usually pay much higher than the indigenous firms in both private and public sectors.

**Internal Consistency**     Compensation policies should take into account the differentials in skills and levels in respect of both responsibility and authority. A sense of proportion needs to be maintained to achieve internal consistency so that wage/salary levels conform to the differences in hierarchy and skills. Ill-conceived differentials may lead to conflict among work groups. In a fabrication unit, after wage revision the welders were getting less than gardners. The technical staff in the organization resented this by raising slogans and protests: Should grass-cutters (gardeners) get more than gas-cutters (welders)? At the macro level similar questions (e.g., should a peon in a rural bank get more than a school teacher in the same village?) arise due to occupational values in the society and skill endowment at a given stage of economic development. But at the micro level, internally within the firm, such questions need careful examination each time decisions are taken to review salary scales.

**External Consistency**     The simplest and most widely used criterion is to consider what is generally known as the *going rate* in the labour market for comparable jobs in the industry/region. While deciding wage rates in public sector, comparison may be made of wage rates in private sector for comparable jobs. It is possible that public sector units may fix relatively lower wage rates than private sector units because the former affords a greater sense of job security. But if the differentials are significant enough, public sector may find it difficult to attract the right talent. For key jobs if the rates are not uniform, inter- and intra-sectorally and among industry groups, there may be imbalances in the distribution of skills and talents.

**Ability to Pay**     As already mentioned, wherever minimum wage legislation is applicable, enterprises should pay minimum wages irrespective of their capacity to pay. Over and above the minimum wages, enterprises pay more depending upon their ability to pay. Also, enterprises vulnerable to union pressures may end up paying more than this due to the coercive bargaining power of the unions. It is not uncommon to see enterprises paying much less than what they can pay just because the employees are not organized.

**Pay and Performance**     Linking pay to performance is sound and makes good sense. However in the organized sector in India, the compensation policies have, unfortunately, a remote relationship, if ever, between pay and performance. Analysis of the components of total wage/salary reveals that over the years a substantial part of the rise in the pay is intended to meet the rise in the cost of living. While basic wage/salary and even bonus is not usually related to performance, many enterprises have a wide range of production incentive systems.

The main problem in linking pay with performance is the absence of criteria and tools to measure performance objectively and the inability to evolve mutually satisfactory norms of sharing the fruits of performance between labour and capital.

*Labour Costs and Productivity*    Wages and salaries can be linked to the productivity and profitability of an enterprise. Growing and profit-earning enterprises find it easier to pay more than stagnant and loss-incurring enterprises though it is the latter category which would be most hard pressed to attract and retain skills. Again wage costs as a percentage to total costs would be higher in labour intensive firms than capital intensive firms and in assembly-type units than in process units. For instance, in India, the labour cost as a percentage of total cost could be around 60 in coal mining against barely two or three per cent in petro-chemicals or fertilizers. In most manufacturing firms it does not exceed 15–16%. Capital intensive process units can thus afford to pay substantially more than labour-intensive units because the impact of higher wages and salaries on output costs is not so acute as in labour intensive units. Also in recent years, productivity bargaining is gaining ground in India too. For example, the ITC increased the pay scales of unionized employees substantially through wage agreement whereby the union agreed to cooperate with the management in maintaining the share of labour cost in the ex-factory cost per cigarette at the same level over a five-year period. Many firms have entered into wage agreements which entailed a trade off between more jobs versus more wages. For example Premier Automobiles Ltd could accomplish a major productivity bargaining agreement. Several other chemical and engineering firms had, in recent years, entered into similar agreements. However, such agreements raise questions about their effects on the level of employment in the economy, particularly in the context of widespread unemployment and on the firm in the event of a recession. The counter argument is, "What is the point in keeping wages low, if you cannot keep the labour costs too low?" Quite often firms in India find labour cheap, but not the cost of labour.

*Cost of Living*    Dearness Allowance (DA) and City Compensatory Allowance (CCA) now form integral part of most wage structures. The general principle underlying these allowances is to neutralize at least a portion of the increase in the cost of living. Where these allowances do not form part of the wage structure, ad hoc and lumpsum, increases in pay are unilaterally announced by managements to partially provide for such neutralization. It may be observed in certain private sector organizations which follow both the systems, the ad hoc pay increases are (usually for staff and managerial employees) at least equal to the increase in DA sanctioned to those governed by the DA scheme (usually workmen) since the time ad hoc pay increase was sanctioned last till the current ad hoc pay increase. Wage and salary increase related to increase in cost of living usually poses additional burden on the employer without corresponding improvement in productivity. The additional financial burden is met by adjusting the prices, if the market can bear and if public policy allows. Otherwise the pressure is on firms to cut costs elsewhere or seek productivity improvements to absorb the increase in wage costs.

**Merit and Seniority Progression**     Merit progression refers to the practice of rewarding a person according to his/her contribution. Merit progression is usually based on annual performance appraisal. When the person's performance is outstanding or distinctively above average, the organization may like to reward him with extra (over and above the normal) increment(s). There are, of course, other less used ways of rewarding merit/superior performance. These include, production-incentive and profit-sharing schemes, bonus, promotions, job enlargement and job enrichment.

Usually most pay-scales provide for step increases over a time scale. Annual increments in basic pay accrue to the employee as he accumulates experience till he reaches the end of the pay-scale. Some organizations provide for time bound promotions and stagnation allowances too. Time-bound promotions refer to the practice of promotion to the next grade after the person completes service in the present grade for a specified number of years. Stagnation allowance refers to the practice of sanctioning extra increments or lumpsum amount after the person reaches the end of the pay-scale.

As a result of the above practices, the senior employees get more pay (higher basic and consequential increases in other benefits like DA, Provident Fund, etc. which are usually expressed as a fraction or percentage of basic pay) than their juniors even though both would be doing same or similar work. The logic for seniority progression is that as a person accumulates experience, his skills get sharpened and productive efficiency goes up. This may, in jobs requiring manual skill and dexterity continue to happen only up to a point and thereafter, because of age and other considerations, the productive efficiency may decline. In jobs requiring mental skills (teaching, for instance), there may not be any similiarly evident saturation or declining point unless the person becomes senile.

**Motivation**     "Money may not be everything but everything else may be way behind!" Company compensation policy can be an effective tool to motivate people for superior performance. There is a lot of debate on whether after a point money ceases to be a motivating factor, due to several reasons such as individual preferences, consequential trade offs (in terms of family and social obligations, etc), taxation policies, etc. A wide variety of non-monetary incentives have, therefore, been devised to compensate, reward, sustain and improve superior performance.

**Integrity**     James Burnham predicted in his famous book, *Managerial Revolution*, which he wrote half-a-century ago, that the future belongs to professional managers who would be the *rulers*. Berle and Means pointed out the divorce between ownership and control, in their well-acclaimed book, *The Rise of the Modern Corporation*. Now, professional managers have access to and control over resources. They do not, of course, usually  own them. As we have seen in Chapter 4, integrity has been identified as one of the most important attributes in selection criteria for managerial employees who wield control over corporate resources. Having given them the power, there are many like the veteran civil servant L K Jha, who argue that it is important to compensate them adequately enough to keep them out of temptation. L K Jha once asked "whether we can afford not to pay more for civil servants who wield such enormous power?" The question is indeed ticklish. To paraphrase Mahatma Gandhi, companies can give enough to meet a person's needs and to let him lead a life befitting the position he occupies, but no company can give a person enough to meet his greed.

## Job Evaluation

Job evaluation is a systematic method of appraising the value/worth of one job in relation to other jobs in an organization. The objectives of job evaluation include the following:

- To determine wage rates for the job irrespective of the attributes of the employee
- To determine and recognize the need to link pay with the requirements of the job
- To provide an acceptable basis for wage differentials taking into account the requirements of knowledge, skills, experience, effort, hazards, responsibilities, etc. required in each job
- To establish a systematic wage structure at organizational level which will be agreeable to the organization and the individual employees

In addition to the above mentioned objectives, the reasons why organizations resort to job evaluation include the following:

- It is a rational, defensible and systematic approach to determine the relative worth of jobs
- To meet employees demand for a rational grade structure
- To replace old systems with new ones based on current objectives, values and job requirements on the eve of negotiating new wage settlements
- To provide a means of employee/union participation in wage determination because usually job evaluation is undertaken by the management as a joint exercise with the union.

Traditionally, labour courts and tribunals have, in the past, recommended different wage rates for different skill/experience/responsibility levels. Over the last five years, however, several techniques have been developed to evolve systematic (not scientific), rational and defensible wage structure through job evaluation as an adjunct to collective bargaining. The recognized union, where it exists, is usually involved in the process. Clarity about the coverage of employees in terms of categories and levels also is an essential preparatory step for job evaluation. Job evaluation can be done internally by the organization's own staff or by an external consultant or through joint experience. Involving external consultant is usually recommended to impart a measure of expertise and objectivity to the exercise. The process of job evaluation entails the following steps:

- Job analysis, job description and job specification for all jobs to be covered in job evaluation;
- Arranging them in a sequence in terms of their value to the organization after

careful scrutiny and comparison;
- Plotting the sequence of jobs on a money scale.

**Methods of Job Evaluation**　Some common methods of job evaluation are briefly reviewed here:

*Ranking*　Jobs are relatively ranked according to their perceived difficulty and value to the organization. They are then classified into different groups based on a gradation of skill intensity, difficulty in effort and responsibility, length of experience, etc. A grade and a wage level is allocated to each group of jobs.

Though this is a simple form of job evaluation it can be used mainly in smaller organizations with clearly defined jobs. In large, complex organizations it is difficult to objectively rank the jobs indicating the degree of difference between each grade.

*Classification and Categorization*　Job categories are determined through certain criteria or rule of thumb and the job Classification and Categorization Committee slots each job in an appropriate category after comparing the job descriptions of each job with those of category descriptions. Different categories are graded on wage scale representing perceived value, worth or importance to the organization. This method, like the ranking method, is simple and treats the whole job. But under classification and categorization method, categories or grades are determined first which become the means to measure the worth of each job. Central Pay Commissions follow this approach, and over the years, successive pay commissions have tried to bring down the number of job categories/grades. The Fourth Central Pay Commission (1986) reduced the number of pay-scales for 52 lakh Central Government employees from 156 to 36. There were complaints about anomalies in categorization of different jobs into certain pay-scales. In coal, ports and docks and several other large undertakings the problems of categorization persisted for decades and still remain to be solved because of the large size and complexity of jobs and operations.

*Rating*　This requires a more detailed examination of the jobs than is done under ranking or classification. First the job requirements in terms of qualifications, experience, training, mental and physical effort, nature and degree of responsibility to men, materials, machines, output, special hazards, monotony, boredom, etc., have to be identified. Each aspect needs to be specified. For example, what type of qualifications? What type of skill? The actual number of factors to be considered depends on the organizational conditions and preferences and may vary from four or five to over 20!

Each factor should be assigned some points in a given range. Then each job is analyzed and points allocated within the given range depending upon the degree of importance, intensity (of skill ?), difficulty (of jobs ?), length (of experience ?), etc. The points are added to denote the value of the job which then is translated into monetary terms by a predetermined conversion formula.

This is more cumbersome and time-consuming than ranking and classification methods. But it attempts to provide logic, rationale and an analytical base to defend the system. However, one can still argue that each of the steps in this exercise – factors, points and weightages – is characterized by subjective *opinion-based* judgement.

*Factor Comparison*　This is an analytical method using certain limited number of factors (e.g. mental effort, skill, physical effort, responsibility and working conditions) and assigns money value to the jobs following a four step process:

(a) Select key jobs (say 15 or more), representative of wage/salary levels across the organization.

(b) Analyse jobs to determine the proportionate share in wage/salary for each factor.

(c) Establish a scale for each factor, and compare factor by factor, each job with all other jobs and rank the jobs.

(d) Calculate the money value for each factor and determine the wage rates for all jobs under consideration.

Since the evaluation is in money terms, it may lead to some bias. This method is normally applied to manual jobs. It is here mostly, that the unions object to the job evaluation exercise determining the wage rates than through collective bargaining.

*Other Methods* Some academics and international consulting organizations have developed modern methods of job evaluation. Among them mention may be made of the *Hay System of Guide Chart Profiles* which some multinationals and large private sector corporations in India seem to adopt or consider adopting. The Hay System uses three compensable factors with sub-components (Table 8.3) defined on a guide chart and a point scale.

**Table 8.3   The Compensable (sub) Components Under the Hay System**

| Know-how | Problem solving | Accountability |
|---|---|---|
| Skill, education and training | Thinking environment (constraints, if any) | Freedom to act |
| Managerial know-how | Thinking challenge (routine or creative) | Scope or magnitude of accountability |
| Human relations skills (Basic, important, critical) | | |

The jobs are evaluated on the basis of factors as in a point rating approach. Each sub-factor has a number of degree levels with point scores. Weightages are assigned to these based on their relative importance to the organization. Ranking or profiling is done to obtain the rank order of jobs. The scores for jobs are plotted against a salary structure developed from a salary of comparable jobs/firms.

The chief merit of the Hay System is that it combines job evaluation with a market survey of salaries to reflect current labour market situation and enable organizations to determine salary levels realistically in a competitive world. However, such linkage may lead to wage-grade drift and anomalies. Therefore, there is need for a constant review, audit and monitoring of grade relativities such that proactive actions can be initiated to prevent possible upsets.

It is seen from the foregoing account of different methods of job evaluation that each method has its pros and cons and is appropriate for a particular purpose/organization. The simple non-analytical methods like ranking and classification will mostly serve the purpose of small organizations with mostly fewer (50 or so) job levels.   The analytical methods like point-rating factor-comparison methods seem to provide rational, defensible base is to deal with the needs of relatively large and complex organizations.   The Hay System is a modern system of job evaluation which reckons the labour market factors also.

***Prerequisites for Effective Job Evaluation***    (i) Well defined system of job and organization design. Job analysis, job description, and job specification provide the basis.

(ii) Participation of recognized union, where it exists is imperative.

(iii) The system should be simple and easy to understand rather than being too technical and complex.

(iv) The industrial engineers should work jointly with the union and management. The wage agreement in the textile units in Coimbatore in the late 1980s provides an excellent example of unions using industrial engineers to defend their demands for wage revision.

(v) The job evaluation to be undertaken as an adjunct to (but not to prevent) collective bargaining.

(vi) Labour market survey to ascertain prevailing wage  rates/salary levels and should preferably be undertaken prior to the commencement of job evaluation.

(vii)Job evaluation exercise should not be viewed as an excuse to cut wages or retrench employees.  It should not adversely affect the terms and conditions of existing employees.

(viii) There could be a system of steering, implementation and evaluation committees with due representation to recognized unions.

(ix) Employees and union should be aware about the objectives and implications of job evaluation.   There should be proper communication in this regard with an effort to seek the active involvement of the employees.

(x) It is appropriate to use outside consultants to provide a measure of objectivity and to bring to bear expertise to the exercise. Organizations like National Productivity Council, Administrative Staff College of India and Defence Work Study Unit have developed vast expertise and experience in job evaluation.

The management's lack of clarity about the nature of the pressures influencing pay policies, and rapid changes in technology, labour and product markets, union structures, etc. create immense problems and difficulties for  job evaluation. Organizations also need to have some policy about the desired levels/degree of internal and external consistency.  Job evaluation should not be taken up as a cost-saving measure or as a means to accept union demands on pay.

# Pay Surveys

One of the major issues in the area of labour market relates to the question of wages. Notwithstanding the ideals enshrined in the Constitution and the statements made in the successive plan documents, distortions in wages have been a major cause for concern resulting in inequalities and exploitation in the labour market.   The absence of a proper data base comprising a long-term series on the trends of money and real wages with provision for timely and accurate analysis of wage share in national income, inter- and intra-sectoral/regional/industry wage differentials, impact of inflation, technological change and productivity on wages and earnings may have contributed to the failure of public policy in this respect accentuating the distortions over the years. Even at firm level, much of the ad hocism could be traced to the absence of a sound data base. In most industrialized countries the world over, labour market surveys of different sorts provide the basis for rational and realistic decisions on pay and benefits.

It is not as though we in India lack in efforts to gather information and data. As we shall note here, there is indeed often a duplication of effort, albeit piecemeal:

(i) The labour bureau and various other government organizations meticulously compile data on the implementation of various legislations such as Minimum Wages Act, Payment of Wages Act etc. and bring out periodical reports. Additionally, information on wages is covered in the course of monitoring implementation of various other legislations. The Reports on Annual Survey of Industries, the various occupational surveys and the data furnished by the National Sample Survey Organization and the Central Statistical Organization also seek to provide information on this subject. Surveys on labour conditions and on special groups of labour such as contract, bonded, women, child and unorganized labour also shed light on this aspect.

(ii) From time to time pay commissions are set up to review the pay in public sector in the Centre and in the States and wage boards are constituted for certain industries. Usually the pay commissions and wage boards take a minimum of 3–4 years time to come out with recommendations which more often than not, are subject to government intervention and intense negotiations by affected groups. Invariably these commissions and wage boards seek to collect once again and all over a plethora of past and current information and data. They even appoint committees and consultants to prepare studies and to provide analytical information and inputs. They send out questionnaires and hold public sessions at different places across the country depending on the scope of enquiry.

(iii) At the industry and firm level almost without exception each time a collective agreement is negotiated, both the union and the management send out their representatives to collect comparable information and data on wages, fringe benefits, etc. and spend a lot of resources and effort in putting together the bits and pieces of information and in trying to identify the discrepancies in the presentations by other parties, to serve their partisan ends. Frequently, they appoint committees and commissions to conduct wage surveys for themselves, but unfortunately such surveys fail to give correct information. Competitive considerations persuade them especially employers, to keep their information secret even as they expect others to share similar information openly. With the result such surveys particularly when they relate to the remuneration of managerial cadres often prove to be disfunctional.

(iv) Of late, the Union Research Group in Bombay has started collecting information across firms in and around Bombay and to disseminate information to unions. For the employers, organizations like the Bombay Chamber of Commerce and the Confederation of Engineering Industries began to carry out wage surveys of member firms once in a while. Local chapters of some professional bodies like National Institute of Personnel Management also conduct surveys of member firms on collective agreements, fringe benefits, etc. Multinational companies for their part, have formed a multinational remuneration club to privately exchange information on remuneration packages for their employees at regular intervals.

(v) In central public sector the Bureau of Public Enterprises supposedly monitors wage trends and issues guidelines periodically.  It is common knowledge that a number of public enterprises flout these norms overtly or covertly and unions have challenged some of these in the Supreme Court which led to the setting up of a High Power Pay Committee for Public Sector (Chairman: R B Mishra) in 1986. The Committee submitted its report in November 1988 while some unions have again moved the court (in April 1989). The latter finally persuaded the government to implement the recommendations of the Committee set up under its directives.

(vi) In individual firms, innumerable problems and vexatious delays surface in translating the wage agreements signed to action for individual employees by way of correct fitment, determination of new pay-scales, calculation of arrears, etc. The slow and inept official communication network breeds grapevine and often results in industrial strife and litigation before the issues, many of which could normally be redundant are settled somehow or other!

The effect of the exercises such as those mentioned above had been to create a data base which is weak and incomplete in many respects.  It suffers additionally from problems for a variety of reasons such as :

(i) Data being selective and serving partisan purposes

(ii) the data being often considered in isolation without regard to parameters relating to individual firms, industry or labour market characteristics

(iii) incomparability over a time

(iv) time lag

(v) conflict over secrecy v. transparency

(vi) non/poor response from target groups

(vii) difficulties in standardization and disaggregation

(viii) doubts and distrust among constituents over the data/information.

## PAY STRUCTURES

As noted earlier, job evaluation provides a systematic basis for determining pay levels. Jobs are usually classified into different groups to reflect broadly the occupational groupings such as the following.

- Managerial and professional: Top, middle and junior
- Technical/supervisory
- Administrative and clerical (staff)
- Manual (workers): Highly skilled, skilled, semi-skilled and unskilled

Company characteristics, labour market situation, wage settlements, opportunities for advancement and motivational strategies influence the design aspects of pay structures in terms of number of grades and the length/range of scale of pay in each grade.

Too few grades limit opportunities for progression. Too many grades cause apprehensions about equity and fairness. Each grade will have a minimum and maximum. Yet, jobs placed in a particular grade carry the same value though the actual pay varies with length of experience and/or performance.

Currently most industrial organizations have 3 – 9 grades each in workers, staff, supervisory and managerial cadres below board level.

The *differentials* in monetary terms between different grades are significant where the number of grades in a particular occupational grouping is smaller and negligible where the number of grades is large. *Overlap* occurs between the grades when the number of grades or the length of pay range is large. The overlap in the pay range also covers the trainees in a grade. The assumption is that the contribution from the trainees in the next grade may be worth less than those at the end of the lower grade and doing a good job. The number of ranges within the structure occupational group depends on the span or the difference between minimum and maximum pay for a job. It is desirable to maintain differential between the mid-points of each salary grade to provide reasonable scope to ensure that the reward for the job is commensurate with the higher responsibilities in the next grade. However, the gap between adjacent grades should not be too wide as to reduce the flexibility if job grades need review.

While designing pay structures, it is useful to conduct job evaluation and ascertain market rates for different jobs through a survey. The pay structure providing number of grades, span/length and upper and lower limits in each grade, differentials, and the overlap between grades depend on company policies, competitor's practices and pressures from unions, etc.

## Components of a Pay Structure

The most comprehensive definition of wage is found in the *Industrial Disputes Act, 1947,* which is as follows:

*Wages* means all remuneration capable of being expressed in terms of money, which would, if the terms of employment expressed or implied, were fulfilled, be payable to a workman in respect of his employment, or of work done in such employment and includes the following.

(i) Such allowances (including dearness allowance) as the workman is for the time being entitled to;

(ii) the value of any house accommodation, or of supply of light, water, medical attendance or other amenities or of any service or of any concessional supply of foodgrains or other articles;

(iii) any travelling concessions;

(iv) any commission payable on the promotion of sales or business or both.

But wages does not include the following.

(i) any bonus;

(ii) any contribution paid or payable by the employer to any pension fund or provident fund or for the benefit of the workman under any law for the time being in force;

(iii) any gratuity payable on the termination of his service.

Under that definition, a wage means all remuneration (express or implied) capable of being expressed in terms of money including all allowances, perquisites, concessions and commissions. In other words, the wage is a remuneration earned by the workman for rendering service or giving his labour and should approximate as near as possible to the living wage in the prevailing socio-economic scene.

Usually, the wage structure in Indian Industry is divided into three components: the *basic wage*; the variable *dearness allowance*; and, the *other allowances and incentives*.

***Basic Wage***    The basic wage provides a stable base to the wage structure.  It is built upon the wage concepts recommended by the Fair Wages Committee (1948) and the 15th Indian Labour Conference (1957) to which references were made earlier.  The pattern was set by tribunals and courts in the post-second World War period.  It now varies and progresses according to periodic job evaluations, wage settlements, awards by tribunals, wage boards, pay commissions, etc.

The basic wage is fixed as price for labour/services rendered. Differentials in basic wages are normally based on a set of criteria which the Fair Wages Committee suggested may take into account. The following is a set of such criteria:

- The degree of skill
- the strain of work
- the experience involved
- the training required
- the responsibilities undertaken
- the mental and physical requirements
- the disagreeableness of the task
- the hazard attendant on the work, and
- the fatigue involved.

***Dearness Allowance (DA)***    The Study Group on wage policy set up by the National Commission on Labour, observed that, "The words *Dearness Allowance* primarily suggest and refer to allowance paid to employees in order to enable them to face the increasing dearness of essential commodities."  The system of DA for employees began during the  Second World War when the government sanctioned a scheme of grain allowance to their lowest paid employees.  Gradually many other classes of employees in organized and partly the unorganized sector began to receive DA as a means to protect, to some extent, the real income of wage earners and salaried employees from the effects of price rise.  Instead of increasing wages as is done elsewhere DA is paid to neutralize the rise in prices.  The expectation was that in time, if prices go back to the earlier level, the DA can be reduced or withdrawn.  But this normally did not happen, and prices generally showed a tendency to continue to rise.  In other countries where similar practice exists, it is referred to as a practice of inflation adjusted earnings or COLA (Cost Of Living Allowance).  Even in India, Section 3 of the Minimum Wages Act refers to it as Cost of Living Allowance.  This forms a *variable* component of the wage packet since the rate of the allowance increases more than once every year whereas the basic pay-scale or wage rate is revised after relatively longer spells of time, synchronizing with fresh wage settlement, pay commission award, etc.

The existing schemes for the determination and sanction of DA usually have three parameters, i.e. the index factor, the time factor and the points factor.  The first parameter i.e. index is usually the All India Consumer Price Index (AICPI) Number for industrial workers (Base 1960 = 100 AICPI). This is compiled and published by the Labour Bureau, Shimla. Since 1977, two committees – one headed by Nilakanth Rath and the other by Seal – have gone into the matter. The findings of both the committees have been hotly debated and disputed by the federations of workers' unions and employers' organizations and this itself has now become a bone of contention in the industrial relations scene in the country. Quite a few organizations use local/regional indices published in the *Indian Labour Journal*, a monthly magazine of the Labour Bureau, Shimla.

The second parameter is the manner in which the variation in the index selected is used. The scheme of DA should be related directly to the rise in the index selected. The allowance may go up with the revision in the index based on the average for a selected period to offset the temporary fluctuations in the index. Thus the time factor also plays a role in determining the allowance and many schemes related to averages ranging from a quarter to a 12-monthly moving average.

The third parameter is related to the points factor. A dose of DA is related to certain prescribed increase in the number of the index points.

There are different patterns of calculating DA, using the above parameters. We shall consider here four major patterns.

*The Central DA (CDA)* Applicable to employees of the Central Government, the index used is the AICPI. The Fourth Central Pay Commission recommended, since 1 January 1986, a pattern whereby DA is sanctioned half-yearly on January 1 and July 1 every year, with reference to the percentage increase above the 12-monthly index average over 608 in whole number with fractions carried forward. Earlier, under the Third Central Pay Commission award in vogue till 31 December 1985, DA was linked to every increase of 8 points in the 12-monthly moving average of the index. Under the Fourth Pay Commission's scheme of DA 100% neutralization is provided for employees drawing basic pay up to Rs 3500, 75% to those in the pay range of Rs 3,500 – 6,000, and 65% to those drawing pay above Rs 6,000 subject to marginal adjustments – some public sector corporations also use this pattern. When the government was reluctant to continue the central DA pattern to the public sector employees who were governed by it, a Committee (High-Powered Pay Committee headed by Justice R B Misra) was appointed which ruled that DA is an entitlement which can not be unilaterally changed. The Supreme Court virtually endorsed this recommendation and employees in about 70 out of nearly 220 central public sector undertakings continue to get central DA. Future appointees in these corporations, however, will be getting only IDA.

*The Industrial DA(IDA)* This is vogue in over two-thirds of central public sector undertakings and a large number of private sector organizations. The Index used is the AICPI. DA is sanctioned at a flat rate, irrespective of pay range, once every quarter. From 1 April 1984 till the end of 1986, DA was being sanctioned at the rate of Rs 1.65 per every point (subsequently raised to Rs 1.90 per every point with effect from 1 January 1987 and a tripartite committee is currently (June 1990) reviewing the subject afresh). The amount of Rs 1.65 was arrived at after hectic bargaining and tripartite consultations at the national level, on the basis of the minimum pay and DA. In Bharat Heavy Electricals Limited (BHEL), a public sector undertaking which was taken to illustrate and work out the rate of neutralization, the minimum pay was Rs 810.50 and the AICPI was 492 on 1 April 1984 (810.50 divided by 492 = Rs 1.65). The IDA supposedly neutralizes fully the price rise in the case of unionized staff drawing pay up to Rs 810. Above that level neutralization gradually tapers off down to about 20% at the senior level.

*DA System in Banks and LIC*   The index used is AICPI. DA is sanctioned every quarter. The rate of neutralization is different from CDA and IDA and varies depending upon basic pay range. This provides for a higher neutralization at senior levels than is possible under IDA.

*Double Linkage*   In certain industries, particularly in chemical and pharmaceutical industries in the Bombay region, DA is paid on the basis of double linkage. Under this system, DA is paid at:

- 100% for the first slab of basic pay of Rs 100
- additional 50% for the next Rs 100. 25% more for every slab of the next Rs 100 or part thereof, and
- a person with a basic pay Rs 400 will get Rs 800 as DA (200%) and the one with a basic pay of Rs 600 will get Rs 1500 (250%) as DA.

Over the years, there have been a variety of rulings on the question of DA. DA is meant to neutralize for rise in cost of living. It is an entitlement for the worker and can not be reduced except in cases of a decline in prices. There shall be no discrimination in DA formula for people drawing similar wages within an organization. The question of ceiling on DA also came up for review many a time. Trade unions have considered freeze or reduction as a temporary measure in cases where a firm faced genuine financial/market crisis subject to the proviso that the earnings foregone may be made good after the organization begins to earn profits. The price increases have assumed menacing proportions. This is increasing inter-sectoral wage disparities. Even the differences in the quantum of DA for a given basic pay have been becoming glaring enough to raise demands for, say, a shift from IDA to CDA. The direct linkage between pay-scales and DA is also not to be missed.

**Allowances**   The successive wage settlements/awards have produced a heterogeneous group of allowances, which have come to form an integral part of the wage structure.

Table 8.4   Illustrative List of Allowances in Organized Employment In India

| | |
|---|---|
| Acting | Heat |
| Attendance | Leave travel |
| Acid and gas | Lunch |
| Books | Medical |
| Car | Night duty |
| Cash | Overtime |
| City compensatory | Paternity |
| Computer | Pension |
| Conveyance/Transport | Provident fund |
| Deputation | Relocation |

| | |
|---|---|
| Driver | Servant |
| Dust | Shift |
| Education | Special |
| ESIS | Strain |
| Family | Tiffin |
| Graduate | Telephone |
| Group insurance | Uniform |

The list of allowances shown in Table 8.4 is illustrative, but not exhaustive. The Fourth Central Pay Commission (1986) and the High Powered Pay Commission (1988) have recommended rationalization of allowances. However, with the passage of time, the new technologies, new materials and new environment have shown a tendency to add more allowances to the list than to rationalize the existing ones.

## METHODS OF PAYMENT

There is a distinct and clear attempt in the remuneration system which seeks to compensate an employee for different types of contribution. Different methods of payment exist. Table 8.5 shows the relationship between contribution and method of remuneration. For most kinds of contributions, be it normal or extra, the methods could be more than one. For example, the normal method of remuneration for contribution measured in terms of time could be an hourly, daily, weekly or monthly rate. Similarly the incentives paid for extra contributions can be calculated in several ways. Some of them are discussed in the following section.

**Table 8.5    Contribution–Remuneration Linkage**

| Kind of Contribution | Method of Payment | |
|---|---|---|
| | For Normal Contribution | For Extra Contribution |
| 1. Time | Basic wage + fixed allowance | Overtime wages |
| 2. Skill | Basic wage based on job evaluation + allowance | Higher basic wage + allowance through promotion |
| 3. Effort | Basic wage based on job evaluation + allowances | Incentive bonus and merit increments |
| 4. Ideas | Suggestion rewards | – |
| 5. Responsibility | Basic wage based on job evaluation + allowances | Higher basic wage + allowances through promotion |
| 6. Working condition | Basic wage based on job evaluation + allowances | Higher basic wage + allowances |
| 7. Cooperation | Continued payment of basic wage + allowances | Incentive bonus |
| 8. Continued service | Time scale increment in basic wage | Promotion and fringe benefits |

Source: National Commission on Labour, 1968. *Report of the Study Group on Productivity and Incentives*, New Delhi, p 40.

## Wage Incentive Schemes/Payment-by-Results (PBR)

Wage is "a fair day's remuneration for a fair day's work," i.e.,standard performance. A wage incentive scheme is described as "a method of payment for work of an acceptable quality produced over and above a specified quantity or standard". Payment-by-Results (PBR) refers to a method which provides for the "direct linking of workers' earnings to a measure of their performance".

Where pay is contingent upon performance, employees usually give their best under incentive conditions rather than under non-incentive conditions. The incentives can be financial or non-financial. Both types of incentives have appropriate role under certain conditions. Where wage levels are low, financial incentives are considered to be more valued. Where wage levels are higher and tax rates progressively increase, employees may prefer non-financial incentives. A cursory review of wage settlements may point to a shift in emphasis in the demands of employees and their unions from financial benefits to non-financial benefits.

PBR systems (wage incentive being one) can be distinguished on the basis of unit of accountability for performance and classified into three categories: (i) individual performance, (ii) group performance, and (iii) plant or enterprise as a whole. These three categories of PBR are briefly outlined here.

*Individual Payment-by-Result Schemes*    Several individual PBR systems are in vogue. Some of the well-known plans are piece rate system, premium bonus system (standard hour/measured work day plans) or work improvement systems. Emerson, Halsey and Taylor (differential piece-rate plan) have contributed significantly to evolve individual PBR systems.

*Piece-rate Systems*    These were the forerunners of modern incentive systems under this category. The unit of measurement can be number, weight or volume of the items produced – reward is based on an agreed rate per unit of output.

Another method of individual PBR considers time as the unit of analysis. Earnings/incentives depend on the difference between the time taken and time allowed to complete a certain job. Such schemes are called as *premium bonus* or *bonus schemes.*

Output (whether measured in terms of number/weight/volume or time allowed) is usually influenced by more than one factor. Also quality, costs, timeliness of completion of job, etc. do count. Therefore, performance must be measured in a holistic sense, taking into account the multiple factors. In response to this, work improvement schemes based on the principles of work study and methods study came into vogue and individuals are rewarded for their contribution to suggested changes, savings in costs, etc. Also, over the years, organizations began to realize the need to measure performance over an extended period of time rather (e.g. week, fortnight, month or longer) than by hour or day and then to award incentive bonus. The purpose is to sustain higher levels of productivity over a period of time and maintain a measure of stability of employee earnings. But if the duration between duration performance and reward is unduly lengthened, it may dampen motivation. Therefore, individual PBR system should provide for incentive earnings at least on a monthly basis.

The schemes may vary in the way in which earnings vary with changes in performance. The earnings may vary (i) in the same proportion as performance; (ii) proportionately less than performance; (iii) proportionately more than performance; or, (iv) in proportions that vary with levels of performance. The first of the above mentioned four schemes is called the *straight-proportional* incentive scheme while the rest are *differential* or *geared* incentive schemes. The gearing is regressive, progressive or constant. The gearing is regressive where the rate of change in earnings falls gradually with increase in performance and *progressive* when the rate of change of earnings gradually increases with increase in performance. It is constant but not identical when the scheme provides for one or more abrupt changes, providing for an increase on reaching a specified level of performance. Each type of variations in the scheme has to be purposive. For instance, the purpose of a regressive scheme is to discourage output beyond certain level, for it may then affect quality, material costs, energy use, etc.

The purpose of individual PBR schemes is to accomplish higher levels of performance with a promise of extra remuneration for the extra effort over the standard. The key considerations here relate to the issues in accurate measurement and the basis for fixing the incentive rates. The individual employee's performance must be under his control. If more aspects of work are outside his control, it may not work. The effects of the scheme on other individuals and groups of workers who are not covered by it but whose support and cooperation is critical should be taken into account.

**Group Payment-by-Result Schemes**    The PBR schemes discussed above can be applied on a group basis also. Group PBR is appropriate where jobs are interdependent, where it is difficult to meaningfully measure individual performance, and where group pressures can influence the output of the members of the group. As in individual PBR schemes, there should be an objective measure of performance for the group which the members should know that they can affect by their performance.

The criticism against group incentive scheme is that the incentive benefits being similar to all members of the group, the best performers may lose incentive. However, a good group PBR will generate peer-level pressure for superior performance and reduces the need for supervision, if not make it partly redundant. Also, the positive effects of making group relatively homogeneous and integrated will have long-term impact in sustaining team spirit and organizational effectiveness. For group PBR scheme to succeed, groups have to be relatively stable. Excessive personal turnover may be disruptive for operation of such schemes.

**Plant or Enterprise Schemes**    PBR schemes could be extended to cover plant or enterprise. These schemes emphasize gain-sharing accruing through reduction in labour and other costs. A performance index based on a ratio of some output costs like labour, material or other costs is calculated. The gains arising out of improvements in performance over and above the base or the norm is shared between the employees and the organization according to a pre-determined ratio. The objectives and scope of plant or enterprise wide PBR can be much wider providing for employee participation and labour-management cooperation.

*Time-Rate Systems*    In situations where individual, group or plant/enterprise based PBR systems are difficult to introduce, pay could be related to time spent on the job. Simple time-rate system does not provide any linkage between pay and performance and, therefore, the latter may become a casualty. Variations like Measured Day Work (MDW) and Merit Rating seek to link performance with time rate payment.

*Measured Day Work (MDW)*    Under MDW pay is determined in the employment contract. The employee is required to put in a minimum specified performance to be eligible to get the pay. Now accomplishment of minimal standards for reasons within the control of the employee may entail sanctions, ranging from warning to dismissal in the event of continued poor performance. Some MDW schemes provide for a one step increase in wage as a bonus to all those who reach or cross the minimal standard of performance. Except that the scheme provides for a measure of stability and predictability in output for the company and earnings of the employee, it does not really induce people to give their best.

*Merit Rating*    This scheme is a method of granting fixed pay increments or regular pay raises linked to performance appraisal. The size of the raise, timing  and the place of the pay range are all aspects on which there is need to establish a policy. Merit pay scheme may also be in the form of a variable bonus. The quantum and the frequency of bonus need to be spelt out. The measure  of performance in either case is the assessment of overall job performance based on selected criteria related to personal traits, actual job behaviour and/or achievement of agreed objectives.

**Managerial Incentive Plans**    Most of the incentive schemes discussed so far have generally been applied to workmen and staff. There is no reason why some or all of these be extended to managerial employees. Typically, however, managerial employees are given the following types of incentives:

- Commission as a percentage of profit
- Stock options where be managerial employees are given shares at a special price, usually lower than market value and/or on a fixed formula
- Bonuses in cash or kind (discount coupons, paid holiday travel, sponsorship to educational programmes, etc).

**Making PBR Schemes Effective**    (a) Standards of performance and criteria for measurement should be objective, fair and clear to all concerned. The aspects of performance measured should be within the control of the employee(s) concerned.

(b) The linkage between pay and performance should be clear, simple and easy to understand.

(c) The sharing of gains should be on a basis agreeable to both the management and the employees.

(d) The schemes should be sufficiently attractive enough to give the employees a feeling that they are being adequately compensated for the contribution made.

(e) Minimum pay to employees be guaranteed and the scheme should not result in deduction in the existing earnings of employees.

(f) The scheme should result in saving of costs and/or improvement in output and quality.

(g) The gap between actual performance and incentive payment under PBR system should not be long.

(h) There should be proper communication of the details of the scheme to all concerned, with provision for review, redressal of grievances, and training for positive attitudinal disposition and proper  measurement and record keeping.

(i) It is desirable to encourage employee participation and consultation and negotiation with the union about various aspects of the scheme.

(j) There should be an overall climate of trust and understanding between employees, unions and management conducive for effective labour-management cooperation.

## FRINGE BENEFITS

Fringe benefits and employee welfare programmes have been in vogue in industry since long.  Some of them like provident fund and gratuity have become statutory while others concerning housing, education, etc., are not statutory  yet. The fringe benefits are non-wage benefits offered by the employer to the employees; they represent "a substantial cost-expense to the employer and a cost-saving to the employee". The money value of fringe benefits may usually account for around 40% if not more of the employee remuneration in certain large organizations.

### Key Considerations

The general corporate objectives for offering fringe benefits to employees are to attract and retain employees.  The specific objectives are related to the nature of each benefit. For instance, an attendance bonus may be introduced to encourage punctuality and regularity in attendance and reduce the incidence of absenteeism.  Reimbursement of tuition and books, extra increments and accelerated promotions for those acquiring higher qualifications/skills may be provided if the purpose is to enhance the qualification/skill mix of the employees.  Nutritious food (milk, etc.) may be provided to certain employees if the purpose is to offset the stamina or deficiency caused by exposure to certain gases, etc. Overall, the reasons for instituting and expanding the list of employee-benefit programmes are several.  Paternalistic or humanistic considerations, statutory requirements, concern for security, hazards of industrial life, tax considerations, utilization of leisure time, and competitive considerations  are some of them which are considered here briefly.

*Paternalistic or Humanistic Considerations*    Historically, employee fringe benefit programmes began as a voluntary effort with a welfare orientation.  "The general shortage of skilled labour, the unattractiveness of industrial employment and urban living, and the location of the company in an area which had no industrial tradition together provided the setting in which the management had to find ways and means to attract and retain"employees.[*]  Paternalistic attitudes, a desire or need to supplement wage compensation with certain infrastructure or facilities to provide for health,

---

[*] C P Thakur, 1985.  *Corporate Strategy on Fringe Benefits*, Spectrum: Patna.

education and housing as also social, cultural, religious, recreational activities induced some employers to take up voluntarily a series of welfare programmes considered beneficial to the employees.

**Statutory Requirements**     Since 1940s a series of social legislations incorporated a wide variety of fringe benefits and programmes. Thus certain benefits became statutory. The Factories Act stipulated number of hours of work and the kind of facilities like canteen, rest sheds, creches, etc. in the premises. The Maternity Benefits Act provides for special leave with pay.

**Concern for Security**     Traditionally in India, the joint family system provided a measure of security for the members of the family as a whole. As industrialization has been progressively replacing it with nuclear families, the employees and unions in the organized sector, together with the government, began to mount pressure on employers to provide for social security needs. Provident fund, gratuity and pension are the kind of benefits which come under this category; the first two have already been made mandatory with the enactment of the Provident Fund Act and the Gratuity Act. With the steady increase in life span and rising concern for sustaining purchasing power in old age in the face of spiralling inflation, employees are worried about post-retirement benefits. A variety of pension programmes linked to group insurance scheme with contributions from employees are now becoming popular in corporate sector. Government employees already have pension schemes.

**Hazards of Industrial Life**     As discussed in Chapter 9, industrial employment poses additional risks to employee health and safety which may lead to occupational diseases, accidents and loss of limb or life. To avoid depletion of savings in such illness, accidents, etc. and to protect the interests of dependants of the employee involved in fatal accidents, certain provisions have been incorporated in legislation like the Workmen's Compensation Act, the Employees' State Insurance Act and the Maternity Benefits Act.

Most large organizations also provide for the normal health care of their employees and their families. This is borne out of realization that aspects like attendance and productivity are linked to the health of the employees and their families, and are reinforced by the pressure of unions who normally raise demands at the time of wage settlements to provide for better health care. Some large organizations have their own hospitals and dispensaries while others have various schemes and schedules of rates for reimbursement of medical expenses, individual/group insurance cover for hospitalisation of employees and their families. Some organizations like Tata Steel, public sector oil companies, etc., extend post-retirement health care benefits to their employees and their families.

**Tax Considerations**     Tax considerations induce individuals and organizations to develop ingenus methods of avoiding tax obligations through restructuring the pay packet. A significant portion of total remuneration includes myriad non-wage benefits and reimbursement for a variety of expenses like house rent, medical, transport, entertainment, education, cheap mortgages, interest free loans or loans at concessional rates, etc. The purpose is to enable the employee to have maximum value for a given remuneration package, without the organization having to incur extra costs. The tax free extras list is ever expanding more prominently in respect of managerial employees. However, in recent years the tax authorities are taking exception to the camouflaging of business expenses and disallowing certain types reimbursements or non-wage benefits in toto or beyond certain limits. One need not be surprised if tax authorities potentially tax some of the allowed expenses retrospectively. So there is need for caution in using employee benefits for tax avoidance.

*Utilization of Leisure Time*  The shortening of the working hours or the phenomenon of extended week-end leads to an increase in leisure time. There is awareness about the effects of off-duty life-style on working life and vice versa. The importance of leave and holidays for rest and recuperation to maintain an agile body and creative mind is also underscored. In view of these, organizations are not only providing for paid leaves of different kinds (casual, privilege, sick, special casual leave, etc.) but also granting facilities for leave travel (usually in the form of reimbursement of travel expenses for holiday travel once in a year or two). To make such holidaying cheap and convenient, large organizations construct holiday homes at resorts or hire hotel or guest house accommodation and make it available to their employees and their families at subsidized rates.

While some organizations have policing mechanism for verifying whether the persons have actually used the amount for the purpose for which it is given, others operate on a system of *trust* and do no policing. Such policing may lead to industrial unrest.

*Competitive Considerations*  Despite unemployment, there is skill shortage. Organizations continuously face problems in attracting and retraining right people. Competitive pirating is not unheard of. There are additional problems for organizations located in backward areas and disturbed areas. A variety of incentives and benefits are being offered to attract and retain people. Township (company housing), liberal loan facilities, self-lease of houses owned by employees, construction of schools or reimbursement of educational expenses (including hostel fees etc. in some cases) of employees children, special pay or allowances (e.g. Disturbed Area allowance), membership in clubs/ professional associations, sponsorship for training and conferences abroad, buy back of company house, car, furniture at discounted rate, are just a few benefits which fall in this category.

# Current Approaches

We have seen that organizations provide fringe benefits to employees to comply with statutory requirements and honour negotiated settlements, besides voluntary considerations such as keeping in tune with competition, build a favourable corporate image, etc. Three main approaches are currently in vogue in the sphere of fringe benefits – innovation, flexibility and harmonization. These are discussed here.

*Innovation*    Organizations are enlarging the scope of fringe benefits and have begun to experiment with innovation. New dimensions are being added to certain benefits with the availability of innovative individual/group insurance benefits for life cover, health care and pension funds. New benefits are being invented to cater to specific organizational problems like redundancy, redeployment and relocation. If people are redundant one option is to retrench them by paying suitable compensation or announcing special benefits under a voluntary separation (*Golden Handshake*) scheme. The other option is to promote *outplacement*. This means, train surplus staff in marketable skills at the cost of the organization, assist them actively in seeking placement outside the organization by meeting interview costs, waiving notice period and grant of lien on jobs for six months to an year so that employees do not stop from availing the new options/opportunities for fear of uncertainty about new job and new organizations. In the event of redeployment, training in multiple skills and special incentives have become common. In the case of relocation, active assistance in disposal of old household belongings, etc., full reimbursements of transfer and transit costs, assistance for house loan, lease accommodation, school/college admissions, etc., have become common. New benefits are being added to minimise tax, overseas travel/education, free holiday travel, etc. New approaches seeking to tailor-make benefits to suit the needs of individual employees and aligning the benefits of blue and white collar employees are also part of innovation in the design and administration of fringe benefits.

*Flexibility*    Organizations are realizing the need to be sensitive to mould the benefits to suit the needs of individual employees rather than offer a common, standard package. With the result, flexible compensation packages have been gaining widespread acceptance among managerial employees. Such flexible packages are still to be extended to worker and staff categories in India.

Typically in a flexible compensation package, the total pay packet is decided or negotiated and employee is given option to distribute it under different items like pay, house rent, conveyance, entertainment, journal allowance, membership in club, furnishing allowance, drivers salary, etc. Most of the items represent a variety of reimbursement accounts which constitute expenses that do not form part of taxable income. The scope of flexible compensation package, as practised in India for managerial cadres, often extends beyond fringe benefits. The purpose is to minimize the adverse affects of taxation and provide a higher value for a diversified group of employees while checking the costs of employee benefits.

*Harmonization*    It is a process of bringing blue and white-collar conditions of service into some kind of alignment. The objective is to have a single status for all employees. In terms of conditions of service, whether it is blue-collar workers getting the same conditions as white-collar workers or vice versa or a compromise between the two is reached is a matter of corporate strategy. Though harmonization process may extend to all conditions of service and even work practices, in practice usually it covers time (working hours, *time-office* practices such as punching in and punching out, deductions for lateness, etc), and a variety of fringe benefits including transport (bus facility), catering, uniforms, medical care and educational facilities for children.

Harmonization seeks to bring in a measure of equity and fairplay and supposedly contributes to improvements in employee attitudes and performance and simplification of pay-roll procedures and fringe benefit administration.

## SUMMARY

Wage and Salary administration is one of the major aspects of personnel function. Organizations need to compensate their employees according to their contribution. But what would be a fair wage for a day's labour? Public policy sets the tone and direction. There should be equal pay for equal work and no discrimination on any ground. Employers are obliged to pay minimum wages irrespective of their capacity to pay. A series of legislations bring a measure of protection to employees against exploitation. Behavioural science theories indicate that rewards could be intrinsic or extrinsic but they need to satisfy a four-fold criteria if they are to motivate people for superior performance: *equity* (wages should be equitable), *valence* (they must be valued), *salience* (they should make a significant difference to the employees) and *contingent* (they should be contingent upon performance). Job evaluation provides a systematic basis for assessing the relative worth of jobs. Pay surveys impart knowledge and understanding about the labour market situation. Together, job evaluation and pay surveys provide the basis to develop a wage structure. The components of wages include basic pay, dearness allowance and other allowance/benefits. Wage incentive schemes/payment-by-results schemes are also introduced to link wages with a measure of performance and improve productivity. Fringe benefits are provided to complement the pay and contribute to the welfare and quality of life of employees. They also have a labour market role and influence the propensity of organizations to attract and retain people. They began on a voluntary note, but a series of legislations introduced a measure of involuntarism. Currently organizations are searching for innovations in the design and administration of benefits, providing for flexibility (particularly in respect of fringe benefits of managerial employees) and endeavouring to harmonize employee benefits to improve employee attitudes and performance as also to simplify pay roll procedures and benefits administration.

## KEY WORDS

| | | |
|---|---|---|
| **Basic Wage** | : | It is the price for labour/services rendered. It is one of the components of wage structure. It provides a stable base to the wage structure. |
| **Dearness Allowance** | : | It is an allowance paid to the employees to enable them to face the growing dearness of essential commodities. |
| **Fair Wage** | : | While the lower limit of the fair wage must obviously be the minimum wage, the upper limit is equally set by what may broadly be called the capacity of industry to pay. Between these two limits the actual wage would depend on (i) the productivity of labour, the prevailing rates of wages, (iii) the level of national income and distribution, and (iv) the place of the industry in the economy of the country. |
| **Incentive Wage** | : | It is the extra payment for above-standard performance. |
| **Job Evaluation** | : | It is a systematic method of appraising the relative worth of jobs. |
| **Living Wage** | : | It represents a standard of living which provided not merely for a |

|  |  |  |
|---|---|---|
|  |  | bare physical sustenance but decency, protection against ill-health, requirements of essential social needs and some insurance against the more important misfortunes and old age. |
| Minimum Wage | : | A minimum wage must provide not merely for the bare sustenance of life but for the preservation of the efficiency of the worker by providing some measure of education, medical requirements and amenities. |
| Need-based Minimum Wage | : | The minimum wage should be need-based and "should ensure the minimum human needs of the industrial worker, irrespective of any other consideration." |
| Nominal Wage | : | It is the wage expressed in money terms. |
| Real Wage | : | It is money/wage deflated by the cost of living index. It denotes the purchasing power of the money/wage. |
| Payment by Results | : | It is a system of linking workers' earnings to a measure of their performance. |

## REVIEW QUESTIONS

1. Review the key public policy considerations in wage policy. Comment on how these are pursued and with what result?
2. What is job evaluation?  Describe different methods of job evaluation.
3. Discuss the major aspects influencing wage and salary administration at company level?
4. What is a salary structure?  How is it designed?
5. Review different approaches to:
   Dearness allowance
   Employee benefits
6. What are the ideal features of effective incentive scheme?
7. Review the major behavioural considerations which influence the reward system in an organization.
8. Distinguish between
   Nominial wage and real wage
   Minimum wage, living wage and fair wage
   Minimum wage and need-based minimum wage
   Ranking and rating methods

# CASE STUDY I:  GRASS-CUTTER v. GAS CUTTER

In one public sector undertaking with a chequered past, a line manager was appointed as the Chief of Personnel. Within a year after taking up the assignment, he had to sign a wage agreement with the workers' union. The union at that time was dominated by non-technical staff.  The union's charter of demands favoured the interests of its dominant member groups.  It asked for a significant revision in gardeners' pay, but was not equally vocal in pressing for the increase in the pay scales of workers in certain technical grades.  The management conceded these demands because the union cooperated with them in keeping the burden of the pay revision well within the guidelines of the Bureau of Public Enterprises (BPE).

Once the agreement was signed and communicated to employees/members by the management and the union respectively, there was commotion among the technical staff.  They walked out of the union, formed a separate technical staff union and marched round the company premises holding placards which read, "Here grass cutters get more than the gas cutters."  In the engineering assembly unit, till the pay revision occurred, welding was a highly-rated job.  But not any longer.  Now gardeners get more than welders.

## QUESTIONS

1. What happens if grass-cutters get more than gas-cutters?
2. Evaluate the pros and cons of the approach of both the management and union in this incident?
3. List the lessons learnt. Suggest a way out of the problem on hand.

# CASE STUDY II:  TWO-TIER PAY STRUCTURE

In 1976, the Indian subsidiary of a multinational refinery became a Government of India company.  The government company had announced an ambitious expansion programme which meant doubling the work force in less than four years.  In 1977 at the time of wage revision, the union and management agreed to a two-tier pay structure.  Those already employed will be eligible for a higher grade and those who are (to be) recruited afresh will get a lower grade though jobs are similar in skill, responsibility and effort. Both the union and the management justified that this is an innovative practice widely followed in deregulated companies abroad, particularly the airlines in North America.

## QUESTIONS

1. Is it a fair agreement?
2. Would it contravene with the concept of equal pay for equal work?

## FURTHER READING

1. Dayal, Sahab, 1980.  *Industrial Relations System in India*, Sterling: New Delhi.
2. Fonseca, A J, 1975.  *Wage Issues in a Developing Economy*, Oxford University Press: Bombay.
3. Government of India, 1969. *Report of the National Commission on Labour*,: New Delhi.

4.  Government of India, 1986. *Report of the Fourth Central Pay Commission*: New Delhi.

5.  Government of India, 1988. *Report of the High-Powered Pay Committee on Public Sector Emoluments* (Chairman: Justice R B Mishra): New Delhi.

6.  ILO, 1984. *Payments by Results, ILO : Geneva.*

7.  Kanungo, R N and Mameel Mindonca, 1987. *Work Rewards and Management of Human Resources, Indian Management*, April, pp 8–19.

8.  Smith, Ian, 1983. *The Management of Remuneration*, The Institute of Personnel Management and   Gower: London.

9.  Subramaniam, K N, 1979. *Wages in India*, Tata McGraw-Hill: New Delhi.

10. Thakur, C P, 1985. *Corporate Strategy on Fringe Benefits*, Spectrum: Patna.

11. Venkata Ratnam, C S, 1986. *Problems of Paying: A Review of the IV Central Pay Commission*, IMI: New Delhi (Mimeo).

12. Venkata Ratnam, C S, 1989.   "Emoluments in Public Enterprises: Review of Pay Committee's Report", *Economic and Political Weekly*, May 27, 1989, M61–M66.

# CHAPTER 9

# Occupational Health and Safety

**LEARNING OBJECTIVES**

After going through this chapter, you should be able to:
● Understand the significance of occupational health and safety;
● Develop a broad awareness about the regulatory environment and coverage (than specific content) of various statutory measures; ● Know the possible measures organizations take to promote occupational health and safety of employees.

Industrialization has brought in its wake a reluctant respect for environment. The people in many societies are exposed to certain health hazards. But the workers and employees in factories and elsewhere are very often exposed to additional risks of environmental pollution, occupational diseases and injuries. These aspects of industrial life, once ignored by employers as a necessary by-product of industrialization, are now being addressed by governments, employers, employees and their unions, besides a host of other public and international organizations.

## WORKING CONDITIONS, OCCUPATIONAL HEALTH AND SAFETY

Working conditions include all aspects of work: physical, social, economic, technical, legal and human. The physical conditions refer to climatic factors and include not only aspects like ventilation and temperature, but also physical facilities at work such as canteen, rest room, creche, etc. The social aspects relate to work group composition etc. The economic aspects relate to wages, benefits, etc. The technical aspects relate to the kind of technology used. The legal aspects relate to contractual obligations, which are mutual and reciprocal. The human aspects relate to the quality of supervision, communication, etc.

**EXHIBIT 9.1**

> **On the Value of Human Life**
> "In a country as populous as ours, there can be a danger of a tendency developing to discount the value of human life. Its loss in accidents or through the slow and agonizing process of an occupational disease may not stir a community as much as it would in countries with chronic labour shortages, though to the near ones it is a tragic occurrence. Relief gets organized after the event, but prevention gets side-tracked. We have noticed, in the years since Independence, a welcome improvement in such public attitudes, but this has been slow and brought about largely through shocks administered by serious happening."
> Excerpts from the *Report of the National Commission on Labour (1969)*.

The Whitley Commission reported in early 1930 about the working conditions which first drew attention to this and a programme of action was drawn up in 1946 with thrust in the following areas:

- Reduction in the hours of work in mines to 48 hours a week as in factories.
- Legislation to regulate hours of work, weekly rest periods and holiday with pay for other classes of workmen not now subject to regulation, namely, those employed in shops and commercial undertakings, road transport services, docks and municipal labour.
- Overhaul the Factories Act with a view to prescribe and enforce standards in regard to lighting, ventilation, safety, health and welfare of workers.
- Strengthening of the inspection staff and inspectorate (particularly mines).

After Independence, the Constitution made special reference to working conditions in The Directive Principles of State Policy.

Section 39(e): That the health and strength of workers, men and women, and the tender age of children are not abused and that citizens are not forced by economic necessity to enter avocations unsuited to their age or strength;

Section 39(f): That childhood and youth are protected against exploitation and against moral and material abandonment.

Section 42: Just and humane conditions of work and for maternity relief.

The successive Five-year Plans of the Union Government were designed to pursue these goals and as we shall discuss later, the government created a regulatory framework, and set up infrastructure and inspectorates to oversee their effective functioning.

Employers are concerned about safety and health because of cost considerations: Compensation laws and their liberal interpretation in recent past meant additional, avoidable costs (if work place can be made safer). The hidden costs of accidents could well be several times more than the direct and obvious costs. Considering the quantum of disruption that a single accident causes, involving not only the affected workmen, but also others in the same plant or work place, every year we may be losing more mandays on account of accidents than due to industrial disputes. And, over 95 per cent of accidents are caused by human failures which may have their roots in bad human engineering, low morale, lack of education or training about safe work practices, poor plant layout or inadequate supervision and maintenance.

Employees and unions are concerned about health and safety at work-place because it concerns the employee/members well-being and security. Loss of limb or life or chronic ailments in the nature of occupational diseases bring enormous grief and problems for the employees and their families. It is only in recent years that employees and their unions  are making demands on employers for better, safe and healthy working conditions. After the Bhopal tragedy, plant safety and occupational health have become the key issues.

## SOCIAL BACKGROUND AND WORKING CONDITIONS

Traditionally, social attitudes towards working conditions in India seem to be lax. The National Commission on Labour observed in 1969:

"They get used to a rhythm of work with all the good and the bad points thrown in, whether they work in transplanting operations in a paddy field in knee-deep mud or in a city or town drainage, in unorganized tanneries or butcher-shops, or for that matter in the cleaner surroundings of factories, particularly in modern units. A worker in unorganized tanneries will not rue over the odours he has to work with, because a worker in a chemical unit is free from them. Even within the same industry a worker recognizes differences between establishments and is at his job without comparing work conditions in better units. He accepts certain environments associated with certain types of work. It is  only when these get changed for the worse, and that too beyond a limit, that protest begins. This limit itself is elastic. If no special hazard is involved, protest can be negotiable for better wage rates."

## ERGONOMICS

Ergonomics is the scientific study of the relationship between man and his working environment. It takes into consideration not only the physical environment in which man works, but also his tools, materials, and the method and organisation of his work. It is concerned with the whole man, physical and mental, biological and behavioural aspects.

In early 1960s ergonomic studies focused on the design of machine controls, levers, knobs, buttons, on the visual displays carried by instruments, on work place, plant layout, on chairs and tables, on the design of hand tools, on manual handling of heavy workloads. Aspects like noise, vibration, ventilation, temperature, etc. began to be taken into account subsequently. Eventually  the entire spectrum of working environment began to be encompassed in ergonomic research so that job design and organisation, stores, monotony and fatigue too could be taken into account.

The rapid industrialization in developing countries led to  a massive transfer of technology and import of plant and machinery that had  high safety standards in western industrialized countries. But when they are put to use in a different physical (climatically), psychological and social environment new problems began to surface in safety and health. Application of ergonomic principles pointed to the need to use different design for factory layout depending upon whether they are built in tropical zones or cooler climates.  For instance, in a hot, dry climate steel rolling mills should be built without walls to allow maximum air movement through the mill, and factory walls constructed of huge louvres which are kept open during the dry season and closed when the monsoon begins. Additional hazards in the use of movable machinery in activities like construction and mining could also be tackled by the application of scientific principles. The most common accidents in mining are cave-ins and root falls due to poor timbering or dangerous tunneling techniques.

Over the years, ergonomic studies have contributed immensely to make the work places not only safer but also convenient and productive. Ergonomic studies teach us how to take full advantage of human beings' finite capacities with the potential of modern technologies. They also seek to put restraints on people working beyond their optimal range of  abilities which may lead to errors that could cause accidents and injuries.

It is futile, however, to expect ergonomics to solve all problems of health and safety. Occupational health and safety problems are often compounded by the lack of safety equipment, awareness and expertise coupled with poor maintenance. Also, usually there is a lag in understanding and coping with the ramifications of modern technologies and materials on occupational health and safety.  The recent revelations on the health effects of asbestos and radiation effects of computer screens point to this.

## REGULATORY ENVIRONMENT

In the early days of industrialization everywhere, accidents, injuries and damage to health were ignored by employers and the responsibility to prevent them as also to bear the consequences was considered to belong to the employee.  In the face of widespread poverty and unemployment workers are made to accept hazardous jobs and poor working conditions even in present times, particularly in developing countries. However, the alarming rise in occupational health and safety and the grim working conditions prompted the International Labour Organisation to produce 25 conventions on occupational safety and health, dealing with occupational diseases, accidents, labour inspections, etc.  The most recent, the Occupational Safety and Health Convention (No.155) was adopted in 1981.  It defines, for the first time, the basic rights of workers for protecting their occupational safety and health. Article 13 states that a worker who has removed himself from a work situation which he has reasonable justification to believe presents an imminent and serious danger to his life or health shall be protected from undue consequences in accordance with natural conditions and practice." The adoption of this legislation will profoundly influence enterprise policies on occupational health and safety.

Government of India, like many other governments, took initiative in setting up international standards by its staunch support of the ILO conventions and recommendations and enacted various protective provisions in Factories Act and other laws. Principally, the regulatory environment for occupational safety and health is encompassed in four legislations.

The Factories Act prescribes measures for the avoidance of accidents and personal injuries to workmen employed in the factory.    The Workmen's Compensation Act and Employees State Insurance Act and the Personal Injuries (Compensation Insurance) Act prescribe the liability of the employer to pay compensation to workmen for injuries by accidents or by occupational diseases.    The salient features of these four legislations are briefly discussed hereunder.    There are other legislations dealing with issues of occupational safety and health in such sectors as ports and docks [Dock Workers (Regulation of Employment) Act, 1948], plantations (The Plantations Act, 1951) and mines (The Mines Act, 1952) which are not discussed here.

## Factories Act, 1948
The physical aspects of working conditions are regulated under the Factories Act, 1948.  Most other aspects of working conditions, including, partly, the physical aspects are sought to be regulated through The Industrial Employment (Standing Orders) Act, 1946. The measures under the Factories Act cover the following aspects.

*Health*    Chapter III of the Factories Act deals with measures devoted to the well-being of the workers inside the factories. Some important provisions concern:
  (i)    Cleanliness (Sec. 11)
  (ii)   Disposal of wastes and affluents (Sec. 12)
  (iii)  Proper ventilation and temperatures (Sec. 13)
  (iv)   Protection against dust and fume (Sec. 14)
  (v)    Precautionary measures in such industries as cotton textiles and cigarette-making where artificial humidification is  necessary (Sec. 15)
  (vi)   Avoidance of over-crowding (Sec. 16)
  (vii)  Protection from glare or shadow in the room (Sec. 17)
The State governments normally prescribe appropriate standards and ensure their compliance through periodic inspections and sanctions against violations.

*Safety*
  (i)    Dangerous parts of the machinery should be securely fenced by safeguards of substantial construction (Sec. 21)
  (ii)   Prohibition of employment of young persons to operate dangerous machines without proper training and adequate supervision (Sec. 23)
  (iii)  Additional safeguards against transmission machinery (Sec. 24)
  (iv)   Minimum distance (18 inches) to be maintained from selfacting machine (Sec. 25)
  (v)    Safe working peripheral speed of revolving vessels, cages, flywheels, etc. where grinding is carried on (Sec. 30)
  (vi)   Prohibition of employment of women or children near cotton openers (Sec. 27)
  (vii)  Responsibility of the employer or occupier for the sound construction of floors, steps, staircases, and gangways (Sec. 32)

(viii) Specific provisions for protection of eyes against glare (Sec. 35) or dangerous fumes (Sec. 36) and protection against explosive or inflamable dust, gas, etc. (Sec. 37)

The Factories Act makes it obligatory on the part of the manager of a factory to send a notice to the prescribed authority, within a prescribed time limit, the details about occurrences causing any bodily injury or disability or death. The Factories Act also prescribed certain notifiable diseases (as listed in the Schedule appended to the Act) which are in the nature of occupational diseases and fixed responsibility on the employer to notify to the prescribed authorities whenever any worker contracts any such disease. The employer's responsibility does not end with prompt reporting of the accidents. Prompt action and post-accident care is a must. The State government has the authority and responsibility to inspect and investigate into causes of any accidents or actual or apprehended incidences of occupational diseases. Section 91(A) of the Factories Act provides for occupational health surveys by a competent government authority of Factory Advisory Service, Central Labour Institute, etc.

## Workmen's Compensation Act, 1923

Occupational diseases are specified and categorized for purposes of determining the compensation payable to the affected workmen or their dependants. Employer is liable to pay compensation if a workmen who, having been employed in certain employments for a continuous period, ceases to be so employed and develops symptoms of an occupational disease peculiar to that employment within two years of the cessation of employment.

Even where an employee is suffering from a disease and if the employment causes acceleration of the disease either by strain or fatigue incidental to employment, the employer would nevertheless be liable for compensation.

However, the following three factors must be established to hold the employer liable for compensation under Sec. 3 of the Workmen's Compensation Act: (a) there must be an injury; (b) it should be caused in an accident, and (c) it should be caused in the course of employment.

The words, 'accident' and 'injury', are not to be viewed narrowly. Several judgements held that accident means an untoward mishap which is unforeseen by the workmen and injury means a physiological injury, not necessarily tangible in character. Accidents and injuries occurring in the course of employment mean not only those occurring when a workman is actually engaged in doing something in the discharge of his duty to the employer, but also when he is engaged in acts belonging to or arising out of it.

The main theme of the Workmen's Compensation Act is to provide security to the workman who receives partial or total incapacity resulting in a loss in earning capacity. The protection so afforded is independent of the acts of grace or mercy which the employer might show to him. Compensation rates vary depending upon whether the injury is leading to: (a) temporary partial disability; (b) temporary total disability; (c) permanent disability; (d) permanent total disability.

## The Employees' State Insurance Act, 1948 (The ESI Act)

The ESI Act provides for certain benefits to employees in case of sickness, maternity, employment injury and related matters. The Act applies to all factories, other than seasonal factories, run with power and employing 20 or more persons. The coverage of the act has been extended to several classes of establishments, viz. electrial power using factories employing 10 or more workers and non-power factories employing 20 or more workers, shops, theatres, cinemas, hotels, restaurants, etc.employing 20 or more persons in several States. It covers all employees whose remuneration in aggregate does not exceed Rs 1600 a month.

The administration of the Employees' State Insurance Scheme, framed under the Act, has been entrusted to The Employees' State Insurance Corporation (ESIC), an autonomous body set up by an act of the central government. The ESIC Board consists of representatives of central and state governments, employers, employees, medical profession and the Parliament.

The ESIS has set up regional boards in all states including a network of offices at various levels and operates from over 520 centres throughout the country. About 75 lakh persons' family units (i.e. insured employee households) have been covered under the scheme.

The scheme provides the following benefits financed through contributions from concerned employers and employees.

*Sickness Cash Benefit*    About half the wages upto 90 days sickness.

*Maternity Benefits*    All insured women are entitled to benefits which are equal to full wages for leave upto 12 weeks, of which not more than six weeks must precede the expected date of confinement.

*Disablement Benefits*    Three categories of benefits—temporary disablement, permanent total disablement and permanent partial disablement—as provided under the Workmen's Compensation Act.

*Dependants Benefits*    These are also provided under the Workmen's Compensation Act. If a person dies from employment injuries, the dependants are entitled to compensation to be paid in a certain ratio to the widow and the minor children and other dependants.

*Funeral Benefit*    When an insured person dies, during the period he is insured, the eldest member of the family or other dependant or friends as the case may be, is entitled to Rs 100 to meet funeral expenses.

The Act contains deterrent provisions including fine and compulsory imprisonment for any default in payment of contributions by the employer.

## Personal Injuries (Compensation Insurance) Act, 1963

This is a supplemental enactment to the Workmen's Compensation Act. It seeks to impose on employers a liability to pay compensation to workmen sustaining personal injuries and to provide for the insurance of employers against such responsibility. This Act is applicable only to certain classes of workmen and not to all categories as defined in the Workmen's Compensation Act, 1923.

## Evaluation of the Regulatory Framework

Since the Whitley Commission reported on the working conditions in the context of health, safety and welfare of workers and the working of the Factories Act then in force, much progress has been made to improve standards, strengthen regulatory measures, streamline inspection services and augment health services. Still, with the rapid strides in industrialization and introduction of new technologies, additional problems began to surface.

With the passage of time, the need for amending the legislations was felt and accordingly almost all these legislations were amended. The problem, however, is that if the new regulations are applied to old factories rigorously, how many of them will meet the test? If they do not, what are the implications to the continued existence of the old factories, to employment and other social and economic aspects.

As in other fields of labour administration, here too, there are many inadequacies in terms of the strength of inspectorates, the qualifications, expertise and commitment of staff, and the absence of deterrent penalties.

The Factories Act and the Workmen's Compensation Act provide for statutory returns and reports. State governments and public institutions as also the offices of the Director-General, Factory Advice Service and Labour Institutes and the All India Institute of Hygiene are engaged in special studies, enquiries and investigations on the subject. Still the data base is inadequate and the available information on occupational health and safety is scanty.

The coverage of the ESIS is low even within the organized sector, largely due to restricted scope and partly because the scheme has not been popular with employees and unions. Several surveys point to the growing dissatisfaction with the scheme, particularly among the employees in view of the inadequacy of facilities and benefits. There is also criticism about the lack of enthusiasm on the part of state governments to augment and properly administer the facilities. Employees are also concerned that besides their contributions to the scheme they have to invariably spend additional amounts of money on medical aid from private doctors and for purchases of medicines not available in ESIS dispensaries.

Some of the large organizations in both public and private sectors have realized the limitations of the ESIS, sought exemptions from the operation of the scheme and started providing much more liberal and better medical facilities through setting up company hospitals/dispensaries, free medical aid, etc. A variety of schemes such as medical insurance, group insurance and death benefit schemes have also become popular in recent years. The medical insurance scheme provides liberal health benefits (including hospitalization) on a graded basis depending upon the quantum of contribution made. Usually the employer makes the contribution for specified categories of employees and their families. In some cases employees themselves share the burden to get the same or similar benefits or to become eligible for upgraded benefits. The group insurance scheme is normally linked with the provident fund and amounts ranging from Rs 10,000 to Rs 25,000 are paid to the legal heirs/nominees of the deceased worker. For executives the benefits, where they exist, are usually much higher. The death benefit scheme is designed to give monetary assistance to the next kin of the member — employee who dies in service. It is funded by nominal contributions from employees with matching contributions, in some cases, from employers.

## ORGANIZATION COMMITMENT

There is a growing awareness about occupational health, safety and working environment. Legislation, trade union pressures and pro-active actions from enlightened employers are influencing the movement toward safer and healthier work places. Yet, ironically, we are unable to fully comprehend and predict the effects of modern technologies on occupational health and safety.

Increasingly, the top management is being asked to take the initiative and accept responsibility for occupational health and safety. Employers started providing machine guards and personal protective equipment. Employees are educated that "the best safety device is to be careful." Senior management personnel are asked to "manage out" accidents. The total commitment of organization should however, result in concrete actions at plant level as laid down in ILO convention 155 on the subject (see Exhibit 9.2).

**EXHIBIT 9.2**

---

**Excerpts from the ILO Convention 155 Concerning
Occupational Safety and Health and the Working Environment
Action at the Level of the Undertaking**
Article 16

1. Employers shall be required to ensure that, so far as is reasonably practicable, the work places, machinery, equipment and processes under their control are safe and without risk to health.
2. Employers shall be required to ensure that, so far as is reasonably practicable, the chemical, physical and biological substances and agents under their control are without risk to health when the appropriate measures of protection are taken.
3. Employers shall be required to provide, where necessary, adequate protective clothing and protective equipment to prevent, so far as is reasonably practicable, risk of accidents or of adverse effects on health.

Article 17

Whenever two or more undertakings engage in activities simultaneously at one work place, they shall collaborate in applying the requirements of this Convention.

Article 18

Employers shall be required to provide, where necessary, for measures to deal with emergencies and accidents, including adequate first-aid arrangements.

Article 19

There shall be arrangements at the level of the undertaking under which:

(a) workers, in the course of performing their work, cooperate in the fulfilment by their employer of the obligations placed upon him;
(b) representatives of workers in the undertaking cooperate with the employer in the field of occupational safety and health;
(c) representatives of workers in an undertaking are given adequate information on measures taken by the employer to secure occupational safety and health and may consult their representative organizations about such information provided they do not disclose commercial secrets;
(d) workers and their representatives in the undertaking are given appropriate training in occupational safety and health;

(e) workers or their representatives, and as the case may be, their representative organizations in an undertaking, in accordance with national law and practice, are enabled to enquire into, and are consulted by the employer on all aspects of occupational safety and health associated with their work; for this purpose technical advisers outside the undertaking;

(f) a worker reports forthwith to his immediate supervisor any situation which he has reasonable justification to believe presents an imminent and serious danger to his life or health; until the employer has taken remedial action, if necessary, the employer cannot require workers to return to work situation where there is continuing imminent and serious danger to life or health.

### Article 20

Co-operation between management and workers and/or their representatives within the undertaking shall be an essential element of organizational and other measures taken in pursuance of Articles 16 to 19 of this Convention.

### Article 21

Occupational safety and health measures shall not involve any expenditure for the workers.

## MEASURES FOR OCCUPATIONAL HEALTH AND SAFETY

### Occupational Health

Occupational health measures call for protecting the workers against health hazards which may arise out of their work or the conditions in which it is carried on; contributing towards the workers' physical and mental adjustment in particular by the adaptation of workers to the jobs for which they are suited; and, contributing to the establishment of the highest possible degree of physical and mental health.

The first measure is indispensable. The remaining two can be developed gradually. There are three aspects of protection: (a) preventive; (b) curative and (c) safety.

**Preventive Measures**    These include pre-employment and periodic medical examination, removal of health hazards to the extent possible, special attention to those who are vulnerable to risks, education of workers in health and hygiene, training in first-aid and emergency treatment for accidents.

**Curative Measures**    The curative aspects will begin once a worker suffers from ill-health or disease. One important hurdle in curative aspect is the general feeling among workers that a medical check-up may result in disqualification for continuing employment if something adverse is detected. Such psychological blocks can be overcome only over a period of time.

### Safety

The measures for safety include the following.

(i) *Active interest and support of top management is sine qua non for promoting safety:* Top management's concern is manifest in its observance of statutory measures and enforcing safety rules, personal attendance at safety meetings, periodic reviews and inspections, and inclusion of safety figures and achievements in the agenda at board meetings and annual reports.

(ii) *Compliance of statutory measures and enforcement of safety rules*: The various statutory provisions under the Factories Act and other relevant legislations need to be implemented in letter and spirit. The managements should adopt a humane and not mere legalistic approach. While the Factories Inspectorate is concerned with the compliance of legal measures on the part of the employer, at the factory level, the management's fundamental approach in enforcing safety rules should be positive in nature. Where necessary, managements should not shun disciplinary action to deal with violations effectively.

(iii) *Appointment of safety officer*: The Factories Act requires that safety officer should be appointed in all factories employing 1,000 or more workers or where the manufacturing process carried on exposes workers to serious risk of bodily disease, poisoning or disease.

The safety officer may be concerned with positive aspects of motivation such as safety education or with functional authority for enforcing safety or both.

(iv) *Constitution of a safety committee:* Every factory employing 100 or more workers should have standing arrangements at the plant level to ensure continued participation of workers in matters connected with safety. The arrangements may be in the form of safety committees.

The various schemes of workers' participation in management announced by the Government of India envisage matters relating to safety to be included among the items on the agenda for participation.

(v) *Engineering a safe plant and operations:* Sound and forward looking arrangements in plant lay-out and human engineering are essential ingredients of a progressive safety programme. The Factories Act prescribes certain measures the standards for which may be laid down by the State Governments concerned. There is probably no engineered safeguard that some employer cannot alter or circumvent and so there is need to be doubly cautious. Conforming to safety precautions usually entails some delay or extra effort and people are often prone to short-cut the engineered device. So there should be proper reward and punishment system for safe and unsafe practices respectively.

(vi) *Education and Training in Safety:* Employers should recognize their responsibility to educate employees to think, act and work safely. The various avenues that this education can take include:
- Induction of new employees
- Emphasis on safety points  during on-the-job  training
- Special attention and efforts by the first-line supervisor
- Establishment of employee safety committees
- Holding special meetings
- Use of house magazines, and other media such as charts, posters, displays, audio-visuals, etc.

Regular meetings with employees will help promote self awareness and evolving improved safety rules, devices and practices.

(vii) *Record keeping and Accident analysis*:  The  Factories Act makes it obligatory on employers' part to report to the government on accidents. The measures which are widely recognized to analyze accidents are: (a) frequency rate; and, (b) severity rate. These can be expressed as:

$$\text{Frequency rate} = \frac{\text{No. of lost-time accidents} \times 1,00,000}{\text{No. of employee-hours during the period}}$$

$$\text{Severity rate} = \frac{\text{No. of employee days lost} \times 1,00,000}{\text{No. of employee-hours worked during the period}}$$

These measures of accidents are arbitrary, but so long as most firms use the same indexes, the results are valuable for comparison.

An accident is an unplanned incident and should be analyzed in terms of both costs and causes. If insurance premiums and compensation can be termed as direct costs, the indirect costs, some of which are listed below, are several times the direct costs.

- Cost of damage to equipment, materials and plant
- Costs of wages paid for time lost by workers not injured
- Costs of supervisors and staff in investigating, recording and reporting
- Costs of replacing the injured employee
- Miscellaneous cost including any overtime caused by accident, loss of income due to delayed delivery and costs of maintaining a first-aid dispensary for accidents that do not technically result in loss of time.

About the costs and consequences to the affected employees and their families, no calculations are adequate, particularly in the case of fatal accidents.

As employers and employees become fully aware and educated about the true cost of accidents their concern and safety consciousness might grow.

The causes of accidents could be technical and human. Technical causes such as defects in plant, equipment, tools and general environment can be eliminated largely through engineering. Human causes such as attitudes, carelessness, recklessness, inability to perform the job, day-dreaming and alcoholism can be minimized by concentrating on personal aspects.

More accidents are caused due to human failures than due to technical or mechanical reasons. And more human failures are caused by relatively smaller fraction of accident-prone employees who need special attention as to their physiological deficiencies and psychological problems. Careful analysis of the causes of accidents will reveal the underlying causes that help managements cure and prevent them than merely tackle the symptoms.

(viii) *Rewarding for Safe Practices*: Safety contests and safety awards are common at plant, industry, regional and national levels. Awards are usually based on the number of hours worked without time lost to an accident, good housekeeping, safety suggestions, etc.

There is a good deal of controversy over the merits of such contests and awards. While awards provide a positive motivation, instances are galore when safety contests have led to abuses. Serious accidents have not been reported and actual events are misrepresented. All incentive arrangements, from the profit sharing system to safety contests, have in them the stimulus to undesirable as well as desirable action. But, if on balance, the good that is stimulated outweighs the ills accompanying the system, then the use of incentive arrangement is justified.

## SUMMARY

Industrial workers are exposed to additional risks of environmental pollution, occupational diseases and injuries; in populous developing countries like India these may easily be ignored and rarely stir the community. The ergonomic researches began to focus on the relationship between man and the working environment with the result the work places are made much more safer. But there is usually a lag in understanding the true ramifications of modern technologies and materials. In the post-Independence era the Constitution, public policy, legislations and union actions have sought to provide specific obligations for employers and employees. The government has also set up infrastructure and inspectorates to monitor the situation.

Regulation alone will not work, particularly because in the context of rapid changes in technology, manufacturing processes, materials and factories, the laws rapidly become archaic. The weaknesses in labour administration also make regulation largely ineffective. What is needed is a strong commitment on the part of every organization, particularly top management towards the health, safety and quality of working environment. The initiatives of International Labour Office in this direction are laudable. And, there is growing tendency towards effective and meaningful cooperation between employers and unions in the design and implementation of measures for occupational health, safety and quality of working environment. These measures not only seek to engineer safe plant operations, but also inculcate an orientation towards health and safety with a wide variety of educational and motivational programmes.

## KEY-WORDS

**Ergonomics** : It refers to the scientific study of the relationship between man and his working environment. It takes into consideration not only the physical environment in which the man works, but also his tools, materials and the method and organization of his work.

**Frequency Rate** : It is a measure of number of hours lost due to injuries and illness as a proportion of number of hours worked.

**Occupational Disease** : Disease or illness resulting from exposure to certain aspects of the working environment.

**Severity Rate** : It is a measure of the number of the employee hours lost due to injury or illness.

## REVIEW QUESTIONS

1. Briefly review the objects, scope and nature of governmental measures to regulate the working environment.
2. (a) Describe the relationship between social background and working conditions.
   (b) Outline how ergonomics contributes to a safer work place.
3. Discuss the measures for occupational health and safety at enterprise level and explain the role of top management, supervisors, unions and workers in this regard.
4. Discuss a few accidents that occurred at your work place. Explain: the causes, how they were dealt with, and how they should have been dealt with.

# CASE I: WAS IT AN ELECTRIC SHOCK?*

Mohanlal, lineman (electrical), was working in the power supply group of the electrical maintenance section of the Mines Department. He had 15 years of experience of repair and maintenance of high tension (6.6 kv) and low tension (440 v) overhead electric lines. From the beginning of the mines operation, he was engaged for erection of electrical lines in the quarry area of the mines. During his service, he acted as leader of the crew whenever the chargeman was absent.

One day at 1 p.m. a message was received in the Mine Control Centre that Mohanlal had a fall from a low tension pole. He was shifted to the mines hospital where he was declared to be unfit for six weeks due to injuries on his shoulder, legs and hands.

On preliminary inquiry from his co-workers, it was gathered that Mohanlal was sent to attend the *fuse call* from the union office in the camp area. He was assisted by two persons. The helpers who were at the site informed that Mohanlal checked the electrical circuit of the premises and upon finding everything in order, concluded that the supply was disconnected from the service lines on the pole near the office. He climbed the pole. But before he could attend to the fault he fell down from a height of about 6.5 metres and sustained physical injuries.

Mohanlal stated in the hospital that while he climbed the pole, his elbow got into contact with some metallic part and he felt some sensation in the nerves due to which he could not hold the pole firmly. Also the grip of one of his legs was lost. Consequently he lost balance and fell down. On interrogation as to why he did not use a ladder and safety belt, he replied that he had not assessed this to be a job of line repair work. Further he had been doing such repairs many times earlier without the ladder and the safety belt. He also quoted the non-availability of transport and manpower for carrying the tools and tackles to the site. Further, he said that safety belt caused more inconvenience while working on the lines.

He also confirmed that he had switched off the main supply lines feeding to that area. He did not know what sensation he got in his body, but it was not an electric shock, he said.

## QUESTIONS

1. What are the issues? What are the lessons?
2. Should Mohanlal be given paid leave and compensated as per the provision in the Workmen's Compensation Act? Should he be penalized for his negligence or violation of safety regulations, if any?
3. What was the role of management, particularly the person who supervises the work of Mohanlal?

---

* Source: Steel Authority of India Ltd, 1989. *Managerial Experiences in Focus: Second Volume of Cases*, New Delhi, pp 117 (Reproduced with permission from the publisher).

# CASE II: DEADLOCK OVER DEATH COMPENSATION

Raju was an apprentice trainee in a large public sector project. While on job during the training period he was involved in a fatal accident. He was not a member of the union. Still the union took up his case and asked for funeral advance. When the management was hesitant to take an immediate decision the union threatened the management with a wild cat strike. The management paid the advance. Two days later the union insisted that the management must pay compensation as per Workmen's Compensation Act. The management maintained that at the time of his death, Raju was not an employee and so he was not eligible for compensation. The management was afraid it would set a precedent. The compensation works out to Rs 20,000. The union maintained that it costs less than the cost of one dinner that the management hosts whenever a VIP visits the project. In the absence of a favourable response from the management, the union went on strike.

## QUESTIONS

1. What are the issues?
2. Is the demand of the union justified?
3. Evaluate the response of the management.
4. Suggest how the problem should be tackled at this stage.

## FURTHER READINGS

1. Texts of relevant legislations.
2. Government of India, 1969. *Report of the National Commission on Labour*, New Delhi.
3. Government of India, 1988. *Indian Labour Year Book, 1988*, Labour Bureau, Ministry of Labour, New Delhi.
4. ILO, 1987. *World Labour Report, Vol. 2* (Ch. 9: Safety and Health), Geneva: ILO.

# Dynamics of Human Behaviour—Role of Personnel

---

**LEARNING OBJECTIVES**

After going through this chapter, you should be able to:
● Understand the internal psychological processes and external situational factors that affect human behaviour.    ● Appreciate the need for adopting multipronged motivational strategies for ensuring high performance and employee satisfaction.    ● Become aware of various factors that need to be considered in designing an effective communication system.
● Discern the causes leading to resistance to change and to suggest ways and means for overcoming them.    ● Describe alternative planned change strategies for improving productivity, human satisfaction and overall effectiveness of organization.

All organizational processes are ultimately human processes being the outcome of human interaction.  Behaviour encompassing all our actions—verbal or nonverbal—is the basic and the only observable unit of interaction between people.  However, human behaviour is the result of a complex set of interacting variables between an individual and his environment.  Understanding human behaviour and discovering the underlying causes are a prerequisite for formulating effective personnel policies and human resource development strategies.  In the following pages, thus, an attempt will be made to analyze the causes of human behaviour both in terms of inner psychological processes and external situational factors.  This will be followed by a brief description of motivational process with particular emphasis on motivational strategies available to managers for creating productive and satisfying conditions for employees. Coordinated action of employees towards a unified goal is made possible through a properly designed communication system. The factors to be considered in designing communication network so as to ensure free flow of information in all directions in organizations are also discussed. In the final part of the chapter, behavioural and attitudinal issues in introducing and managing change in organizations have been highlighted and alternative strategies of planned change have been briefly described.

## UNDERSTANDING HUMAN BEHAVIOUR

It is through behaviour that employees give expression to their commitment to work, level of motivation and their attitudes. Behaviour includes all our actions—overt or covert and verbal or nonverbal—and thus directly affects our performance in organizations. In order to discern why different people behave in different ways, it is necessary to understand the causes underlying such behaviour. The causal analysis of behaviour provides necessary conditions for enabling us to direct the behaviour of employees in desired direction.

There are basically two schools of thought in psychology which attempt explanations of human behaviour. One school believes in the psychic inner causes of behaviour which states that the actions or behaviour of a person emanate from the internal psychological structure often called personality. As employees differ in their personality so do they differ in their behaviour. It follows then that change in behaviour can only be brought about by changing the personality of individuals. According to the second school led by B F Skinner, the behaviour of a person is primarily determined by the external situational factors, often called the stimuli, and the reward associated with one's response. By changing or rearranging the external situational factors including the reward system, one can redirect and mould the behaviour of employees. The underlying principle of this theory can be stated as: (i) individuals learn by repeating their behaviour, (ii) behaviour is repeated if it is immediately rewarded or reinforced, and (iii) repetition of behaviour strengthens that behaviour which becomes a conditioned response.

The two points of view mentioned above are in sharp contrast with each other and neither extreme is sufficient enough to provide a fuller insight into the complexities of human behaviour. Attempt, therefore, has been made to explain the behaviour in terms of both the internal psychological processes and external situational variables. At a given point of time, the behaviour of a person is the result of a complex set of interactions between an individual personality and the situation in which he finds himself. The framework combining both viewpoints can be presented as $B = f(P)(S)$; where B stands for behaviour, P for the person and S for the situation. Behaviour thus is a function of the person in relation to the situation.

## Variables in the Concept of Person

The internal psychological structure of a person consists of a number of interacting processes through which one organizes, interprets and responds to external stimuli such as information, physical conditions of work and the behaviour of other persons like superior, subordinate or colleague. Some of these internal processes are explained below.

*Motivation*    This is a process of need-arousal, propelling a person to channelize his energies and efforts in the direction of seeking satisfaction of that need. The concept and process of motivation will be discussed in detail later on.

*Perception*    It is a process by which one experiences external reality, selects part of numerous stimuli present in one's environment, interprets that stimulus and incorporates the new understanding into one's perceptual framework. Individuals differ in their perception of the same given reality as they tend to interpret the situation in terms of their respective perceptual frameworks. Also, as humans we have a limited capacity to handle a variety of information at the same time, so we tend to *selectively* respond to only those pieces of information which fit into our beliefs and experiences. Thus a change in the personnel policy of the organization may be perceived as desirable by middle managers but undesirable by a section of workers or vice versa.

*Cognition*    This is a process by which individuals remember perceived information using memory, seek to establish new sets of relationship amongst various pieces of information and recall the stored information. It involves one's rational thinking process, reasoning capacity and intellectual manipulation of abstractions. Each one of us, based on our perception of the experience, develops a unique cognitive map which provides consistency in our attitudes, thought, action and so behaviour.

A piece of information which is consistent with an employee's cognitive map will be readily acceptable whereas any action on the part of management which disturbs the consistency of the cognitive map of employees is likely to be resisted.

*Emotion*    This is a process by which individuals experience both positive and negative feelings at a given point of time. Emotion refers to subjective states of feeling unlike cognition which is the thinking and logical part of one's personality. The feeling of joy and satisfaction one experiences in accomplishing a challenging task in organization is what gives rise to commitment to work and encourages employees to put in more and more efforts in their work. The feeling of boredom and dissatisfaction with one's repetitive task would lead to frustration and withholding of one's efforts. Emotions are great reservoir of our energies. When negative emotions like anger or hate are aroused, lot of our energies are wasted in containing those feelings. When we experience positive feelings like joy and love, much of our energies are productively channelized.

*Learning*    This is a process by which an individual modifies and enriches any or all of the components like perceptual framework, cognitive map and emotive states and seeks to redefine relationships amongst them. Learning must be manifested in changed behaviour, adoption of new approaches and search for new alternatives leading to adaptive response to situations. Individuals obviously differ in their capacity to learn and the pace at which they learn. A person is said to be rigid when he finds it difficult to modify and adapt his behaviour to meet the demands of a new situation.

These analytical concepts are organized into certain integrative concepts such as attitude, personality structure, and the self concept. These processes are interactive in nature and are arranged in a consistent manner. Before a person behaves or acts, he processes the stimulus present in his environment through the internal psychological processes. The person, thus, acts as a whole and his action is determined by the complex set of interaction among the internal processes. These processes differ from one person to another, which results in difference of behaviour among people.

## Variables in the Concept of Situation

A person's inner psychological processes get activated when he or she is confronted with varied situations. His capacity to interpret accurately and respond to situations in adaptive ways or otherwise will depend on the characteristics of the situation prevailing at a given point of time. Some of the situational factors that have impact on employee's behaviour are briefly summed up here.

**Organization Structure**    The structure of an organization provides a framework and outlines a network of relationships among role occupants within which employees are expected to behave. A tightly structured organization creates a situation for employees which limits their interaction with a few persons and leads to routine and often impersonal behaviour. A loose, flexible structure, on the contrary offers a great deal of opportunities to expand interaction with large number of people and behave in innovative and personalized manner. The latter encourages individual employees to develop problem-solving orientation, to take initiative and to experience personal and professional growth.

**Organizational Processes**    The organizational processes such as leadership, decision-making and control, communication and motivation also influence the personality and, therefore, behaviour of the employees. If the decision making is centralized at the upper echelons of the hierarchy, the employees at lower levels do not learn to take responsibility and to exercise authority delegated to them. They would prefer to refer the problems to the top management rather than take the risk of solving problems themselves. The decentralized and participative decision-making, on the other hand, helps employees to develop their personality in the direction of exercising independent judgement, accepting responsibility and getting committed to organizational objectives.

**Socio-cultural Milieu**    The value system, norms and practices existing in the socio-cultural environment do affect the personality characteristics of a person. The diversity and heterogeneity of social experience in terms of family background patterns, ethnic differences, age group, sex and reference groups account for differences in behaviour amongst employees. For example, in Indian culture, power-distance among people on account of caste system, wealth, authority, age and sex has been traditionally legitimized through social norms and sanctions and even today a vast majority of people tend to accept it as a part of reality. This has, thus, given rise to dependency syndrome in our culture where employees of older generation at least expect a higher authority to give direction and take decisions. An employee's capacity to function autonomously is hampered as he or she is likely to look to someone higher up to give direction.

## Implications

The framework discussed above suggests that there are at least two ways by which behaviour of employees could be directed towards productive pursuits in organizations. One is by changing the personality, that is, the internal psychological structure of the person, which is a long-drawn and uncertain process. The personality development, in the formative years, takes place in  home and in the community which has a lasting effect on our behaviour. The experiences that have gone into moulding one's personality are unique to oneself and quite distinct from those of the other individuals. Changing the behaviour of each employee through personality modification is an uphill task for organizations. Despite these limitations, most of the management development and training programmes are designed to achieve the change in personality structure of employees. No wonder, most managers who undergo these training programmes are often skeptical about transferring their learning into work situation.

Another strategy of changing behaviour of employees is to modify the characteristics of the situation prevailing in an organization. The assumption here is that given a situation conducive to eliciting positive behaviour, most employees will develop desirable attributes in their personalities. Situational factors like organizational practices and the nature of work have tremendous influence in shaping one's personality. For example, work of a routine, repetitive type tends to have a degenerative effect on one's personality while challenging work provides ample opportunities for realization of one's potential for growth. Thus by modifying the situational variables, one can bring about changes in behaviour in a predetermined desirable direction. Finding an optimum fit between the person and the situation by altering the latter is the challenge that a personnel specialist must accept for ensuring high performance-oriented and adaptive behaviour on the part of the employees.

## EMPLOYEE MOTIVATION

Most human resource management strategies are eventually meant to optimally utilize the capabilities of individuals and groups towards achievement of organizational objectives. Performance of an individual is a function of his ability and willingness or desire to use his ability in achieving personal or organizational goals. This willingness or desire to act, and to behave,  is what may be called motivation. Thus a person may have the ability but little motivation to use that ability in a desired direction.

Motivation or lack of it gets manifested in behaviour. It is by observing the behaviour of employees that a manager draws inference regarding their motivation level. Most behaviour is purposeful or goal-directed and may involve a deliberate or conscious decision on the part of a person. Thus undesirable behaviour cannot be dismissed as of no consequence. A person indulging in undesirable activities is trying to work towards achieving his personal goal which may be at variance with the organizational goals. This person is highly motivated but channelizes his energies in an undesirable direction from the point of view of the organization. Given the same socio-cultural environment and the organization climate, it is not unusual to find people who, despite difficult conditions, are able to put in their best in work situation while there are others who even in the best possible conditions prefer to remain on the side lines and contribute only that minimum which they consider necessary to their survival in the organization. Both these groups of people are motivated— what makes the difference, however, is the direction in which they are willing to expend their energy.

Individuals also differ in terms of intensity of their behaviour. Some are high on activity level while others are low; some are fast while others slow. The intensity of behaviour is also a function of the strength of the need and the energy level an individual possesses at a given point of time. Motivation thus is a personalized phenomenon which can be shaped by prevailing situational characteristics. In work organizations, by changing the situational characteristics, it is possible to channelize the energy of people in desirable productive pursuits and maintain that behaviour at high intensity level. Motivation provides a set of tools, a conceptual framework to the manager which can be used to diagnose the direction and intensity of behaviour of employees and to take corrective measures to change the behaviour in desirable direction.

## Basic Principles of Motivation

Based on research and experimentation for the last four decades or so in the field of motivation; it has been possible to derive certain basic principles underlying human motivation.

These principles can be stated as follows:

(i) All reasonably healthy adults have a considerable *reservoir of potential energy*. Differences in the total amount of potential energy are important determinants of motivation.

(ii) All adults have a number of *basic motives* or *needs* which can be thought of as valves or outlets that channel and regulate the flow of potential energy from this reservoir.

(iii) Most adults within a given socio-cultural system may have the same set of motives or energy outlets; they differ greatly in relative strength or readiness of various motives. If a particular motive is strong, it forces the energy outlet to open easily, while a weak motive allows limited flow of energy.

(iv) Actualization of motive depends on specific situation in which a person finds himself.

(v) Certain characteristics of a situation arouse or trigger different motives, opening different valves or outlets. Each motive or energy outlet is responsive to a different set of situational characteristics.

(vi) Each motive leads to a different pattern of behaviour.

(vii) By changing the nature of the situational characteristics or stimuli, different motives are aroused or actualized, resulting in the energizing of distinct and different patterns of behaviour.

## Motivation and Job Satisfaction

Several attempts have been made through empirical and exploratory research for the last half a century to identify motives that play an important role in  determining individual and group performance.  One of the most widely discussed *theory of motivation* is that of Maslow which looks at *motivation* in terms of *a series of relatively separate and distinct drives*.  Five *basic needs* are identified:

(i) The physiological needs such as hunger, thirst, sex, etc.

(ii) The safety needs for protection against danger, threat and deprivation.

(iii) The love needs for satisfactory association with others, for belonging to groups, and for giving and receiving friendship and affection.

(iv) The esteem needs for self respect and for respect of others, often referred to as the ego or status needs.

(v) The self-actualization or self-fulfilment needs to achieve the potential within oneself, for maximum self-development and for creativity and self-expression.

According to Maslow these needs are arranged in a hierarchy.  The most potent need will monopolize consciousness and will tend to evoke behaviour in response to it.  Once this need is satisfied, another higher level need is likely to become activated and so on.  A need is never satisfied completely except for a short time.  People, therefore, are continuously in a motivational state, but the nature of the motivation is fluctuating and complex.  All needs are never completely satisfied—they recur periodically—and if their satisfaction is deprived for any period of time, they become important to him. Yet, they are usually not significant until lower-level needs are reasonably well satisfied.  The deprivation most people experience with respect to lower-level needs diverts their energies into the struggle to satisfy them and the need for self-actualization remains dormant.  A few supporting features of the need hierarchy theory as postulated by Maslow are given below.

(i) The higher needs are a later evolutionary development.

(ii) The higher the need and the less imperative it is for sheer survival, the longer can the gratification be postponed, and it is easier for the need to disappear permanently.

(iii) Living at the higher need level means greater biological efficiency, greater longevity, better sleep, appetite, few chances of disease, etc.

(iv) Higher needs are less urgent subjectively.

(v) Higher need gratifications produce more desirable subjective results such as more profound happiness, serenity and richness of inner life.

(vi) Pursuit and gratification of higher needs represent a general trend toward good health.

(vii) Higher needs require better outside conditions (educational, economic, etc.) to make their activation possible.

(viii) Satisfaction of higher needs is closer to self-actualization than that of lower-needs.

Although there is reasonable support for the hypothesis that to some extent human needs do have hierarchical order, questions have been raised regarding the generality of Maslow's formulation. Nonetheless, the theory advanced by Maslow contributes significantly to insight into the dynamics and complexity of human motivation.

**Motivation-hygiene Concept**    One attempt at operationalizing the insight provided by Maslow's formulation in work situation was made by Herzberg and his colleagues which has come to be known as two-factor theory of motivation and satisfaction.

In essence, the theory proposes that the primary determinants of employee satisfaction are factors intrinsic to the work that employees do, i.e. recognition, achievement, responsibility, advancement, personal growth in competence. These factors are called *motivators* as they encourage employees to obtain satisfaction of these needs through better job performance. The motivators are also called *job-content factors*. Absence of these needs in one's own job will not lead to dissatisfaction but to a lesser degree of satisfaction or even to apathy and indifference. Dissatisfaction is seen as being determined by a separate set of factors which are extrinsic to the work itself. These aspects of the work environment are called *hygiene* factors and include: company policies, supervisory practices, working conditions, salaries and wages, and interpersonal relationships on the job. The hygiene factors are also called *job-context factors*. Thus, Herzberg theory suggests that a job should enhance positive work motivation and employee satisfaction to the extent that it provides opportunities for employees to achieve, gain recognition and responsibility, advance in the organization, and grow in competence. The presence of hygiene factors will lead to less dissatisfaction among employees but will not provide sufficient conditions for them to experience satisfaction on the job. The employees, therefore, in the absence of motivators will not be able to give their best to their respective organizations.

The theory has gained wide acceptance among managers throughout the world and has been used in numerous organizations to enrich the content of jobs by building in the *motivators* in work situations. However, empirical evidences do not always support the two-factor theory of Herzberg. For example, both intrinsic as well as extrinsic factors have been found to be related to both satisfaction and dissatisfaction.

There seems to be certain similarity in the two theoretical postulates that have been presented above. An attempt is made here to establish the relationship between the two sets of motives identified and their impact on the utilization of human capabilities in Table 10.1. which is self-explanatory.

In Table 10.1 two basic systems are involved: physical systems which include physiological and anatomical functions, and psychosocial systems, which include the individual in organizational and societal contexts. If we relate the need hierarchy to these systems, we find that physiological and safety needs are related to physical system while other higher level needs to psychosocial system. Safety need, in part, also relates to psychosocial system.

Table 10.1  Relationship of Motivation to Individual Performance

| Systems | Need-hierarchy | Hygiene Dissatisfiers | Motivator-Satisfiers | Capacity |
|---|---|---|---|---|
| Psychosocial | Self-actualization Esteem social | | Achievement Recognition Work itself Responsibility Advancement (Job-content factors) | Latent human capacity |
| Physical | Safety and security | Company policy and administration Supervision Salary & wages Interpersonal relations Working conditions (Job-context factors) | | Normal output |

The hygiene and motivator factors also relate to the need hierarchy. The two systems somewhat overlap. Dissatisfiers include love, safety and physiological needs, while satisfiers reflect self-actualization, esteem and love needs. In relating these to individual performance we see that both satisfiers and dissatisfiers are involved in motivating the individual to *normal* performance. In tapping latent human capability and moving beyond the normal range of output, the satisfiers become relatively more important.

## Motivational Strategies

Given the complexities of human behaviour, existence of multiple needs and goals among employees, differences in the priorities of individual goals and differential expectations, it is imperative that the strategies to be adopted for motivating employees should be multipronged and multifaceted. Some of the strategies adopted in organizations are discussed here.

**Performance-based Reward System**    The reward system used to elicit desirable response from employees must be perceived as equitable. As employees, we always compare ourselves with others in the same organization besides others outside and if we perceive that we are getting less reward than our colleagues with similar qualifications and expertise, then the reward is perceived as inequitable. If the contribution is perceived to be more than the inducement, the principle of equity is disturbed and an imbalance is created in our mind. In order to return to a balanced state, either an employee reduces his contribution or pressurizes the management to increase the inducement. Seeking to maintain balance between contribution and inducement is a continuous subjective process and is a necessary condition for achieving the purposes for which reward system is developed. Such a balance can be perceived and equity can be maintained if the reward system is based on predetermined and widely shared performance criteria.

**Enrichment of the Content of Jobs**    Herzberg's two-factor theory discussed above provides the basis by which job enrichment as yet another strategy of motivating employees has been extensively used. In recent years, the emphasis has shifted away from job-context factors to enriching the content of job in terms of providing higher responsibility, adequate challenge, advancement and learning opportunities and the like.

**Job Redesign**    The redesigning of jobs on the basis of self-regulating autonomous groups with emphasis on group responsibility is being widely used as a strategy of improving productivity and employee satisfaction. The concept of job redesign and the principles involved have already been discussed in detail in Chapter 2.

**Operant Conditioning**    Based on Skinner's theoretical formulation on understanding human behaviour as discussed in the beginning of this chapter, a number of organizations have used principles of positive reinforcement to direct the behaviour of employees in desirable direction.

In order to operationalize the positive reinforcement approach, the following steps are necessary.

(a) Specific desirable behaviour such as coming on time, regular attendance, production norms and the like are identified.

(b) For each of the specific behaviour identified above, a reinforcement schedule is worked out in such a way that as and when such behaviour occurs, the employee is rewarded and that piece of behaviour is thus reinforced. The reinforcement could be in the form of monetary reward, other forms of award, recognition or appreciation. The reinforcement schedule could be fixed as in salary or variable as in production incentive. Likewise, the reinforcement could be continuous, that is, everywhere an employee exhibits the behaviour he is rewarded or it could be intermittent, that is, at intervals. The reinforcement could be also based on *ratio*, the number of items, or *frequency*, the number of times. The choice of a particular reinforcement schedule or a combination of it will depend on the type of behaviour desired by the organization. It is not desirable to use negative reinforcement, often called punishment, as a strategy for inducing the desired behaviour. The likely unintended consequences of punishment will be discussed in the next chapter. However, in order to reduce the recurrence or continuance of undesirable behaviour, ignoring that behaviour by withholding positive reinforcement has been found to be more effective.

**Achievement Motivation**    Yet another development in motivation theory has been the identification of certain intrinsic motives that are determinants of work-related behaviour. These motives are; need for achievement, need for power and need for affiliation. The need for achievement gives rise to the desire to excel in relation to competitive or internalized standards in work situations. The need for power leads to such behaviour as increased control over other people, commanding attention, controlling the channels of communication so as to remain in charge of things. The need for affiliation refers to such behaviour as sharing of warmth, establishing friendly relations. belonging to social groups, and so on.

Out of the three needs, the need for achievement plays an important role in determining the performance of an individual. Like any other attribute, the degree of achievement motivation tends to vary among individuals. Some individuals rate very high, while others very low in this need achievement. As a matter of fact research in this area by McClelland and his colleagues has established that not only individuals but groups, organizations or even societies could be rated according to the degree of achievement motivation evident in the total system. McClelland emphasizes a positive relationship between achievement motivation and economic growth in various countries. Businessmen, particularly entrepreneurial-managers tend to have relatively more achievement motivation than other identifiable groups in society.

There are at least four characteristics of the individual with high achievement motivition :

(a) He likes situations in which he takes personal responsibility for finding solutions to problems.

(b) He has a tendency to set moderate achievement goals and to take *calculated risks*.

(c) He wants concrete feedback on how well he is doing.

(d) He considers the sense of personal achievement, challenge and excellence in work as the most important rewards.

McClelland and his group have developed methods and techniques whereby achievement motivation of employees of an organization could be considerably increased on a planned basis.

We have so far presented some of the theories of work motivation which have been applied in numerous organizations with varying degrees of success in the optimum utilization of human capabilities and skills. There are obviously considerable differences with regard to emphasis on certain aspects of motivation over others and also the approaches that are adopted in bringing about change in organizations. Despite the differences in approach, a common factor that has come to be recognized as the central core of motivation is the nature of work itself. Attention is being shifted away from the factors which do not directly constitute essential aspects of work to factors which make work inherently challenging and satisfying.

## EMPLOYEE COMMUNICATION

Communication involves transmission of information, ideas, emotions, skills by the use of symbols-words, pictures, and figures from one person to another. More precisely communication refers to transfer of meaning between sender and receiver. Communication is thus the most basic of all the organizational processes through which coordinated effort of large number of employees can be directed towards unified purpose, shared meaning and expectation developed and commitment to organizational goals generated. It is necessary, therefore, to design an effective employee communication system in an organization to ensure that the purpose of communication is adequately met. In the following pages we will discuss some of the major factors that must be given due consideration in designing communication system.

## Characteristics of Communication Networks

In designing the communication system in an organization, the following characteristics of communication network must be kept in mind.

**Information Need**    The type of information required by individual role occupants, group, departments, units and vertical levels need to be ascertained so as to enable each of the components of the organization to function with optimum efficiency.

**Number of employees/groups to be covered by given type of information**    Certain types of information particularly those relating to personnel policies may have to be shared with all the employees. Thus the communication circuit will cover the entire organization. Some type of information may be specific to a department or to a particular hierarchical level, in which case the communication circuit should include only those departments and levels. If the communication circuit is too large, intended messages may not reach every one. Also, filtering and distortion of intended message at successive levels takes place.

**Type of Messages**    There are certain messages which are of repetitive type in that at successive levels, the same message has to be repeated. A large information loop may reach many members of the organization through a repetitive pattern of transmission. A policy directive from the top management may go down the line through repetition at each level. Certain messages, however, are of modification type that at successive levels the messages need to be interpreted and modified to meet the requirement of the particular level. A different pattern of transmission needs to be used and the communication circuit for these types of messages will have to be small. The message of the management has to be suitably modified to make it relevant to the workers operating on machines.

**Feedback Mechanisms**    All processes of communication are cyclical in nature and, therefore, the communication circuit must have a built-in feedback mechanism to enable the original transmitter of message to ensure that the message has been received as was intended. The larger the communication circuit, the more difficult it is to get the feedback. That is why opinion surveys are conducted amongst workers to obtain their feedback on organizational policies, practices and procedures.

**Communication Networks and Task Efficiency**    The number of communication links or levels to be covered in a communication circuit will affect the efficiency of the circuit for a particular task. The smaller the number of communication links in a group, the greater is the efficiency of the group in task performance. At least four types of communication networks can be identified, each suited to a particular task.

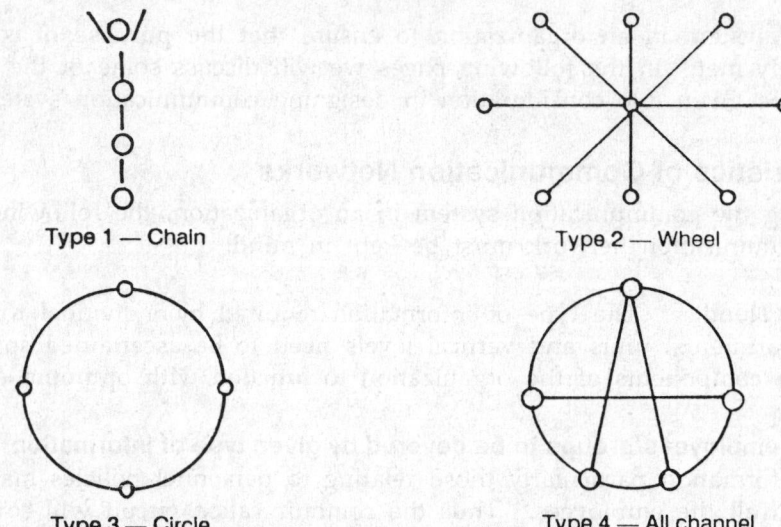

Type 1 — Chain

Type 2 — Wheel

Type 3 — Circle

Type 4 — All channel

The *chain network* can cover a large number of employees and is more appropriate for messages of simple repetitive type. The *wheel network* is more efficient for tasks of additive or coordinative nature, where the chairman in a meeting collects the viewpoints of various members and announces the collective view. The *circle network* is suited to tasks which require building on the idea of the other or supplementing the effort of each other. *All channel network* is primarily meant for solving complex problems wherein unrestricted interaction and interchange of ideas are required.

**Communication Circuit and Organization Efficiency**    A communication circuit may be too large, involving unnecessary people with messages irrelevant for their roles and tasks. This creates a situation of *information overload*. It is not an uncommon experience for many executives who often deal with this problem of information overload by throwing circulars and other written messages in the waste-paper basket. On the contrary, if the communication circuit is too small, leaving out the relevant people, it is the task that suffers.

It is essential to continuously find an optimum fit between the communication circuit and organizational efficiency. Moreover, the communication circuit must be open to feedback and adaptive so as to respond to exigencies of changing situation.

## Direction of Communication Flow

Communication system in an organization should be so designed as to meet the information requirement of vertical levels and horizontally differentiated departments or units. In order to ensure free flow of relevant information throughout the organization, appropriate mechanisms will need to be developed for: (i) downward communication, (ii) upward communication, and (iii) lateral communication. The types of information that need to be considered for the three directions of communication flow are listed below.

**Downward Communication**    There are two methods that can be adopted for facilitating downward communication— written and oral.

| *Written* | *Oral* |
| --- | --- |
| Letters | Face-to-face communication |
| Memos/reports | Performance counselling |
| Newsletter | Conferences/meetings |
| Magazines | Speeches |
| Manuals/handbooks | Closed circuit TV |
| Bulletin/posters | |

*Job Instructions*    Specific directions to employees to enable them to perform their tasks efficiently, that is, *how* and *What* have to be done.

*Job Rationale*    Information  providing rationale for the task and its relationship to other tasks in organizations, so as to develop an appreciation of the relevance and meaningfulness of the task, that is, *why* it has to be done.  What organizational *purposes* will be achieved through the task?

*Organizational Policies, Procedures and Practices*    Information regarding the norms, rules and procedures to enable employees to learn the *do's* and *don'ts* as expected by the organization.

*Feedback*    Information,  both positive and negative, to the subordinates regarding their performance so as to help them monitor their own efforts.  Also information about subordinates' strengths, weaknesses and potential for growth and development so that they can operate from their areas of strength, improve in areas where they are weak and make efforts towards realizing their potential.

*Identification with Organization*    Information of an ideological character to inculcate a sense of mission, pride and commitment in employees towards the organization as a whole.

**Upward Communication**    Some of the methods for facilitating upward communication are: suggestion boxes, quality circles, joint participative fora like shop council and plant council, attitude/opinion surveys, grievance-handling machinery, meetings, formal progress reports, and, open-door policy wherein any employee is allowed to directly approach the chief executive to share information and ideas.

*Feedback on Attitudes and Feelings of Employees*    Information as to how employees feel about their jobs, about supervision, about peers and about the mission of the organization.

*Information regarding Production and Targets*    On a regular basis which will provide input to the management in planning and target-setting process.

*Feedback on Organizational Policies, Procedures and Practices*    On the basis of these the management can bring about suitable modifications, if necessary, or else can initiate corrective action.

*Employee Grievance*    Small individual grievances if left unnoticed or unattended to often lead to collective grievance which may become a source of major industrial relations problem.

*Suggestions for Improvement and Innovation*    The employees are in a better position to provide suggestions for improvement in the work procedure and to think of innovative ways to do the work more efficiently. These suggestions often lead to remarkable improvement and innovation in the work place.

*Lateral Communication*     In this procedure, communication flows across the departments.

The methods for ensuring horizontal flow of communication are regular meetings, task forces, written communication, productivity-improvement group, social events, telephone, etc.

*Inter-departmental Coordination*     The goals, tasks and activities of functionally differentiated departments need to be integrated to ensure unity of efforts towards overall objectives of the organization.

*Sharing Information*     Information can be shared with colleagues with greater accuracy and speed as compared to the use of vertical channels which invariably cause delays and distortions. Also, information on innovations being experimented within one department needs to be shared with other departments on a continuing basis.

*Solving Problems*     Organizations encounter problems like low productivity, high costs, absenteeism and the like which require multi-disciplinary approach to solve them. A problem of this type needs to be examined from a variety of perspectives, which is made possible through lateral communication.

*Resolution of Conflicts*     Inter-departmental conflicts do arise due to communication distortion, lack of understanding and competition for scarce resources. Horizontal communications promote cooperative attitude and collaborative orientation.

*Sense of Belonging*     Lateral communication facilitates awareness of one another's constraints and aspirations, thereby creating conditions for working even under the worst conditions. It is the feeling of belonging to the team that makes it possible for one department to accommodate the request of the other even if one's departmental priorities have to undergo a change.

In designing communication system, the types of information to be shared under downward, upward and lateral channels need to be matched with the characteristics of the communication circuit discussed above. For example, in downward flow of communication, information relating to job instructions and job rationale should be shared with a small number of employees directly engaged in that task; whereas, information about identification with organization needs to be shared with a large number of employees covering the entire organization. The choice of method will depend on the extent to which a particular method conforms to the characteristics of communication circuit mentioned above.

## PLANNED CHANGE STRATEGIES

Organizations are created and designed as instruments of socio-economic development in a society. As instruments of development. they are affected by the changes that take place in the environment. Changes can occur also in the internal environment of an organization due to changing expectations and aspirations of the work force or introduction of new technology like computers. Change has today become a pervasive phenomenon affecting practically every aspect of organizational life. Management of change, therefore, has assumed far greater significance in view of its rapid pace and increased unpredictability of direction both in the internal and external environment of the organizations. Since organizations are characterized by complex network of interdependent individuals and groups, change in any one aspect of organization will obviously have repercussions on other aspects as well as on the entire organization. It is imperative, therefore, that change, no matter how seemingly insignificant, must be carefully planned so that its negative consequences on other organization subsystems are anticipated and corrective action can be taken on time.

## Need for Change

Some of the factors in the internal and external environment of the organizations necessitating change are:

(i) Need for improvement in productivity and quality,

(ii) increased uncertainties in social, political and economic environments,

(iii) rapid pace of change in technology and knowledge,

(iv) globalization of business and standards of goods and services; beneficiaries compare the indigenous goods and services with international standards,

(v) increase in the number of stake-holders and pressure groups within and outside organizations,

(vi) increased competition at national and international levels,

(vii) consumer/customer-orientation,

(viii) obsolescence likely to increase, thus necessitating continuous learning by organizational members,

(ix) decision-response time for organizations shrinking,

(x) adaptation through adjustment, search and creating options,

(xi) value-based normative training and education to develop the culture of work commitment.

## Resistance to Change

Although the need for change arising out of the factors mentioned above is perceived yet it is an uphill task to implement changes in existing systems. All changes in final analysis involve transformation and modification of people's attitudes, knowledge, skills and practices acquired in the process of coping with existing complexities. Any change in belief system and habit, therefore, is likely to be resisted as it requires adoption of such new, untried coping mechanisms. More specifically, change is resisted on account of the following factors.

*Evaluation of Outcome*    The employees' assessment of the effect of and the goal to be achieved by change is likely to be different depending on, for example, the hierarchical levels to which they belong. The same change proposal may be perceived differently by managers and workers in terms of its likely impact on organization.

*Adaptability to Change*    Individuals differ in terms of certain psychological characteristics such as risk-taking ability, proneness to anxiety tolerance of ambiguity flexibility and the like.  Those employees who have not developed the characteristics required for responding positively to change are likely to resist change efforts.

*Personal Goals*    Change may be perceived as a threat to one's personal goals like security, prestige, money, power and professional competence, in which case it is likely to be resisted.

*Misunderstanding of Purpose and Lack of Trust*    Lack of understanding of the purpose of change and low degree of trust amongst various sections of employees may result in resisting effort towards change.

## Dealing with Resistance to Change

Resistance to change can be minimized if not completely eliminated by adopting the following measures.

(i) The nature of change should be made clear to the people who are going to be affected by it.

(ii) commonality of purpose and meaning of change can be achieved through education and communication.

(iii) the interest or pressure groups resisting change can be co-opted in the decision-making structures, thus absorbing their resistance and making them a partner in the change process.

(iv) people should be encouraged to actively participate and get involved in deciding about the nature and direction of change.

(v) change has to be initiated not on personal grounds or for personal benefits of a few individuals but for objective requirements of the organization.

(vi) the already established institutions, norms, customs and  social relations should not be ignored but incorporated to the  extent possible, in the change process.

(vii) opportunities for developing facilitative and supportive skills for management of change such as counselling, individual and group therapy, and consensus building in groups are to be provided.

## Organization Development (OD)

Organization Development (OD) is by far the most widely used strategy of planned change in organizations.  Based on the insights derived from researches in behavioural sciences in the last four decades, OD provides a normative framework within which changes in the climate and culture of the organization towards harnessing the human potential for realization of organizational objectives is brought about.  Organization Development thus aims at developing and revitalizing the adaptive capacities of organizations so as to enable them to respond to their internal and external environments, in a pro-active manner.

*Objectives of OD*    Some of the major objectives of OD are listed below.

(i) create an open problem-solving *climate* throughout the organization, so that employees develop a high degree of problem-solving orientations.

(ii) develop *relationships* based on trust and collaboration among individuals and groups vertically, horizontally and diagonally.

(iii) inculcate *team spirit* amongst employees and to develop a culture of consensual decision-making.

(iv) make *competition positive* where it exists, and so contribute to excellence in meeting the work goals as opposed to win/lose competition.

(v) locate decision-making and problem-solving *responsibilities* as close to the information source as possible.

(vi) increase the sense of *affiliation* with  organization objectives amongst employees throughout the organization by adopting strategies geared to integrating the individual needs with organizational requirements.

**Characteristics of OD**    The major characteristics of OD are as follows.

*Planned Change*    A great deal of effort is directed towards planning for change in a systematic manner as it is focused on people.  Interdependence amongst individuals as also other constituent elements of organization is  recognized and planning is attempted so as to deal with  unintended consequences of change efforts.

*Systematic Change*    The OD efforts usually involve the organization as a whole or an identifiable unit within it.  The emphasis is on *total system* change.

*Relational Thrust*    The OD programmes have a relational thrust; they seek to relate individual needs with organization goals by activating work groups and teams and using them as medium and target of change.

*Long-range Change*    Since OD aims at bringing about a culture change, the time span for such a change is much larger, sometimes two to three years or more.

*Catalyst for Change*    The catalyst for change often called the *Change Agent* with professional expertise in applied behavioural sciences must be involved while introducing OD programmes. Though an external change agent needs to be involved, however, a major thrust of OD effort is to prepare a cadre of internal change agents from within the  Organization who sustain, maintain and strengthen the change efforts.

*Intervention and Action Research*    The organization development approach places emphasis on making appropriate intervention in the ongoing activities of the organization.  In action research, the change agent establishes collaborative relationship with the clients and works jointly with them in diagnosing problems, setting change goals, making intervention and evaluating the outcome.  The process is continuous and cyclical and, therefore, requires active involvement and commitment of both the change agents (external or internal) and the clients for a longer time duration.

**Interventions**    A wide variety of interventions have been developed to assist the organization to move towards its change goals.  The choice of an intervention, however, depends on the target group, that is, the level at which change is desired.  The levels could be individual, dyads/triads, teams/groups, inter-group and organization as a whole.  At the level of *individual*, interventions like life and career planning counselling, sensitivity training (T-Group) for heightened self awareness are used; while for *dyads* (superior-subordinate), process consultation and third party peace-making are considered to be more appropriate. At the level of *group*, team-building workshops, family, T-Group and survey feedback are some of the interventions which have proved effective. The most widely used interventions are sensitivity training, process consultation and survey feedback. These three taken together can be used for any target group. In OD, while one may begin at any one level (individual, interpersonal, group, intergroup, organization) because of the interdependent nature of these levels, interventions must be directed at all subsequent levels.

## Management-by-Objectives (MBO)

Management-by-objectives (MBO) is yet another approach which has been widely used to integrate individual and group goals with the overall organizational goals. The emphasis in MBO is on involvement of employees in goal setting process. The overall goals of the organization are broken down into unit or departmental objectives. Each unit and department in turn assigns individualized objectives to its own members. Individualized objectives are set in consultation with the departmental or unit head and mechanisms for monitoring and review of these objectives are also specified. Thus, every employee, as a part of the MBO process, has a set of agreed objectives, concrete plans of action for achieving those objectives, and mechanism for continuous monitoring, periodic and final review. Figure 10.1 outlines the basic process of MBO.

MBO programmes if effectively implemented tend to improve communication within departments and increase mutual understanding between superior and subordinate. Managers tend to develop a more positive attitude towards performance evaluation and feedback systems and learn to monitor their own progress towards predetermined objectives. The performance appraisal system based on MBO tends to be more objective and provides useful data which can be used for career planning, reward distribution, job allocation and management development plans and programmes.

## Quality of Work Life

One of the major problems facing the developing and the developed world is the quality of work life of a vast majority of employees engaged in productive pursuits. The issue is not just one of achieving greater human satisfaction but it also aims at improving productivity, adaptability and overall effectiveness of organizations. The quality of work life movement in a broader sense seeks to achieve integration among the technological, human, organizational and societal demands which are often contradictory and conflicting.

The quality of work life is not based on a particular theory. It does not advocate a particular technique for application. Instead, it is more concerned with the overall climate of work and the impact that the work has on people as well as on organization effectiveness. Direct participation of employees in problem-solving and decision-making, particularly in areas related to their work, is considered to be a necessary condition for providing greater autonomy and opportunity for self-direction and self-control. The ultimate objective is of upgrading the quality of life at work. The recognized purpose is to change the climate at work so that the human-technological-organizational interface leads to a better quality of work life and eventually to an improved quality of life in community and society.

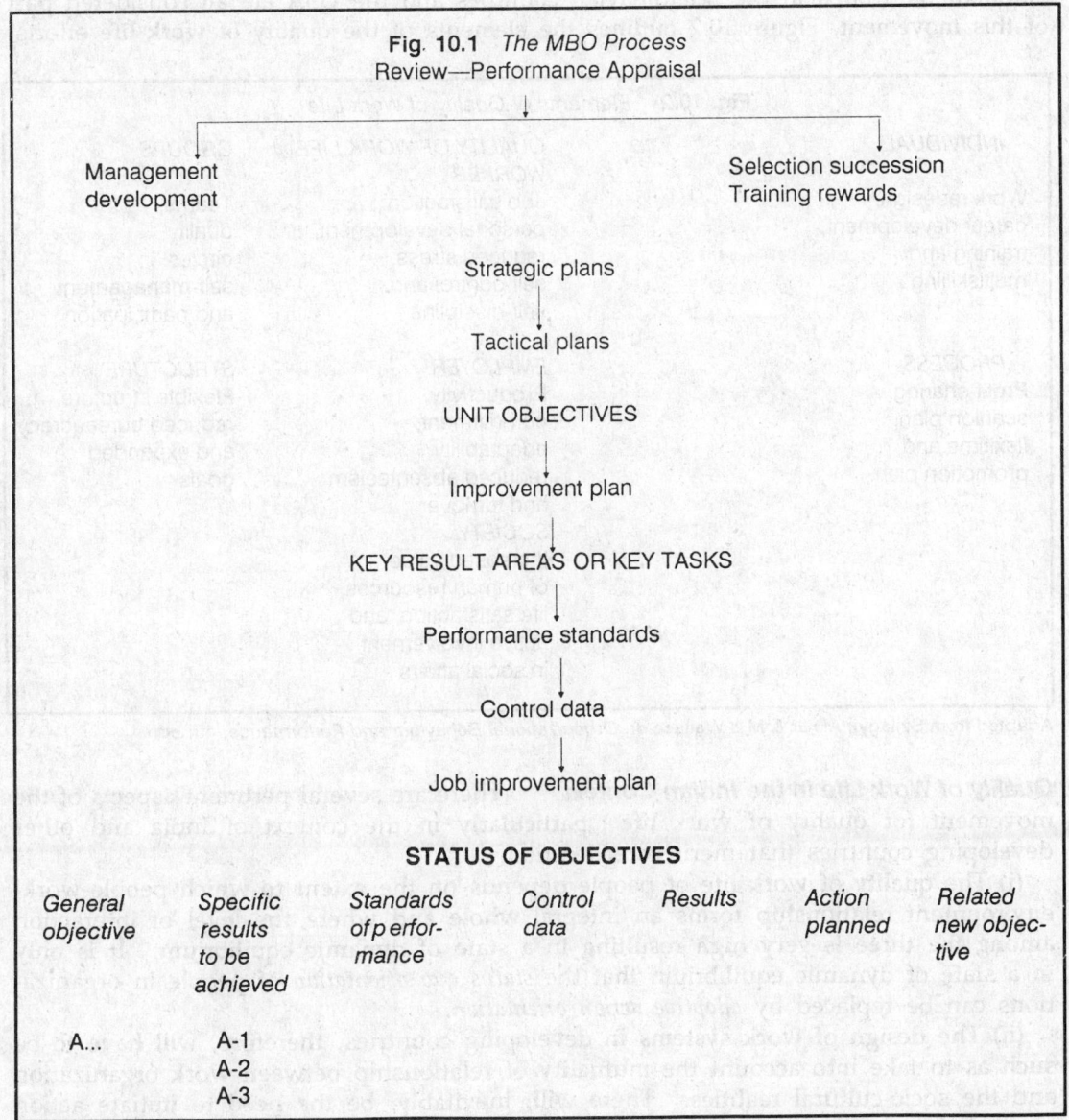

**Fig. 10.1** *The MBO Process*

Review—Performance Appraisal

Management development

Selection succession Training rewards

Strategic plans

Tactical plans

UNIT OBJECTIVES

Improvement plan

KEY RESULT AREAS OR KEY TASKS

Performance standards

Control data

Job improvement plan

**STATUS OF OBJECTIVES**

| General objective | Specific results to be achieved | Standards of performance | Control data | Results | Action planned | Related new objective |
|---|---|---|---|---|---|---|
| A... | A-1 A-2 A-3 | | | | | |

**Approaches to Quality of Work Life**    The quality of work life movement traditionally has been closely identified with the job redesign efforts based on socio-technical systems approach. However, during the 1980s the concept of quality of work life has been broadened to include a number of approaches aimed at joint decision-making, collaboration and mutual respect between management and employees, increased autonomy at work place, and self management.  Thus the quality circles adopted by Japanese and Indian industries as well as democratization of work process through self-regulating autonomous groups in the Scandinavian countries and the USA are all considered part of this movement. Figure 10.2 outlines the elements of the quality of work life efforts.

**Fig. 10.2**  *Elements of Quality of Work Life*

| INDIVIDUAL | QUALITY OF WORK LIFE WORKER | GROUPS |
|---|---|---|
| Work redesign, career development, training and multiskilling | Job satisfaction personal development, reduced stress, self-control and self-discipline | Teams, quality circles self-management and participation |
| *PROCESS*<br>Profit-sharing, scanlon plan, flexitime and promotion plan | *EMPLOYER*<br>Productivity, commitment, adaptability, reduced absenteeism and turnover<br>*SOCIETY*<br>Increased value of human resources, life satisfaction, and active involvement in social affairs | *STRUCTURE*<br>Flexible structure, reduced bureaucracy and expanded goals |

Adapted from Szilagyi, AD Jr & M J Wallace Jr, *Organizational Behaviour and Performance*, 4th edn.

***Quality of Work Life in the Indian Context***     There are several pertinent aspects of the movement for quality of work life  particularly in the context of India and other developing countries that merit consideration.

(i) The quality of work life of people depends on the extent to which people-work-environment relationship forms an integral whole and where the level of interaction among the three is very high resulting in a state of dynamic equilibrium.  It is only in a state of dynamic equilibrium that the *status quo orientation* of people in organizations can be replaced by *adaptive action orientation*.

(ii) The design of work systems in developing countries, therefore, will have to be such as to take into account the mutuality of relationship between work organization and the socio-cultural realities.  There will, inevitably, be the need to initiate action research in a variety of settings and on a large scale which alone can provide an insight into the nature and dynamics of interlinkages between the work system and the socio-cultural system.

(iii) In most developing countries, work redesign can become a powerful instrument of cultural and attitudinal change.  Certain values, attitudes and cultural attributes acquired in the new work system can manifest themselves in the socio-cultural and political system as well. Thus, while in the case of India, the bureaucratic form of work organization reinforces the authoritarianism of traditional society, the redesigned work system based on participative principles will tend to foster democratic values in the society at large.

(iv) While it will be necessary to inculcate new values and attitudes in the work place, it will also be equally desirable to design such systems which will sustain and strengthen the predominant patterns of behaviour that already exist in a given culture. Thus, in case of India, proposed alternative form of work organization with semi-autonomous group as unit is more geared towards incorporating the main orientations of people as also some of the characteristics of socio-cultural conditions prevailing today.

The movement for the quality of work life aims at integrating the socio-psychological needs of human beings, the unique requirements and constraints of a particular technology, the structure and processes of the organization and the existing socio-culture milieu. The purpose of the movement is to create a culture of work committment in organizations and society to ensure higher productivity, greater job satisfaction and active involvement in community and social life.

Work plays a central role in the life of people engaged in productive pursuits. The nature of work one is involved with has, therefore, a profound impact on shaping not only his personality or determining his performance level in the organization but also on his commitment to his fellow beings in the society. Thus, it is imperative to bring about improvement in the quality of life at work which can and even does lead to qualitative improvement in other facets of one's life. The prevailing socio-cultural conditions in India leave no option but to bring about such a change.

Various approaches have been adopted in different socio-cultural contexts to improve the quality of work life such as quality circles, team work, autonomous group working, flexitime and self-management. Central to all these approaches has been the direct participation of employees in affairs relating to their work leading to increased autonomy, self-control and self-direction.

In developing countries such as India only superficial attention has been paid to such a vital area of concern. The quality of work life movement provides a value framework and a philosophy which has a long-term implication for the human resources development.

## SUMMARY

The personnel function, concerned as it is with management and development of human resources, must address itself to the behavioural and attitudinal issues affecting productivity and employee satisfaction. An indepth understanding of employees' behaviour in a wide variety of situations can lead to initiating search for alternative ways of channelizing human actions towards productive pursuits. Several frameworks for diagnosing human behaviour, its intensity and its direction have been presented. Motivational strategies including communication, although present provide the basis for coordinated action but not enough attention is paid to ensure the availability of relevant information to the right people at the right time. Thus, the need for designing a proper communication system in organizations has been highlighted and factors to be considered for developing such a system have been discussed. Alternative strategies for introducing planned change and approaches to quality of work life in organizations have also been presented.

---

## KEY-WORDS

| | | |
|---|---|---|
| Cognition | : | An act or process of knowing or rational thinking involving recall memory, intellectual manipulation, etc. |
| Emotion | : | An affective state of consciousness in which joy, sorrow, fear, hate or the like is experienced, as distinguished from cognitive or volitional states of consciousness. |
| Learning | : | A process of training, practice or experience by which a person modifies behaviour. |
| Management-by-Objectives | : | An approach involving employees in the goal-setting process with a view to integrating individual and group goals with the overall organizational goals. |
| Motivation | : | A kind of inducement. It is a process of need arousal propelling a person to channelize his energies and efforts in the direction of seeking satisfaction of that need |
| Organization Development | : | A planned change strategy aimed at developing and revitalizing the adaptive capacities of organizations so as to enable them to respond to their internal and external environments, in a pro-active manner |
| Perception | : | A single unified awareness derived from sensory processes while a stimulus is present. |
| Quality of Work Life | : | A movement concerned with the overall climate of work and the impact that the work has on people as well as organization effectiveness. |

## REVIEW QUESTIONS

1. Discuss with examples, if any, how internal psychological processes and external situational factors affect human behaviour.
2. Critically examine the implications of various motivational strategies in ensuring high performance and employee satisfaction in your organization/Indian context.
3. Why does a communication system need to be designed? What factors need to be taken into account to make it effective?
4. Identify the factors that lead to changes in the organization. Enumerate the conditions giving rise to resistance to change. Suggest ways and means to overcome resistance to change.
5. Discuss the objectives and salient features of various planned strategies in making organizations effective.

# CASE: LATE OR NOT LATE

---

Kailash reported for work at 10.40 a.m. Madan, Kailash's boss, was angry with Kailash for being late without permission and yet saw him signing in the register quietly even without a word of apology. Madan felt that probably this was not the first time he was behaving like this. He, therefore, called Kailash. The following conversation took place between them.

| | |
|---|---|
| *Madan:* | Kailash, what is wrong with you? |
| *Kailash:* | Why? Nothing. |
| *Madan:* | I want to know why you are late and still signed in the register quietly? |
| *Kailash:* | I am not late. What do you mean when you say "I have signed quietly"? |
| *Madan:* | What time is it now? |
| *Kailash:* | 10.40 a.m. |
| *Madan:* | What time does the office open? |
| *Kailash:* | 9 a.m. |
| *Madan:* | Then? |
| *Kailash:* | Then, what? |
| *Madan:* | You are late by 100 minutes. |
| *Kailash:* | No, I am not late. Yesterday Ghai Saab (Madan's boss) gave me an envelope and asked me to deliver it in person before going to the office. I started off at home much earlier than I normally do and this is the reward I get! |
| *Madan:* | Is that so? I do not know about it. O.K. Forget it. You are not late. |

Kailash leaves the place. After a while, Madan gets a nagging doubt. Is he (Kailash) telling me the truth? Or, is he pulling a fast one on me? So, he picks up the receiver and speaks to Ghai. Ghai was busy at that time and fails to recollect having sent Kailash on some work. Instead, he retorts, 'Why would I send your man?'. Madan is furious. That fellow, Kailash, not only came late but also bluffed blatantly. So he called Kailash again and gave him a mouthful.

| | |
|---|---|
| *Madan:* | You not only came late, but also bluffed to me so blatantly. How dare you do that? I can have you charge-sheeted. |
| *Kailash:* | What is it you are talking? |
| *Madan:* | I am referring to the incident in the morning. You came late. |
| *Kailash:* | I thought you also agreed with me, earlier, that I was not late. |
| *Madan:* | Yes, I did because I foolishly believed your words. Now I realize I should not have. |
| *Kailash:* | You guys feel that you are the only virtuous people and we are all cheats. Come. Let us go and speak to Ghai and sort out the matter. |
| *Madan:* | That is not necessary. I already checked with him. |
| *Kailash:* | Since you don't believe me, I cannot believe you either. |
| *Madan:* | How dare you say that to me? |
| *Kailash:* | Why should I be afraid of speaking the truth? Let us go to Ghai *Saab*. He is not like you. Let me prove to you that I am honest and truthful. |
| | (Both go to Ghai's cabin) |

As they open the door, Ghai looks at them, figures out why they came and even before they could walk nearer and explain the purpose of their visit, he beams and says loudly:

| | |
|---|---|
| *Ghai:* | Oh Boy ! I know why you people are after me. I did send Kailash on some work. And, Madan, I am sorry neither did I inform you yesterday nor could I recollect it today when you rang up. You see, these days I am so much preoccupied with the deal we are trying to clinch. |

Kailash stares menacingly towards Madan. Madan tries to be cool in the presence of his boss and says:

| | |
|---|---|
| *Madan:* | Kailash! I am sorry about it. But you know the confusion occurred because I did not know anything about it. O.K. Let's forget. You are not late. |

## QUESTIONS

1. What are the issues? What lessons can be learnt from this incident?
2. Identify the internal psychological processes and external situational factors affecting the interpersonal relationship and behaviour in this case.
3. Discuss whether there was a communication gap? How has it occurred? How could it have been avoided?
4. Discuss whether employee-related decisions are often nearly as complex? How do situations like this affect human behaviour?
5. Discuss what can be done to retrieve situations such as this?

## FURTHER READING

1. Child, John, 1984. *Organization: A Guide to Problems and Practice*, Harper & Row: London.
2. Dayal, Ishwar, 1976. *Change in Work Organization*, Concept: Delhi.
3. French, Wendell and Bell, Cecil H Jr, 1983. *Organization Development (2nd edn)*, Prentice-Hall: New Delhi.
4. Luthan, Fred C, 1989. *Organizational Behaviour (5th edn)*, McGraw-Hill: Singapore.
5. Maheswari, B L, 1982. *Management By Objectives*, Tata McGraw-Hill: New Delhi.
6. Sharma, Baldev R, 1986. *Not By Bread Alone*, Shri Ram Centre for Industrial Relations and Human Resources: New Delhi.
7. Udpa, S R, 1988. *Quality Circles in India: Participation for Progress*, Tata McGraw-Hill: New Delhi.

# Employee Relations

### LEARNING OBJECTIVES

After going through this chapter, you should be able to:
- Identify major organizational factors and processes that adversely affect employee relations  • Understand the meanings of terms like discipline, employee grievance, job stress and counselling  • Familiarize yourself with judicio-legal approaches to dealing with problems of indiscipline and employee grievance  • Appreciate the need for effective management of discipline and employee grievances using positive managerial approach  • Describe the organizational stressors causing job stress among employees and strategies for managing stress effectively  • Understand the meaning, usage and steps involved in non-directive counselling  • Develop awareness of efforts made in handling problem employees in the Indian context.

## MANAGEMENT–EMPLOYEE RELATIONS

Organizations are collective bodies of individuals engaged in a common purpose through individual and group efforts. Channelizing human energies in a predetermined desirable direction is not possible unless harmonious relations are maintained among organizational members. Relationship among employees provides the context in which organizational roles assigned to members are performed, team spirit inculcated, expectations clarified, conflicts resolved and shared norms of behaviour developed. Maintenance of harmonious relationship among employees across the vertical and horizontal levels of the organization is thus a necessary condition for enabling organizations to move towards excellence.

Despite the significance of healthy employee relations, there are occasions in the life of every organization when relationships are strained, particularly between the management and the individual employee. The management has certain expectations of the employees in terms of standards of behaviour and performance, code of conduct, desirable actions and behaviour which are made known to the employees through formal or informal, written or verbal means.

Failure to meet these expectations or deviations from the laid down norms of behaviour on the part of the employees leads to the problem of indiscipline. In such situations, the management must initiate action to ensure that an employee's behaviour is in conformity with their expectations.

Likewise, the employees also have certain expectations of the management in terms of their conditions of service, working environment, satisfaction of their variety of needs, freedom of expression and operation, and equitable, just and fair treatment which are often made known to the management through various means of upward communication. Failure on the part of the management to meet those expectations leads to what is called employee grievance.

Thus both the problems of discipline and of employee grievance are two sides of the same coin. They result from the mismatch of the expectations of the management and the employees and failure of one group to meet the expectations of the other. If the problems relating to discipline and employee grievance are not properly managed, the relationship is strained and harmony disturbed. The strained relationship affects adversely the productivity, efficiency and effectiveness of the total organization.

Yet another set of factors leading to strained relationship is the stress that employees experience in carrying out their day-to-day affairs. Failure to meet one's own expectations in terms of career goal, achievement and challenge, life goals, and self-esteem may lead to stress among the individuals. The stress can be caused by several factors some of which are extra organizational in nature while others arise from organizational policies and structures, work pressures, group pressures, quality of interpersonal relationship and nature of job. Stress leads to anxiety and tension which in turn affects relationship among employees. Productive capacities of individuals under stress and their ability to establish meaningful relationship with others are considerably reduced.

The problems relating to discipline, grievance and stress are of continuing nature in the life of any organization. Moreover, being basically human problems, they are complex in nature in that they cannot easily be predicted and controlled by conventional managerial actions or by legal-judicial process. What is required is a new set of skills—counselling skills—the use of which can go a long way in resolving those issues on a continuing basis. Counselling then becomes an important managerial and personnel function.

## MANAGING DISCIPLINE

### Positive Approach

The concept of discipline has undergone significant change in view of our enhanced knowledge and insight into the complexities of human behaviour.  Discipline in the context of modern management process needs to be viewed as a behavioural control mechanism.  The process of behavioural control like any other forms of control is an important managerial function.    Viewed in this context, the behavioural control mechanism entails a number of processes like:

(i) Formulation of goals/objectives

(ii) setting of standards of performance

(iii) developing appropriate norms

(iv) actual performance and behaviour

(v) evaluation of performance/behaviour in terms of standards of performance and norms

(vi) ascertaining the extent of deviation from standards of performance and norms

(vii) determining causes for deviation

(viii) initiating corrective measures which might include in addition to removing the causes of deviation, reformulation of goals/objectives, revision of standards of performance and modifications and/or development of new norms.

Thus, the process of behavioural control is cyclical and calls for continuous monitoring of the activities of employees with a view to determining deviation from standards and norms of conduct or *desirable behaviour* and taking appropriate corrective measures so as to minimize the effect of such deviations on organizational goals. Viewed in this sense, several issues common to mechanisms of managerial control in organizations are of relevance. These are listed below.

(i) Participation of employees in formulation of goals/objectives, setting standards of performance and development of appropriate norms.

(ii) psychological acceptance of the above by all employees.

(iii) agreement on the methods of evaluation and determination of deviation.

(iv) reduction of time lag between the occurrence of deviation and initiation of corrective mechanisms—early sensing, warning and detection system as a pre-requisite.

(v) a movement away from reliance on external control to emphasise on developing internal control among employees so as to minimize the economic and psychological costs involved in policing function.

(vi) output orientation, procedure or time orientation.

Discipline in industry, in the light of the above, therefore, cannot be seen as *maintenance of proper subordination* or *obedience to rules* but as willing acceptance of the norms of conduct of the organization and a commitment to behave or act in an appropriate and desirable manner so as to contribute towards the overall effectiveness of an organization.    Promotion, maintenance and strengthening of discipline presupposes the following conditions.

(i) Change in organizational culture based on punitive and/or legal orientation to a culture based on development of shared value system and norm-based positive orientation. It is important for people to actively *participate* in defining, developing, evaluating and changing appropriate norms of behaviour on a continuing basis.

(ii) Inculcation of positive attitudes towards oneself, other people and the work organization through what Kelman has called the process of *internalization* rather than compliance and identification.    Internalization as a process of attitude change leads towards development of self-control and self-discipline.

(iii) Providing opportunities for continuous learning so that employees behave and act in a manner expected of them.   Discipline essentially is a learning process and the appropriate climate and right opportunities must be provided so that employees develop *problem-solving*, constraint-overcoming orientation rather than escapist and constraint-avoiding orientation.

(iv) Creating conditions whereby employees can experience *satisfaction* of a variety of their socio-psychological needs and pursue fulfilment of personal goals in the process of doing their work and meeting demands of their roles.   Nonfulfilment of the multiple needs often leads to frustration manifested in such behaviour or actions which are traditionally labelled as indisciplined or undesirable behaviour.

## Traditional Approaches to Deal with Indiscipline

***Traditional Approach***     The traditional approach to deal with problems of indiscipline tends to emphasize the coercive and punitive methods within the rational-legal framework.   The underlying assumptions behind such an approach are:

(i) that people need to be coerced or forced to conform to the norms of a group or organization thereby necessitating policing functions on the part of supervisory and managerial personnel; and

(ii) that punishment is necessary for correcting deviations and changing behaviour of people in a desirable direction.

These assumptions are unrealistic as they are based on inadequate and superficial understanding of the complexities of human behaviour.   Coercion as a means of ensuring conformity will ultimately lead to alienation and apathy on the part of employees. They will conform to rules and regulations only to the extent to which they can safeguard their own interest rather than give their best.   Threat of punishment induces people to channellize their energy towards nullifying and/or removing the threat rather than correcting their own behaviour.   The behaviour change is at best temporary and is subject to one's perception when threat of punishment is present. Numerous cases of indiscipline occurring when the supervisory staff or leader is not present illustrate the above points.

***Judicial Approach***     The Judicial approach has yet another serious limitation in dealing with the problems of indiscipline in a constructive manner.   It is invariably resorted to as an *after-effect*, that is, when the situation of indiscipline has already arisen.   Thus the corrective action creates a time lag between the occurrence of indisciplined behaviour and the initiation of necessary action.   Despite several limitations, however, this approach is quite frequently adopted in Indian industries.   This has advantages too in the sense that it follows the law of natural justice and it provides the offender every opportunity to state his side of the case.

It is a well-known fact that judicial approach and disciplinary proceedings are time-consuming processes leading to unusual delays.   There may be reluctance on the part of the disciplinary authority to get involved unnecessarily.   Management at times resorts to strategic leniency under conditions of apprehension that a disciplinary action might provoke reactive responses like stoppages of work, etc.   Strict compliance with requirements of discipline may become an end in itself at the cost of the over-all interest of the organization. Discipline tends to connote strict adherence to rules and regulations rather than meeting the organizational objectives. In normal course, therefore, taking recourse to judicial approach in dealing with problems of indiscipline does not create conditions for the optimum utilization of human potential toward constructive pursuits.

***Humanistic Approach***     Due to the problems mentioned above, there is yet another school of thought which advocates a more humanistic approach while dealing with the problems of indiscipline. This approach is often labelled as *human relations* approach where the emphasis is on establishing a healthy interpersonal relationship between the leader and the employees. The offending employees are treated as human beings and their total personality and behaviour are taken into consideration. An attempt is made to probe deeper into the causes leading to acts of indiscipline. Even the causes of personal nature are considered to be of relevance. Corrective mechanisms involve being considerate to the employees and helping them to get over their personal difficulty by change of assignments, shifts etc. Punitive actions are avoided to the extent possible.

This approach which is basically oriented towards establishing a good relationship with subordinates and being sympathetic towards them is often perceived as a *soft* approach. Individual and personal factors like interpersonal attractiveness, biases, stereotypes, etc. may influence the decision, leading to perceived inconsistency in dealing with deviations among other employees.

## Alternative Approaches to Deal with Deviations

Developments in behavioural sciences for the last three decades indicate a growing emphasis on and trend towards preventive and constructive approaches to dealing with problems of indiscipline and deviancy in organizations. In the 1950s, Douglas McGregor,* a behavioural scientist studied in detail the limitations of both judicial and the human relations approaches. Instead, he advocated the use of what he called *Hot Stove Rule*. According to this rule, a sound disciplinary system in an organization should possess the following characteristics:

- advance warning
- immediacy of action
- consistency
- impersonality

Like a hot stove, the sound disciplinary system must be capable of giving advance warning to employees as to the consequences of non-conformity to certain norms and rules of the organization. If the rules and penalties are clear and well understood, a violation would lead to some natural consequences. Further, just as a stove, the penalty for violation is immediate and automatic. The hot stove burns anything touching it in the same manner. Likewise, high degree of consistency is yet another characteristic of a sound disciplinary system. Impersonality needs to be maintained by

---

* McGregor, Douglas, 1967. *The Human Side of Enterprise*, McGraw-Hill, New York.

keeping away subjective or personal feelings.

If these principles are not followed, the morale of the employees gets affected and their faith in the disciplinary system gets eroded. There are a number of factors which make it extremely difficult to follow these principles in most organizations. One of the guiding principles of the above approach is rationality. Human beings, however, are capable of rational and logical thinking only to a certain degree beyond which their emotional and subjective personality takes over. This is called the phenomenon of *bounded rationality*. This process of differential perception makes it difficult for employees to comprehend in totality the intention of the management and can lead to perceived inconsistency. Most organizations tend to neglect explicit communication of disciplinary actions which is a necessary condition for the success of this approach. Many other factors like strategic leniency, compassion, need for flexibility etc. make it difficult for organizations to follow the principles enunciated above in an objective manner.

### Human Resources Development (HRD) Approach

Yet another approach of relatively recent origin in managerial discipline may be called *human resources development* model. The emphasis in this approach is to treat employees as the most important resource in an organization. Like any other resource, a human beings can be an asset or liability to an organization depending on how they are utilized and developed. Human beings are assumed to be basically active, willing to put in hard work, responsible and disciplined. Most people prefer and enjoy situations which are characterized by discipline and order rather than indiscipline and chaos.

Through a system of appropriate training and education, multi-pronged motivational strategies, proper job allocation etc. the efficiency level of employees can be raised and their commitment to organizational goals enhanced. Viewed in this context, the causes of indiscipline among employees are inadequate and in-appropriate training, motivation system and personnel policies.

Indiscipline may also occur due to failure on the part of the individual to measure up to the requirements of conduct prescribed or established. The objectives of the disciplinary process are to create conditions whereby employees can willingly contribute their best to organizational objectives. While extreme forms of penalty like dismissal and discharge are rarely resorted to analysis is made of the working conditions, supervisory and managerial practices, match between technology and the employee, etc., to provide insight into the causes of indiscipline. The emphasis is on self-control and self-discipline as opposed to external control. In this approach, the penalty imposed is for a particular action or behaviour and not the total personality. Punishment is more in the nature of reminder to an employee that as a human being he has several options by which he can avoid behaviour which is neither desirable for him nor the organization. The basic aim is to re-educate and not to penalize.

There has been a growing tendency to use groups as effective instruments in dealing with problems of indiscipline and deviations. Both formal and informal Groups, have tremendous influence on their members and demand conformity to certain central norms as a price of retaining membership. It is a well-known fact that peer group influence plays a greater role in controlling and influencing one's behaviour. Reference groups, likewise, act as catalysts for employees to emulate norms and behaviour of group members. Thus if organizational norms are accepted by groups in an organization, the task of maintaining conformity to those norms can be left to the groups. This is likely to be more effective than managements or formal leaders trying to control adherence to norms from a distance and by imposing occasional penalties. Several examples are available where work groups have successfully and effectively developed norms of absenteeism and of helping relationships and have adhered to those. Pride and prestige attached to groups are powerful factors for which members adhere to groups and they will not like to lose their membership. Leadership as a process of influencing employees to act and behave in the desired manner and in accordance with the norms laid down plays an important role in strengthening positive and constructive discipline in an organization. Every manager or supervisor regardless of the position he occupies in the hierarchy of an organization plays a leadership role in shaping and directing the behaviour of his subordinates and, therefore, he is directly responsible for maintaining high standards of discipline among his people. A leadership style based on mutuality of interaction, persuasion, healthy interpersonal relationships and participation and involvement in standard setting process ensures conformity to the norms and generates commitment to organizational policies and objectives.

The leader's personal behaviour as perceived by his subordinates will obviously determine not only the quality of interaction between a manager and his subordinates but will also affect the extent to which employees exhibit norm-based disciplined behaviour. Leadership effectiveness of a supervisor is likely to be eroded if his behaviour is seen not in conformity with the disciplinary norms of the organization. A supervisor, either under pressure or otherwise, may resort to a collusive behaviour in order to get along with or please the men he controls. He may avoid taking appropriate actions when required or may indulge in favouritism. This sort of behaviour on the part of the leader has serious implications for his ability to maintain a disciplined staff.

## Diagnostic Skills

All behaviour and actions of human beings are purposive. When a person behaves in a manner inconsistent with the desired mode of actions, he is doing so apparently to achieve certain goals for himself, which he feels he cannot achieve if he behaved otherwise.

Every piece of behaviour – desirable or undesirable, therefore, is a symptomatic manifestation of some deep-rooted deprivation of need and perceived blockage to achievement of certain goals. There is, therefore, the need to probe deeper into the causes – external or internal to the person – that tend to lead to certain forms of behaviour and not others in a given situation.

Diagnostic skills to look beyond what is manifested in observable behaviour, i.e. the needs, the goals, the value and attitude systems, process of perception and as a matter of fact, the whole personality structure of the individual needs to be considered and developed. Directionality of behaviour and its intensity can only be explained in terms of the interaction among a number of variables such as, motive structure of the individual and the situational factors like organizational culture, socio-cultural milieu and the overall standards of discipline in a given social system.

In constructive discipline, causal analysis of deviant behaviour is important as the remedial measures adopted are not based on apparent symptoms but on a careful and insightful diagnosis of the cause of such behaviour. The changes and learning achieved through this process are more meaningful and stable.

## Intervention Skills

A culture of work commitment and positive attitudes to organization as a whole needs to be developed by providing opportunities to people to learn to be autonomous, responsible, self-directing, self-controlling and self-disciplining in their respective work places and organizational life.

Various approaches have been tried out in different organizations to achieve the above. Some of these are work redesign and job enrichment programmes. In the redesign of the work system, a group of employees not only collaborate in setting and achieving targets, but also develop norms of absenteeism and codes of conduct and ensure the adherence to such norms by group members. The basic idea is to provide opportunities for satisfaction of higher-level needs of employees on the job, so as to enable them to experience satisfaction of these needs in the process of participation in the organizational life.

Behaviour modification techniques with emphasis on positive reinforcement has also been used to help employees learn desirable behaviour and strengthen the norm-based behaviour in the context of an organization. Developmental counselling and group therapy provide yet other approaches to dealing with problems of deviant behaviour.

Inducing change in behaviour presupposes effective use of influence by the leader. In hierarchical organizations an important source of influence generally used is authority that a manager has by occupying certain position in the hierarchy of an organization. However, the authority-based influence does not seem conducive to creating a climate of genuine acceptance on the part of the employees. At best changes, if any, are temporary as they are based on external sources of rewards and punishments. Other sources of influence including persuasion have been found to be more meaningful in helping employees to direct their behaviour in desirable directions.

## Disciplinary Action: Process and Limitations

Despite the efforts made by the management to develop a culture of positive discipline, there could still be a few employees who would not conform to the norms and standards of behaviour, and the policies of the organizations. In such cases, disciplinary action will have to be administered.

As a matter of fact the Industrial Employment (Standing Orders) Act 1946[*] requires all industrial establishments of 100 or more workmen to define its service rules and prepare standing orders which should also include the procedures for disciplinary action. In the absence of its own standing orders, the company has to follow the model

---

[*] Government of India, 1946. *The Industrial Employment (Standing Orders) Act 1946.* Ministry of Law and Justice and Company Affairs: New Delhi.

standing orders. The *model standing orders* spell out specifically the terms and conditions governing day-to-day employer–employee relationship. It is the duty of the employer to make the provisions of standing orders known to the employees. The employees in turn are required to comply with these provisions. Failure to do so can result in a change of misconduct. Thus the standing orders provide the basis for disciplinary action against employees in an organization.

The model standing orders also contain provision for disciplinary action for misconduct. Misconduct on the part of an employee includes such acts like wilful insubordination or disobedience to any lawful and reasonable order of the superior, theft, fraud, or dishonesty in connection with the employer's business or property, and the like. Any action or behaviour can be defined as misconduct if it adversely affects the interests of the industrial establishment, or is prejudicial to the interest of other employees. The definition of misconduct including examples provided in the model standing orders is not exhaustive; it is only indicative. An employee taking leave on false grounds, workers deciding on go-slow or *gherao*, complaint to the police against management without reasonable justification, etc. could constitute misconduct. The agreement among concerned parties as to what constitutes a misconduct in some cases poses a problem as the terms and the act and the behaviour are subject to interpretation.

**Domestic Enquiry**   The first step is to find out through preliminary investigation whether a prima facie case for misconduct against an employee is evident. The next step is to conduct domestic enquiry into the allegation of misconduct within the organization. Principles of natural justice must be followed while conducting the enquiry which would mean that no person shall be the judge in his own cause or be condemned unheard. In the context of domestic enquiry these principles have following implications:

(i) The enquiry against the employee must be fair and conducted by an impartial person

(ii) the employee has the right to present such witnesses in whom he has faith

(iii) the employee has the right to cross-examine the management evidence

(iv) the evidence of the management should be taken in his presence

(v) no material should be used against him without giving him an opportunity to explain

(vi) the punishment awarded should not be out of proportion to the misconduct committed.

If at all the case goes to the tribunal or a labour court, for adjudication, the court will seek to establish (i) whether proper domestic enquiry was conducted; (ii) whether the principles of natural justice were followed; (iii) whether there was lack of bias or not in the enquiry proceedings, and (iv) whether the other party was heard in good faith. If the domestic enquiry has not been conducted properly, then the labour court itself conducts fresh enquiry on its own following the principles of natural justice.

**Punishment**   Various forms of punishment for different types of misconduct and their gravity are often specified in the standing orders of organizations where the Industrial Employment (Standing Orders) Act is applicable. The punishment, in such cases, can be awarded according to the specification of the standing orders. Among the penalties available are:

(i) Warning or censure

(ii) fine

(iii) withholding of increments

(iv) demotion to a lower grade

(v) suspension

(vi) discharge simpliciter – termination of service for loss of confidence; does not necessarily imply any act of misconduct

(vii) discharge

(viii) dismissal.

Of the above forms of punishment, suspension, discharge and dismissal are severe penalties, while warning, fine and withholding of increments are considered minor punishments.

*Adjudication*     The 1971 amendment (Sec. 11A) of the Industrial Disputes Act, 1947 made provisions for industrial disputes relating to the discharge or dismissal of a worker to be referred to a labour court, tribunal or national tribunal for adjudication. In case the court is satisfied that the order of dismissal or discharge was not justified; it may set aside the order of discharge or dismissal and direct reinstatement of the workman on such terms and conditions, as it thinks fit, or give such other relief to the workman including the award of any lesser punishment in lieu of discharge or dismissal.

The above provision has made the task of the disciplinary authorities more difficult. The disciplinary authorities now normally avoid the penalties of dismissal or discharge, instead they inflict such penalties which would not come under the purview of the above Act. Also, there is a realization that the domestic enquiry must be conducted in a fair and methodical manner, records be maintained properly and the punishment awarded must be commensurate with the evidence available.

The procedure to be followed in initiating disciplinary action within the legal framework is a lengthy, tedious and time-consuming process. The limitations of this approach have already been highlighted in the previous section. The adoption of this process and the accompanying legal intricacies require one to be trained in the procedure and be aware of the implications of each type of punishment.

## MANAGING GRIEVANCE

In a broader perspective, grievance would include any discontent or dissatisfaction experienced by an employee which affects the performance of the organization. An employee can be aggrieved at the treatment meted out to him by his superiors or the management, on his conditions of service, the nature of job and a host of other organizational factors.

The feeling of dissatisfaction sometimes may be verbally shared or kept within or

it may be expressed in written or oral forms. Nevertheless as long as the dissatisfaction with the system persists, an employee's performance may be adversely affected. At times the discontent may be on account of inadequate or distorted information
or even on imaginary grounds. The fact, however, remains that whenever dissatisfaction exists, necessary action must be initiated by the management to remove the
causes—real or imaginary—for such discontent so as to ensure the employee's continued commitment to his work.

There are several ways in which employees express their dissatisfaction ranging
from a passive indifference or apathy to a more aggressive reaction of hostility or
violence. Acts of indiscipline, absenteeism, loitering, restriction in output and the like
are some other forms of behaviour which can be attributed to feelings of frustration
and dissatisfaction among employees. All these actions are often expressions of some
deep-rooted problems encountered by the employees. They, thus, provide useful data
on the basis of which the management can diagnose the problem and initiate corrective action. Unexpressed dissatisfactions also need to be monitored so that corrective
action could be taken before they are expressed in undesirable behaviour.

In formal organizations, however, employee grievance has a restrictive connotation
particularly in view of the need to develop a formal mechanism for grievance redressal. Usually distinction is made between a complaint and a grievance in organizational context. A discontent or dissatisfaction is said to be a complaint when (a) it
has not assumed a great measure of importance to the complainant and (b) it is voiced
in a highly informal fashion. We all have complaint against several things around
us, but they do not become as serious to merit most of our attention. A complaint,
however becomes a grievance when (a) the employee feels that injustice has been
done to him, (b) it is formally expressed either verbally or in writing, and (c) it is
related to policies, procedures and operations of the organization. The reasons for
grievance could be, as stated earlier, either real or imaginary. In most organizations,
these grievances are more often related to conditions of service and other contractual
obligations. The Model Grievance Procedure (The National Commission on Labour,
1969)* for example provides the following definition of grievance:

"Complaints affecting one or more individual workers in respect of their wage payments, overtime, leave, transfer, promotion, seniority, work assignment and discharge
would constitute grievance. Where the points at dispute are of general applicability
or of considerable magnitude, they will fall outside the scope of this procedure."

## Nature and Causes of Grievance

As it can be seen from the above, the meaning of grievance is restrictive in nature
and the decision as to what constitutes a grievance in an organizational context is arrived at collectively by the management and the union of that enterprise. When the
individual grievances are not redressed and if other workers get affected by the same
situation, they may become a collective grievance. The collective grievances normally come under the purview of collective bargaining.

---

* Government of India, 1969. *Report on the National Commission of Labour*, Ministry of Labour,
Employment and Rehabilitation: New Delhi.

Although the precise nature of the causes of a grievance differs from one organization to another, in general they tend to fall under the following categories in most Indian organizations:

(i) Promotions
- Supersession
- Acting promotion
- Seniority
- Pay fixation

(ii) Compensation
- Increments
- Payment
- Recovery of dues

(iii) Amenities
- Inequitable distribution
- Entitlement
- Medical benefits

(iv) Service matters
- Transfers
- Continuity of service
- Superannuation

(v) Disciplinary action
- Punishment
- Fines
- Victimization

(vi) Nature of job
- Job allocation

(vii) Condition of work
- Safety
- Hazards

(viii) Leave.

The International Labour Organization (ILO) classifies a grievance as a complaint of one or more workers with respect to wages and allowances, conditions of work and interpretations of service stipulations, covering such areas as overtime, leave, transfer, promotion, seniority, job assignment and termination of service.

The causes of grievances mentioned are necessary to identify the nature of a grievance and to decide whether that grievance can be formally taken up for redressal through the formal grievance handling machinery. The deeper causes leading to those grievances need to be analyzed so that preventive as well as corrective steps could be taken by management. This diagnostic approach will be discussed later in this chapter.

## The Grievance Procedure

Most large organizations in India have a formal grievance procedure which enables the organization to redress those grievances which come under their purview. The advantages of having a formal procedure are listed below.

(i) It provides established and known methods of processing grievances and keeps this channel of communication open

(ii) The redressal of a grievance is attempted by:
- establishment of facts pertaining to the grievance
- collection of facts and evidences
- asking probing questions relating to the grievance
- analysis of facts and data generated
- taking decisions on impartial basis.

(iii) Role of emotion which may have caused the grievance in the first place can, however, be minimized by following the process of objective analysis.

(iv) The process covers several levels in the organization including reference to outside institutions or individuals, if so desired or provided in the contract.

(v) Its existence provides confidence among employees that they can be heard and that their grievances could be impartially redressed. The mere existence of this procedure, therefore, is satisfying even though an employee may never have an occasion to use it.

(vi) Even if a grievance is not settled in an employee's favour, still the employee may feel satisfied because of the opportunity to communicate and to be heard by the management.

(vii) Involving various hierarchical levels like middle and senior management in the grievance redressal process provides a safeguard against the possible arbitrary or biased decision of the immediate supervisor.

(viii) Various levels in the organization get to know of the kinds of issues that concern workers and managers.

It is advantageous for large organizations, therefore to adopt a formal grievance procedure. The National Commission on Labour (1969)[*] has suggested a model grievance procedure which can be adapted to suit the requirements of specific organizations. The Tata Iron and Steel Company (Works),[**] for example, has a grievance procedure which consists of several stages as shown below:

| Stage I | Worker fills grievance form submits to | Shift In charge |
|---|---|---|
| Stage II | Worker not satisfied | Department Head |
| Stage III | Worker not satisfied, unanimous decision binding on both parties | Zonal Works Committee 5 Management + 5 Union representatives |
| Stage IV | If no unanimous decision binding on both parties | Central Works Committee Top Management and Union Officials |
| Stage V | Final Decision | Chairman of the Company |

Having a formal grievance procedure is a necessary but not sufficient condition for effective handling of grievances. Like many other formal mechanisms, the grievance procedure also tends to become procedure-oriented rather than outcome-oriented. In

[*] Ibid
[**] Monappa, Arun, *Industrial Relations*, Tata McGraw-Hill: New Delhi, 1985, pp 153–155.

other words, following laid down procedures rather than the speedy redressal of grievances tends to become the primary concern. This causes delays which only increase frustration among the employees and in turn affect the productivity as also the morale of other employees. The social costs of delay in redressal of grievance are quite high which are not usually appreciated by those responsible for making the procedure operationally efficient and effective. The members of the grievance-handling committees at various levels lose interest when the problem solving efforts are replaced by a tug of war between interested parties. If the climate of trust and mutuality of concern for employees' grievance do not exist, people down the line lose faith in the procedure. This state of affairs leads to a situation where employees take recourse to extra-organizational methods such as union pressures, personal contacts and the like for redressal of their grievances. Or else grievances are not voiced in appropriate form and in course of time they tend to become collective disputes.

## Alternative Approach to Handling Grievance

As discussed earlier, grievance is indicative of discontent and dissatisfaction among employees with the management policies, practices and procedures. It forms a significant part of the upward communication flow in an organization and therefore is an important source of feedback to the management on the reactions that various managerial actions evoke among the employees. The grievances, even if biased or subjective, provide useful diagnostic data to the management to assess the health of the organization, to evaluate impact of its policies and to initiate corrective actions wherever necessary. Even when dissatisfaction is not expressed in overt terms, it is necessary for management to develop ways and means to identify the sources of dissatisfaction rather than allowing it to take the form of an expressed grievance. By not initiating timely action, the organization tends to lose the productive efforts of a discontented employee. It is indeed unrealistic to assume that a dissatisfied employee will perform at his best.

The feeling of dissatisfaction among the employees, whether expressed as a grievance or not, thus requires immediate attention by the management. As a matter of fact it becomes an important part of the managerial function which more often than not is neglected particularly in large organizations. The managerial approach to dealing effectively with employees' grievances can be stated as follows:

*Immediacy of Action*     The grievances or dissatisfaction of employees must be recognized and settled immediately as and when they arise. The first line supervisors, therefore, need to be trained to handle a grievance or complaint properly and promptly. If grievances are settled at the first stage itself, corrective actions can be immediately taken and the possible adverse effect's on employees' performance can be minimized.

*Acceptance of Grievance*     A grievance when presented to a supervisor must initially be accepted as expression of genuine feeling on the part of the employee. Acceptance does not necessarily mean agreeing with the grievance; it simply conveys the willingness of the supervisor to look into the complaint objectively and dispassionately.  A supervisor who tends to show greater concern for his employees creates a climate where the number of grievances get drastically reduced.

**Problem Identification**    The complaints stated by an aggrieved employee usually have emotional overtones and may, therefore, be vague, exaggerated statements of the problem.  The supervisor needs to listen to the complaints properly and to provide help in identifying the real problems.

**Getting the Facts**    It is necessary for the supervisor to collect relevant and adequate facts relating to the nature of grievance.  The facts must be separated from opinions, inferences and feelings.  It is also useful to maintain records of these facts so that these could be utilized at later stages of grievance redressal in case the grievance is not settled at this stage.

**Causal Analysis of the Grievance**    An attempt must be made to identify the real causes, after ascertaining the facts, leading to the grievance.  It will require a deeper analysis of the problem in terms of its frequency of occurrence, past records relating to the individual and to similar problems, management practices, union practices, nature of job, relationship with other employees and above all the individual attitudes to and behaviour at work.  Identification of causes helps the management to adopt corrective measures to prevent its recurrence.

**Taking Decision**    The impact of various causes on the nature of grievance needs to be evaluated with a view to generating alternative courses of action.  After examining the consequences of each alternative solution on the current and future practices of management, on the individual and the union; a decision needs to be taken which is best suited to the situation.  It will be necessary for the supervisor to keep in mind that the decision he takes might become a precedent both within the department and the organization.

**Implementation and follow-up**    The decision, whether favourable or unfavourable to the employee concerned, must be immediately communicated and implemented preferably by the supervisor. This adds further to the credibility of the supervisor in the eyes of the employees. The decision thus implemented should be followed up and reviewed to see whether the grievance has been satisfactorily resolved or not. In case, it is discovered that the clash of interest has not been satisfactorily resolved, then one has to go back to the first step of redefining the problem, collecting facts and follow through the subsequent steps.

The problem-solving approach to handling grievances has obvious advantages over the formal legally-oriented grievance procedure.  While it provides useful diagnostic data to management about the state of affairs in work place, it also leads to the development of a climate of trust, openness and mutual concern between the management and the employees in the organization.

## MANAGING STRESS

The stresses and strains that employees experience in their jobs often get reflected in behaviour that are not conducive to optimal performance. The resulting behaviour at times may also be undesirable, affecting adversely the relationship among employees. In the following pages an attempt will be made to explore the meaning of stress, to identify various causes and to suggest strategies to cope with this growing phenomenon.

### What is Stress?

Stress usually has a negative connotation and the term that one uses to describe this state in a person is called *distress*. For example an employee experiences distress when he is reprimanded by his superior or when he has to meet an urgent deadline amidst heavy demands on his time. There is also a positive aspect to stress which is signified by the term, *enstress*. Enstress denotes good feeling experienced by a person when he suddenly comes to know of rewards for his outstanding performance. Stress is, therefore, not something damaging which should be avoided. It is more a question of handling stress situation in such a way that a person experiences positive feelings and reduces the negative effects of distress.

Stress can be defined as "an adaptive response, mediated by individual characteristics and psychological processes, that is a consequence of an external action, situation or event that places special physical and psychological demands upon a person".[*] Beehr and Newman define *job stress* as "a condition arising from the interaction of people and their jobs and characterized by changes within people that force them to deviate from their normal functioning".[**] From the above definitions, we can outline the following features of stress.

(i) Stress is an adaptive response to an external situation.

(ii) The response to external situation represents physical, psychological and behavioural deviations from the normal functioning.

(iii) Since stress can have damaging physiological and psychological effects on employees, it will affect their health and their performance.

(iv) Stress has been identified as a major cause of absenteeism.

(v) Stress experienced by one employee affects the safety of other employees or the public in cases where an employee handles dangerous or public safety equipments.

In the light of the above it is necessary therefore to manage stress effectively so that its dysfunctional effect on employees and their organizational performance can be minimized and controlled.

### The Effects of Job Stress

The stress that an employee experiences in the job has several undesirable effects on

[*]   Ivancevich, John M and Michael T Matteson, 1980. *Stress at Work*, Scott, Foresman: Glenview, pp 5-9.

[**] Beehr T A and J E Newman, 1978. 'Job Stress, Employee Health and Organizational Effectiveness," *Personnel Psychology*, Winter, pp 665–699.

the individual and the organization. The capacity of an individual to perform at his best under conditions of stress drastically reduced. Performance usually drops sharply when stress rises to high levels. The problems arising out of high stress can be described as:

*Physical Problems*      A high level of stress gives rise to high blood pressure and high levels of cholesterol and can result in heart disease, ulcers and arthritis.

*Psychological Problems*      High levels of stress may be accompanied by anxiety, anger, nervousness, depression, tension and irritability. These psychological states in job situations lead to lowering of self-esteem, resentment of supervision, inability to concentrate and take decisions, and job dissatisfaction. The outcomes of these psychological problems can be highly dysfunctional for the organization.

*Behavioural Problems*      The behavioural problems associated with high stress include sleeplessness, overeating or undereating, excessive drinking and smoking, and drug abuse. These problems may be manifested by tardiness, absenteeism and turnover. Increasing incidence of alcoholism and drinking in place of work are behaviours which could be the result of high job stress experienced by those employees.

## The Causes of Stress

The factors causing stress in a person are called *stressors*. As the social and organizational demands on us tend to increase with complexities, so do the intensity of stressors for an employee. The common stressors acting on employees can be summarized as follows:

*Extra Organizational Stressors*      The forces lying outside the organization have significant impact on job stress experienced by employees. The fast pace of modern living has increased stress and decreased the sense of personal well being. The environmental forces to which an employee must respond are:
- fast pace of social and technological change
- economic and financial conditions including inflationary pressures
- caste system, ethnic identity, minority issues
- family demands and social obligations
- relocation and transfers.

*Organizational Stressors*      As the organization becomes large and complex, more and more organizational factors constitute potential stressors for individual employee in their jobs. These organizational stressors are listed below.
  (i) *Policies*:
- unfair, arbitrary performance reviews
- inequity in pay
- rigid rules and ambiguous procedures
- frequent transfers necessitating relocation

(ii) *Structures*:
- centralization and formalization
- lack of involvement in decision making
- little opportunity for career advancement
- high degree of specialization
- interdepartmental conflict
- line staff conflict

(iii) *Processes*:
- poor communication
- inadequate feedback on performance
- ambiguous and conflict goals
- unfair control systems
- inadequate information

**Group Stressors**     In organizations, employees are members of various formal groups and informal. The department or section to which one belongs for example is the formal group.  The nature of task that one is supposed to carry out may necessitate working in groups like task force and problem solving teams.  The group, therefore, can also be a potential source of stress. The group stressors are explained here.

*Lack of Group Cohesiveness*   If an employee is denied the opportunity to develop a sense of belonging, if supervisory style prevents cohesiveness, if attitudes and behaviour of other members does not allow the acceptance of an employee, it may produce stress in an individual.

*Lack of Social Support*    As members of groups, we always look for support from co-members in times of happiness or sorrow.  If such a support is not forthcoming, it can also cause stress.

*Interpersonal and Intergroup Conflict*   The incompatibility of needs and values between superior and a subordinate and between colleagues usually leads to interpersonal conflict.  Likewise the objectives and goals of two groups may be at variance leading to intergroup conflict.  These conflicts can also lead to considerable stress in individuals.

**Job-related Stressors**     The nature of job, whether routine or innovative, the working conditions, and hazards related to a particular job tend to create conditions in which the job holder can experience a lot of stress.  The job-related stressors are:
- unrealistic job description
- crowding and lack of privacy
- excessive noise, heat or dust
- safety hazards
- routine nature of job
- presence of toxic materials.

**Individual Stressors**     All context related stressors eventually affect the individual. There are, however, other individual stressors which are quite significant in enhancing our understanding of the concept and process of stress management.   The individual stressors are:

*Role Stressors*   The individual employee performs multiple roles within as well as outside the organization.  Roles are a set of expectations that other members (family, superior, subordinates, and colleagues) have of an individual.  When these expectations are not properly conveyed and understood in the same way as intended by the other members, the employee concerned experiences role ambiguity.  Likewise, if these expectations place contradictory demands on an individual, the individual concerned experiences role conflict.  Both the situations of role ambiguity and role conflict cause considerable stress to the individual.  The individual's responses to these stressors are often dysfunctional to the organization as well as the individual.

*Personality Characteristics*   Individuals differ in terms of personality traits and dimensions like authoritarianism, rigidity, tolerance of ambiguity, need for achievement, and many other characteristics.  One such personality dimension is Type A or Type B, the profiles of which (Table 11.1) are as follows:

**Table 11.1   Profiles of Type A and Type B Personalities***

| Type A Profile | Type B Profile |
| --- | --- |
| Is always moving | Is not concerned about time |
| Walks rapidly | Is patient |
| Eats rapidly | Doesn't brag |
| Talks rapidly | Plays for fun, not to win |
| Is impatient | Relaxes without guilt |
| Does two things at a time | Has no pressing deadlines |
| Can't cope with leisure time | Is mild-mannered |
| Is obsessed with numbers | Is never in a hurry |
| Measurers success by quantity | |
| Is aggressive | |
| Is competitive | |
| Constantly feels time pressure | |

* Brief, Arthur P, et. al., 1981, *Managing Job Stress*, Little, Brown: Boston.

The research has shown that employees with Type A profile tend to experience more stress which ultimately might lead to serious physical consequences like heart attacks, and hypertension.  The individuals of Type B characteristics, on the other hand are patient and take a broader view of things.

*Life and Career Changes*   The slow changes in life like ageing process or sudden changes such as loss of dear ones can be highly stress-producing.  The more the person experiences life changes, the poorer will be his subsequent health.  The same can be said for career changes as well.  Frequent and sudden changes in one's career or nature of job and responsibility, underemployment or over employment, etc. can be stress-provoking.

## Management of Stress

The stress that employees experience on the job affects adversely the psychological health of the individuals, their performance and their relationship with other employees in the organization. Stress, therefore, needs to be managed effectively to minimize its undersirable consequences.   Two strategies of coping with stress can reduces undesirable consequences. Two strategies of coping with stress can be thought of: one, where the focus is on helping the individual employee to overcome the negative effect of stress and the other is to bring about organizational changes aimed at removing or preventing the occurrence of stressors on the job.* A brief discussion of both the strategies follows:

**Organizational Strategies**    The most effective way of managing stress calls for adopting such measures as will reduce the already existing organizational stressors and prevent occurrence of potential stressors.   In the previous pages major organizational stressors like policies, structures, processes and nature and conditions of job have been identified. The presence or absence of these stressors will differ from one organization to another. The first step, therefore, should be to identify, through diagnostic analysis, the major stressors in the context of an organization and then to bring about appropriate change in the organization to minimize their effects on employees. In general terms, however, the following strategies can be adopted:

*Creating a Supportive Organizational Climate*    Creating a climate of mutual support and trust among employees throughout the organization is likely to reduce job stress.  This will call for restructuring of organization towards greater decentralization of authority, opening up of channels of communications and free flow of information, and participation in decision-making process, changes in the organizational policies relating to performance appraisal and equitable distribution of reward also are necessary.

*Job Redesign*    As discussed in Chapter 2, job redesign is increasingly being used as a strategy of enriching the content of various jobs in organizations. The formation of semi-autonomous work groups provides opportunities to employees to experience satisfaction of a variety of higher level needs like responsibility, recognition, learning and growth. The work group also provides necessary mutual support and help to its members. As a result, stress caused by routine nature of job, lack of mutual support and lack of control over  one's own job is considerably reduced.

*Role Clarity*    Role ambiguity and role conflict arising out of unclear and contradictory expectations of various employees with whom one has to work have been identified as major sources of stress. As discussed in Chapter 2, role analysis technique can be meaningfully used to bring about role clarity in various roles that employers are called upon to perform in an organization. Role clarity is achieved through a joint negotiation with other employees on ambiguous and contradictory expectations. Similar technique can be used in dealing with interdepartmental or intergroup conflicts.

**Career Planning and Development**    Lack of career planning and development opportunities tend to be a source of considerabe uncertainty and stress among the employees. The stress is created by not knowing what the next move is and how they are going to make it. Carefully worked out plans for career paths and develop-

---

* Luthans, Fred, 1985. *Organizational Behaviour*, 4th edn, McGraw-Hill: Singapore.

ment taking into account both the individual capabilities and aspirations on the one hand and the organizational requirements on the other can lead to considerable reduction in stress experienced by employees.

***Individual Strategies***    Individual coping strategies are used when an employee under stress exhibits undersirable behaviour on the job such as poor performance, strained relationship with co-workers, absenteeism, alcoholism and the like. Employees under stress require help in overcoming its negative effects. The strategies used are:

*Behavioural Self-control*    In ultimate analysis, effective management of stress presupposes exercise of self-control on the part of an employee. By consciously analyzing the causes and consequences of their own behaviour, the employees can achieve self-control. They can further develop awareness of their own limits of tolerance and learn to anticipate their own responses to various stressful situations. The strategy involves increasing an individual's control over the situations rather than being solely controlled by them.

*Cognitive Therapy*    The cognitive therapy techniques such as Ellis's rational emotive model and Meichenbaum's cognitive strategy for modification have been used as an individual strategy for reducing job stress. The approach adopted in one study was as follows.

The Participants were taught that much of their experienced strain like anxiety, tension, etc is caused by their cognitions that is *self-talks*. This part of the treatment programme then consisted of lectures and interaction discussions designed to help participants to:

(i) recognize events at work and what cognitions they elicit

(ii) become aware of the effects of such cognitions on their physiological and emotional responses

(iii) systematically evaluate the objective consequences of events at work, and

(iv) replace self-defeating cognitions that unnecessarily arouse strain (e.g., I'am an incompetent worker who cannot handle the workload) with more adaptive appraisals (e.g. "I handle this workload as well as any one else.")*

*Networking*    Networking is based on the assumption that people need and benefit from social support from significant others. Building of social support therefore can be used as a strategy for reducing job stress. Employees experiencing stress are encouraged to establish close associations with trusted colleagues who are good listeners and confidence builders. These co-employees provide the necessary social support to the person to get over the stressful situations. Developing such alliances in the work organization is called networking which is increasingly being used to helping employees to deal with stress.

*Counselling*    Yet another strategy that has been widely used in organizations for dealing with problems of adjustment of employees is the familiar technique of counselling. Employee counselling can effectively be used to dealing with problems relating with stress as well. Career counselling for example can provide clarity to one's career goals and opportunities, thereby reducing the uncertainty in this regard which is a

---

* Ganster, Daniel C, et al. 1982. *Managing Organization*, October, pp 535-537.

major source of job stress. Likewise, the employees can be helped through counselling to identify their own strengths, weaknesses and response patterns and develop a plan of action for changing their behaviour. The details of the concept and technique of counselling will be discussed in the following section.

---

## COUNSELLING

---

As we have seen in the preceding sections, if the problems relating to indiscipline, grievance and job stress are not effectively resolved, they invariably tend to lead to strained employee relations; which in turn affects the performance and satisfaction levels of organization members. Several strategies have been suggested for resolving those problems. One thing however, that emerges is that ultimately the individual employee's capacity and willingness to respond positively to a problem situation will determine the effect on organizational performance and individual well being. The effective management of these problems presupposes development of problem solving orientation and positive attitudes to work and people among the employees. Counselling is primarily used for this purpose and thus it acquires the status of an important managerial function.

### Counselling Defined

Counselling is a professional form of interpersonal communication whose purpose is to assist the employee with which eventually to question the knowledge store. It is a planned systematic intervention in the life of an individual who is capable of choosing the goal and the direction of his own development. Counselling, therefore, is aimed at maximizing human freedom by increasing one's long term control over his environment and responses which are evoked by it. It is liberating in nature, develops responsible independence, increases autonomy, and assists an individual to help himself.

### Theoretical Model for Counselling

The capacity of an individual to adapt to different situations depends on his *behaviour repertoire* which is made up of three elements— experience, perceptions and generalizations. If the behaviour repertoire of an individual is broad and rich, he has within himself access to a variety of response patterns and depending on the demands of the situation he can choose a response which is appropriate, realistic and adaptive for that situation. In other words, he has the flexibility to respond to varying situational demands. The behaviour repertoire is said to be broadbased when an individual has had access to variety of experiences, his perceptions are in tune with existing realities and the generalizations that he had made or conclusions that he has arrived at regarding himself, the other people around him and the situation are based on validated information and interpretations. In case a person does not have the opportunity to get exposed to varied experiences his response pattern will be limited and his behaviour repertoire will be inadequate. Such a person with inadequate behaviour repertoire will not have the flexibility to choose appropriate response to met the demands of the situation. On the contrary his responses are likely to be repetitive, routine and rigid regardless of the situational demands.

The behaviour repertoire may thus be inadequate for any three reasons: lack of experience, distortion in perception or erroneous generalizations. Given the inadequacy of behaviour repertoire, an individual's adaptive ability will be considerably reduced. The objective of counselling is to discover and correct inadequacies in behaviour repertoire. These discoveries can be made by either the person himself, the client or the counsellor. The counselling methods, therefore, can be grouped into two types :

(i) *Directive counselling* in which the counsellor discovers and provides interpretations of the inadequacies, and

(ii) *Non-directive counselling* in which the client discovers his own inadequacies and develops plan of action to deal with them. The counsellor only facilitates the self-discovery on the part of the client.

Any one counselling method will not be equally effective in discovering and correcting inadequacies in behaviour repertoire. Choice of a particular method needs to be based on the diagnosis of the problem. For example, lack of experience can be most effectively dealt with by directive counselling or counsellor discovery, whereas distortions in perceptions or erroneous generalization by non-directive counselling or client self-discovery.

## Nature of Counselling

Non-directive counselling is being more widely used in dealing with problem employees who exhibit maladaptive behaviour in organizations. Counselling has been described as a helping relationship between the person seeking help (client) and the person providing help (counsellor). It uses a positive approach. The underlying assumptions of counselling are as follows :

(i) People can grow; they can improve. The counsellor must believe in the worth of the individual and in that person's ability to do better.

(ii) Counselling is an investment in the individual which will result in future pay offs for both the parties.

(iii) Counselling is a learning process. The client is encouraged to diagnose his own inadequacies and to become aware of the need for initiating corrective steps. The change achieved is more lasting than any change that is imposed.

(iv) Counselling involves confrontation. The client must learn to confront his own inadequacies and problems. The problems therefore will have to be brought out. Confrontation can cause stress, which is a necessary condition for change.

(v) Acceptance of an individual as he is by the counsellor is important. The client must be accepted as a worthy human being capable of growth and development.

(vi) Counselling is a continuous and time consuming process that is likely to involve several sessions.

(vii) The effectiveness of counselling is determined by specific change in behaviour taking place in the client.

## Facilitating Characteristics of Helping Process

Establishing helping relationship with the client is a prerequisite for effective non-directive counselling. Like all human relationships, helping relationship between the client and the counsellor needs to be developed, nurtured and strengthened for effective behavorial change in the employee seeking help. The responsibility for establishing such a relationship obviously lies with the counsellor who needs to develop behavioural skills that will facilitate the helping process. These facilitating skills or characteristics are :

*Empathy*    The first step in counselling is to establish empathic relationship with the client. Empathy means putting his problems and feelings in his terms and according to his perspective. It is different from sympathy. Sympathy means that one experiences the same feeling as the other person. However, for empathy, the counsellor does not have to feel the same way as the client would, it is more an understanding of the feelings of the client that matters for providing help. The understanding thus achieved must be put into words. Three steps are necessary in developing empathy:
    (a) to listen carefully to what the client is saying about how he feels on account of his problems.
    (b) thinking of words that can represent the client's feelings and situation.
    (c) to communicate to the client one's understanding of his feeling and situation.
    Listening with understanding requires the counsellor to give full attention to the client, to suspend his own judgements, and tolerate his own anxiety of accepting or rejecting whatever is being said. Giving attention to the other person is the biggest compliment that one can give. Communicating one's understanding of client's problems and feelings provides an opportunity to the counsellor to check whether the understanding was in tune with what the other was trying to say. Thus it keeps the channel of communication open between the counsellor and the client.
    Establishment of relationship of empathy involves three stages:
*Stage I*    The counsellor summarizes his understanding of what the client is saying and presents this summary. The summary is an interchangeable formulation reflecting the same feeling and meaning conveyed by the client. No additions or subtractions are made in the statement. Such interchangeable formulations allow the client to determine how well the counsellor can comprehend his world as he has expressed experience of it.
*Stage II*    The counsellor extends the limits of his own understanding particularly in areas where the client does not demonstrate a depth of understanding. The counsellor encourages depth reflection on the part of the client by raising probing enquiries. Moderate interpretations of the client's problems are also attempted by the counsellor. The purpose is to encourage him to develop deeper understanding of his own situation which is a first step to discovery of alternative courses of action.
*Stage III*    The highest and ultimate form of empathetic understanding is action. At

this stage the concentration is on problem solving activities that emanate from a deep understanding of the problem area. Various alternatives are explored and direction for change is provided so that shared discoveries result.

**Respect**     The counsellor must have respect for the feelings and experiences of the client and this respect must be communicated to him. Respect refers to an unconditional positive regard for the other person. The respect or the regard that we have for others are often conditional. For example, we tend to accept people who agree with us and reject those who may be in vehement disagreement with us. For a counsellor, it is important to have unconditional positive regard for the helpee.

Imposition of views, domination and devaluation of others by the counsellor will indicate lack of respect for the client. Involved and committed responses with warmth are indicative of respect.

Respect can be communicated in three stages.

*Stage I*   In the first stage, the counsellor must suspend potentially negative feelings, attitudes and judgements that might have restrictive or destructive effect on the expressions and behaviour of client. This establishes a basis for secure relationship. The message that the counsellor sends is: *with me you are free to be who you are.*

*Stage II*   The counsellor identifies the strengths of the other and positively responds to those strengths. Specific aspects of the other's experiences that are indicative of his strength are highlighted, emphasized and reinforced by the counsellor. This is done to develop in the other's respect for his own capacities for making appropriate discrimination and acting with responsibility in relevant areas.

*Stage III*   After having identified and reinforced the strengths, the client now is in a position to concentrate on his weaknesses and the negative aspects of his behaviour. The counsellor thus provides help in identifying the areas of personality which cannot be accepted but must be changed for improved effectiveness.

**Concreteness**     Concreteness refers to specificity of expression of feelings and experiences on the part of the helpee. For counselling to be effective, the counsellor has to ensure that the problem is understood in concrete and precise terms and that his response does not become too far removed emotionally from the client's feelings and experiences. The counsellor's own behaviour directly influences the other who is encouraged to attend specifically to problem areas and emotional conflicts. Vagueness and inaccuracy in communication are avoided.

The concreteness has also three stages:

*Stage I*   The counsellor's reflective and interrogative communications must be specific and direct which encourages the other to make his own relevant discrimination and keep his search on for identifying his problem in specific way.

*Stage II*   The emphasis on specificity is decreased and the helpee is encouraged to explore other areas relating to the problem. This is the stage for general exploration of the issues in order to get insight into other possible causes that might be relevant to the problem. The counsellor asks probing questions allowing the client to examine other aspects of his life–work, family, community, and the like.

*Stage III*    After having explored the problem in general terms, there may be the need to redefine or reformulate the problem in concrete terms again.  At this stage alternative courses of action are considered, and the details of advantages and disadvantages of each alternative are explored and discussed.

**Genuineness**        The counsellor must have integrity and be able to reflect on his true feelings.  Being honest with oneself and the other establishes the credibility of the counsellor.  Genuineness refers to authenticity and spontaneity in a person.  Since the purpose of counselling is to help the other person become genuine and authentic in his own life and in dealing with others, the counsellor must set an example himself.  This has two stages:

*Stage I*    In the initial stage of counselling, the counsellor cannot openly share his feelings as these might have restrictive effect on the helpee.  But at the same time he can not supposed to be inauthentic by telling a lie.  Therefore, if the counsellor cannot be authentic, he should not be inauthentic either.  There should be minimum degree of authenticity or at least absence of inauthenticity.  The counsellor should minimize playing the role of a professional; he should instead behave like and relate to the client as a person.

*Stage II*    It is in this stage that the counsellor takes initiative in self-disclosure by sharing his feelings, concerns and experiences.  By doing so he also encourages the other to talk about himself and his feelings more freely and openly.

**Confrontation**        As stated earlier to effect change in behaviour, confrontation between undesirable and desirable, appropriate and inappropriate and irrelevant and relevant must take place.  Confrontation is necessary for leading towards action.  The counsellor brings into open the discrepancy between things that the client has been saying about himself and things he has been doing.  Confrontation provides the other with another point of view to consider in the process of self-evaluation, allows him to make a choice, and take responsibility for that.

The confrontation can be pursued in two stages:

*Stage I*    The counsellor provides  tentative formulations concerning discrepancies in communications from the client. These tentative formulations are stated in the form of probing inquiries rather than directional confrontation.  Pointing out directly the discrepancies between the client's intentions and actions, between what he is and what he wants to become, his own expectations vis-a-vis expectations of others and the like is likely to elicit defensive behaviour (anger, withdrawal, projection, etc) on the part of the other.

*Stage II*    This stage is marked by the counsellor taking the lead in providing opportunity to the client to directly confront various discrepancies in thought and action and in various aspects of his personality, attitudes, and value system.  Conflicts are brought in the open and he is encouraged to resolve those conflicts.  Confrontation of self and others is a prerequisite to an healthy individual's encounter with life.

**Immediacy**        Immediacy refers to the quality of interpersonal relationship between the counsellor and the client existing at the time of interaction. If the relationship is such which evokes anxiety in the counsellor as to what the client is going to say about him and the value of the relationship, it may be an indication that the counsellor is in the relationship primarily to meet his own needs and not for the benefit of the client. The strength and nature of relationship need to be evaluated on a continuing basis. Every relationship will have positive and negative aspects; both these aspects need to be evaluated. If the relationship between counsellor and client is strained or not meaningful to the latter, goal of counselling is unlikely to be achieved.

## HANDLING PROBLEM EMPLOYEES– INDIAN EXPERIENCE

The modern approaches in dealing with problems pertaining to employee relations are increasingly being adopted in different parts of the world. Indian organizations have not lagged behind this either. The efforts that are being made in managing effectively such factors as discipline, grievance and job stress, however, do not match with the enormous problems that Indian organizations face in these areas. The same case exists with the use of professional counselling which has tremendous potential in bringing about qualitative improvement in human resources at the disposal of various organizations. Three cases from Indian organizations are being described to highlight the use of professional managerial strategies in handling problem employees.

# COUNSELLING IN INDUSTRY*

Counselling is a recent concept in the field of employee welfare which progressive managements are increasingly accepting. Counselling services for employees originate from the basic acceptance of the idea that an employee is not just an 8-hour responsibility of the Management. His mental and physical well-being has an important role to play in his working life. His social and family life has a strong influence on his level of production, attendance, his behaviour at work and accidents too. The same holds true of the influence of his working life beyond the work place. He tends to carry home to the family and society the happenings from his work place. Treating an employee as a precious human being, taking care of one aspect of his environment, apart from enriching his life also influences other aspects, leading to all round improvement in the quality of life.

If there is a problem, experience bears out that it is better to solve it rather than to ignore it hoping it will solve itself, or pretend that it does not exist. Problems faced by individual employees or their families can be solved by well meaning friends, union and management personnel, but a specialist's touch works better in combination with theirs.

---

* Mahendra, Ms M, 1986. *Counselling in Industry, Social and Family Welfare in Industry: Survey*, Bombay Chamber of Commerce and Industry, Bombay, pp 145–147.

If every management takes the responsibility of looking after the welfare of its employees and their families, this will make for closer interpersonal relationships and a stronger feeling of belonging. Such an initiative places less strain on the social institutions in society which the industrial community supports eventually.

The professionally trained counsellor helps in various concrete problematic areas like absenteeism, alcoholism, mental disorder, medical problems, indebtedness, interpersonal problems faced by people at the work place.

The counsellor can also work in the wider field of family planning, social-education, employee development; hold social and educational programmes for the families of the employees enriching the lives of both.

Here is an example which supports the claim for professional help.

An employee was referred to the social worker for bad attendance at work.  He was being pulled up constantly by his superiors.  All assurances by the employee that it would improve his attendance seemed to fail.  The apparent cause seemed to be his drinking habit.

After just two sessions with the social worker, the employee revealed that he suspected his wife of being unfaithful to him.  The wife was unhappy because she felt the husband drank and sat at home.  The husband picked fights with her.  She retaliated by going off to her parent's home, which aggravated the situation further.  This went off for about six months.

After the social worker understood the root of the problem, she spoke to both the husband and wife.  She made them speak about and understand each other's problems.  The wife decided to play an active part in the problem solving process by not leaving home after in unpleasant incident.  The husband decided to contribute his mite in easing out the problem.  He discussed his doubts with his wife and with her help, within a month, showed improved attendance.

His drinking was cut down considerably.  With both putting in effort and guidance from the counsellor they could circumvent their problem which resulted in the employee showing an uninterrupted attendance of six months.

A regular income at home made for less tension and lesser unpleasantness.

If this problem had not been handled on time or in a professional way, it may have resulted in a broken family and a dismissed employee.  We as human being do have problems, most of which do get solved on their own, but in certain cases professional help is required. Since we are all striving to lead better lives, it is natural that we should help each other along in the right direction.

The premise on which programmes on employee welfare are based is that the management accepts that an employee's well-being is its concern.  If management provides for this professional help, it will help ease human suffering at an early stage with more satisfying results.

Organizations which have counselling services do bear out the usefulness of these services.

**Employment of a Counsellor**     The persons should be professionally qualified. Recommended strength would be one counsellor for approximately 1,000 employees.

**Wage Scale**     As per post-graduate, professionally qualified post.

**Designation**        Social counsellor/family counsellor/social welfare officer.

# REHABILITATION OF ALCOHOLICS IN INDUSTRY*

Although alcoholism is an age old problem in industry, its conception as a disease, rather than a moral problem, is of recent origin. It is roughly estimated that any industry has about 4% to 6% alcoholics on its pay-rolls. ALcoholism has been found to be a primary cause in several problems faced by industry, such as absenteeism, poor performance on the job, low productivity, proneness to accidents and low morale.

In the mid-50s in the USA, the loss to industry due to alcoholism was referred to as a *billion dollar hang-over*. Today an accurate estimate of this loss is fifteen billion dollars. The pattern in Indian industry should be more or less similar. As such, rehabilitation of alcoholics in industry is a management concern and needs to be handled with urgency and efficiency.

With the increasing realization that alcoholism is an illness and not a moral problem. Managers are realizing their special role and responsibility towards alcoholics. Whereas the traditional approach has been either to dismiss the alcoholic or to tolerate him indefinitely, professional and forward-looking managements today are emphasizing the rehabilitation of alcoholics on the job itself.

This approach serves a number of purposes. An employee is hired with a view to establish a long term relationship in the company. The management invests in an employee by way of money, time and training. Dismissal of an alcoholic employee involves considerable personnel costs, as once again the procedure of recruiting and training goes on for a new recruit.

Further, there is no guarantee that the newcomer may not develop the same problem.

Secondly, the rehabilitation of the alcoholics without dismissal saves society an additional burden of unemployment. The rehabilitation programme can be a mutually enriching experience for management and the employees. Employees would appreciate the management's approach of maintaining the dignity of the individual and his job. This would enhance employer-employee relations.

Before commencing a programme or rehabilitation, the management has to adopt certain attitudes towards alcoholism.
1.    Alcoholism is an illness, not a moral problem
2.    Alcoholism can be treated and, as such, is worth treating
3.    A change of attitudes on the part of management, staff and fellow-workers, towards the suffering alcoholic is essential.

The non-alcoholic world looks upon a alcoholic as a good-for-nothing person. Some

*Rege, Panna K, 1986. *Rehabilitation of Alcoholics in Industry, Social and Family Welfare in Industry: A Survey*, Bombay Chamber of Commerce and Industry, Bombay.

people in the company may take a paternalistic attitude and shield an alcoholic employee, fearing that he may be dismissed if notified.  Others are critical.  They feel it is a moral failing.  They may even blame the Management for *mollycodding* alcoholics and view the recovery programme with cynicism.

The significance of having an in-factory rehabilitation programme of alcoholism is that its contribution is unique.  A job is not only a source of economic strength but also of emotional satisfaction.  Dismissal from a job means a double loss of face to an alcoholic.  Hence, a job carries with it an authority which is binding on the employee and enables him to face facts squarely as the alternative of dismissal is dreaded.

# THE VOLTAS EXPERIENCE

Voltas Limited started an experiment in the rehabilitation of alcoholics at its Works at Thane, on the outskirts of Bombay.  The experiment commenced in 1980, with a survey of absenteeism.  By absentees are meant those employees who consume the leave due to them and lapse into loss of pay for various reasons, acceptable or unacceptable to the company.  It has been observed that the same employees lapse into loss of pay absence every year.  These are termed chronic or habitual absentees.

The survey undertaken in the year 1980–81 at Voltas on 160 chronic absentees showed that 94 had a drinking problem.  A recovery and rehabilitation programme was launched for these employees.  The programme was conducted by the welfare department.  It had three important aspects:

1.  An individual approach to the counselling of an alcoholic
2.  A group meeting of the alcoholic employee once a week
3.  Educating the rest of the employees regarding alcoholism.

Individual counselling is necessary to educate the alcoholic regarding the disease aspects of alcohol and to give him an insight into his behaviour and motivate him to participate in his recovery.

Taking into account the differences between individuals, alcoholics are dealt with accordingly.  A tough alcoholic is confronted with data regarding his poor attendance, poor quality of his work and at times his rowdy behaviour.  Often the threat of losing a job acts as a *constructive confrontation* which motivates him to face reality and change his behaviour.

Initially, an alcoholic will blame his poor attendance on several extraneous factors but will rarely admit that it is due to his drinking habit.

Some alcoholics may be in an advanced stage of alcoholism and may require hospitalization for detoxification and drug therapy.  However, after discharge from hospitals, they have to be motivated to join the recovery programme.

Individual counselling is not enough.  It has to be backed by a group approach.  The group meetings are organized on the basis of *Alcoholics Anonymous (AA)*.  This approach gives the individual alcoholic the strength of numbers.  He obtains acceptance and companionship in the supportive climate of the group. In the group, the drinking alcoholic learns through a process of sharing experiences from recovered alcoholics that he is a sick person as far as alcohol is concerned, and that sobriety and recovery can be achieved only by keeping away from that first drink. This sharing is a guiding force to the suffering alcoholic. It is often an identification with the recovered alcoholic and a feeling that *if he can make it, why can't I*, and so begins the recovery from alcohol.

No programme is complete unless the cooperation of others in the factory is forthcoming. The involvement of the Management, the Union, the supervisory staff and fellow-workers is very significant. It is essential to acquaint the supervisors with the different stages of alcoholism. The shop floor personnel can contribute a great deal in identification of alcoholics. An early detection of alcoholism saves a lot of misery to the employee and to his family. Non-alcoholic employees should also be invited to attend group meetings. AA meetings serve a dual purpose. To the drinking alcoholic, it is a therapy and to the non-alcoholic employee, it is an educative experience.

Informative literature on alcoholism should also be circulated amongst employees to modify stereo-types and misconceptions about alcoholics. It is essential to include members of the alcoholic family in the recovery programme. Hence, orienting them about alcoholism and encouraging them to attend AA meetings is very important.

The experience of the Voltas' recovery programme has been that out of the 94 detected employees with drinking problems, 34 employees showed an improvement in sobriety and in attendance; 9 employees showed an initial improvement and, then, lapsed; 51 employees did not show a significant and consistent improvement.

It takes time to develop a recovery programme in an industrial organization. Management should not expect quick results. But, in the long run, it certainly improves attendance and reduces loss traceable to alcoholism.

# PRODUCTIVITY AND ABSENTEEISM*

A large engineering organization having a work force of 19,300, embarked upon a process of organization development. One of the areas of improvement identified was tackling of absenteeism in the plant. The process of tackling absenteeism was started in early 1980 and is still continuing. The results achieved in short period in reducing the rate of absenteeism are as under:

1978: 20%, 1979: 20%, 1980: 19%, 1981: 16.5%, 1982: 14.3%

Besides reduction in the rate of absenteeism, there are numerous benefits that accrued to the habitual absentees as well as to the organization. Man-hours/days saved due to reduction of absenteeism yearwise are as under:

*Bhatia, S K, 1984. "Productivity and Absenteeism", *The Management Review*, Vol. II.

| Year | Reduction of Absenteeism Rate over Previous Year | Manhours Saved | Equivalent to Mandays |
|------|--------------------------------------------------|----------------|------------------------|
| 1980 | 1% | 2,06,094 | 25,762 |
| 1981 | 2.5% | 5,53,663 | 69,208 |
| 1982 | 2.2% | 6,18,824 | 77,353 |

These extra manhours saved during 1980, 1981 and 1982 are equivalent to 575 employees, without extra costs to pay roll.

## Approach to Tackling Absenteeism

An effective approach, which has been developed and tested for tackling absenteeism at micro-level has two facets. Firstly, absenteeism is essentially management's problem. Attitude of the management towards absence behaviour of employee is of utmost importance. The management should have concern and awareness of the effects of absenteeism. A positive attitude and determination that this problem is unavoidable evil to live with and thus to be ignored, will have to be radically changed. The second aspect of the approach is of creating awareness in the habitual absentees of their absence. The more the employees are kept informed about their absence the greater is the chance of a reduction in the rate of absenteeism. Absentee is to be made aware of his absence and also made to feel that he is not only important but is needed. Simultaneously, absenteeism is viewed seriously as it comes in the way of attaining the goals of the organization. It adversely affects him also. This approach for managing the absenteeism can be summed up in a formula as A2. Translated, this formula A2 means: The attitude of the management (a) and creating awareness amongst the chronic absentees (a). This recipe can bring positive results in the reduction of absenteeism. In this golden rule, the focus is on the individual withdrawing from work.

### SUMMARY

Maintaining healthy employee relations is a prerequisite to higher productivity and human satisfaction. The three organizational factors that affect employee relations are discipline, employee grievance and job stress, which if not managed effectively lead to strained relationship among employees. Discipline means conformity to the norms, rules, regulations and expectations of the management by the employees. In case of deviation from norms particularly the formal one contained in standing orders, disciplinary action is initiated by the Management. Domestic enquiry is an important part of disciplinary proceedings. This legal approach has serious limitations. A positive approach to developing a culture of discipline based on shared norms by the employees is needed.

Employee grievance is a complaint against the management for the latter's failure to meet the expectations of the employees. It is a form of upward communication which provides useful feedback to management on the impact of the policies on employees. Individual grievances, if not resolved, may take collective form and become a major industrial relations issue. Formal grievance-handling procedures existing in most large organizations are not very effective in handling grievances. Effective redressal of grievance presupposes relationship of mutual trust and concern between the management and the employees, in the absence of which no formal procedure could be effective. Grievances, therefore, need to be managed at the source of their origin.  The first line supervisors and managers need to be trained in skills and techniques of grievance-handling by adopting problem-solving approach. Job stress is a relatively new area of study the effects of which on employee relations are being established. Stress experiences on job have several physical and psychological consequences for the job holder, his co-workers, and the organization.  Various organizational stressors have been identified.  Strategies for managing job stress have to be based on both helping the individual to cope with the stress and bringing about appropriate changes in the organization in the direction of greater decentralization, job redesign and supportive climate.

Counselling is a form of interpersonal communication aimed at helping individuals develop their adaptive capacities by enriching their behaviour repertoire.  Two types of counselling are identified in terms of methods–directive and non-directive.  Non-directive counselling is increasingly being adopted to deal with problems of adjustment.  Such counselling necessitates establishing a helping relationship between the counsellor and the client.  Characteristics of and steps involved in the establishment of helping relationship have been described. Three cases from Indian organizations where counselling and other managerial strategies were used to deal with employee problems have been presented.

## KEY WORDS

**Discipline** : Conformity by the employees to the expectations of management in terms of standards of behaviour and performance, code of conduct and desirable actions and behaviour made known to them through formal or informal, written or verbal means.

**Discipline Positive Approach** : Developing a culture of constructive discipline based on shared norms and values which generates willing acceptance of the norms of conduct and a commitment to behave or act in a manner leading to improved effectiveness of an organization.

**Disciplinary Action** : Failure of an employee to comply with the provisions of standing orders results in a charge of misconduct.  The management may take action to determine the extent of punishment to be awarded.

**Standing Orders** : They spell out specifically the terms and conditions governing day-to-day employer–employee relationship which employees are expected to comply. Procedures for disciplinary action and award of penalties are also included.

**Domestic Enquiry** : An enquiry into the allegation of misconduct against an employee conducted within the organization based on the principles of natural justice.

**Grievance** : A complaint expressed verbally or in writing where an employee feels injustice has been done to him by the management.  Usually a complaint based on interpretation or application of the provisions of negotiated contract between the union and the management constitutes a grievance.

**Grievance Procedure** : The procedure, mutually agreed upon between the management and the union, to be adopted for prompt redressal of grievances after full investigation.

**Job Stress** : A condition arising from the interaction of people and their jobs and characterized by changes within people that force them to deviate from their normal functioning.

**Stressors** : Factors on the job, within the organization and in the external en-

|  |  | vironment, causing stress in an employee. |
|---|---|---|
| **Counselling** | : | A professional form of interpersonal communication aimed at helping an employee to cope with or resolve his personal problems of adjustment at work, within family or in the community reflected in undesirable behaviour and poor performance. |
| **Helping Relationship** | : | Relationship between counsellor and client in non-directive counselling characterized by equality and personalized interactions and directed towards helping the client to become aware of his problems and adopt appropriate measures to overcome them. |
| **Empathy** | : | Skill to listen non-evaluatively and to understand the problems and feelings of the other person exactly the way the other person has experienced them. |
| **Respect** | : | Unconditional positive regard and non-possessive warmth communicated to the other person. |
| **Genuineness** | : | Authentic and spontaneous expression of one's thoughts and feelings to the other person. |

## REVIEW QUESTIONS

1. In what ways is a positive approach to managing discipline more effective than the legal approach?
2. What are the limitations of using punishment as a strategy for dealing with problems of indiscipline?
3. Why is it necessary for management to find out the deeper causes of grievances of employees?
4. What steps does the management ought to take for effective redressal of employees' grievances?
5. As a student or an employee of an organization reflect on your experiences and fill in the following table:

| Stress factors present | Specific behaviour exhibited | Effects on yourself | Coping strategies to be adopted |
|---|---|---|---|
|  |  |  |  |

6. What are the types of problems in an organization that can be effectively handled by the use of non-directive counselling and why?

## FURTHER READING

1. Baer, W E 1970. *Grievance Handling: 101 Guides for Supervisors*, American Management Association: New York.
2. Bombay Chamber of Commerce and Industry, 1986. *Social and Family Welfare in Industry: A Survey*, BCCI: Bombay.
3. Chatterjee, N N, 1978. *Management of Personnel in Indian Enterprises*, Allied Book Agency: Delhi.
4. Monappa, Arun, 1985. *Industrial Relations*, Tata McGraw-Hill Publishing Co: New Delhi.
5. Quick, James C and Jonathan D Quick, 1984. *Organizational Stress and Preventive Management*, McGraw-Hill: New York.
6. Rogers, Carl, 1961. *On Becoming a Person*, Houghton-Mifflin: Boston.

# CHAPTER 12

# Industrial Relations Implications of Personnel Policies

Personnel policies have industrial relations implications. Several of the aspects relating to the contractual relationship between individual employee and employer are now determined through legislation and collective agreements. Management's efforts to unilaterally change the terms and conditions of agreement will be questioned by unions along with their legal validity. The turbulence and uncertainty in the environment requires organizations to be flexible enough to adapt themselves to the changes. Unions resist such changes for a variety of reasons (see Chapter 10). Even as there are myriad problems in deciding upon the representative union, the scope of collective bargaining is extending to many of the aspects once considered to be managerial prerogatives. When management resists such impingement upon and abridgement of their rights, conflict ensues. In such a scenario managing for good industrial relations, though desirable, is not easy. The motives, strategies and actions of management speak louder than their proclamations.

# NATURE OF EMPLOYMENT RELATIONSHIP

Over the years the relationship between employer and employee has changed from master and servant to one of employer and employee. Earlier it was a one-sided relationship with employer wielding absolute power to hire and fire employees. Gradually government and unions intervened to prevent one-sided exploitation by the employer and to wield countervailing power over them. Today the relationship between employer and employee is contractual, reciprocal and mutual. The employee has certain rights and obligations and so does the employer. While the laws, courts and unions have, over the years, limited the rights of management, the rights of employees have been preserved and furthered by managerial indiscretions, laws, courts and unions. The obligations of the employer are relatively precise and specific whereas those of the employees are imprecise and elastic. The substantive terms of the contract of employment prescribe wages, hours, holidays, etc. in definitive terms. But the obligations of the employee to provide an honest, efficient and faithful service and to obey orders are not easily measurable and therefore application of sanctions against workers for non-fulfilment of obligations often becomes difficult. Also managerial authority and power needs to be accepted by the subordinates. Tolerance to non acceptance of managerial authority or arbitrariness in the exercise of managerial authority can cause further problems.

**Table 12.1   Sample Lists of Employer Rights and Employee Rights**

| Employee Rights | Employer Rights |
|---|---|
| Job security | Right to formulate rules for recruitment, etc. |
| Entitlements to pay and benefits (under various statutes and within the framework of standing orders, collective agreements, etc.) | Right to discipline (within the framework of standing orders and Industrial Disputes Act) |
| Freedom of association (India did not, however, adopt the ILO convention on the subject) | Expect the employee to work and behave within rules as per agreed norms |
| Refusal to work if workplace is unsafe | |
| Right to strike | |
| Right of appeal to redress grievances | |
| | |
| *Obligations* | *Obligations* |
| To be loyal, diligent, faithful and committed to work as agreed | Meet all contractual obligations. Almost all managerial rights are limited by statutory provisions, court decisions and collective agreement. Past commitments usually become permanent liability unless bought back through productivity agreements, etc. |

In any case, in the employment relationship employees expectations become employer's responsibilities and employers' expectations become employees' responsibilities. So, there is bound to be certain area of friction or dissatisfaction where either party is not able to live up to the other's expectations. When employee's expectations are not fulfilled we call them grievances and when employers' or management's expectations are not fulfilled, it becomes the subject matter for discipline. Both grievances and discipline are thus two sides of the same coin. (see Chapter 11, for a detailed discussion).

The objective of management should be to integrate the interests of both employees and employers and work for collective well-being.

## PLACE OF UNIONS IN ORGANIZATIONS

The scenario of exploitation of employees by employers led to the birth of unions and introduced the era of government regulation and control over employment relationships.

Now, unions are a part of modern industrial societies. There are various explanations about the place and role of unions. These point to a commonality, though unions seek to pursue and further the interests of employees as a collectivity.

While radicals see trade unions as an inevitable response to capitalism, some regard them as a countervailing power against employer seeking to influence management decisions to further the interests of employees. Yet others view unions as being in competition with the management for employees' loyalty.

In countries like India where there is no union-shop situation, the organization comes first and recruits people. Then the people in that organization may form into one or more unions. The relationship between the organization and employee is primarily that between the employee (as a member of the union) and the union remains secondary. The organization compensates employee for services rendered. The employee compensates the union for services rendered on his behalf. The question then arises: Are employees alienated from the organization showing greater affinity to the union? If so, why do primary relationships get neglected and secondary relationships become important? Why do employees seem to trust the union more than they trust the organization which employs them? These questions may or may not apply to all organizations in the same way or to a similar degree.

The simplistic response is that job of the unions is easier than that of the managements. Unions teach their members about their rights while management has to harp on the duties and responsibilities of the employees. Some may say that in large organizations it becomes difficult to deal with a large mass of employees and so the management would deal with the union and the union in turn with the employees. Therefore, there is no question of primary or secondary relationship, alienation and affiliation and trust or the lack of it.

But such arguments do not hold much water. Union's job is not easy. They too have to deal with virtually as many people as the management. They cannot afford to raise the expectations of members because union members are known to be pragmatic in their orientation and do not hesitate to shift allegiance as necessary. Union policies and actions too have to weigh the pros and cons of individual versus group interests.    Unions too have a hierarchy which, perhaps, roughly parallels that of management hierarchy.

Considering that unions are there for ever, it is appropriate for organization to acknowledge their place and role and learn to deal with them appropriately.

## Dealing With Unions

The trade union movement emerged in India between 1918 and 1920.   In 1918, with the intervention of Gandhiji, an industrial dispute was settled in the Ahmedabad Textile Industry and after this incident the Ahmedabad Textile Labour Association was born.   During the same period, similar development took place in Madras when the Madras  Labour  Union was formed under the leadership of B P Wadia.   The International Labour Organization (ILO) was established in the year 1919 which influenced the formation in  1920 of an All India Federation of Trade Unions, viz., the All India Trade Union Congress.   The passing of the Trade Union Act, 1926 meant formal recognition of workers' right to organize.

The advent of Independence quickened the pace of growth of the unions. The years since Independence, particularly the period 1947–57 witnessed a rapid increase in the number of Unions, an increase brought about by a variety of factors such as the changed outlook towards labour organizations, the spirit of awakening in the country, and the economic distress that followed World War II.   The desire of political parties to help labour, as much as to seek help from it, was a contributing factor.

The increase in the number of unions and their membership, over the years, however, did not reflect their real strength.  Considering that the average Union membership has shown a gradual decline from over 1000 in 1947 to about 600 in 1980s, the increase in the number of Unions would seem to suggest rather a splitting of Unions or their inability to absorb workers in new units.  The degree of unionization varies widely from industry to industry.

## Central Organization of Workers

The events which led to the setting up of the All India Trade Union Congress have already been noted.  For sometime, the organisation worked as a strong united body. A section of its leadership had revolutionary urges.  Those who opposed this revolutionary leadership had formed the All-India Trade Union Federation in 1929.  In 1946, when attempts to restructure the AITUC failed, those believing in the aims and ideals of the AITUC separated from that organization and established the Indian National Trade Union Congress (INTUC) in the year 1947.  As the INTUC had, since the beginning, shared and supported the political outlook of the Indian National Congress, its popular image was identified with that of the Congress.   When the socialist group broke away from the Congress in 1948 and formed a new political party, the socialist trade union leaders who were operating within INTUC  also separated from it and formed a new Central Trade Union Organization called Hind Mazdoor Panchayat. This organization and the Indian Federation of Labour formed during World War II came together under the title of Hind Mazdoor Sabha (HMS) in the year 1948. Some splinter groups from the HMS and the AITUC set up a separate organization viz., the United Trade Union Congress. The government has recognized these four central organizations of workers for the purpose of representation at national and international conferences and occasional consultations. Besides the above four organizations, Bharatiya Mazdoor Sangh (BMS) and Hind Mazdoor Panchayat came into prominence in 1955 and 1965 respectively. The Centre for Indian Trade Unions (CITU) came into prominence in 1965 as a result of the bifurcation of the then Communist Party of India (CPI).

## Outsiders in Unions

In all parts of the world overt and covert involvement of trade unions in politics is discernible. The nature, form and extent of involvement may, however, vary depending upon the economic system, stage of development and socio-cultural and other aspects. Indian situation is rather peculiar. In India, unions are bound up in Government and politics much too glaringly and palpably. Indian trade unions were largely organised by nationalist leaders many of whom directed the workers against the British regime. Today in the federal set-up one finds the INTUC being more vocal in states where Congress(I) is not in power and AITUC, CITU and other unions with leftist ideology turning their members' dissatisfaction against the government in states where the parties to which they are affiliated are not in power. Unionized employees have been generally showing preference to people with political clout. Politicians generally show a tendency to cultivate trade union leaders who have significant control over an important section of vote banks in their constituencies. Almost all national trade union federations have been affiliated to one political party or the other. And, the number of such federations has been increasing since mid-70s, in tune with the increase in the so-called national political parties. It is not an exaggeration to say that almost each political party has its own trade union wing.

## Trade Union Legislation

The Trade Union Act 1926 provided that any seven workers may form a union and seek registration with the Registrar of Trade Unions. The registered trade unions are protected from civil and criminal proceedings arising out of the conduct of trade disputes. In turn, the unions must file annual returns of their membership and finances with the Registrar of Trade Unions.

Under Section 10 of the Trade Unions Act, 1926, the certificate of a union can be withdrawn or cancelled if the Registrar is satisfied that the Union has wilfully, and after a notice from him, contravened any provision of the Act.

The Trade Union Act, 1926 does not make the processing of applications for registration, time bound. There is no provision which regulates an application for re-registration from a union, the registration of which has been cancelled.

Under the present law, registration of unions is not compulsory. Several unions/associations have remained outside the purview of provisions of the Act.

## Inter-Union and Intra-Union Rivalry

The splits in the trade union movement had their origin in the twenties when a section of the AITUC leadership broke away and formed a separate organization. After Independence, union rivalry based on political considerations have become sharper. The splitting up and formation of new unions having sympathies with political parties have permeated unions operating at different levels. Attempts to bring about trade union unity have failed to bear fruit. Since legislation permits formation of several unions covering the same group of workers, a voluntary basis was sought to regulate inter-union relations. An inter-union code of conduct was evolved in 1958 at a meeting. They, however, remained on paper.

## Issues and Problems in Trade Union Recognition

Industrial democracy implies that majority union should have the right to sole representation i.e., right to speak and act for all workers and to enter into agreements with the employer. The provision for union recognition has been realized. Labour is a concurrent subject upon which both the central and state governments can legislate, with some state governments legislating for statutory recognition. The Bombay Industrial Relations Act 1946 provided for the recognition of the largest trade union in an undertaking/region with a membership of at least 15% of the work force. Madhya Pradesh and Rajasthan followed suit, while in most other states in the country there is no statutory provision for union recognition. The main issue centres round the modality to be adopted for verification of members of unions out of one of the following methods:

(i)    Verification of fee paying membership of the unions;

(ii)   Election by secret ballot;

(iii)  Check off system.

The issue in question has long been debated in central and state legislatures, tripartite forums and public platforms, but without reaching unanimity. The need for a provision for recognition of unions was again stressed in the Second Five-year Plan. Because of the desire to go slow on legislation, recognition was provided on a voluntary basis in the Code of Discipline in Industry (effective from 1st June, 1958). The most important criteria laid down in the Code are:

(i) A union claiming recognition should have been functioning at least for a period of one year as a registered union and should have the specified membership. In case more than one union is functioning in an establishment, the membership of all eligible unions is verified by the Chief Labour Commissioner of the central or state government as the case may be depending upon the jurisdiction;

(ii) The membership of the union should cover 15% of the workers in the establishment concerned;

(iii) When a union has been recognized, there should be no change in its position for a period of two years;

(iv) Only unions which observed the code of discipline would be entitled to recognition.

However, since the acceptance of this code is not mandatory, the entire purpose of the same has been defeated. With the result, the Trade Union Act, which is supposed to regulate and strengthen the trade union movement, has contributed greatly to weaken it.

Generally managements have not given serious thought towards recognition of unions within the industry. The main problem in granting recognition is to find out a foolproof method of verification of membership. In case of verification by using the membership register, it is very difficult to identify whether the same worker is shown as a member in the register maintained by different unions. This problem can be eliminated by the check off system. However, this has its own weaknesses. Individual workers allegiance to a particular union becomes a matter of public knowledge. This will put pressure on individual employees by rival union leaders who want to increase their strength. Normally an individual worker would not like his management to be aware of his loyalty to a particular union. In view of this, a workable solution would be to determine the strength by secret ballot. The existence of multiple unions is now a fact of life, and however much one may desire, they cannot just be wished away. Hence the task before today's manager is to find out

(i) the basis for recognition of trade unions,
(ii) strategies for dealing with multiple unions and,
(iii) strategies for preventing minority trade unions from creating conflicts.

If these tasks are accomplished even with some degree of success, the present day manager can live in a climate of industrial peace and harmony and avoid major conflicts (see Exhibit 12.1).

**EXHIBIT 12.1**

---

**Possible Criteria for Recognition of Unions**

1. Where there is more than one union, a union claiming recognition should have been functioning for at least one year after registration. Where there is only one union, this condition would not apply.
2. The membership of the union should cover at least 15% of the workers in the establishment concerned. Membership would be counted only of those who had paid their subscriptions for at least three months during the period of six months immediately preceding the reckoning.
3. A union may claim to be recognized as a representative union for an industry in a local area if its membership is at least 25% of the workers of that industry in that area.
4. When a union has been recognized, there should be no change in its position for a period of two years.
5. Where there are several unions in an industry or establishment, the one with the largest membership should be recognized.
6. A representative union for an industry in an area should have the right to represent the workers in all the establishments in the industry, but if a union of workers in a particular establishment has a membership of 50% or more of the workers of that establishment it should have the right to deal with matters of purely local interest, such as, for instance, the handling of grievances pertaining to its own members. All other workers who are not members of that union might either operate through the representative union for the industry or seek redress directly.
7. In the case of trade union federations which are not affiliated to any of the four central organizations of labour, the question of recognition would have to be dealt with separately.
8. Only unions which observed the Code of Discipline would be entitled to recognition.

**Issue of Recognition**    There should ideally be a legal provision for mandatory recognition of trade unions which have a specified membership base expressed as a percentage of the total workforce.  In the absence of legal provisions, managers should take initiative to put this into  practice.

For the purpose of verification of membership, secret ballot seems apporpriate and in 1990 consensus seems to have emerged on this among all central federations of trade unions, including the INTUC.

Strategy in dealing with multiple unions involve,

(i)    Identify areas of agreement and negotiate on them

(ii)    Identify areas of disagreement between Unions and have individual discussions with them to reduce the discord;

(iii)    Give equal and fair treatment to all unions on the basis of well-defined personnel policies.

In dealing with minority unions,

(i)    Keep them informed on all major issues of agreement with recognized unions.

(ii)    Give a greater weightage to the genuine individual grievances brought by them, and

(iii)    Never allow them to have a sense of isolation.

The above strategies cannot be termed as instant remedies or magic solutions in dealing with multiple unions. These can be some sort of workable hypotheses whose validity can be tested in a work situation.  At worst, this can be an honest attempt to solve problems with chances of a variable degree of success.  A word of caution is required. Decisions cannot be taken in isolation without relation to the environment, culture of the organization, culture of the unions and inter-personal dynamics.

To reduce increasing conflict, the management should take upon itself the task of educating and training both, the workers and the leaders of the trade unions, covering the following aspects:

(i)    responsibilities of trade unions;

(ii)    rights and obligations of individual workers;

(iii)    impact of external environment on day-to-day activities; and

(iv)    need for joint effort of management and the union(s) to increase the prosperity at the industry as well as national level.

**Recognition Agreement**    The problems in union recognition have already been reviewed. The union which enjoys the support of the maximum number of employees in an organization should be given recognition which entails the union to represent the employees.

Organizations can not wait for the government to decide or legislate on the subject.  They need to resolve the issue themselves, within the legal framework. The government can play a useful role in defining the role and rights of registered and recognized unions, by making registration somewhat difficult to prevent the mushrooming of small and unviable unions and also conferring trade union rights only to recognized/representative unions.  Where a single union does not have the majority support, more than one union may be recognized and a bargaining council can be formed with a consortium of unions.

The purpose of trade union recognition is to acknowledge the representative character of a union to  negotiate and bargain with the management on behalf of the workers/employees it represents and to establish the foundation for a continuing relationship between the management and union.  Since recognition entails changes in handling industrial relations matters, with a balance of both, employers and employees rights, and involves mutual expectations and obligations, it is desirable for the management and the union(s) to enter into a recognition agreement.  Such a recognition agreement may cover the following aspects:

- The parties to the agreement
- The group of employees covered by the agreement
- The purpose of the agreement
- The rights of both management and the union(s)
- The scope of disclosure of information, negotiations and collective bargaining
- The role and facilities of trade union office-bearers
- The policy and procedure for arbitration on problems arising out of implementation of the provisions of the agreement
- The duration, procedure and conditions for termination of the agreement

Management will insist on its right to management. Union will insist on its right to represent negotiate/bargain on behalf of its members. The clauses relating to unfair practices are stated elsewhere in this chapter and aspects of the code of discipline (Exhibit 12.2) would provide a useful framework to determine the do's and dont's with respect to each other's roles and rights.

**EXHIBIT 12.2**

---

### Code of Discipline in Industry

1. To maintain discipline in industry (both in public and private sectors) there has to be (a) a just recognition by employers and workers of the rights and responsibilities of either party, as defined by the laws and agreements (including bipartite and tripartite agreements) reached at all levels from time to time, and (b) a proper and willing discharge by either party of its obligations consequent on such recognition.

   The central and state governments, on their part, will arrange to examine and set right any shortcomings in the machinery they constitute for the administration of labour laws.

2. To ensure better discipline in industry, management and union(s) agree:

   (a)  that no unilateral action should be taken in connection with any industrial matter and that disputes should be settled at appropriate levels;

   (b)  that the existing machinery for settlement of disputes should be utilized expeditiously;

   (c)  that there should be no strike or lock-out without notice;

   (d)  that affirming their faith in democratic principles, they blind themselves to settle all future differences, disputes and grievances by mutual negotiation, conciliation and voluntary arbitration;

   (e)  that neither party will have recourse to (i) coercion; (ii) intimidation; (iii) victimization; or (iv) go-slow;

   (f)  that they will avoid (i) litigation; (ii) sitdown and stay-in- strikes and (iii) lock-outs;

   (g)  that they will promote constructive cooperation between their representatives and abide by the spirit of agreements mutually entered into;

   (h)  that they will establish, upon a mutually agreed basis, a grievance procedure which will ensure a speedy and full investigation leading to settlement;

(i)     that they will abide by various stages in the grievance procedure and take no arbitrary action which would by-pass this procedure; and

(j)     that they will educate the management personnel and workers regarding their obligations to each other.

3.  *Management(s)agree:*

(a)     not to increase workloads unless agreed upon or settled  otherwise;

(b)     not to support or encourage any unfair labour practice,  such as (i) interference with the right of employees to enroll or continue as union members; (ii) discrimination, restraint or coercion against any employee because of recognized activity of trade unions; and (iii) victimization of any employee and abuse of authority in any form;

(c)     to take prompt action for (i) settlement of grievances,  and (ii) implementation of settlements, awards, decisions;

(d)     to display in conspicuous places in the undertaking the  provisions of this Code in local languages;

(e)     to distinguish between actions justifying immediate  discharge and those where discharge must be preceded by a warning, reprimand, suspension or some other form of disciplinary action which should be subject to an appeal through the normal grievance procedure;

(f)     to take appropriate disciplinary action against its officers and members in cases whose enquiries reveal that they were responsible for precipitate action by workers leading to indiscipline; and

(g)     to recognize the union in accordance with the criteria  (Appendix) evolved at the 16th session of Indian Labour Conference held in May 1958.

4.  *Union(s) agree:*

(a)     not to engage in any form of physical duress;

(b)     not to permit demonstrations which are not peaceful and  not to permit rowdyism in demonstration;

(c)     that their members will not engage or cause other employees to engage in any union activity during working hours, unless as provided for by law, agreement or practice;

(d)     to discourage unfair labour practices, such as (i)  negligence of duty; (ii) careless operation; (iii) damage to property; (iv) interference with or disturbance to normal work; (v) insubordination;

(e)     to take prompt action to implement awards, agreements, settlements and decisions;

(f)     to display in conspicuous places in the union offices, the provision of the code in the local language(s); and

(g)     to express disapproval and to take appropriate action against office-bearers and members for indulging in action against the spirit of this Code.

# Collective Bargaining

There was a time when the employer/management had unfettered authority.  The employer was a law unto himself.  This resulted, at least in some cases in indiscrete use of authority which led to exploitation. Thus, the employees began to organize to wield countervailing power.  This led to disputes and unrest.  The government became concerned and began to prescribe do's and don'ts through legislation.  Still, collective bargaining continued to be a preferred form of settling disputes since that was the best way to avoid unilateral decision-making by either party on matters relating to wages, working conditions and other aspects affecting the employees and at the same time keeping the third party at bay.  Gradually, managements began to negotiate and bargain with unions even if it meant limiting their tradition-bound prerogatives which have mostly become archaic any way.

Having resolved the problems of identifying the representative union(s) and entered into recognition agreement (formal recognition is optional, though desirable), it is important for the management to bargain in good faith.

***Scope/Issues***     What should be the scope of collective bargaining and what kind of issues it should cover?   There are some like Alan Fox who sought to distinguish between market relations (wages and working conditions) and managerial relations (direction, surveillance and discipline) and advocate a say for employees and the trade union in the former, but not the latter.   There are others like Alwin Gouldner  who observe that the efficacy of rules, norms and conventions depend on the manner of their formulation.   Sociological and behavioural research evidence seems to suggest that there is a world-wide movement away from unilateral regulation to joint determination.   Managements must, in the long run seek to bargain for the voluntary cooperation of employees; otherwise, they may be forced to accept in some form or the other, sooner than later, some limitation on their  authority at the workplace.

To begin with, the scope of collective bargaining used to be limited to negotiation on wages, benefits and working conditions. Subsequently, the scope has been widening to cover aspects like overtime, job classifications, introduction of new technologies, multi-skilling, discipline, etc.  The practices vary from organization to organization. But the general trend seems to point to a situation where nothing is not bargainable!

In recent years there is a growing emphasis on productivity bargaining.

***Check-list***     (i) Management should be clear about some aspects before they start, in the course of and even after the conclusion of negotiation and administration of the contract.

(ii) *Negotiation strategy–*  Union-management relationships, particularly in the context of bargaining  evolve and revolve around the power equilibrium.  The management should adopt a win–win strategy than a win–lose or zero–sum strategy.  Given the fact that cordial relations require a high degree of mutual trust and reciprocity, no other strategy works in the long run, though in the short-run, manipulative strategies may bring some advantages.  The cooperation of the union is vital and, therefore, nothing should be done with the objective of weakening or hurting the interests of the union.

For long, unions used to submit charters of demands, managements used to bargain and unions collect at the end.  There were occasions when both the parties were busy seeking to bar the gain for the other party.   Now the trend is that both, the union and the management may serve charter of demands on each other. Management should be clear about the objectives of negotiation/bargaining (see Chapter 14: the section on Personnel Productivity through MBO).

- What objectives it considers are  vital and hence cannot be abandoned or compromised
- What it can concede and to what degree, and in exchange for what
- What it needs to do to meet/cope with unreasonable demands/postures of the union.

The approach should be one of give and take, but not giving-in under pressure. There should be some flexibility to cope with unexpected developments. Management should be careful while conceding management rights. For once conceded, it is hard to win them back. Usually, unions insist on consent clauses before implementing certain clauses in the agreement. Consider for example, the difference in the wording of the two agreements.

### Excerpt from Agreement A

As a result of this agreement, union will not object to and will instead cooperate with the management in keeping the labour cost per unit at the same level as the average for 1989 for the next 3 years; if the labour cost per unit goes up, union will cooperate with the management to make good the difference or agree to a proportionate reduction in wages as per the formula worked out in the annexure to this agreement.

### Excerpt from Agreement B

The management and the union realize the need for improvement in productivity. Management may bring in appropriate changes in technology, production processes, equipment, work methods, etc. with the consent of the union as and when the need arises.

In Agreement A the management has specified the task and the result to be achieved. In Agreement B, it is envisaged that before it can act, the management must obtain consent of the union on each occasion.

**The Management Team**    The size and composition of the negotiation team and the spokesman of the team are to be decided in advance. In organizations exposed to pressures of change, and those operating in chemical and high-tech industries they should compose of not only specialists in personnel and industrial relations but also of technical representatives with an intimate knowledge of shopfloor intricacies. They should have a proper brief about what the organization expects from the negotiations and leave enough room for exercise of discretion and show of fexibility during the negotiations. The negotiating team should have the requisite authority to spontaneously respond to atleast some of the demands, rather than have to say "we will get back to you after checking with the Board/Chief executive" each time.

Differences in the management team, if any, should be discussed when they meet in private than before the union at the negotiation table.

**Preparation**    Preparation is a must. Facts are important. Management should be ready with data on various aspects likely to come up for negotiation from competing/comparable firms and the industry/trade associations or the local chamber of commerce. Pay and benefit surveys will help.

The management team should also try to know and understand the union team and adjust appropriately. Watch out for conciliatory gestures and confidence winning efforts. Deal bluffs and threats tactfully. Keep an eye on the flow of communications about the negotiations to employees and if it becomes absolutely necessary reach out to the employees  through formal communication channels, to share facts and explain the management point of view.

## Negotiation Agreement

*Review Union Demands*   Get a control on negotiations by asking for more information and data to get a full picture of the nature of each of the proposals.

*Avoid Outright Rejection of Demands*   Prepare counter proposals, incorporating company demands.  Let the other party know that any agreement on specific provisions/demands is only tentative and subject to agreement on the total package.  The negotiations should spell out mutual obligations.  It means that the provision will be binding on one party when the other is honouring its side of the commitment and vice versa.  For instance, there could be a clause in the agreement which might say that "the management may withdraw additional pay and benefits to the employees accruing under this agreement if during the pendency of this agreement employees shift their allegiance to a different union or leader."  Such clauses ensure that the obligations are not one-sided.  When an agreement is reached during the negotiations, it is signed and usually registered with the Commissioner of Labour.  Then it becomes a contract which is binding on both the parties.  The signed agreement and its implications on the concerned employees should be widely communicated with necessary clarifications,if any.  The supervisors should be explained the rationale, content and implications of the agreement, both to the organization and the individual employees so that they (the supervisors) are better equipped to clarify the issue to their subordinates.

**Implementation of the Agreement**   The agreement should clearly and adequately provide for arrangements to implement the agreement and to attend to complaints and grievances arising out of interpretation of its various provisions.  The more care one takes to be clear, specific, explicit, appropriate, precise and accurate about the technical terms, subject matter, specific actions, responsibility and accountability, the less the problems in interpretation and implementation.  It is useful to specify the modus operandi to resolve disputes or problems arising out of or in the course of implementation of the agreement.

**Renewal and Revision of the Agreement**   The agreement should specify the period of operation, i.e. when it comes into operation and when, how and in what conditions it is terminated.  It should also provide for contingencies arising from changes in the environment during the period of operation of the agreement.  It is desirable to have dialogue with the unions on a regular basis, even after the agreement is signed so that problems, if any, can be proactively dealt with.  The discussions on renewal should commence a few months (some professionally managed companies start the process six months) before the expiry of the agreement.

**Prerequisites**   For negotiations and collective bargaining to succeed, the conditions necessary within the organization. These are called prerequisites and they include the following:
- Both the employer(s) and union(s) should have freedom of association.

- There should be mutual trust, confidence and respect between the management and the union.
- There should be a semblance of parity in the strength of both the parties. Otherwise, negotiations may lead to one-upmanship or a *see-saw* game.
- The rights and responsibilities of both employer(s) and union(s) must be recognised and respected. In this context, some consider that the right to strike (of employees and unions) and lock-out (of employers) should be recognized.
- Both the parties should select representatives who are duly authorised to negotiate and bestowed with the authority to take decisions.
- The parties should demonstrate unity of purpose at least within each group. They should show good demeanour and avoid personal abuse. Parties may be allowed to let the steam out, but when tempers run high, it is desirable to adjourn negotiations and reopen dialogue when the parties cool down.

## INDUSTRIAL CONFLICT

Conflict is endemic to industrial society. Notwithstanding the advantages of labour–management cooperation, the interests of labour and management seem to be opposed in a large measure. Conflict may either be sustained and organized or sporadic and unorganized. It may manifest itself actively in a strike or a go-slow, which are calculated attempts to apply pressure so as to alter the situation. The passive expression of conflict consists in the withdrawal of effort resulting in poor productivity, absenteeism, and poor time-keeping. Strike, considered to be the weapon of last resort, is the proverbial tip of the iceberg. Below this tip lies the entire range of relationships between labour and management in which is embedded the divergence of interests between them. Figure 12.1 indicates the various manifestations of industrial conflict.

Among the various manifestations of industrial conflict, strike is the most dramatic expression. As Gouldner observes, "A strike is a social phenomenon of enormous complexity, which, in its totality, is never susceptible to complete description, let alone explanation". There can be enormous variations in the reasons for strikes as well as their manifestations. Smelser has succinctly summarized different accounts for the occurrence of strikes under five heads.

***The Economic Advantage School***     It maintains that labour unions are in business and attempt to maximize the wage gains of their members.

***The Job Security School***     This is a variant of the economic advantage school, focuses on the desires of the workmen to protect the conditions of their work in the long-run rather than on short-term wage gains.

***The Class Warfare (or Marxist) School***     This school attributes workers' unrest to the fact that the working classes suffer from systematic exploitation at the hands of the capitalists.

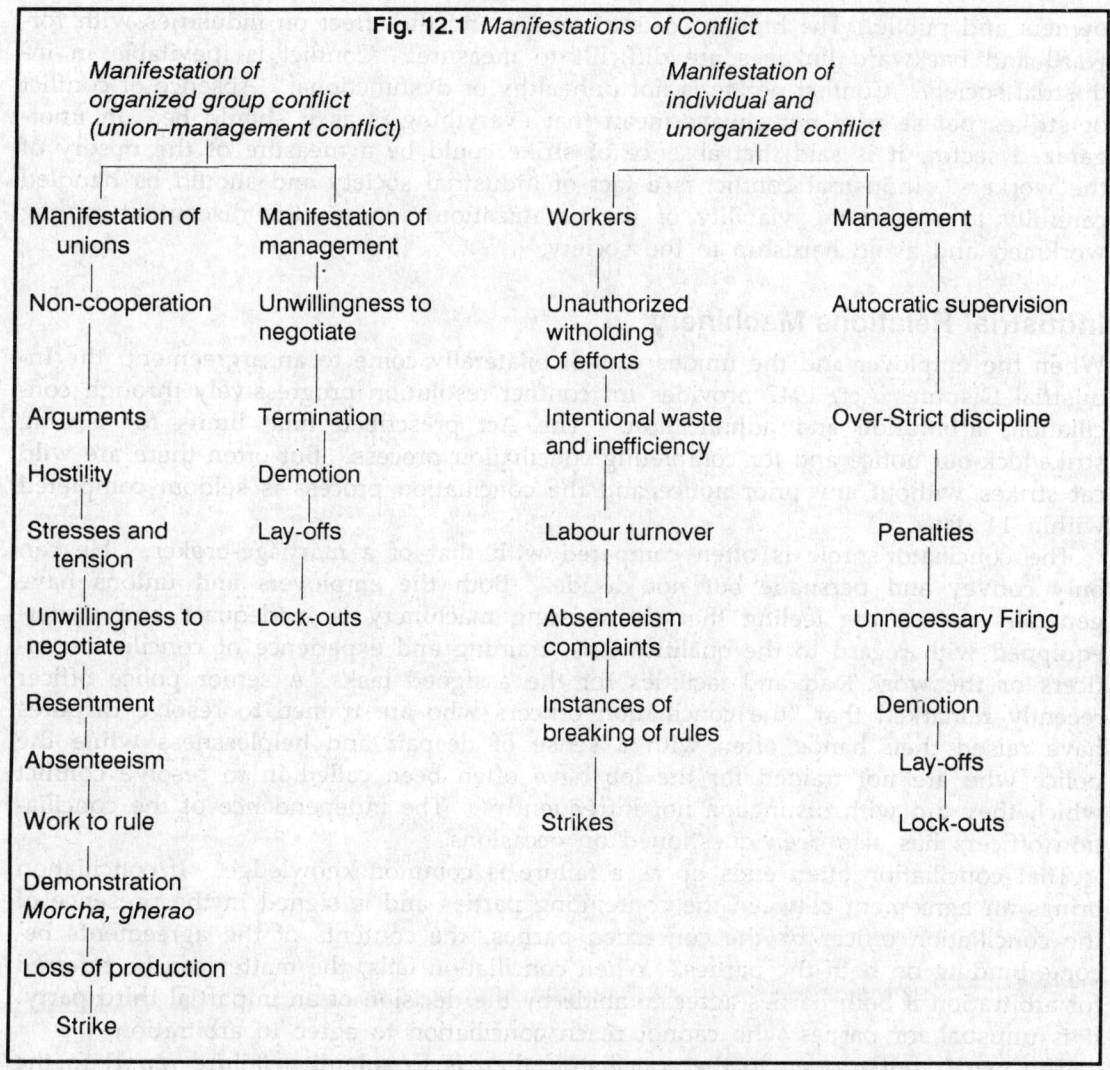

**Fig. 12.1** *Manifestations of Conflict*

Source: Kornhauser, A Dubin, R, and Ross, A M (Ed.), 1954. *Industrial Conflict*, McGraw-Hill: New York, p 14.

***The Political School***    This emphasizes the conflict between unions and management over the recognition of unions and collective bargaining, jurisdictional disputes among unions, internal leadership rivalries and influence of communism on unions.

***The Human Relations School***    This is associated with the industrial sociology of Elton Mayo and his associates. Broadly speaking, this school traces the basic dissatisfaction among labourers to the breakdown of primary groups among workers and lack of communication and understanding between management and workers.

Industrial conflict has been a source of major concern because of the disruption to economic development and the losses involved for everyone concerned——workers, owners and public. The hidden costs of strikes and the effect on industries with forward and backward linkages are difficult to measure. Conflict is inevitable in industrial society. Conflict per se is not unhealthy or dysfunctional. Absence of conflict or strikes per se may not always mean that everything is as it should be. In unorganized sector, it is said that absence of strike could be a measure of the misery of the workers. Industrial conflict is a fact of industrial society and should be handled carefully to ensure the viability of the organization, remove the discontent among workmen and avoid hardship to the society.

## Industrial Relations Machinery

When the employer and the unions cannot bilaterally come to an argreement, the Industrial Disputes Act, 1947 provides for conflict resolution progressively through conciliation, arbitration and adjudication. The Act prescribed time limits for issuing strike/lock-out notice and for completing conciliation process. But often there are wild cat strikes without any prior notice and the conciliation process is seldom completed within 14 days.

The conciliator's role is often compared with that of a marriage-broker. He can only convey and persuade but not decide. Both the employers and unions have generally voiced the feeling that the existing machinery is inadequate and under-equipped with regard to the qualifications, training and experience of conciliation officers or the work load and facilities for the assigned tasks. A senior police officer recently remarked that "the conciliation officers who are trained to resolve disputes have raised their hands often with a sense of despair and helplessness while the police who are not trained for the job have often been called in to resolve conflict which they did with distinction not infrequently". The independence of the conciliation officers has also been questioned on occasions.

That conciliation often ends up as a failure is common knowledge. If conciliation brings an agreement between the contending parties and is signed in the presence of the conciliation officer by the concerned parties, the contents of the agreements become binding on both the parties. When conciliation fails, the matter can be referred for arbitration if both parties agree to abide by the decision of an impartial third party. It is unusual for parties who cannot reach conciliation to agree to arbitration.

The usual course open to the conciliator, then is to submit a failure report to the government. The government may, at its discretion, refer a dispute to adjudication. The adjudicator's verdict is binding on both the parties. The Industrial Disputes Act provides for adjudication through labour courts (in case of personnel disputes over matters such as dismissal and disciplinary action involving individual workers), labour tribunal (matters such as wages, bonus, rationalization, etc.) and national tribunals (if the dispute has a wider significance or concerns establishments in more than one state). It is not open for either or both the parties to bring a dispute before a labour court or tribunal. The matter is left entirely to the discretion of the government. The Government need not give reasons for referring a dispute for adjudication. Even the Supreme Court has no jurisdiction over this matter. At best it can persuade the government, but not compel it to refer the matter for adjudication. This is indeed the bone of contention and concern is expressed about the arbitrary nature of this provision in the Industrial Disputes Act which gives considerable leverage to manipulate with the power politics of unions and union-management relations at work place.

The Indian Labour Year Book provides data about the industrial disputes referred to the Industrial Relations Machinery (both central and state spheres), failure reports received, disputes referred for adjudication, arbitration and awards in favour of and against the workers. Though the data is incomplete due to poor response from most states and union territories, it is adequate to draw some broad conclusions.

As already noted, most disputes are referred to conciliation. In recent years most disputes referred for conciliation could not usually be resolved at that stage and have therefore had to referred adjudication. Barely one per cent of the cases were referred for arbitration, since 1940s. The existing machinery for the investigation and settlement of industrial disputes, as provided under Industrial Disputes Act 1947, is inadequate and needs to be strengthened in the following areas:

(i) Trained and experienced officers, who have been exposed to the working problems of the industry should man the conciliation machinery. The conciliation machinery may be made independent of the government's control and influence.

(ii) The adjudication machinery provided under the Industrial Disputes Act should be substituted by setting up Industrial Relations Commission both at the central and the state level, broadly on the lines suggested by the National Commission on Labour with suitable modifications. The IRCs should also oversee the conciliation machinery.

(iii) Arbitration machinery provided under Section 10(A) of the Industrial Disputes Act should be increasingly made use of by employers, trade unions and the workmen. Even where financial demands are involved, arbitration machinery may be tried on an experimental basis. The arbitrator or panel of arbitrators so chosen for such purposes should be mutually acceptable to both the union and the management. The government and the trade unions can jointly prepare a panel of experienced arbitrators at the national and the State levels from whom the employer can choose.

(iv) The government should refrain from actively intervening in industrial disputes except when the disputes resulting in prolonged work-stoppages have a wide impact on the economy.

## Consultative Machinery

Apart from the industrial relations machinery discussed above, the Government has also constituted a consultative machinery. This consultative machinery now exists at every level, at the level of the undertaking, industry, state and nation. It aims at bringing the parties together for mutual settlement of differences in a spirit of cooperation and goodwill. At the undertaking level, the machinery is bipartite in character. These include the works committees (the Industrial Disputes Act, 1947 stipulates that works committees are to be set up in units employing 100 or more persons) and joint management councils (since 1958, following the thrust laid down in the Industrial Policy Resolution, 1956). At the industry level there are wage boards (now only for a couple of industries) and Industrial Committees; at the state level there are labour advisory boards and at the national level there are the Indian Labour Conference and the Standing Labour Committee. The machinery at state and central level is advisory in nature and tripartite (representing government, labour and management) in character.  Important legislative proposals are discussed and recommended by the Indian Labour Conference and Standing Labour Committees.  The 16th session of the Indian Labour Conference held in 1958 displayed a great deal of initiative and enthusiasm and evolved a Model Grievance Procedure, a Code of Discipline and adopted an Industrial Truce Resolution stressing the need for settling industrial disputes through voluntary arbitration.  Subsequently till 1977 the Conference was not held.  The tripartite labour conference has since been revived but needs to be continued on a regular basis.  The Industrial Disputes Act Amendment Bill of 1982 listed the following as unfair labour practices.

### By Employer

(i)    Threatening workmen with discharge or dismissal if they join a trade union or threatening a closure or lockout if a trade union is organised.
(ii)   Granting a wage increase to workmen at crucial periods of  trade union organization with a view to undermine the efforts of the trade union.
(iii)  To establish an employer sponsored trade union
(iv)   To encourage or discourage membership in any trade union by discriminating against any workman.
(v)    To discourage or dismiss workmen by way of victimization due to the exercise of employer's rights, by falsely implicating a workman in a criminal case for misconduct of a minor or technical nature, etc.

### By Workmen or Trade Unions

(i)    To force workmen to become members of a trade union
(ii)   For a recognized union not to bargain collectively in good faith with the employer
(iii)  To stage, encourage, coercive actions such as wilful go-slow, and to stage demonstrations at the residence of the employers or management staff members.

---

# MANAGING FOR GOOD INDUSTRIAL RELATIONS

The industrial relations scenario presents a grim picture because the relations which should have been handled in a mature *adult* way have largely been adulterated by myopic considerations.  The reactive approaches of the *actors* in a *tit-for-tat* spirit bred zero–sum games even where there was an opportunity for both the parties to come out winners, if only they had the wisdom and foresight to accommodate, compromise and collaborate rather than confront.  If the workman stays away from work unauthorizedly or resort to *go-slow* and *work to rule*, managers would threaten to keep the workmen out of work by suspension, dismissal, discharge of lay off and retrenchment.  If workers have grievances against management, management has grievances against workers about the latter's indiscipline and disregard for norms.  If workers are accused of sabotage, managers are held to be guilty of making the units sick.

The buck may not stop, and this is a game where everyone loses. It is time that the strategy is revised. Managements get the unions they deserve. If the personnel function is weak and does not take care of the genuine needs and expectations of the employees in an organization, that organization will have more industrial relations problems. Some organizations have handled their human resources function so well that the unions could survive without having to fight with the management and efficiency in industrial relations function was measured not in terms of strikes and disputes handled, but in terms of the contribution made to make conditions for conflict redundant. Here are ten golden rules for good industrial relations.

1. Managements should have harmony as a goal. If they genuinely want *harmony* and *good* relations they must let it happen.

Analysis of the official statistics on industrial disputes in the manufacturing sector published by the Labour Bureau, Shimla, for the period, 1974–83, reveal that during the 10 year period, an average 50% of the strikes in India were either fully or partially successful from the union point of view. This raises the question as to whether the management is genuinely interested in harmony. One often hears employees and trade union leaders accusing management of instigating strikes, be they in private or public sector, to survive recessionary market situation or a weak order book position. There may be cases where managements may not bother much.

2. Having defined harmony as goal, managements should pursue it vigorously. Harmony in industrial relations may be difficult, but not impossible. In industry, the relationship between employee and employer are contractual. So, there are mutual expectations and obligations. Employees' rights are employers' obligations and vice-versa. Hence, conflict is inherent but need not be dysfunctional. It is the responsibility of the management to take the initiative in all facets of industrial relations to mitigate conflict. Employees lose freedom when they join an organization. The need for freedom would be dormant so long as they get a *just* treatment. If they think that they are given a *raw deal* real or imaginary, the conflict surfaces: it may even escalate, if not promptly dealt with. If employees' perceptions about *raw deal* or *lack of fair play* are true, management must change its ways. If employees perceptions are imaginary, management must not only to be fair but also appear to be fair and seek to change the perceptions.

3. Full acceptance by management of its accountability in industrial relations in the same way that accountability is accepted for the quality of product or marketing strategy.

4. A distinction, based on the concept of accountability, between the functions of union and functions of management is necessary.

5. Setting up norms and following them up with exemplary standards and transparent honesty.

If organizations were to have order and to function in harmony with a sense of purpose and achievement there is need for norms that are just and humane. These norms will gain acceptance and respect if they emerge from a consensus among all concerned rather than when they are imposed from above.

6. Uniform applicability of the policy and procedures, after considering the varying local conditions in a multi-plant situation. Every organization and manager is faced with problems resulting from past practices. Operational experiences result in a set

of *past* practices, which when accumulated become part of the culture of the organization. These unwritten but nonetheless real policies exist apart from contracts and policy manuals and owe their origin to the countless informal decisions and actions taken by management. Hurried or casual responses to seemingly unimportant situations and employee requests set precedents that make a dent on the policy. Granting a request to one employee and denying it to another will lead to charge of favouritism. The chief source for the loss of managerial prerogatives is indiscretion.

7. There is need for bargaining in good faith with the majority union of the employees on matters concerning compensation and working conditions and having joint consultation on all other matters affecting the employees. *Union shopping* practices would be costly in the long run though it may appear that there is a short-term pay off because weak unions create more problems than strong ones. The management should neither seek to exploit the weaknesses of the unions in the organization nor submit meekly to its coercive tactics. Bargaining outcomes should be viewed in a spirit of partnership and *give-and-take* than in an adversarial win-lose mood. As for the need to institutionalize joint consultation, we may recall what Field Marshall Montgomery said: "Even a man regimented in every sense of the term would carry out his duties with more vigour and spirit if treated as someone who really mattered, and who understood the over all importance of the project in which he was involved".

8. Maintain direct two-way flow of communication between management and employees. The relationship between employees and organization is primary and that of employees and the union in which they become members at a later stage is secondary (except in *closed shop situation* which does not prevail in India). If employees are alienated from the organization and begin to primarily demonstrate their allegiance to the union the management should blame itself. The secondary relationship becomes important and valued when the primary relationship turns sour. In such an event whether real or imaginary, management should show concern, not apathy.

One of the main reasons for the alienation is the breakdown in communications. Management should establish rapport with the rank and file rather than only with the union leadership.

9. There is need to maintain a systematic data base on all aspects concerning human resource management to ensure objectivity in managerial actions that will help bridge the gap between employees and management in terms of credibility and confidence through better communication of information and promotion of knowledge about the organization.

10. Respect for and acceptance of the industrial relations function in an enterprise depends upon the quality and competence of the industrial relations professionals and their involvement in strategic planning with adequate responsibility, authority and accountability. If there is lack of respect it may be due to lack of expertise. If there is lack of acceptance, it may be because they play their role assuming the union to be their adversary. If there is lack of involvement in strategic planning it may be because they have failed to convince the top management about their intrinsic worth in a pro-active role. In an organization, if the union appears to be doing its job better than managers in managing, one may conclude that union leaders commitment to their cause is greater than the managers commitment. Introspection is necessary so that we do not lose time and perspective by continuing to project outward and be

on the defensive.  Those who are responsible for managing for *good* industrial relations should change first if they expect the relationships to change, for the better.

## SUMMARY

Over the years, the master and servant relationship between owner and worker has evolved into employer–employee relationship.  This change is significant in more ways than one.  The employment relationship is no longer one-sided.  It is contractual with elements of reciprocity and mutuality. Laws, courts and unions have limited managerial authority.  Trade unions, despite their chequered history, multiplicity, inter-union rivalry, and confusion about their recognition as representative bodies have come to stay and act as countervailing power.  Managements must learn to deal with them appropriately.  A recognition agreement would help bring clarity in respective roles and mutual expectations.  The scope of collective bargaining is extending beyond pay, benefits and working conditions and infringes upon managerial authority and decision-making.  Managements too have learnt to put forth counter proposals and demands and paved way for give-and-take to enhance productivity through collective bargaining.  The success of collective bargaining entails, among others, recognition of certain rights of both the parties.  For the employees, this means, among other things, right to unionize and right to strike.  Conflict thus is inherent in industrial life.  Ways and means have to be found to cope with conflict.  Apart from recourse to the industrial relations machinery set up under the Industrial Disputes Act, 1947, the management should think and act pro-actively as good industrial relations also form an integral part of the core objectives of an organization.

## KEY WORDS

| | | |
|---|---|---|
| **Closed-shop** | : | It is a practice, not formally prevalent in India, whereby recruitment is restricted to members of the union. |
| **Employee Relations** | : | Relations between employer and employees as individuals. |
| **Industrial Relations** | : | Relations between employers (associations) and employees (associations) as a group. *Union–management relations* and *industrial relations* are used synonymously. |
| **Union Recognition** | : | Recognition of a union as being representative of a certain group of employees, determined through one or more of the following methods: secret ballot, membership verification and/or check-off. |
| **Union Registration** | : | The Trade Union Act, 1926 provides for registration of unions. Registration is not mandatory; but, registered unions enjoy some benefits (immunity from civil and criminal prosecution for participation in industrial disputes) and have some obligations (to conform to such provisions as filing annual returns, etc). |

## REVIEW QUESTIONS

1.  Critically review the changes in the concept of employment relationship and their effects on human resource management.
2.  Discuss the place and role of trade unions in organizational context.  Suggest approaches to deal with them.
3.  i) Are unions necessary?

ii) Should unions be recognized? If yes, how?

iii) Should there be a recognition agreement? Why? What aspects should it cover?

4. Describe and comment on:

i) Code of Discipline

ii) Unfair labour practices.

5. What are the guide-posts in managing for good industrial relations? Are they practicable?

# CASE STUDY : PIONEER INDUSTRIES LTD[*]

Pioneer Industries Ltd (PIL) is a custom-built assembly type industry. Established in 1941 as a private enterprise, the organization ran into trouble due to financial vicissitudes and conditions peculiar to this industry the world over. When the Government of India was approached for help by way of subsidy, they initially placed orders on a cost-plus formula and subsequently, in 1952, acquired two-thirds controlling interest. The Government acquired full control and ownership over the enterprise in 1961. Since then the Government has been extending generous financial help and seeking overseas technical help from a host of countries to strengthen the organization.

In 1965, a visiting team from Japan studied the organization and observed that it can hope to double the output merely through re-organization of work which required no additional inputs by way of capital or technology. But the organization did everything except change work methods. A sum of over Rs 100 crore was invested, new equipment and facilities acquired, technical collaboration entered into with internationally renowned firms and manpower increased from 5,000 to 7500. The quality of workmanship of the firm was lauded when the product stood up to severe tests, and the engineers and officers of the organization achieved a major breakthrough in product design capability. Yet, the level of production stagnated and the length of the production cycle more than doubled between 1973–82.

The government had been giving substantial help to the organization by protecting the market and liberally increasing the prices to cover costs. In the early 1970s the administered price was virtually doubled on a cost-plus-profit basis to help the organization tide over its losses. As a result, in 1979–80 the firm could show a surplus of about Rs 1.8 crore even though the output was merely one-third of rated capacity. The cushion of liberal price policy soon evaporated, and in 1984–85 alone the company incurred a loss of over Rs 15 crore. There is a general feeling among the employees and the junior and middle managers of the organization that its personnel and industrial relation practices and policies have been principally responsible for the poor performance.

In the early years, soon after the organization began operation, the management sent one of its officers to register a trade union for the workers in order to forestal the emergence of a communist union. The communist union which nevertheless came

[*]C S Venkata Ratnam, 1988. "IR and Productivity", *Indian Management*, May, pp 47–49.

into existence had eventually to wind up because of the tactics of the management. However, the communists ensured that their loyal supporters infiltrated into the management-sponsored union. As a result, although the firm has all along had only one union for workers and an association for the staff, there have been persistent factions in both bodies based on political cleavages. Among the several groups, the marxist communists and right wing BJP command sizeable support. Although both the union and association have been independent of outside affiliations and leadership, the employee leaders have often been identified with specific groups in the wider environment.

The leadership kept changing during the two decades from 1947 to 1967 because there has been no wage revision during this entire period. It is significant to note that two other organizations in the public sector which manufacture a similar product had revised wages during this period. The wage increase given way back in 1947–48 was made by a cut in the DA in 1948–49 because of financial stringency. The cut was restored only in 1963 but in the same year DA was delinked from the cost of living, once again off-setting whatever benefits had accrued. While the workers' union kept a low profile through these turbulations, the association picked up a draftsman by name AK who they believed could take on the management, and made him general secretary. AK studied the various issues in depth and submitted a list of seven collective and 116 individual demands. After much reluctance the management constituted a bipartite committee, but limited its brief to an examination of anomalies in pay scales. Although the committee submitted a unanimous report, the management dragged feet because the finance ministry did not concur with the recommendations. The bureaucrats eventually opted for an adhoc settlement by elongating pay scales, and that too only with regard to 7 out of the 47 categories. The outcome did not satisfy the association but nevertheless raised hopes of securing a more favourable outcome through a confrontation. The association gave a strike call and over 95% of the members participated in the longest ever strike lasting 58 days. This was in 1967. The strike was withdrawn on the assurance of the government that a sub-committee of the Engineering Wage Board would be constituted to examine the special features of this industry. Encouraged by this favourable outcome, the workmen joined hands with the staff and a Joint Action Committee (JAC) was formed with AK as the convenor.

Worried by this unity of workers and staff, the management influenced the government to back out of the promise to appoint a special sub-committee. The management's strategy was to create the impression that AK had failed to force the government into a special consideration of their claims and thereby sow discord. The government eventually backed out of its commitment and handed over the matter not to a special sub-committee but to the Engineering Wage Board. The employees protested vehemently that the special circumstances obtained in their industry needed separate consideration. The more the management tried to forge disunity, the harder the attitude of the leadership became. They began systematic efforts to prepare workers for conflict.

AK conducted a survey of 4000 employees and came out with disturbing conclusions. One out of every four workers had no pay to take home after the statutory deductions and various other cuts. Many had to absent themselves on pay day to escape from their creditors. The indebtedness among majority of the workers ranged between five to ten times their gross annual earnings. There was widespread resentment against the management among both workers and staff. Marshalling these facts and sentiments, the leaders insisted that they had been denied a wage increase although similar other enterprises were benefited.

Analyzing that AK was the backbone of union militancy, they decided to suspend him for irregular attendance. Construing this as an act of victimization, the staff walked out of work. The management cut the wages of those who walked out, which sparked yet another walkout with the workers also joining. The JAC ultimately submitted a strike notice over a charter of demands, the first being the reinstatement of AK. The strike lasted 27 days. The strike ended at the instance of the local Congress MP who got the concerned minister to assure satisfactory solution. A one-man commission was apointed. AK pulled political strings and a commission was appointed which awarded better benefits than the workers themselves had asked for. The employees virtually deified AK for getting them such impressive benefits and his influence rose to dizzying heights.

Soon after the settlement, a new CMD was appointed. Concerned at the growing popularity of AK, he lured the leader to accept promotion from the staff category to junior manager. As a manager AK was miserable and frustrated. He had to sever his connections with the association and the union. His disciples, mostly with strong Marxist leanings, assumed the mantle of leadership, gained prominence and gradually sidelined him. Two years went by and his frustration mounted. Apart from the loss of influence he had enjoyed as a union leader, the management had not lived up to the promise of creating a separate department for him to preside over. Soon, AK asked the CMD to demote him to his original position, but the latter refused to oblige.

AK now pulled strings through a top national level leader of the INTUC who happened to be on the Board of PIL. He offered to affiliate both the union and association to the INTUC if only his demotion could be secured. Enamoured by the prospect of building a base for his union in this important city, the leader accomplished AK's demotion as draftsman. The leadership of the union which was in the hands of strong Marxist sympathizers did not immediately invite him to take over leadership, though they were once his disciples. However, AK put up a panel of candidates headed by one PS who had INTUC leanings for the 1973 elections and trounced the Marxists. A wage revision became due subsequently in 1974. AK was invited to be the chief negotiator on behalf of both the union and the association although he held no formal position. As the negotiations were under way a state of Emergency was promulgated in the country. In November 1975 a draft agreement giving several benefits was finalized with the Joint Secretary in the concerned ministry.

As the agreement was pending for approval by the government, the INTUC leader pressurized AK to affiliate both the bodies to his union as had been promised. The leader's fear was that once the settlement was through AK would become all powerfull and might refuse to affiliate. AK pleaded that since PIL was a stronghold of communists, and he himself had no formal position, he had to first secure a favourable settlement and win confidence before moving towards formal affiliation. The INTUC leadership grew suspicious of AK. They offered to send him on a tour of some Asian countries if he formally affiliates the union to the INTUC, but he was silent.

In tripartite negotiations held in January 1976, the government went back on the draft settlement reached in November 1975 on the ground that the Bureau of Public Enterprises (BPE) had certain objections. AK believed that there was foul play. The enterprise level management could not persuade the government to stand by the promise. In the meanwhile, the undertaking got a new CMD. Taking advantage of the Emergency, the new CMD introduced a second shift to augment production, besides introducing a multi-trade system to make better use of skilled manpower.

Negotiations were started afresh and a new wage settlement was worked out by December 1976 within the framework of BPE norms, providing for an incentive system instead of DA based on the local cost of living index. The agreement was to take effect from September 1974 from which period arrears were to be calculated. The workers expected that the arrears would be substantial. The union wanted a quick implementation of the settlement but the CMD wanted time. Soon there was a change of heart and pay slips were prepared for the month of January with the EDP facilities of a neighbouring enterprise(although PIL had its own EDP). The pay slips came as a rude shock to the workers since hardly anyone benefited financially inspite of the many commitments made in the settlement and conveyed to the workers by the leadership. Most workers got no arrears and in some cases excess payments were sought to be recovered.

AK wrote to the CMD immediately to stop the distribution of the pay slips, pointing to the *grave consequences of such manipulation of trade union affairs* and called for discussion to sort out the discrepancies arising out of the *arbitrary understanding of the management in calculating the arrears*. Management paid no heed to his letter. Irate workers beat up AK and his associates within the factory premises. In an emergency meeting of the union's general body held soon after, the leadership was seized by the Marxists.

With the workers' hopes dashed, production and productivity began to slide down. The downstream has continued unbated. The second shift had to be reduced to a skeleton shift. The multi-trade system became inoperative. A study conducted by the BPE acknowledged that the 1977 wage agreement was principally responsible for the strained industrial relations and low productivity.

## QUESTIONS

1. Identify the personnel policies which affected industrial relations climate in this case.
2. Which of the problems in this case are a creation of the enterprise level management and which are a result of the public enterprise environment?
3. What is your assessment of the management's way of handling the unions and union leadership?
4. Could the management have avoided political intervention at various levels?
5. Was the 1977 wage agreement principally responsible for the strained industrial relations and low productivity? How could it have been handled?

## FURTHER READING

1. Kornhauser, A, et al. (Ed.), 1954, *Industrial Conflict* (Chapters 1 and 4), McGraw-Hill: New York.
2. Ramaswamy, E A, and Uma Ramaswamy, 1981. *Industry and Labour*, Oxford: New Delhi.

3.    Salamon, Michael, 1987. *Industrial Relations: Theory and Practice*, Prentice-Hall: Hertfordshire.
4.    Venkata Ratnam, C S, 1986. *Industrial Relations Environment in India*, International Management Institute, India (Mimeo): New Delhi.
5.    Venkata Ratnam, C S, 1989. *Employers' Dilemma*, EFI-SOLAR Foundation: Bombay.

# CHAPTER 13

# Employees' Participation in Management

In organized sectors of human activities, participation of people in areas which are of vital concern to them is not a new phenomenon; as a matter of fact the concept of participation embodies within itself relentless effort of mankind throughout history to seek meaningful interaction with people with whom they work and to enhance the sense of *being in control* of their immediate environments. In India, as abroad, various participative mechanisms have been evolved, nurtured and strengthened to inculcate a sense of involvement among employees in their spheres of work so as to generate positive commitment and appropriate motivation towards desirable and legitimate productive pursuits. Participation as a conscious and deliberate choice in designing human systems has come to be recognized as a predominant value in most social systems, not only because participative designs of social systems create conditions conducive to the release of human potential and constructive use of human resource, but also because it enhances through collective action, the quality of life of people at work and in the community. For the best in man to come out, it is necessary for him to know why he is doing certain things and not the others, and participation is precisely a quest toward that end.

## CONCEPTUAL FRAMEWORK OF EMPLOYEES' PARTICIPATION

There are at least four types of participation that can be developed at enterprise level so as to provide opportunities to all levels of employees to get involved in issues and areas that affect their work and lives. These can be categorized as: information sharing, consultative, joint decision-making, and self-managing groups (Table 13.1). Various groups of employees can be associated with different types of participation depending on their areas of concern, their expertise as well as their willingness. It will be necessary, however, for each enterprise, to make its own assessment of organizational constraints and opportunities and take into account the existing mechanisms for participation, to define the purpose, scope and content of the joint councils.

From an ideological point of view, participation may be viewed as either integrative or distributive. It is integrative where the purpose is to develop common goals and joint problem solving approaches. It is called distributive where the purpose is to distribute power and authority among rank and file.

Employees' participation can be ensured through representative system or through direct participation and involvement of all employees. In a representative system usually the elected or nominated (nomination can be by union in most cases and in some by the employer) representatives of one or more employee groups (workers, staff, officers, etc). Both direct and representative systems of participation may coexist.

### Table 13.1   Different Types of Participation

| Type | Level | Means | Scope |
|------|-------|-------|-------|
| Information sharing | All levels | Communication meetings newsletter suggestion scheme, etc. | Information about policies, changes, etc. |
| Consultation | Enterprise/plant/ shop-floor level | Works Committees, shop-floor, plant councils, joint management councils, etc. | Work, working conditions and welfare |
| Join decision-making | Board/plant/ shop level | Representation at board, plant and shop level decision-making bodies | Work-related issues |
| Self-management | Enterprise— wide | Same as above | All strategic, policy and operational issues |

Where the intention is to combine thinking with doing within the existing framework, employee participation is ensured through creation of parallel organizational structures like quality circles, etc.

Employees' participation can be voluntary or statutory. Usually government sponsored schemes bring in compulsion or involuntarism through statutory and other means. Alternative approaches to participation like direct participation and parallel organizations like quality circles have been voluntary. One would wonder whether legislation would ensure effective participation. But employees' participation is no longer an idealistic and ideological conception. It is considered imperative for organizations to cope with the myriad changes in the environment and make the rising expectations of employees compatible with the requirements of high performance.

# Government Policy and Participation[*]

More than the employers and workers, the government has been at the forefront in encouraging workers' participation in management for the realization of the ideals enshrined in the Constitution, objectives of planned economic development, industrial productivity and harmony in industrial relations. Since Independence, various schemes have been formulated by the Government of India to encourage workers' participation in management, which are briefly reviewed here.

*Works Committee 1947*     The Industrial Disputes Act 1947 provided for limited participation of elected representatives of workers in Bipartite Works Committee. The main aim of these committees was to promote measures for securing and preserving amity and good relations between employers and workmen. Though a large number of committees were set up and at the end of 1987, 530 such committees were operating in the central sphere, the scheme by and large has not been successful in achieving the desired objectives.

The functions of works committees were not clearly defined. There was frequent conflict between the elected representatives of works committees and the trade unions operating in the enterprises. Participation was mainly limited to aspects of welfare management.

*Joint Management Councils (1958)*     In 1958, Joint Management Councils (JMCs) were introduced. JMCs were to be entrusted with administrative responsibility for various matters relating to welfare, safety, vocational training, preparation of holiday schedules, etc. They were to be consulted in matters of change in work operation, amendment or formulation of standing orders, rationalization etc. to encourage smooth work operations and enhance productivity. Representation of workmen to the JMCs was based on nominations by the recognized trade union.

JMCs did not receive much support from unions or management. It was alleged that JMCs and work committees appeared similar in scope and function and that multiplicity of bipartite consultative bodies served no purpose. And where the membership strength of unions was disputed, composition of the council became a contentious issue.

*Employee Directors in Nationalized Bank Boards (1970)*     Subsequent to the nationalization of banks, under the Nationalized Banks (Management and Miscellaneous Provisions) Scheme 1970, the government required all nationalized banks to appoint employee directors to their boards, one representing workmen and the other representing officers. The scheme required verification of trade union membership, identification of the representative union and the appointment of a worker-director from a panel of three names proposed to government by the representative union. The tenure of an employee director was to be three years.

---

[*] The description of various schemes and issues is largely taken from: Government of India, 1990, Seminar on Labour Participation in Management: Status Paper, (Ministry of Labour): New Delhi, Jan. 8–9.

This was the first major attempt to place representatives of workmen on the boards of public sector corporations. The process of membership verification and appointment of worker directors was carried through smoothly in 1971, but the second round of appointments were completed in all the 14 banks only in 1981. Membership verification continues to remain a major difficulty and the process of appointments has been delayed. In retrospect, it is also evident, that while the scheme clearly laid down procedures for appointment, etc. there was no clear enunciation of the objectives of such participation or of the role and functions a worker director had to fulfill.

**Constitutional Amendment and 1975 Scheme**     In 1975 the Constitution was amended and Section 43A was inserted in the Directive Principles of the Constitution. This section provided that "the State shall take steps by suitable legislation or in any other way to secure the participation of workers in the management of undertakings, establishments or other organizations engaged in any industry". In accordance with this amendment, the Scheme of Workers' Participation in Management in manufacturing and mining industries was introduced in 1975. The scheme provided for formation of joint councils at shop and plant levels and covered only those manufacturing and mining units which employed 500 or more workers. The scheme was required to be implemented in both public and private sectors, as well as in departmentally run units. Shop and plant level councils were assigned specific functions relating to production and productivity, reduction of absenteeism, safety, maximizing machine and manpower utilization, etc.

The scheme did not lay down norms for the nomination of representatives to the councils. This made for considerable confusion and it was left to management to work out an acceptable formula for representation to the councils. Providing for flexibility in the nomination of representatives only seemed to make matters more difficult, except where a single union was the dominant union and interested in such bipartite functioning.

**Scheme of Workers' Participation in Management (1977)**     Two years later, commercial and service organizations with 100 or more employees were brought within the purview of a participative scheme, broadly similar to the 1975 scheme. It was applicable to institutions like hospitals, the P & T, railways and state electricity boards. While both the 1975 and 1977 schemes generated considerable enthusiasm initially, with a large number of organizations constituting such forums, there was a sharp decline, after 1979. Various problems surfaced. Apart from the perennial controversy about the criteria for determining representation to the forums, the exclusion of grievance redressal, the restriction to consideration of only work-related issues, the inadequate sharing of information, the lack of a supportive participative culture, the indifference of management, the involvement of second-rung union officials, etc. contributed in different ways to the ineffective functioning of many forums and their subsequent closure.

**Comprehensive Scheme for Employee Participation (1983)**     In December 1983, following a review of the progress of participative schemes in industry, a new scheme was prepared and notified.

This scheme was applicable to all central public sector enterprises, except where specifically exempted. It envisaged constitution of bipartite forums at shop and plant levels. In enterprises considered suitable it was also to be implemented at the board level. The mode of representation of worker representatives was to be determined by consultation with the concerned unions, and parity in representation between management and unions continued to be the norm.

The scheme brought within the ambit of the councils a wider spread of work-related issues. At the plant level, the council could discuss issues relating to personnel, welfare environment and community development, plant operations and functioning, and also take up financial matters relating to profit and loss statements, balance sheets, operating costs, plant financial performance, labour and managerial costs, etc.

A standing tripartite committee was also set up by the Ministry of Labour to facilitate review and corrective measures. Implementation of the schemes was left to the administrative ministries, while state governments were requested to introduce the scheme in their public sector enterprises.

*Workers' Participation in Management Bill, 1990*　　Article 43A of the Constitution requires the State to take steps, by suitable legislation or in any other way, to secure the participation of workers in the management of undertakings, establishments or other organizations engaged in any industry. So far, all the schemes pertaining to participation of workers in management have been non-statutory. At present (July 1990) there is no central law on the subject. The non-statutory schemes have not been able to provide an effective framework for a meaningful participation of workers in management. Therefore, the government has introduced a bill in the Parliament on 25 May 1990 to:

(i) Provide for specific and meaningful participation of workers in management at shop-floor level, establishment level and board of management level in industrial establishments;

(ii) provide for formulation of one or more schemes to specify detailed criteria such as the manner of representation of workmen on the shopfloor and establishment level councils, and of workmen and other workers on the Board of Management, nomination of representatives of the employers on the shop floor and establishment councils and conducting their business, etc.

(iii) provide for the principle of secret ballot for determining the representation of workmen on the shop floor and establishment level councils, and of workmen and other workers on the Board of Management;

(iv) provide for rules to specify the power which an inspector may exercise, the number of members of the monitoring committee and the manner in which they shall be chosen, etc. to oversee compliance of the provisions under the Act.

## Issues in Participation
Certain critical issues emanate from our experience of participation in the last few decades which are briefly discussed here.

***Mode of Representation***    Deciding the means by which worker representatives should be nominated to the forums has been probably the most critical difficulty in the implementation of participation. This issue has been contentious as it is related to union membership strength. Some favour periodic secret ballot to decide this matter, while others argue that secret ballot would only create further problems, and that membership verification would do. There can be no real progress in workers' participation unless this is decided. Also, a view should be taken whether the workers' representative should be nominated by trade unions functioning in the enterprises, or they should be selected from all the workers including those who do not belong to any union. If former is the case, a specific mode of representation may have to be prescribed if there is no consensus among the trade unions otherwise the scheme would remain incapable of implementation whenever there is no consensus. If, however, the idea is to select a workers' representative from among the workers, secret ballot may be the only way.

The 1990 Bill provides that the workmen's representative shall be elected by, and from amongst, the workmen of the industrial establishment, by secret ballot or nominated by the registered trade unions, in accordance with the scheme.

***Scope of the Forums***    Is the 1983 scheme broad enough in the coverage of issues? Can the categorization in the 1983 scheme provide the basis for further improvements? While some financial matters were brought within the purview of the 1983 scheme, it was primarily with the intent of information sharing. Are there other issues to be covered in this area?

It has been repeatedly pointed out that the participative forums exclude interest-related issues and that this exclusion has hamstrung the working of the forums. What kind of interest-related issues should be brought in? Grievance redressal has figured prominently in this regard.

At another level, is the distinction made between work-related and interest-related issues relevant to the logic of participation? Also, is it relevant and in consonance with the organizational needs?

The matters falling under the jurisdiction of shop floor and establishment councils under the 1990 bill are specified in Schedules I and II respectively (see Exh. 13.1).

**EXHIBIT 13.1**

---

**Excerpts from Workers' Participation in Management: 1990 Bill**

## Schedule I: Powers of Shop Floor Council

1. Production facilities
2. Storage facilities in a shop
3. Material economy
4. Operational problems
5. Wastage control
6. Hazards and safety problems
7. Quality improvement
8. Cleanliness

9. Monthly targets and production schedules
10. Cost reduction programmes
11. Formulation and implementation of work system
12. Design group working
13. Welfare measures related particularly to the shop.

# Schedule II: Powers of Establishment Council

## Operational Areas
1. Evolution of productivity schemes taking into account the local conditions.
2. Planning, implementation, fulfilment and review of monthly targets and schedules.
3. Material supply and its shortfall.
4. Storage and inventories.
5. Housekeeping.
6. Improvements in productivity in general and in critical areas in particular.
7. Encouragement to and consideration of suggestion.
8. Quality and technological improvements.
9. Machine utilization knowledge and development of new products.
10. Operational performance figures.
11. Matters not resolved at the shop-level or concerning more than one shop.
12. Review of the working of the shop-level bodies.

## Economic and Financial Areas
1. Profit and loss statement and balance sheet.
2. Review of operating expenses, financial results and cost of sales.
3. Plant performance in financial terms, labour and managerial costs, market conditions, etc.

## Personnel Matters
1. Absenteeism.
2. Special problems of women workers.
3. Initiation and supervision of workers' training programmes.
4. Administration of social security schemes.

## Welfare Areas
1. Operational details.
2. Implementation of welfare schemes, medical benefits and transport facilities.
3. Safety measures.
4. Sports and games.
5. Housing.
6. Township administration, canteen, etc.
7. Control of gambling, drinking and indebtedness.

## Environmental Areas
1. Extension activities and community development projects.
2. Pollution control.

*Levels of Participation*    Board-level participation has found few takers. The primary problem faced in a multi-union situation relates to who should be on the board. Can we really think of board-level participation unless and until we decide how to determine union membership strength? And is it sufficient to give board representation only to workers and exclude officers?

What other lessons have we learnt from our experience at shop, departmental, plant or establishment levels? And when organizations want to make a beginning in participative forums, at which level should they begin? The 1990 bill provides for a three-tier participation, including at the board level. The proportionate share of workers' representatives and the persons representing other workers in the Board of Management of every corporate establishment is put at 13% and 12% respectively.

**Coverage of the Scheme**     How wide a segment of industry should be brought within the purview of workers' participation? So far the earlier schemes were made applicable on the basis of a minimum number of workers. Should this be continued? Or, should the scheme be applicable only to large organizations? Should the schemes be different based on the size of organization?

The 1990 bill seeks to extend the coverage to all corporate establishments.

**Voluntarism or Legislation**     All schemes, other than the Works Committee and Bank employee directors, have been based on the principle of voluntary implementation. There are however many who feel that voluntary implementation has failed and that participation needs to be legislated. But will legislation succeed against attitudes that are deeply ingrained and run counter to the logic and culture of participation? Legislation can be complied with in form, without any change in inner content and process. Can legislation make any headway unless there is also legislation on the criteria for determining union membership strength?

Legislation would be comprehensive and cannot easily account for exceptional circumstances. Nor can legislation provide for modification of a scheme to suit an individual organization's needs. Statutory provisions would have to extend equally to both the private and public sectors of industry.

**Workers' Share in Equity**     The 1985 Union Budget made provision for the offer of stock options to employees. Should equity participation form a major element for enhancing workers' participation in management? Unions oppose linking participation schemes with workers' share in equity. Also, nowhere in the world has there been a positive correlation between workers' share in equity and performance of the firm.

**Appropriateness of the Scheme**     Some enterprises which are not in the manufacturing sector but are consultancy or service organizations, or who have too few employees feel that the scheme is not relevant to them  even at shopfloor or plant levels. Similarly, companies engaged in construction very often get their work done through the contractors and do not employ workers on regular basis. Efforts have been made by the Ministry of Labour to discuss how employees' participation in management can be evolved even in such organizations but there has not been much progress.

It is imperative to recognize that participative forums only provide a means to encourage democratic decision-making. The mere constitution of such forums guarantees nothing. If the forums are to be organizationally relevant, both unions and management have a joint responsibility to generate and sustain a democratic temper. This democratic temper is a process which requires intensive information-sharing, clear stating of differences, understanding the premises of positions taken, and then proceeding to work out commonly acceptable alternative which meet mutually agreed organizational goals. The institutionalization of such processes would go a long way in developing healthy relations in the organization between workers, unions and management.

***Changing Composition of the Work Force***        Not much cognizance is taken of the rapidly changing composition of our work force.  Research evidence indicates that the average age of our industrial worker is declining,  and is well below 40 years of age at present.  Correspondingly, educational and technical skill levels attainments are rising.  All this accounts for greater awareness in the work force, and a greater desire to be involved in decisions relating to their work and career management.  Can these needs be met through representative participative forums?  Does this also not call for greater information-sharing and more participative work systems and processes?

***Limitations of Representative Participation***        Representative participation in the form of joint councils although desirable and necessary has its own limitations in so far as its role in improving productivity is concerned.  It does not and cannot ensure participation of all the employees, particularly the grassroot workmen, in the decision-making and production processes. It also poses a dilemma for the representatives. While on the representative bodies, they have to identify with the total objective of the organization and take decisions jointly within the overall framework of organization's plans and policies. But at the same time they have to continue to maintain their credibility among the workmen by protecting the latter's interest.  Often these two clash leading to a situation where representatives become apathetic and indifferent to the process of participation itself.  On the other hand, the representative groups may develop elitist orientation resulting in wider gap between them and the people whom they represent.

## Prerequisites to Make Representative Participation Work

Some of the steps that facilitate introduction and effective functioning of the joint councils can be stated as follows:

(i)   Developing a common framework of purpose, content, level and  types of participation among the members of joint councils so as to take care of differential expectations.

(ii) Need to jointly evolve and agree upon the processes of  agenda setting in terms of content and theme, as well as the  methods of identifying problem areas and collecting relevant information.

(iii) The need to begin with areas where it is relatively easier to have successful experience and then to add on other areas   gradually.

(iv) Delineating boundaries and defining relationship among the  existing nominated and/or elected committees vis-a-vis shop and plant councils. There is the need to agree on ways and means to keep the channels of communication open among not only the committees and councils but also among the rank and file.

(v) Developing guidelines for decision-making by the councils and fixing responsibility and time-frame for implementation of the decisions.

(vi) Need to identify centre of responsibility for decision implementation in the existing organizational structure so as to avoid situations where managements may give priority to their own tasks over the council's decisions.

(vii) Defining roles, status, authority, and facilities for members and office-bearers of the councils in relation to the trade unions.

(viii) The need to keep the employees informed of the decisions arrived at, their implementation and the outcome so that the employees are able to develop confidence and faith in the working of these forums.

(ix) Continuous evaluation of the functioning of these councils by various mechanisms like employee opinion poll, meetings of all the council members at certain intervals, utilization of suggestion boxes, etc.

# ALTERNATIVE APPROACHES TO PARTICIPATION

## Direct Participation

The representative system can be strengthened, if self-management is introduced to begin with at the shopfloor level which would ensure direct and personal participation of employees in areas of their own activities. To achieve this the work system will have to be restructured so as to provide the workers with greater autonomy and control over the total production process. This will be a step towards industrial democracy at shop-floor. Several attempts to develop alternative forms of work organization have been made in India in various sectors of industries and service, the detailed accounts of which are available elsewhere (Srivastava, 1976; De, 1979; *et al.*). The need for redesigning the work systems in the light of adoption of new technology has been already highlighted in the preceding pages. Restructuring of work at shop-floor level necessitates corresponding changes in the organization structure with emphasis on group functioning and interdisciplinary team work. A trend is already visible particularly in the industrialized nations for new technology which help restructuring their organizations on the basis of socio-technical design principles.

## Parallel Organization

The introduction of new technology will put tremendous pressures on the management and the employees to design and develop innovative productivity programmes, in ways that are not detrimental to the needs and interest of the workers. This will necessitate introduction and management of change on continuing basis at enterprise level. The organizations designed on bureaucratic and scientific management principles will not be able to meet the demands placed on them by the new technology nor will they be able to respond positively to changing social ethos and milieu.

Programmes for improving productivity within the framework of rigid hierarchical organization structure have not led to significant or stable improvement in the direction of higher productivity and employee satisfaction. Since the existing organization structures are geared to maintain stability by ensuring utilization of a largely predetermined production processes and operations, they cannot easily sustain and strengthen changed programmes. New types of structures need to be created to cope with increasingly changing technologies and uncertain and environments. These structures could be group based, formalized, permanent, cross-functional, vertically integrated and consisting of members from the management, the unions and the employees belonging to different levels, run parallel to the existing operating structure of the organization. The composition of these groups and membership depends on parallel structures which manage change innovatively and effectively, to identify problem areas and to develop creative ways of solving those problems, to overcome resistance to change, and to enhance the adaptive capabilities of individual and groups. They provide mechanisms whereby employees at all levels can actively and meaningfully participate in decision-making process and develop their potential in activities that are not necessarily part of their regular functional jobs.

Parallel organizations have been designed to deal with problem areas like cost saving, productivity and quality, quality of working life, organization climate, strategic decisions and similar other productivity-related issues. The new structures facilitate continuous processes of gathering data, diagnosing problems, generating alternatives, making recommendations, monitoring and implementing change in specific problem areas. Some of the examples of the parallel organization include the Scanlon Plan, Quality Circles, and Quality of Working Life Councils (Moore, 1986).

*Scanlon Plan*        The Scanlon Plan is a group-incentive plan rewarding all employees with bonuses derived from their cost-saving suggestions. At the department level there are a number of production committees usually consisting of the supervisor and a couple of employees of the department. The suggestions which are accepted and are under the control of that department are immediately implemented. Other suggestions involving concurrence of higher levels or other departments are passed on to the next level *steering committee* which is a plant-wide committee consisting of top management, union leaders and representatives from different departments and levels in the organization. In between the production committees and the steering committee there may be a *screening committee* consisting of supervisory middle management personnel.

*Quality Circles*        The Quality Circles concept can also be seen as yet another illustration of parallel organization which has been so successful in Japan and has received world-wide attention as a unique approach to voluntary participation in matters relating to innovations and improvement in productivity, quality, working conditions and the like. A small group of workers constitute a quality circle on voluntary basis several hundreds of which could exist in an organization at any given point of time. The circle groups can meet both during and after the working hours and discuss issues and problems relating to their work unit and their own jobs. Statistical methods and various techniques of problem analysis are used. In India attempts have been made to develop parallel structures for implementing and operationalizing the Quality Circles concept. The structure that has been developed is somewhat similar to the one discussed under Scanlon plan. In addition to the quality circles, there are facilitators, co-ordinators, and the steering committee who play their respective roles at various stages of the functioning of quality circles.

**Quality of Working Life Councils**     The Quality of Working Life Councils consist of a steering committee and several departmental level committees. The members of these committee are drawn from both the management and the union. These joint councils run parallel to the traditional collective bargaining processes of negotiating and grievance-handling machinery. The major concern of these councils is to bring about improvement in the quality of life of people at workplace through restructuring of work system and other interventions intended to increase productivity and employee satisfaction.

As can be seen from the preceding description, there are several participative mechanisms that are being developed and experimented with for involving employees for higher productivity in India and abroad. A number of alternatives have emerged based on the experience of managers and union leaders for the last several decades. None of the alternatives, however, is universally applicable. Each enterprise has to develop its own mechanisms of participation depending on the prevailing situation and taking into consideration the type of technology, expectations and aspiration level of employees, and above all, the state of union–management relations.

## SUMMARY

Employees' participation in management is no longer an idealistic or ideological conception. It is an imperative need to cope with change in organizations in the context of changing profile of people with high expectations and the demands for high performance. There are at least four types of participation than can be developed at the enterprise level: information-sharing; consultative, joint decision-making and self-managing groups. It can be integrative or distributive, direct or representative, voluntary or statutory. Since Independence, the government has introduced a number of schemes of representative participation which did not always produce desired results due to a variety of dilemmas and the absence of certain prerequisites. In 1975, the Constitution was amended and Section 43A was inserted providing for workers' participation as one of the Directive Principles of State Policy. For the first time, in 1990, the government introduced a bill to make three-tier representative forums of participation. In recent years, there is growing awareness about the potential of alternative approaches to participation such as direct participation and parallel organizations.

## KEY WORDS

| | | |
|---|---|---|
| Direct Participation | : | This is a system of participation of individual employees especially in aspects relating to their work and working environment |
| Representative Participation | : | This is a system of employees' participation through elected or nominated representatives of the concerned group(s) of employees |
| Distributive Participation | : | This is a system of participation which seeks to distribute power and authority from top, downwards in organizations |

| Integrative Participation | : | This is a system of participation which seeks to integrate the employers and employees into organizational purposes for adopting problem-solving approach for common good |

## REVIEW QUESTIONS

1. Critically review the government schemes of workers' participation in management and suggest the prerequisites to make them work.
2. What are the key issues in representative schemes of participation? Discuss whether and how they can be resolved.
3. Distinguish between direct and representative systems of participation. Suggest whether or how they can coexist and what steps are necessary to make participation work.

# CASE : XYZ CORPORATION

XYZ Corporation is the pseudonym for a plant in eastern India in the core sector in public sector which was formally commissioned in 1959. For over a decade the organization did not consider any measure to formally involve employees to participate in management. It experienced serious industrial relations problems during 1960s and early 1970s. In early 1970s a bold experiment was made in the organization by appointing a trade union leader as General Manager of the plant which at that time became notorious for inter-union rivalry, chronic industrial unrest and persistent sickness. Due to the well-meaning efforts of the union leader-turned-General Manager, the concerned Union Minister and the State Labour Minister a tripartite agreement was signed in 1972 to set up a three tier consultative machinery to deal with the labour management problems in the plant. Unions affiliated to the three central trade union federations, i.e. Indian National Trade Union Congress (INTUC), Centre for Indian Trade Unions (CITU), and All India Trade Union Congress (AITUC), were signatories to this agreement. The major features of the agreement were:

1. To set up a state-level council (SLC) consisting of equal representatives of the management and of the three participating unions. The state government was also represented on this council with the labour minister as the Chairman. This council was entrusted with the task of supervising and regulating industrial relations in the plant and to discuss major issues and problems.

2. To set up a bipartite plant level committee (PLC) consisting of equal number of representatives of the three unions on the one hand and of the management on the other for resolving specific problems and disputes arising in the plant.

3. Bipartite floor level committees (FLC) in agreed units or departments to deal with day-to-day matters arising at the floor level.

4. Work stoppages should not be resorted to or encouraged by the unions without first seeking redress through the three-tier machinery.

5. It was recommended that the parties should take recourse to voluntary arbitration if other efforts to resolve a dispute did not succeed.

The three-tier machinery was launched with fanfare and was expected to usher in an era of qualitative change in union management relationship,with the climate of distrust and hostility being replaced gradually by a sense of trust and participation.

The state-level consultative council had a few meetings and later became virtually defunct because the State Labour Minister could not devote much time as the Chairman of the Committee. After initial hesitation the Bipartite Plant Level Committee started functioning. While this committee made some favourable impact upon labour–management relations its most important contribution, perhaps, was that it brought the three feuding unions to a single bargaining table. The FLCs, however, could not be formed as the unions could not agree on the mode of election of the workers' representatives in the committees.

While the inactivity of the SLC did not affect the working of the three-tier machinery too seriously, the non-formation of FLCs did. A large volume of small problems affecting various groups of workers, large and small had no forum to come up to except the PLC. The PLC, as a result, got burdened with a vast number as well as variety of problems which it could not possibly resolve in a reasonable period.

The agreement had run for about 18 months when INTUC union terminated it in 1973 by a formal notice according to law because it wanted a single bargaining union to be recognized for the organization by verification of membership under the code of discipline in industry. Its real intention was to wrest that status from the CITU union. The state government took no action on this demand. CITU was affiliated to the ruling party in the state at that time. Though the formal machinery lapsed, the negotiating framework continued without the label of FLC. The INTUC did not come in the way because having failed in persuading the state government to agree to membership verification and wresting sole representative status, it thought it good enough to retain some status to involve, interact and influence in aspects concerning union–management relations.

Through perseverance and lobbying throughout 1974, an Apex Committee could be formed in January 1975 with the representatives of the three unions and management to design and implement a simplified incentive scheme for the plant.

The Apex Committee on Incentives was followed by the adoption of a four-stage grievance procedure and constitution of a Central Grievance Committee in August 1975. A number of committees have also been created to discuss the production and productivity of each major shop with an Apex body at the plant level headed by the Managing Director. Plant Joint Consultative Committees were also formed for canteen, hospital, safety, etc. In all, 78 committees with the involvement of 467 representatives from the three forum unions were constituted. Not even a day passes without one or the other committee holding its meeting. The committees are constituted on the basis of equal representation from management and the three *major* unions, affiliated to CITU, INTUC and AITUC. The scope of functioning of the different committees seems to have been expanded taking into consideration the scheme for employees' participation in management as outlined in the government's order dated 30 December 1983.

There are three standing committees in the organization to deal with the existing aspects of human problems connected with commissioning of new assets and incentives schemes. There is also a standing committee for sharing information with the remaining four other unions which have not been represented on any of the remaining 77 joint committees. One of these was affiliated to Hind Mazdoor Sabha (HMS) and the rest to lesser known political parties.

To oversee the working of the consultative machinery, a monitoring cell has been created with one of the Deputy General Managers as Chairman and Chief General Manager (personnel),Chief of Training, Chief Industrial Engineer and a representative from Finance Department. All the committees are supposed to meet on fixed dates and time as per a calendar prepared much in advance and recommendations of various committees are to be implemented on a time-bound basis. Occasionally, training for participation is imparted to members of these committees. Thus the institutional arrangements for participation through joint consultation are quite elaborate. But a discerning analysis of the working of the system makes one suspect whether there is much ado about nothing. In a multi-union situation there is continuous pressure from all unions to include them in the participative processes. Of the seven registered unions, only three affiliated to CITU, INTUC and AITUC have been accorded representation in 77 out of 78 committees. The rationale was to maintain status quo and not disturb the arrangement first made while registering the tripartite agreement in 1972. But during the last decade the trade union dynamics in the organization changed considerably. CITU, being the only union with formal recognition, appears to feel a loss of status in participative forums as equal partners. Together these three unions are regarded as forum unions. Among them, the union affiliated to AITUC has much smaller following than the union affiliated to HMS. Though this fact is widely known throughout the organization, the management is reluctant to open the issue of the composition of forum unions. The HMS thus feels let down by the arbitrary approach of management. The remaining three non-forum unions did not have any following worth reckoning. The three forum unions enjoy security. The management seems to pursue a policy of status-quo unmindful of the trade union dynamics in the plant. The unrecognised non-forum unions have been blocking implementation of decisions at participative forums in departments/sections, where they enjoy sizeable following. The union representatives on the committees do not necessarily enjoy popular support of the employees in the respective departments.

## QUESTIONS

1. Critically evaluate the approach of XYZ Corporation towards implementing the scheme of workers' participation and identify the major issues.
2. Outline what needs to be done to make participation work in XYZ Corporation?

## FURTHER READING

1. Cherry, Richard, 1982. "The Development of General Motors Team-based Plants" in Robert Zager and Michael (Ed), *The Innovative Organisation: Productivity Programmes in Action*, Pergamon Press: New York.
2. De, Nitish R, 1983. "Workers' Participation in Formal Sector in Developing Countries: A Balance Sheet". *Economic and Political Weekly*, August, pp M 118–125.

3.     De, Nitish R, 1979. "New Forms of Work Organisation in India", *New Forms of Work Organisation*, ILO: Geneva.

4.     Emery F E and Thororud E, 1966.  *Form and Content in Industrial Democracy* (Tavistock: London).

5.     Government of India, 1990. *Seminar on Labour Participation in Management: Status Paper*, (Ministry of Labour): New Delhi.

6.     Gyllenhammar, P G, 1977. *People at Work*, Addison-Wesley: Reading, Massachussetts.

7.     ILO, 1984. *World Labour Report, Vol. I and II*, Geneva.

8.     ILO, 1983. *Workers' Participation in Decisions within Undertakings*,  Geneva.

9.     Kanawaty, G, 1981. *Managing and Developing New Forms of Work Organisation*, ILO: Geneva.

10.    Kavdia, I S, 1989. *Salvation Through Employees' Participation in Management, Profit Sharing and Ownership*, JEML: Jaipur.

11.    Maccoby, Michael and Dougles Carnichal, 1984. "Issues of Participation and Ownership in Productivity and Development", *American Labour News Supplement*, January.

12.    Moore, M L, 1986. "Designing Parallel Organisations to Support Organisational Productivity Programmes" Joseph J Famularao (Ed.) *Handbook of Human Resource Administration*, 2nd edn, McGraw-Hill: New York.

13.    Nayar, Meenakshi, 1982. *Workers' Participation in Management — The Case of Employee Director in Nationalised Banks*, National Labour Institute: New Delhi.

14.    Pais, H, 1988. *Employee Participation in Management*, National Labour Institute: New Delhi.

15.    Sharma, B R, 1986. *Not By Bread Alone*, Shri Ram Centre for Industrial Relations and Human Resources: New Delhi.

16.    Srivastava, Bhupen, 1976. "Conditions and Organisation of Work" *Proceedings of the National Seminar on Quality of Working Life*, National Labour Institute: New Delhi.

17.    Vahcic A and T Pertin, 1986. "Economics of Self-Management, Self-managed Enterprises and Public Enterprises", *Public Enterprise 6(2)*, February, pp 135–146.

18.    Venkata Ratnam, C S, 1983. "Review of Researches in Industrial Democracy in Public Enterprises in India". T L Shankar *et al. (Ed.) Public Enterprise: Research in Focus*, Himalaya: New Delhi.

19.    Virmani, B R, 1980. *Workers' Participation in Management: Annotated Bibliography*, Commonwealth Secretariat: London.

# Measurement of Personnel/Human Resources

**LEARNING OBJECTIVES**

After going through this chapter, you should be able to:
- Understand the broad approaches to controlling manpower costs
- Familiarize yourself with the rationale and use of computerized Human Resource Information Systems (referred to as CHRIS or HRIS) and the system design aspects of HRIS ● Examine the concept and approaches to human resource accounting

Measurement is very important in management, yet, it is the weakest aspect of personnel. It is only in recent times that personnel began to realize that the business of personnel shall be business and began to focus on relating its objectives to the business goals and the bottomline. For personnel to provide the competitive advantage, organizations are attempting various approaches like MBO, Ratio Analysis and Productivity Analysis. Proper and systematic information system is important for analysis, review and improvement of various aspects of personnel. Computerized personnel systems have a greater role than mere pay roll preparation and should aid human resources planning and various subfunctions of personnel. With employees now being reckoned as the most important asset of any organization, there is growing interest to reflect them also on the balance sheet. Various approaches have been developed in the last two years and some Indian organizations have begun to show interest in the subject. This chapter briefly deals with these aspects.

## CONTROLLING MANPOWER COSTS – RATIONALE

According to classical economic theories labour surplus developing countries like India ought to have had comparative advantage in labour-intensive production. But technological developments over the years made such classical theories lose much of their relevance. The method of managing usually rendered even *cheap labour* costly due to inefficient use of labour and other inputs and low morale, motivation and mismanagement. As already mentioned, the labour cost varies across firms. In India they vary from around a mere two percent in petro-chemical industries to about 60% in coal. Therefore, it can be argued that manpower costs assume criticality and provide firms the much needed competitive edge in industries where they account for a somewhat significant total cost of production. However, it is a widely held belief among employers that even in firms where manpower costs are supposedly insignificant, they continue to be critical. How? They cite the example of the weak link in the chain which brings the vehicle to a grinding halt frequently until that link is removed. In a growing, competitive and uncertain world, for most firms, manpower costs have become the focal point among various strategies to restore competitive advantage to firms.

With the result, organizations began to look at manpower costs more discerningly. Three broad approaches have been used to analyse and control manpower costs through the extension of the following three concepts to the management of personnel:
1. Management-by-Objectives
2. Ratio analysis
3. Productivity analysis
The three approaches are briefly discussed here.

## Management-by-objectives (MBO)

The rationale for extending MBO approach to personnel function is simple. Peers in other departments are focusing on income, assets, liabilities, sales, costs and profits, while personnel continues to talk about feelings. This will no longer be adequate. The business of personnel shall be judged in terms of business goals: Peter F Drucker and others began to argue that few factors are as important to the performance of an organization as measurement. And, especially in personnel, measurement is the weakest area. Personnel professionals tried to live up to the challenge. Applying the principles of MBO, it was argued[*] that a *Personnel Manager's Result Guide* will have the following examples for Performance Standards:
(i) Employee costs per unit of production/service shall be held at...(Base Year) and indexed to ... as a percentage of fixed and semi-variable expenses.
(ii) At least 66.6% of increased cost of improvements in the Long Term Agreement shall be met through improvement in employee productivity.
(iii) During the next ... years, there shall be reduction of....% in down time of plant and machinery ...% in the avoidable waste of materials and ....% in absenteeism beyond authorised leave.

---

[*] K N Randeria, 1982. *Cost of Employee*, National Institute of Personnel Management: Calcutta.

(iv)  Ensure that 33.3% of savings arising out of (3) above will be distributed to ensure improvement in the individual employee's earnings.

(v)  An individual employee must move up ... grades in his work span of ... years through careful manpower and succession planning.

(vi)  At least 25% of vacancies in the managerial cadre shall be filled from amongst the lower job holders through appropriate training and development programmes.

This is one approach to analyse manpower costs.

## Ratio Analysis

This approach suggests identification of certain key performance indicators for manpower. These may relate to utilization of manpower (e.g. labour cost as a percentage of total cost) or to personnel functions within an organization (e.g. cost of recruitment). The ratios may cover, broadly the following areas.

### Cost of Recruitment and Replacement

*Cost per hire:*   The costs of recruitment include:

- cost of time spent by personnel at various levels in recruitment process
- cost of advertisement (including agency fees)
- costs of conducting, screening tests (preparation, administration, evaluation, etc)
- costs of travel, etc. of interviewers and interviewees
- costs of medical examination
- Administrative and other costs (telephone, stationery, venue for tests, interviews, etc.)

Not all costs are easy to identify. There could be complexities in allocating and appropriating costs. Costs vary on definition of hiring process. For example, whether to include costs of induction and placement including joining expenses, etc. It also depends on whether the recruitment costs are to be expressed in terms of number selected or number retained. And, if number retained is the variable, what is the time factor to determine whether a candidate is retained? Till training is completed and/or probation is confirmed: one year, two or three?

Once these issues are resolved, the costs of recruitment can be expressed in terms of the following equation:

$$\text{Cost per hire (in Rs.)} = \frac{\text{Costs of recruitment}}{\text{No of recruitees retained}}$$

If the purpose is to determine actions that could lead to a reduction in this ratio, the attention should be focused on different stages of recruitment process:

- Whether to conduct recruitment *in-house* or to contract it out to a recruitment agency or head-hunting firm? Much depends on the availability of expertise (inhouse or outside agency) volume, and frequency of recruitment effort, relative cost comparisons, judgement on reliability, etc.
- Whether  advertisement costs could be cut down by resorting to sources like employment exchanges, campus interviewing, etc.? Is there any trade-off in-

volved in terms of drawing the net closer than keeping it wide open?

- Should fewer candidates be called for interviews by being highly selective in early stages of screening so that interview costs can be cut down? Some times this is done not so much to cut down costs as to induce qualified people to appear for interview by meeting travel costs, etc.
- Should the organization be more careful in offering jobs so that a higher proportion accept the jobs and stay on for a long enough (though it is difficult to determine what length is 'long enough' and even if it is, it may vary from job to job) period?

*Recruitment Cycle Time*    It refers to the time taken from commencement to completion of recruitment process. This helps to determine the lead time required to initiate and complete the recruitment process.

Also, break down analysis of time taken at each stage in recruitment process will help initiate specific actions to cut down the recruitment cycle time. For instance, for certain jobs the date of interview is communicated in the advertisement itself (though this is not always desirable and may preclude preliminary screening). Informal recruitment processes, and maintaining lists of active job seekers for different jobs also helps reduce the recruitment cycle time. Tight job specification, proper design of application bank, computerization of application blank and certain types of tests also help to reduce the cycle time.

*Cost of Turnover/Replacement/Retention*    Turnover could be defined as any permanent departure beyond organizational boundaries. Transfers within the organization and temporary layoffs are not usually reckoned in determining the rate of turnover. The rate of turnover could be calculated by the following formula:

$$\text{Turnover rate (in \%)} = \frac{\text{Number of separations}}{\text{Average strength of employees}} \times 100$$

The main component of cost involved is separation pay (where applicable). Other costs include those relating to administrative functions, conduct of exit interviews, etc. The indirect costs of the consequences and resulting effects on morale and motivation are, of course, hard to quantify.

The replacement costs include all costs associated with recruiting an employee. Additionally, some other aspects such as the following have cost implications:

(a) If a young person replaces an old one, the wage costs could be low, particularly for jobs at unskilled level. The reverse may be true for skilled and professional jobs.

(b) There is usually a time lag before a person begins to give optimal performance.

(c) There are costs in training and orienting the new person.

(d) How well the new person would be integrated into existing structure and work groups. If, over all, the change results in improvement for the individual, group and the organization, there are no additional costs on this count, but only benefits. If the reverse is true for one or all the three mentioned (i.e. individual, group and the organization) it means additional costs.

***Training and Retraining***     The cost of training is usually expressed in terms of the following equations:

(a) If the purpose is to determine per employee expenditure on training:

$$\text{Training expenditure (per employee)} = \frac{\text{Total training expenditure}}{\text{No. of employees}}$$

(b) If the purpose is to determine per trainee expenditure on training:

$$\text{Training expenditure (per trainee)} = \frac{\text{Total training expenditure}}{\text{No. of trainees}}$$

(c) If the purpose is to relate training costs to training activities one or more of the following formulae become relevant:

$$\text{Training cost per day} = \frac{\text{Training costs}}{\text{Training days}}$$

$$\text{Cost per trainee} = \frac{\text{Training costs}}{\text{No. trained}}$$

$$\text{Trainee ratio} = \frac{\text{No. of trainees}}{\text{No. of employees}}$$

The following questions need to be addressed while looking at costs of training:
● What costs? Whether and how does one allocate and apportion fixed investment costs (building, equipment, etc) and input cost (time spent by line managers in providing training, top management time in giving policy-direction, monitoring, etc.).
● Evaluation of training is extremely difficult and complex (see Chapter 7).
● Quality is not free. Cost reduction in training cannot be at the expense of quality.  Sometimes, it may cost more (in terms of after affects of training). Wasteful training costs can be reduced, where it becomes possible to identify. Perhaps it is less costlier to defer or avoid training than make any compromise in 'inputs' merely on cost considerations.

# PERSONNEL PRODUCTIVITY

Personnel's potential to contribute to productivity is overwhelming. Let us cite examples.
● Using socio-technical systems approach in 1970s BHEL, Haridwar could minimize idle time and improve plant utilization from 30% to 70% in less than a year.  It is a different story that the momentum was not sustained.  Similar experience, though short-lived relates to Calico mills.

- Between 1957 and 1976 Caltex oil refinery at Vizag could halve manpower (from 700 to 353), yet improve throughput by 10% without additional technology or investment. Simple O & M studies, productivity bargaining and management style made it possible. In another company, manpower strength had gone up by 30%, over Rs 100 crores were invested, design and technology improved but method of work organization was not reviewed and personnel policies were neglected; with the result production cycle and cost of production virtually trebled in less than a decade.
- In Coal India the proportion of cost of labour per tonne of coal increased from 38% (in 1973) to about 60% (by mid 80s).
- ITC, on the other hand paid its workers about 25% more wages than before and yet maintained the share of labour cost per cigarette at the same level.
- Premier Auto paid the workers substantially more than it did before, but could bring down labour costs by increasing productivity. The problem is not so much with wage rates as with manpower utilization. Manpower utilization is better not when it is more intensively used as when it is intelligently used.
- Some major hospitals in Bombay carried out an analysis of the time spent by their nurses. They found over 70% is devoted to filling and filing reports. The *raison d'etre* for nurses was different. Through O & M studies, brainstorming and simplification of paper work they could bring down the time spent by an average nurse in filling and filing reports to about 30%. The time so released is made available to attend to patients.
- In Jaipur Metals and Electricals, a sick unit, through labour–management cooperation, employees agreed for a wage cut, DA denial and deferment of bonus and traded the sacrifices for productivity gain sharing and share holding in the company. In two years the emoluments (inclusive of productivity earnings) trebled besides employees acquiring 50% shareholding in the company.

Several companies are reporting substantial savings through quality circles. Examples abound. There are various ways in which personnel could help reduce costs.

There is a problem with figures and ratios. This can lead personnel into an activity trap! Don't we hear of cases where a personnel man may seek to justify his existence by engineering a problem and then proceeding to settle it? If the person in charge of grievance handling is assessed against number of grievances processed, he may, like the proverbial policeman causing crime to book criminals, create and process grievances. When the corporate headquarters insisted on achieving zero-overtime at short-notice, the plant management made similar payment under a different head and got away with substantial window-dressing. Our measurement and control systems are weak enough to let such permissiveness loose. In another case, when recruitment was banned in the company, the maintenance staff began to subcontract several maintenance jobs and gradually even the routine work which the existing staff had been carrying out.

# COMPUTERIZED HUMAN RESOURCE INFORMATION SYSTEMS –RATIONALE

Human Resource Information Systems are needed basically for three purposes:

(i)   To store information and data for each individual employee for reference
(ii)  To provide a basis for decision-making in day to day personnel issues, (e.g. grant of leave) as also for planning budgeting, implementing and monitoring a host of human resource functions
(iii) Supplying data/returns to government and other publics.

# Information Needs in HRD and Related Activities

The information needs of each activity in HRP and its complementary activities are varied.   The following is an indicative list:

## Manpower Planning
(a)   Inventory of existing and future needs
(b)   Reliable performance standards
(c)   Possible changes which affect manpower use
(d)   Location and matching of skills available with skills required.

## Recruitment
(a)   Valid measures for testing and selection
(b)   Costs of recruitment and replacement

## Development of People
(a)   Valid measures of performance levels of employees
(b)   Training and development—cost-benefit calculations
(c)   Career and succession plans
(d)   Linkages between individual aspirations and organizational needs

## Compensation
(a)   Linkages between wages, productivity and profits
(b)   Determining impact  of money on employee motivation to work
(c)   Assessing the effect of technology and inflation on wages and productivity levels.
(d)   Analysing employee costs in terms of turnover, contribution, etc.
(e)   Deriving more value for the organization through collective bargaining, fringe-benefit programmes, etc.

## Integration and Maintenance
(a)   Analyzing various indicators of organizational health such as rate of absenteeism, turnover, accidents, mandays lost, grievances and discipline.
(b)   Setting up environmental standards for physical  and mental health of the employees.
(c)   Adapting to changes in the environment
(d)   Studying the impact of changes in markets, organization and technology
(e)   Examining the causes of changes in productivity and profit performance
(f)   analysing the communications climate in the organization.

### Separations

(a) investigating the causes and costs of separation

(b) developing incentives for voluntary separation, if need be, and monitoring their effect of such schemes. The list, as already mentioned, is indicative, but not exhaustive.

A variety of company records are maintained to meet each of the above information needs not only for internal control, feedback and corrective action, but also to meet the various statutory obligations.

## Use of Computers in Personnel

Human resource information/inventory/records can be based entirely on a manual system. However, with the growing criticality and complexity of human resources in rapidly changing context, premium is attached to discern clearly and comprehensively the various inter-linkages and build scenarios for a wide range of alternatives. The speed at which the information is retrieved, processed and analysed for decision-making also counts. Well-designed, comprehensive, business-based computerised HRIS alone can provide the needed information and analytical capabilities with the shortest time lag to provide strategic advantage for organizations undergoing or planning change. Information management is the key to employee productivity, competitive strength and corporate excellence. Therefore, there is an increasing preference in the industrialized countries to move away from manual systems to computerised systems.

The shift from industrial society to information society is discernible in the developed world also. We currently have technologies which are not fully used. However, surveys in developed and developing countries revealed that human resource information systems are not as extensively used as is possible for decision-making purposes. By and large, till recently in India, computers are used mainly for processing pay rolls alone. Now quite a few large firms have already begun to use them for HRP and several other human resource functions. The advent of micro-processors and personal computers have accelerated the transition from manual to computerized HRIS. Also, they hold records in a compact manner enabling access and retrieval in a flexible way, promptly. Computers can be used with profit in a wide variety of situations covering the full range of human resource management functions (see Table 14.1). Historically, the pay roll function was the first to be computerised because it was more definitive, repetitive and labour intensive. Gradually, however, the system began to be put to several other uses, including those with increasing complexity. Some of the recent examples of competitive advantage to companies using information technologies in human resource function include the following:[*]

***Employee Information***     With 80,000 employees in more than 200 sites worldwide, Texas Instruments, the Dallas-based electronics leader, faced the need to provide immediate information on changes in policies and procedures. The company's executives decided to automate its standard employee policies manual by putting it on mainframe computer. The automated manual can be directly accessible to  employees

---

[*] Also see: *Personnel*, May 1985.

anywhere in the world 24 hours a day. Because the system provides readily accurate, consistent, up-to-date information, it allows managers to make quality decisions.

***Collective Bargaining***    Companies may bring a computer terminal linked to a data base to meetings so that negotiations can be expedited by referring to computer printouts that immediately project the impacts of pay increases, inflation, and benefit packages on costs and so forth. The system is an extremely effective way of eliminating guessing and basing proposals on solid facts that are readily available to both sides.

**Table 14.1    Computerised Applications for HRIS**

| *Least Complex Application* | ← | | | *Most complex Application* |
|---|---|---|---|---|
| * Payroll preparation | * Automation of basic Personnel data | * Salary analysis | * Skills inventory | * Collective bargaining |
| * Cheques preparation | * Preparation of scheduled reports e.g., seniority | * Performance planning | * Human resource planning | * Information sharing |
| * HR reports | | * High-flier tracking | | * Teletraining |

Adapted from the reading materials prepared by the School of Management Studies, Indira Gandhi National Open University, New Delhi, 1987 (MS.7 Block 2, Unit 8: Computers in Human Resource Management, p 38)

Companies who care to improve their image among the rank and file may install a telephone system that can handle mass call-ins simultaneously. Employees could call whenever they wanted to get an update on the issues and any progress towards a settlement in negotiation process.

***Teletraining***    Companies may link their regional offices through a communications network for training purposes, simply by combining existing telephone lines with special audio and graphic equipment. They could connect trainees and classrooms all over the country to a single location with one instructor. Such distance learning could be completely interactive.

***Performance Appraisal***    One of the most innovative uses of technologies is the use of computer-based performance-appraisal systems. The rating of employees' performance is more objective and the data base can be used to maintain information on staffing and training, and for wage and salary administration.

## System Design and Software Packages

The type and range of HRIS depends on the organization, its needs and top management preferences. Smaller firms may only need a basic card system for individual employees and simple set of forms to discern trends on key aspects of human resources as also to comply with statutory returns. Larger firms, however, may require a more comprehensive data base depending upon the rationale for computerization, potential uses and aspects of personnel decision-making within the organization. Further aspects of system design depend upon:

- The use of computers (types, extent, location, whether on-line, etc)
- the design of the basic records, forms and input material (concern for secrecy, government regulations, etc., may some times limit the use)
- the procedure and programme for collecting, recording, updating, retrieving, analysing and disseminating information

There are a number of software packages readily available in the market to suit the general needs. Several large firms in different sectors (BHEL, NTPC, ONGC, ITC, Voltas, for instance) have developed comprehensive packages to suit their needs. Table 14.2 gives an indicative list of some programmes, but there are many other package available in India and abroad for a wide range of computer applications. Most of the packages are menu-driven which can also be customized to a limited extent at the customers' site.

**Table 14.2   Indicative List of Software Packages**

| Name of the Inventory | Supplier | Operating System/Language |
|---|---|---|
| Personnel inventory | MANTEC | CP/M, DBASE-II |
| Payroll accounting | (Several Sources) | Almost every system/language |
| Skills inventory | MECON | COBOL |
| Manpower planning | MECON | COBOL, FORTRAN |
| Personnel inventory and Records | SONATA | WORDSTAR, LOTUS |

## Setting Up HRIS

Top level commitment is essential for the successful use of computer-based Human Resource Information Systems. Employee attitudes and skill shortages are also problems. In the USA, legislation limits the use of HRIS. But the advantages of HRIS are many. Timely retrieval of the available information, however, voluminous it may be, provides competitive advantage through better handling of human resources. A firm which wants to set up HRIS should:

(i)   Determine the potential contribution it can make to the strategic needs of the organization

(ii)  appoint a senior manager to review and integrate the relevant issues as major components of corporate plans.

(iii) formulate a prioritized development strategy and determine what effect it should have on the firm's competitive posture

(iv)  make people throughout the organization aware of the advantages of HRIS.

## Personnel Inventory

Inventory is a detailed list *in stock*. Personnel inventory refers to a list of personnel, their background in terms of age, skills, experience, abilities, aspirations, etc. HRIS contributes to the development of a personnel inventory for HRP. An integrated HRP system requires not only an inventory of existing personnel but also a forecast of future human resource needs.

The type of information built into personnel inventory depends upon the possible uses to which it can be put, some of which are listed below.

- Career and succession planning
- Compensation planning
- Training
- Personnel decisions–transfer, promotion, rewards, etc.
- Organization analysis, etc.

Organizations may choose to mention more detailed inventory for certain groups of employees, (e.g. management staff) than others (say temporary staff) depending upon its perceived use. The major input in early stages comes from individual employees in terms of the initial information they supply in application blanks, etc.. Later, organizational data supplements the personnel inventory, with appropriate linkages with payroll preparation and other subsystems of human resource management. Information should be generated to update the inventory by asking each employee to complete a standardized update form once in a year or so. *It is impor tant to uphold the need to maintain privacy and protect the rights of employees.*

Information on certain aspects of personnel has to be maintained in every organization. Organizations require this to deal with employees as individuals in everyday employment relationship. Information relating to individuals is needed as inputs to take decisions on sanction of leave, placement, transfer, training, promotion, etc. as also for such purposes as preparing the monthly pay cheque. Similarly, organizations also will have to maintain data for groups of employees to deal with collective bargaining and other aspects of union–management relations. It also helps to understand the specific issues among different groups of employees (based on age, skill, function, grade, etc.) or to comply with government regulations, etc. (e.g. returns on occupational health, disadvantaged groups, etc).

Typically, *individual data* cover the following types of information:

(i) Name and Address
(ii) Demographic and Family particulars (age, sex, marital status, number of dependents, etc.)
(iii) Whether employee belongs to special category (SC, ST, etc.)
(iv) Qualifications (educational, technical, languages known etc.)
(v) Experience (past employers)
(vi) Current career information (experience in current designation, department etc.)
(vii) Total experience
(viii) Transfer, promotion details
(ix) Training, skills, etc.
(x) Salary, allowances and benefits
(xi) Seniority
(xii) Due date for increment
(xiii) Eligibility for promotion
(xiv) Personnel record: (rewards, distinctions, grievances, discipline, punishments, etc.)

(xv) Employee potential

(xvi) Due date for superannuation

(xvii) Other aspects, if any.

*Collective or group-based* data may cover information to generate different kinds of reports that seek to review operations, check conformity with regulations or to provide analytical perspective.

The reports are typically those which present information on manpower status (new recruits, vacancies, retirements, promotions), compensation (e.g. wages and salary, benefits, recovery of advances), training, etc.

The *regulatory reports* are mainly returns to be submitted to various public authorities to fill certain statutory obligations, (e.g. reports on accidents, industrial disputes, provident fund, Employees' State Insurance Scheme, etc).

The *analytical reports* are those which seek to establish relationship between ratings in selection tests and job performance, age distribution and skill mix of employees, etc. They help management to review policy and take up affirmative or proactive measures.

## Personnel Audit

Audit, in accounting parlance, refers to the official examination of accounts. Personnel audit refers to examination, review or evaluation of personnel policies and programmes. In HRP, personnel audit refers to the efforts that seek to discern the extent to which the human resource planners are tuned into personnel problems and opportunities. The purpose is to identify the deviations, if any, from the plan and their causes.

If there are specific goals (goal-oriented approach), norms (normative approach) or basis for comparison with other comparable firms (comparative approach), system type audit can be used in HRP. Personnel might also use compliance audit to study whether and to what extent the organization is complying with legislation and union agreements and employees with policies, procedures, and rules. Such an internal audit on a continuous basis or at regular intervals would help personnel to simplify and standardize policies and procedures. Rationalization is important because regulations that cannot be implemented or monitored may breed indifference that could percolate into the core area as well.

Personnel audit should focus on study and analysis. There is the classic example that William F White provides of how on careful analysis a small spindle could virtually eliminate conflict in a restaurant. A proper analysis of grievances should lead us to blind spots in personnel policies whose correction could make grievances on that count redundant. In HRP, ability to keep track of skills and potential will help the organization to harness the internal resources to the maximum. This, is turn, builds morale and motivation and contributes to productivity.

There is no typical or ideal approach to personnel audit. Nevertheless, the effectiveness of the audit improves, if those who perform the function address themselves to the following questions:

1. What domain of activity should be the focus? Relations with employees and the union(s), concern for productivity, compliance with regulations or concern for cost-

saving? Sometimes, in the short-run, some of these may not be complementary. The thrust of the organization may vary, over time. Organizations may be having strained industrial relations but may not adversely affect productivity and profitability. Conversely, *good* industrial relations may not necessarily lead to good business results.

2. Whose perspective? Owners and management, unions and employees, customers and public (authorities)?

3. What level of analysis? Individual, group or organization? Sometimes effectiveness at one level may adversely affect effectiveness at other level.

4. What time factor? What is necessary for long-term effectiveness (good human relations) could sometimes be incompatible with what is expected for short-term efficiency. The trade-offs in the choice of time needs to be recognized.

5. What type of data to be used? Facts or feelings? Subjective perceptual data or objective organizational data or a blend of both. Perhaps a blend of both for a wider perspective.

# HUMAN RESOURCE ACCOUNTING

Most organizations aver, *People are our most important asset*. Yet the human assets are usually not reflected in company balance sheets. The traditional accountants believed that human resources unlike physical assets, are not capable of being owned, retained or utilized in the business at the pleasure of the organisation, except in rare cases of contracted or bonded in terms of employment which too have either been regulated or abolished. Notwithstanding the similarities and dissimilarities, it is argued that men should not be equated with machines. Therefore, human resources were not considered amenable to financial reporting. However, during the last two decades several efforts have resulted in idenifying various measures of the valuation of human assets.

Human Resource Accounting (HRA) may be referred to as a process of identifying, measuring and communicating information about human resources in financial terms to aid HRP and control.

## Rationale

The rationale for HRA is provided in a series of arguments.

(i) Most organizations devote considerable time, money and effort to maintain and improve the quality of human resources. This occurs through performance appraisal, training and development, counselling, career and succession planning and a variety of employee benefits and services. Earlier, most human resource related investments were made based on certain faith, philosophy or compulsion (statutory, unions, competitive pressures). But gradually cost-consciousness is spreading to human resource function too.

(ii) Now there are techniques available to systematically rate jobs and evaluate employee performance just as machines are rated as to their capacity.

(iii) It is important to know whether human assets are appreciating or depreciating over a period of time and identify causal factors for proactive actions.

(iv) Changes in the value of human resources may indicate changes in the trends of employee turnover. Such changes may prompt organizations to relook at cost of hiring, pay and benefit programmes, leadership styles, etc.

(v) HRA can help quantify the allocation of human resources in monetary terms for budgeting purpose, using concepts such as profits centre, etc. as part of management planning and control strategies.

(vi) The HRA data would also be relevant to investors, financiers, creditors, etc for decision making purposes. Strategic decisions concerning mergers and acquisitions could be based on the quality and skills of people available.

## Approaches to HRA

Several approaches to valuation of human resources have been developed during the last two decades or so. They may be classified as monetary and non-monetary measures.

*Monetary Measures*    These measures focus on cost or economic value. The monetary measures include the following:

*Historical Cost of Acquisition*   The expenditure incurred to recruit, train, induct and develop an employee is accumulated and  capitalized to reflect the cost of that employee. The costs of recruitment, induction and the like are amortized over the expected tenure of the employee while costs of training and development are amortized over a short period.

*Replacement Cost*   It is the cost of replacing an existing employee. The elements of cost include the cost of recruitment, induction,training and development, opportunity cost involved in the gestation period till the new employee reaches the level of performance put in by the old employee, the differences in wage\salary payment etc (in certain cadres, particularly where skill shortage is pernicious, organizations have had to pay substantially higher wages to the new employee than what was paid to the person whom such new employee is replacing).

*Opportunity Cost*   This may be determined in respect of employees possessing rare skills or skills in short supply, based on bids (offers) made by various departmental heads competing for certain skilled persons to work in their departments. The bids reflect the price they are willing to pay to acquire (the services of) a certain employee. The bid price is supposedly  determined based on actual or assumed rate for capitalization of the differential earnings expected to be earned by the employee.

*Economic Value*   The aggregate of the expected future earnings (or payments to be made to the person by the employing organization by way of pay and benefits, etc.) and the expected productivity of the employee are taken as the basis to arrive at an estimation of the future contributions of the employee. The future contributions are discounted by a suitable discounting rate to arrive at the present economic value of the individual to the organization.

*Discounted Present Value of Future Wages and Salaries*  Employees are classified into homogeneous groups based on age, skill, experience, nature of job, level of responsibility, etc. into unskilled and skilled workers, office staff, technical staff, supervisors and managerial staff, etc. The present value of future earnings of employees till retirement is taken as the value of human resources.

The earnings of employees in organized sector have shown a tendency to double once every four to five years, because of grade increases, periodic wage settlements and increases in DA due to rising inflation. The present value is determined by discounting the future earnings at a suitable rate like the cost of capital. Usually most firms in India which employ this method use a 12% discount rate.

*Non-monetary Measures*      The proponents of HRA suggest the value of human resources could be quantified in terms of the present worth of their expected future services to the organisation.   However, behavioural scientists suggested a model for measuring changes in the effectiveness of individuals, groups and the organisation. Rensis Likert identified three sets of variables — causal, intermediate and output – which are useful in discussing effectiveness over a period of time.   It is held that causal variables like leadership style and behaviour affect intermediate variables like commitment to objectives, morale and motivation which in turn affect output variables like production, sales, net profit, etc.   Therefore, there is merit in using non-monetary measures.   Some of the non-monetary measures used in HRA include:

(i) *Expected realisable value based on skill, ability, altitudes, etc*:  The value of human resources is derived from the expected realisable value of employees in terms of variables such as the ones indicated above. Considerable work has been done on Human Resource Instrumentation to develop systematic social and psychological measures.

(ii) *Discounted net present value of future earnings*  based on the type of measures suggested by Rensis Likert.

(iii) *Value of employees based on attitude scores in respect of knowledge, skill, etc, and the annual earnings*  The attitude score of an employee is multiplied by annual earnings and the difference between the resulting value and the actual earnings of the employee's annual earnings in considered to reflect the gain or loss of retaining the person.

## Evaluation of Different Approaches

The monetary measures are based on costs and assigned values developed by Brummet, *et. al.* (1969), Giles and Robinson (1972) and several others. The costs may be historical replacement and opportunity costs. Historical costs are easy to measure but bear little relevance to reflect future value. Replacement and opportunity costs are dynamic in nature and difficult to quantify.

Most measures use employee earnings as a surrogate. But they hardly bear any relationship to an individual's worth to the organization. Where the laws of market forces are subordinated to political decision making processes, it could well be that company's may report high on human assets.  The increase in wage\salary payments normally form part of value added, even if there is no intrinsic addition to the value in the manufacturing process. Thus the prevailing conceptions about cost and value have their own limitations.

Some have tried to incorporate productivity (Flamholtz,1971), length of service and promotability (Jaggi and Lau, 1974) based on Markovian flows, optimal allocation through opportunity cost calculation and competitive bidding (Hekimian and Jones,

1971). Since individual measurement processes are difficult, group basis of valuation was suggested by some.  While others like Likert commend  individual and organisational behavioural parameters. Myers and Flowers (1974) too emphasized group valuation on full parameters, viz. knowledge, skill, health, availability, and atitude; but they neglect cost considerations. Most approaches suffer from problems in classification, aggregation, statistical estimation and inference and interpretation of results.

# INDIAN EXPERIENCE

A few large enterprises in India like ACC, BHEL, CCI, EIL, ONGC and NTPC have, in 1980s began to take interest in extending financial reporting system to human resources also.  Almost all of them have thought it appropriate to base their HRA along the model developed by *LEV* and *SCHWARTS*. Under this model the discounted value of employees' future earnings are treated as the value of the human assets of the organization.  The following assumptions are usually made, in Indian context, while applying the model:

- Present pattern of employee compensation including direct and indirect benefits and prospective wage revisions are to be reckoned;
- Normal career growth as per present policies, with vacancies filled from the levels immediately below;
- Weightage for changes in efficiency due to age, experience and skills; and,
- the present value of future earnings is calculated on a discount factor of 12% per annum.

The implications of this model are several.  The present value of future earnings may go up significantly due to high rate of inflation and for periodic wage settlement.  Its effect or the contribution per rupee of human capital depends on changes in other factors of production and the market situation (cost plus pricing or competitive pricing).  The company policies may remain the same.  But when business situation becomes tight due to recession, etc. the employees' experience changes–tight HRP, cuts, bans or freezes on various aspects concerning human resources such as staffing, recruitment and training, pay and benefits, etc.  Subjectivity in assigning weightages and appropriateness of the discounting factor used are other aspects which influence the calculations.

Currently the companies providing HRA information merely work out the discounted future earnings of employees in their balance sheets and add a para or two on the changes in values.  The usefulness of this, except for budgeting purpose, remains to be seen.  Perhaps companies may like to see whether the gross value of all individuals employed in an organization exceeed the value of their earnings.  But they also need to develop wholehearted orientation towards every aspect of human resource management if the organization really considers them assets.

## SUMMARY

It was noted that strategic human resource management which seeks to provide competitive edge to firms through better human resource planning and utilization is concerned, among other things, with controlling manpower costs.  This could be accomplished through one or several approaches—Management-by-Objectives, Ratio Analysis and Productivity Analysis.  Not all costs are easily quantifiable. But emphasis on measurement in personnel will enhance accountability in the function.  One has to be careful, however, in dealing with figures and to avoid falling into an activity trap.  Large, growing and complex organizations are finding it useful to extend the application of new information technologies in dealing with human resource planning and problems.  The basic purposes of computerized human resource information systems are to maintain and use information for informed decision-making and compliance with statutory and other obligations for record-keeping.

We have considered the variety of information needs covering each of the activities considered key and/or complementary to HRP and the possible uses of computers in information sharing, negotiations, training, performance appraisal, etc.  The system design aspects of personnel inventory and personnel audit also were considered.  Finally we have stressed the prerequisites for HRIS to aid HRP.

During the last two decades or so, there is a growing interest in Human Resource Accounting (HRA) which may be described as a process of identifying, measuring, and communicating information about human resources in financial terms to aid HRP and control.  While the rationale is well established, the different approaches to valuation using monetary and non-monetary measures suffer from serious limitations.

## KEY WORDS

| | | |
|---|---|---|
| **Historical Cost** | : | The expenditure incurred to recruit, train, induct and develop an employee. |
| **Opportunity Cost** | : | The actual or assumed rate for capitalization of the differential earnings expected to be earned by an employee. |
| **Human Resource Accounting** | : | It is the process of identifying, measuring and communicating information about human resources in financial terms to aid HRP and control. |
| **Human Resource Information System** | : | It is a systematic way of storing information and data for each individual employee to aid planning, decision-making and supply of returns to external agencies. |
| **Replacement Cost** | : | It is the cost of replacing an existing employee. |

## REVIEW QUESTIONS

1. Describe the broad approach to analyze and control manpower costs.
2. Outline the rationale and uses of computers in HRP.
3. a) Examine whether and how MBO concept can be extended to any aspect of personnel?
   b) Write notes on:
      (i) Personnel inventory
      (ii) Personnel audit

4.  Define and describe the rationale and approaches towards Human Resource Accounting. Critically evaluate different approaches and comment on Indian experience in this regard.

## FURTHER READING

1.  Brummet R Lee, Flamholtz E G, *et al.*, 1960. "Human Resource Accounting in Industry", *Personnel Administration*, 32(4).

2.  Cascio, Wayne F, 1985. "Costing Human Resources", *World Executive Digest*, October, pp 35–54.

3.  Fitz-enz Jack, 1984. *How to Measure Personnel Management*, McGraw-Hill, New York.

4.  Flamholtz, E G, 1971. "Should Your Organisation Attempt to Value its Human Resources". *California Management Review*, Winter, pp 40–45.

5.  Flamholtz, E G, 1971. "A Model for Human Resource Valuation: A Stochastic Process with Service Rewards", *The Accounting Review*, April, pp 253–267.

6.  Giles W J, D F Robinson, 1972. *Human Asset Accounting*, Lawrence Allen, Great Britain.

7.  Gupta, R K, 1988. *Human Resource Accounting*, Anmol: New Delhi.

8.  Hekimian J S, C H Jones, 1967. "Put People on the Balance Sheet", *Harvard Business Review*, January–February.

9.  Jaggi B, H Lau, 1974. "Toward a Model for Human Resource Valuation", *The Accounting Review*, April, pp 321–329.

10. Kolay, M K, 1986. "Human Resource Accounting", *ASCI Journal of Management*, March, pp 262–276.

11. Likert, Reusis (1967). *The Human Organisation*, McGraw-Hill: New York.

12. Randeria, K N, 1982. *The Cost of an Employee*, NIPM: Calcutta.

13. Spiring, John E, 1988. "Selling HRIS to Top Managements", *Personnel* (USA), October, pp 26–34.

14. Wille E, 1981. *The Computer in Personnel Work*, IPM: London.

# Personnel: The Future Scenario

In this final chapter, we take note of the changing scenario by merely listing the emerging areas of concern and highlight the expectations and responsibilities of top management. The future scenario for personnel calls for a major reorientation in philosophy, policy and practices. Some of them are reflected in the new emphasis and thrust being given to the developmental role of personnel in the name of HRD.

## THE CHANGING PERSONNEL MANAGEMENT SCENARIO

Changes in almost every aspect of human life are rapid, pervasive and profound. Change is engulfing technologies, products, processes, materials and above all, People!

There is concern about the following aspects which have implications for personnel/human resources in an environment marked by turbulence and uncertainty, giving rise to high expectations from people and high performance standards from organizations:

1.   Rapid changes in technologies
2.   New manufacturing technologies and obsolete organization structures
3.   The phenomenon of the knowledge worker and demographic changes in employee profile
4.   Competition—people edge
5.   Globalization
6.   Internationalization of business and strategic alliances
7.   Growth of service economy
8.   Customer orientation
9.   Concern about total quality management
10.  Concern about environment and ethics
11.  Concern for participation and quality of working life
12.  Concern about de-skilling, re-skilling and multi-skilling
13.  Demand for better job security and better social security
14.  Practices leading to the phenomenon of working non-employees (part-timers, domestic workers, outsourcing and the like)
15.  Need for creativity and innovation in personnel/human resource practices.

Given this scenario, over 20 personnel directors and chief executives had deliberated on the expectations and responsibilities of top management and the direction of changes in the approaches to personnel/human resource management, at the Second IMI-India Round Table of Personnel Directors held at New Delhi in November 1988. The summary of the deliberations is presented here.

## Expectations of Top Management

1.   Personnel should be integrated into the company's mainstream and linked to business goals.
2.   Personnel has responsibility for top team effectiveness. Though personnel may sometimes find it difficult to take the initiative in this area because of fear of being a part of the problem or reluctance to expose the top management, treading into aspects considered as taboos, this responsibility is something that is basic to the function itself.
3.   Human resource is often a major barrier towards a company's success. Personnel should help organizations gain a competitive edge through effective human resource planning, development and utilization.
4.   Personnel should attract and retain people with relevant skills, knowledge and attitudes as required.
5.   Personnel should contribute towards the stability and growth of the organization by developing and effectively maintaining a succession planning system.
6.   Personnel is required to design a compensation package that is competitive yet viable; individually motivating yet equitable; beneficial in service and after retirement.
7.   Personnel should strive to create a conducive organizational climate that sustains high level performance. Personnel should periodically audit its policies and systems and take timely remedial measures. Systematic feedback to top and senior levels of management must also be provided.

8.  Personnel should foster a climate of mutual trust and confidence between management and unions so that it results in industrial harmony whereby productivity is maximized.
9.  Personnel should develop and deliver a disciplined and productive work force.
10. Personnel should undertake research and diagnostic analysis of personnel-related problems for moving away from fire fighting to provide pro-active policies and responses.

## Responsibilities of Top Management

1.  Personnel should be inducted into the mainstream of business operations by ensuring its representation on all major decision-making forums/bodies.
2.  Clearly define the corporate philosophy and objectives which form the basis of personnel policy.
3.  Support the preparation and implementation of personnel policy, systems and practices at all levels.
4.  Incorporate the necessary accountability on personnel related matters into the role of all managers.
5.  Play a leading role in building an appropriate culture.
6.  Make available adequate resources to facilitate effective functioning of the personnel department.

## Towards a New Approach

The discussion pointed to the need for changes in the role of the personnel function as outlined in Table 15.1.

**Table 15.1   Current and Suggested Role of Personnel**

| Current Role | Suggested Role |
|---|---|
| **1. Strategic orientation** | |
| (i)   Independent goals, not clearly linked to that of the organization leading to an activity trap | Strategic linkage with the goals of the organization |
| (ii)  Standardization of personnel policies, etc. | Flexibility. Human resource policies to be tailored to fit with the targeted market niche in view of rapid changes in environment and growing emphasis on competition |
| **2. Management philosophy** | |
| (i)   Emphasis on direction and control | Seek to achieve consensus and commitment of people through people's participation |
| (ii)  Employees as a cost | People as a resource |
| (iii) Hire and fire | Attract and retain people |
| (iv)  Maintain discipline and seek compliance to organization needs | Build positive work ethos and organization culture for employee motivation |

(v)    Hierarchical personnel policies and practices — Emphasis on horizontal personnel practices with a view to harmonize employee pay, benefits and working conditions

3. *Performance management*

Emphasis on feelings and reliance on subjects appraisal systems with an eye on harmony — Develop data-base for objective measurement of facts for analysis with an eye on the bottom line

4. *Relationships*

Master and servant relationship reinforcing the negative, apartheid features of our social system in workplace — Emphasize reciprocity and mutuality in relations

5. *Change in approach*

(i)    Power centre — Service centre

(ii)   Fire-fighting role — Pro-active approach

(iii)  Labour intensive — Capital intensive (in the hope that robots cannot unionize but being myopic to the dangers of computer virus!)

(iv)   Building organizational pyramids to take care of employee aspirations — Restructuring organization to make them flat/horizontal

(v)    Employee orientation — People and business orientation (to include care of customers and other constituents)

(vi)   Employee training — People training (includes not only employees but also vendors, dealers, customers, etc.) and retraining

(vii)  Contractual employment relations — Contractual working non-employee relations with a view to minimize legal obligations and union pressures (However, this will remain a short-term strategy. For, the groups of domestic workers, subcontractors, part-timers and franchisees will, when they grow to form a critical size, may begin to unionize and bargain.)

# HRD: THE DEVELOPMENTAL ROLE OF PERSONNEL TO THE FORE

There is as yet no proper understanding about the concept of Human Resource Development (HRD). Some view this as the new role or the developmental role of the old personnel function which has hitherto been neglected. Some maintain personnel and HRD are two different concepts altogether. In the absence of agreement on the subject companies are wondering whether to keep them distinct or integrate HRD not only into personnel but into the generic managerial functions in the organization. To understand the issues better, it is appropriate to have clarity over the concept. T.V.Rao, one of the staunch proponents of the concept defines HRD in the organizational context as a process by which the employees of an organization are helped, in a continuous, planned way to:*

---

\* T. V. Rao, *Integrated Human Resource Development Systems in the 1985, Annual of Developing Human Resources*, University Associates, An Arbor, pp 227–231.

- Acquire or sharpen capabilities required to perform various functions associated with their present or expected future roles;
- Develop their general capabilities as individuals and discover and exploit their own inner potentials for their own and/or organizational development purposes;
- Develop an organizational culture in which supervisor-subordinate relationships, team work, and collaboration among subunits are strong and contribute to professional well-being, motivation and pride of employees.

But while discussing the goal and mechanisms of HRD, T V Rao identifies subsystems which begin with performance appraisal and include potential appraisal and development, feedback and performance coaching, career planning, training, organization development (OD), rewards, employee welfare and quality of worklife and human resource information.

The list of subsystems enumerated above cover some of the traditional personnel functions in the new role of HRD Manager, yet ignoring important aspects concerning prerecruitment and post retrenchment, which may well constitute the head and tail respectively of the body of HRD.

One may take the view that human resources in an organization could be taken as given and so the HRD effort in the organization could begin after selection and recruitment. But, a more logical approach, at the micro level, would be to consider Human Resource Planning and Organization/Design as integral parts of HRD, if the goal indeed is to develop the capabilities of an employee as an individual and in his present and future role in harmony with organizational needs and expectations. It is possible that relevant concerns could be taken care of in a comprehensive OD programme, but it is important to state the prerecruitment activities as the starting point of HRD subsystems. The HRD effort becomes more meaningful and effective if due care is exercised at the acquisition stage itself in terms of recruitment, numbers and nature of jobs. This applies not only to new organizations but also the existing organizations which are willing to consider lessons from experience and conduct O & M exercises, from time to time. Similarly, the HR policies, programmes and procedures also need to be reckoned as a distinct subset of HRD.

The linkage between HRD and industrial relations also needs to be properly appreciated and recognized and trade unions should be actively involved. HRD efforts should not be construed as management strategies to wean the employees away from the union.

The human resource policies should focus on:

- horizontal human resource management policies based on trust, openness, equity, consent and consensus than those based on hierarchical control and direction
- build stake and say for people at all levels in jobs and organizations
- develop objective performance review and management systems
- restructure reward systems that are contingent on performance and sustain motivation
- information sharing, grievance redressal and participation.

Many surveys and studies point out that people in organisations expect equitable and fair treatment and prompt redressal of grievances. They do not crave for lenience. They can put up with hard work and harsh conditions (as farmers ungrudgingly work in mud and slush, exposed to the vagaries of weather) provided they are not discriminated against. The five-fold challenges listed above may at the outset appear as plain and simple rhetoric. The future challenge lies in making them happen.

## SUMMARY

The rapid changes covering almost every aspect of organizations infringe heavily in reshaping the thrust of personnel/human resource management. The future scenario will be marked by turbulence and uncertainty, competition and globalization, giving rise to high expectations from people and high performance standards from organizations. The situation calls for clarity on what the organizations expect from personnel and what would be the responsibilities of the top management. The consensus reached at a round-table conference of personnel directors was presented as a framework for discussion along these lines. All things seem to portend to a significant and perceptible change in personnel philosophy, policies and practices. The personnel objectives need to be linked to business results and personnel should look beyond the interests of employees of the organization and orient its services to the other constituents of the organization in a pro-active way. Personnel will have to think of a variety of innovative and creative policies and programmes, organization structures and management styles to make the people in the organizations adapt themselves to the changes and challenges that lie ahead. The developmental role of the traditional function, which has hitherto been neglected has already come to the fore in the form of HRD.

There is a need to look at HRD concepts, components and mechanisms more comprehensively and in an integrated way as people-related functions rather than isolate them from personnel functions or industrial relations aspects.

## KEY WORDS

| | | |
|---|---|---|
| **Reactive Approach** | : | Taking action after the event. |
| **Pro-active Approach** | : | An approach which seeks to accomplish preventive care in human/industrial relations. |
| **Human Resource Development** | : | It is a process by which the employees of an organization are helped to help themselves and the organization. |
| **Horizontal Human Resource Practices** | : | Human resource practices which seek to eliminate or reduce hierarchical differences and bring about greater integration between people and tasks. |

## REVIEW QUESTIONS

1. Outline some of the major changes (at least five) which seem to impinge on the role of personnel and discuss the implications.
2. Do you subscribe to the statement of the expectations and responsibilities of top management towards personnel? Do you find it adequate to meet the future scenario?
3. Comment on the suggested changes in approach to personnel/human resource management in organizations.
4. Critically examine the concept of HRD. Comment on the linkage between HRD, personnel, industrial relations and organization development.

## FURTHER READING

1. Fox, Alan, 1974. *Man Mismanagement*, Hutchinson: London.

2. Rao, T V and D F Pereira, 1986. *Recent Experiences in Human Resource Development*, Oxford and IBH: New Delhi.

3. Rowland, Kendrith and Gerald R Ferous, 1986. *Current Issues in Personnel Management*, Allan and Bacon: Boston.

4. NIPM and Indian Institute of Science, 1990. *National Round Table Conference on Perspective Plan for Human Resources Function: Conference Papers*. Department of Management Sciences, Indian Institute of Science: Bangalore, 25–26 June.

5. Venkata Ratnam, C S, 1988. *Report of the 2nd IMI Round Table Conference of Personnel Directors*, IMI: New Delhi (Mimeo).

6. Venkata Ratnam, C S, 1989. *Management Strategy and Industrial Relations*, IMI: New Delhi (Mimeo).

7. Walton, R E, 1984. *From Control to Commitment in the Work place*, HBR Reprint 85219.

# Index